The Rise and Fall of Public–Private Partnerships

The Rise and Fall of Public–Private Partnerships

Finance, Infrastructure and Developing Countries

James Leigland

Strategic Advisor, SAEx International Management Limited, Mauritius

Edward Elgar
PUBLISHING

Cheltenham, UK • Northampton, MA, USA

Published by
Edward Elgar Publishing Limited
The Lypiatts
15 Lansdown Road
Cheltenham
Glos GL50 2JA
UK

Edward Elgar Publishing, Inc.
William Pratt House
9 Dewey Court
Northampton
Massachusetts 01060
USA

A catalogue record for this book
is available from the British Library

Library of Congress Control Number: 2024944485

This book is available electronically in the **Elgar**online
Economics subject collection
https://doi.org/10.4337/9781035345052

MIX
Paper | Supporting responsible forestry
FSC® C013604

ISBN 978 1 0353 4504 5 (cased)
ISBN 978 1 0353 4505 2 (eBook)

Printed and bound by CPI Group (UK) Ltd Croydon CR0 4YY

Contents

Figures

Tables

Boxes

About the author

James Leigland is the former Technical Adviser and Head of Technical Assistance at the Private Infrastructure Development Group (PIDG), where he designed and managed PIDG's Viability Gap Funding program. He served as the Public–Private Partnership Adviser on the PIDA Panel of Experts, a peer review team that evaluated the outputs of the Program for Infrastructure Development in Africa (PIDA) on behalf of the African Union, NEPAD, and the African Development Bank. He is the former Africa Team Leader of the World Bank's Public–Private Infrastructure Advisory Facility (PPIAF) and the founding manager of PPIAF's Sub-National Technical Assistance program. The USAID-funded project development team that he led in South Africa in the early 2000s concluded 35 private investment projects, including South Africa's first modern municipal bond issue and what have become the two longest-lived water concessions in Africa. He has authored or co-authored 45 professional publications and over 50 consulting reports on private investment in infrastructure, and delivered over 80 public addresses on these topics. He holds a Ph.D. in political economy from Columbia University in New York.

Preface

The performance of infrastructure public–private partnerships (PPPs) in developing countries has been a controversial topic since the development community began widely promoting these mechanisms in the late 1980s. The topic is especially important now because the private sector is being urgently called on to help finance achievement of the Sustainable Development Goals (SDGs) and efforts to reduce the impacts of climate change. PPPs are the principal mechanisms used to facilitate this kind of private participation. But the performance of PPPs in the developing world has substantially failed to meet expectations over the last three decades. These mechanisms have proved to be expensive, fragile, often unsustainable, and rarely able to achieve socio-economic development objectives. A growing body of evidence-based research confirms this. As a result of these shortcomings, PPPs have never played more than a minor role in the financing and management of infrastructure in developing countries, as they do in industrialized economies. This well-documented track record offers little support for expectations that private participation of this kind is likely to make a significant positive difference going forward, for infrastructure service delivery improvements, much less for SDG achievement or climate change mitigation and adaptation.

However, despite this history, leading members of the international development community—including bilateral donors, multilateral development banks (MDBs), development finance institutions (DFIs), and international organizations like the G20 and the United Nations—continue to promote private participation as a mechanism that is essential for closing the infrastructure investment gap in poor countries. Since the 1990s, "PPP advocacy" has become a global enterprise involving thousands of public and private entities (project preparation facilities, project development funds, PPP units, etc.) created to promote, design, and develop infrastructure PPPs in these countries. These entities have spent billions of dollars in this effort. Most of them work exclusively on PPPs without evaluating alternative mechanisms. Many focus only on transactions without considering the legal, regulatory, and policy reforms necessary to take full advantage of private investment.

The only types of PPPs for which advocates can claim some success in developing countries are known as "greenfield projects," like Build–Operate–Transfer (BOT) and Build–Own–Operate (BOO) PPPs, largely for power generation and toll roads. To the extent that PPPs have been successful in other sectors, they have mostly relied on these same greenfield BOT/BOO structures. But the dominance of greenfield projects is hardly a success of PPP advocacy in terms of development benefits. These projects maximize the mitigation of private sector risks by allowing private partners to build, operate, and own new assets for wholesale service provision in exchange for guaranteed, long-term payments usually made in hard currency. Meanwhile, the retail management of end-user services is typically left to the same government departments and utilities responsible for sector mismanagement in the first place. As a result, these public entities are often unable to efficiently use the expensive power or transport services they purchase from private wholesale suppliers. The few PPP projects of any kind which reach financial closure in low-income countries usually cannot be replicated without the same levels of concessional funding and expertise supplied by development partners, which was needed to prepare and finance the pioneering examples of these projects.

This book traces the 30-year evolution of PPP advocacy in an attempt to provide a political economy analysis of the reasons for what often seems like blind faith in the power of PPPs to solve infrastructure investment and management problems in developing countries. The analysis demonstrates how that blindness has been enabled by a series of failures of bilateral donors and multilateral development banks—failure to insist on rigorous program evaluation, reluctance to curtail funding for programs that do not produce expected results, and impatience with longer-term efforts to build the institutions necessary to support equitable and sustainable growth. At a time when the SDGs and climate change seem like such important challenges, it is remarkable that the international development community is willing to continue spending so much money on activities clearly unlikely to succeed beyond the completion of small numbers of opportunistically selected, heavily subsidized projects.

This book is an appeal to leading development institutions to pay attention to what many of their own senior researchers have been trying to tell them and to reflect on the reasons why the message has been ignored—public institutions in developing countries will continue to dominate the financing and management of infrastructure investment, as such institutions do in most industrialized economies. An overwhelming share of this investment will be paid for from government revenues, money borrowed from banks and capital markets, and development partners. But these public institutions in the developing world desperately need strengthening. PPPs circumvent that problem, while achieving very little in terms of narrowing the investment gap. The single-minded advocacy of PPPs means that a huge amount of development aid continues to be diverted from efforts to deal with the real obstacles to infrastructure investment in developing countries.

Abbreviations

AfD	Agence Française de Développement (French Development Agency)
AfDB	African Development Bank
AICD	*Africa Infrastructure Country Diagnostic*
AIIB	Asian Infrastructure Investment Bank
ANC	African National Congress
APEC	Asia-Pacific Economic Cooperation
APPF	Afreximbank Project Preparation Facility
AsDB	Asian Development Bank
ASI	Adam Smith International
AU	African Union
AUC	African Union Commission
AUDA	African Union Development Agency
BLT	build–lease–transfer
BMZ	German Federal Ministry for Economic Cooperation and Development
BOO	build–own–operate
BOOT	build–own–operate–transfer
BOT	build–operate–transfer
BPE	Bureau of Public Enterprise (Nigeria)
BRICS	Brazil, Russia, India, China, South Africa
BROT	Build-rehabilitate-operate-transfer
CAPEX	capital expenditure
CBN	Continental Business Network (PIDA)
CBO	community-based organization
CDC	Commonwealth Development Corporation (U.K.)
CEPA	Cambridge Economic Policy Associates
CFR	Country Framework Report (PPIAF)
CLIFF	Community-led Infrastructure Finance Facility (DFID)
COI	conflict of interest
COMESA	Common Market for Eastern and Southern Africa

CPIA	Country Policy and Institutional Assessment (World Bank)
DAC	Development Assistance Committee (OECD)
DANIDA	Danish International Development Agency
DBSA	Development Bank of Southern Africa
DEG	German Investment and Development Corporation
DevCo	Infrastructure Development Collaboration Partnership (PIDG)
DFAT	Department of Foreign Affairs and Trade (Australia)
DFI	National and bilateral development finance institutions (e.g., AfD, CDC, Proparco, DBSA)
DFID	Department for International Development (U.K.)
DGIS	Directorate-General for International Cooperation (The Netherlands)
DOE	Department of Energy (South Africa)
DRC	Democratic Republic of Congo
EAIF	Emerging Africa Infrastructure Fund (PIDG)
EBRD	European Bank for Reconstruction and Development
ECA	Europe and Central Asia
ECOWAS	Economic Community of West African States
EIB	European Investment Bank
EMDE	Emerging Market and Developing Economy
EOI	expression of interest
EPC	engineering, procurement, construction
ESMAP	Energy Sector Management Assistance Program (World Bank)
ESP	Expert Service Pool (PIDA)
EU	European Union
EWSA	Energy, Water, and Sanitation Authority (Rwanda)
FASA	financial advisory service agreement (IFC)
FCDO	Foreign, Commonwealth and Development Office (U.K.)
FIAS	Foreign Investment Advisory Service (World Bank)
FiT	feed-in tariff
FMO	Netherlands Development Finance Company
G20	Group of Twenty
G24	Group of Twenty-Four
GET FiT	Global Energy Transfer Feed-in Tariff
GIF	Global Infrastructure Facility (World Bank)
GOI	Government of India
GPOBA	Global Program on Output-based Aid (World Bank)

GPRBA	Global Program for Results Based Approaches (World Bank)
GTAC	Government Technical Advisory Centre (South Africa)
HAM	hybrid annuity model
HDV	high development value (PIDG)
HH	household
HIPC	Heavily Indebted Poor Country
HLP	High-Level Panel (G20)
IA	implementation agreement
IBRD	International Bank for Reconstruction and Development
ICA	Infrastructure Consortium for Africa (AfDB)
ICED	Infrastructure and Cities for Economic Development (DFID)
ICR	implementation completion report (World Bank)
ICRC	Infrastructure Concession Regulatory Commission (NIGERIA)
ICT	information and communication technology
IDA	International Development Association
IDB	Inter-American Development Bank
IEA	International Energy Agency
IEG	Independent Evaluation Group (World Bank Group)
IFC	International Finance Corporation
IMF	International Monetary Fund
IPP	independent power producer
IsDB	Islamic Development Bank
IUK	Infrastructure U.K.
KfW	Kreditanstalt für Wiederaufbau (German development bank)
LAC	Latin America and the Caribbean
LDC	least-developed country
LIC	low-income country
LMIC	lower middle-income country
M&E	monitoring and evaluation
MCC	Millennium Challenge Corporation (U.S.A.)
MDA	ministries, departments, agencies
MDB	multilateral development banks (e.g., World Bank Group, AsDB, AfDB, EIB, IDB)
MDG	Millennium Development Goal
MDRI	Multilateral Debt Relief Initiative
MENA	Middle East and North Africa

MIC	middle-income country
MIGA	Multilateral Investment Guarantee Agency
MLTSF	Medium to Long Term Strategic Framework
MOU	Memorandum of Understanding
MW	megawatt
NAO	National Audit Office (U.K.)
NEPAD	New Partnership for Africa's Development
NERSA	National Energy Regulator of South Africa
NGO	non-governmental organization
NIAF	Nigeria Infrastructure Advisory Facility
NORAD	Norwegian Agency for Development Cooperation
Norfund	Norwegian Investment Fund for Developing Countries
NPCA	NEPAD Planning and Coordinating Agency
NRW	non-revenue water
O&M	operations and maintenance
OAU	Organisation of African Unity
OBA	output-based aid
ODA	official development assistance
ODI	Overseas Development Institute
OECD	Organisation for Economic Co-operation and Development
OPIC	Overseas Private Investment Corporation (U.S.A.)
PAD	project appraisal document (World Bank)
PAP	Priority Action Plan (PIDA)
PBC	performance-based contract
PCG	partial credit guarantee
PDF	project development fund
PDPA	Project Development and Procurement Agency (Nigeria)
PFI	Private Finance Initiative (U.K.)
PHRD	Policy and Human Resources Development (World Bank)
PIDA	*Program for Infrastructure Development in Africa*
PIDG	Private Infrastructure Development Group
PIM	public investment management
PPA	power purchase agreement
PPDF	Project Preparation and Development Facility (SADC)
PPDU	Project Preparation and Development Unit (ECOWAS)

PPF	project preparation facility
PPI	private participation in infrastructure
PPIAF	Public–Private Infrastructure Advisory Facility (World Bank)
PPIU	Project Preparation and Implementation Unit (COMESA)
PPP	public–private partnership
PPPLRC	Public–Private Partnership Legal Resource Center (World Bank)
PQL	PIDA Quality Label
PRC	PPP Resource Center (Nigeria)
PRG	Partial Risk Guarantee (World Bank)
Proparco	*Group Agence Française de Développement*
PRSP	Poverty Reduction Strategy Paper (World Bank)
PSAS	Private Sector Advisory Services (World Bank)
PSC	public sector comparator
PSI	private sector infrastructure
PUK	Partnerships U.K.
REC	Regional Economic Community
REFIT	renewable energy feed-in tariff
REIPPPP	Renewable Energy Independent Power Producer Procurement Program
RFP	request for proposal
RIDMP	Regional Infrastructure Development Master Plan
RMB	Rand Merchant Bank
RSA	Republic of South Africa
SADC	Southern Africa Development Community
SDG	Sustainable Development Goal
SDIP	Sustainable Development Investment Partnership
SDM	Service Delivery Mechanism (PIDA)
SECO	Swiss State Secretariat for Economic Affairs
Sida	Swedish International Development Agency
SME	small and medium enterprise
SOE	state-owned enterprise
SPV	special-purpose vehicle
SSA	sub-Saharan Africa
STAP	Short-Term Action Plan (NEPAD)
SUF	Slum Upgrading Facility (DFID)
TAF	Technical Advisory Facility (PIDG)

The share of private investment in sub-Saharan Africa (SSA), long a focus of PPP promotional efforts by the development community, was only about 5

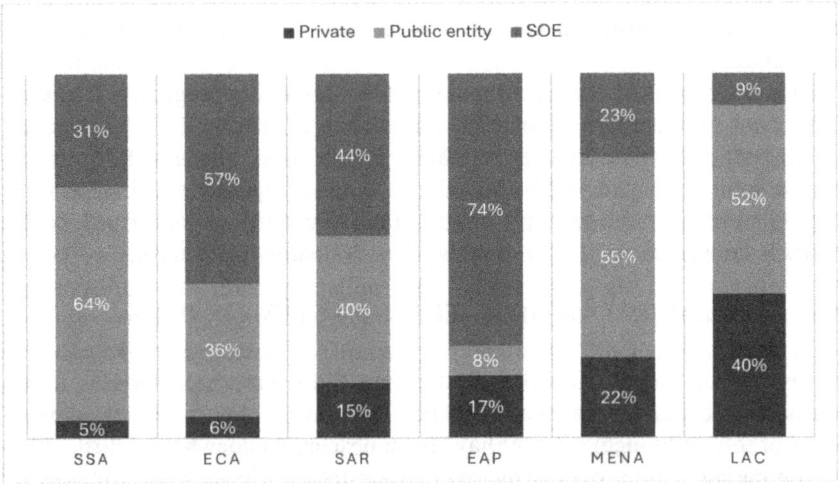

Note: Percentage investment by region. EAP=East Asia & Pacific; ECA=Europe & Central Asia; LAC=Latin America & Caribbean; MENA=Middle East & N. Africa; SAR=South Asia Region; SSA=sub-Saharan Africa.
Source: World Bank (2019c).

Figure 1.1 Public vs. private infrastructure investment, 2017

percent. The study also found that even in cases of investments classified as private, most of the finance in developing countries actually came from governments or development partners—with private debt and equity contributing only about 45 percent of total investment in these "private" projects (World Bank 2019c). The authors of the study later characterized this share of private investment in infrastructure projects to be "overwhelmingly low" (Saha and Ibrahima 2020).

That study identified Latin America and the Caribbean (LAC) as by far the most active region in terms of private participation, but even in LAC private sector entities accounted for less than 40 percent of total investment. A separate World Bank LAC study conducted about the same time concluded that private participation projects "… do not leverage significant amounts of private capital and are best seen as a complement to, rather than a substitute for, public investments" (Fay et al. 2019, 8).

Other studies have attempted to determine the extent to which PPPs have been used in industrialized countries. But these studies have also failed to provide evidence of a revolutionary new paradigm of private infrastructure provision. Burger and Hawkesworth (2011) surveyed 22 countries (19 high-income countries and three middle-income countries) regarding the percentage of infrastructure investment taking place via PPPs. Of these, half (11 countries) reported using PPPs for 5 percent of investment or less. Another seven countries reported that less than 10 percent of infrastructure investment took place via PPP arrangements. These countries included the United Kingdom (U.K.), where the government's Private Finance Initiative (PFI) had long been active in promoting the use of infrastructure PPPs.

A survey of 24 member countries of the Organisation for Economic Co-operation and Development (OECD) published in 2018, found that in 19 countries less than 5 percent of total infrastructure investment took place via PPPs over the previous three years (OECD 2018). In two countries, Australia and New Zealand, PPPs accounted for 5–10 percent of investment. Other studies have produced similar results. One international consulting firm has summarized the overall global share of infrastructure investment via PPPs at about 5 percent (Arthur D. Little 2020).

Finally, available data show that the performance of PPPs in the poorest countries has been especially disappointing. Figure 1.2 uses data from the World Bank's PPI Database to illustrate this.[1] The figure contrasts PPP-related investments in countries classified by the OECD as "least-developed countries" (LDCs) and "low-income countries" (LICs), with investments in countries classified as middle-income (MIC).[2] By 2021, there were nearly twice as many MICs as LDCs and LICs, so the total amount of PPP investment in MICs could be expected to be larger. But from 1995 to 2021, the number of infrastructure PPPs in MICs was over 30 times the number in LCDs/LICs, and the total amount of PPP investment was over 70 times larger (World Bank 2022). Least-developed and low-income countries need the most help with

---

1 This World Bank's PPI Database defines "PPI projects" to include infrastructure PPPs as well as non-PPP projects like utility privatizations, merchant projects, and asset rentals. But Figure 1.2 omits data on non-PPPs to focus directly on more traditional types of PPPs, involving public–private risk sharing formalized in contractual relationships. Throughout this book, PPI Database information has been adjusted in this manner.

2 The OECD Development Assistance Committee prepares a list every three years which identifies all countries and territories eligible to receive official development assistance (ODA). The list includes all low- and middle-income countries (columns 2, 3, and 4 of the list), based on gross national income (GNI) per capita as calculated by the World Bank. The list also includes all of the "least developed countries" (LDCs—column 1 of the list) as defined by the United Nations.

infrastructure investment, but they have attracted less than 1.4 percent of total PPP investment in developing countries since 1995 (World Bank 2022).

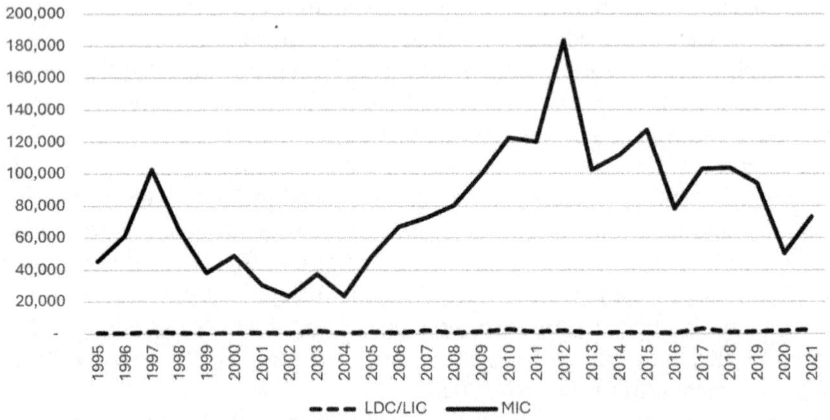

Note: US$ millions—2021 dollars.
Source: Adapted by the author from World Bank (2022).

Figure 1.2 *PPP investment in developing countries by income status, 1995–2021*

1.3 THE EVIDENCE-BASED CRITIQUE

Regardless of confusion about the precise size of PPP-related investments, their generally lackluster performance has been documented in compelling evidence-based project accounts over the past 30 years. These accounts have been accumulating in project reports, working papers, and academic studies.[3] The list of shortcomings is substantial: In the developing world, especially in low-income countries, PPP operational project costs have been higher than expected and private profits much lower than anticipated. PPP project preparation costs have also been much higher than were expected in the 1990s, and certainly higher than the costs of preparing projects for traditional public investment. In the poorest countries, development benefits generated by PPPs have been far from automatic. This is partly a reflection of the fact that about two-thirds of PPP-related investment in LDCs and LICs is associated with electricity generation, mostly via independent power producer (IPP) projects

3 For a more detailed discussion of this, see Leigland (2020b).

that primarily benefit customers already connected to power grids. People classified as poor in these countries typically do not have grid access. The United Nations Economic Commission for Europe (UNECE) now acknowledges that "quality infrastructure investments" resulting from "people-first PPP projects" are exceedingly rare and need to be actively promoted with the use of special PPP project evaluation criteria (UNECE 2021).

BOX 1.1 INFLUENTIAL RESEARCH ON PPPS IN OECD COUNTRIES, SELECTED EXAMPLES

1. Hodge and Greve (2007)
2. Brinkerhoff and Brinkerhoff (2011)
3. Boardman and Vining (2012)
4. Hellowell and Vecchi (2012)
5. Siemiatycki (2015)
6. Verhoest et al. (2015)
7. Boardman and Hellowell (2016)
8. Klijn and Koppenjan (2016)
9. Geddes and Reeves (2017)
10. Bel et al. (2017)
11. Stafford and Stapleton (2017)

Source: Compiled by the author.

Most of the seminal research on PPPs has been focused on projects in the U.K., Australia, Europe, and North America (Box 1.1). Research on the PPP experience in developing countries has been less robust, often conducted or sponsored by development institutions, and focused largely on how and why such projects are attempted rather than why so few of them have been successful (Hammami et al. 2006; Ministry of Foreign Affairs of the Netherlands 2013; Hyun et al. 2018).

But research done to identify the definitive characteristics of PPPs, regardless of the kind of country hosting the projects, suggests multiple reasons for their lack of success in the poorest countries, as documented in the practitioner accounts cited in Box 1.1. In a seminal paper on the micro-economics of PPPs, Iossa and Martimort (2015) characterized PPPs in terms of three main features: (i) the bundling of tasks like design, building, finance, and operation; (ii) the substantial transfer of risk and responsibility to private partners; and (iii) long-term contracts.

In 2021, the United Nations reminded the world that "Developing countries require a boost in private investment if they are to achieve sustainable development goals" (UN 2021, 59). The growing need for infrastructure investment in clean energy at the scale necessary to limit global warming to internationally agreed targets also prompted calls for increased private sector investment (*Washington Post* 2021). Private investment could of course come in the form of bank or capital market financing for traditional public investment activities. But PPP arrangements were expected to do much more because they also promised to use private participation to improve the efficiency of project preparation, financing, construction, operation, etc.

As PPP advocacy has responded to the challenges and obstacles encountered over the last 30 years it has steadily expanded its constituency of true believers, led by the donors and development banks who have backed their faith in PPPs with billions in aid funding to pay for capacity building, reforms, and transaction assistance in developing countries. Much of the aid funding that fuels this advocacy is used to pay for the operations of "project preparation facilities" (PPFs), the foot soldiers of PPP advocacy. PPFs make up a very large, diverse, and fragmented assembly of programs and facilities. The key characteristic shared by these PPFs is their focus on work in developing countries to facilitate the mobilization of private participation for infrastructure investment and management, almost exclusively via PPP mechanisms.

The assemblage includes large, high-profile facilities like Africa50, established by the African Development Bank (AfDB), the Global Infrastructure Facility (GIF), created and hosted by the World Bank, and the Public–Private Infrastructure Advisory Facility (PPIAF), established and funded by donors like the U.K.'s Department for International Development (DFID). But now there are also hundreds of other large and small PPFs, country-focused or geographically diverse, targeting specific sectors or infrastructure in general, financially self-sustaining or dependent on subsidies. PPFs may work on upstream legal and regulatory reforms needed for PPPs, or on one or more aspects of project development, with some of the larger, better funded PPFs supporting the entire project development process leading to the financial closure of projects—some PPFs also provide post-closure support. A large variety of hosting and management models are used for PPFs (Table 1.1).

The multitude of PPP advocates now also includes hundreds of specialized government entities, commonly referred to as "PPP units" and "project development funds" (PDFs), which are expected to guide, regulate, and sometimes finance the PPP development process in their respective countries. A World Bank website lists over 150 PPP units active in developing countries (World Bank 2023). PPP units and PDFs often benefit from traditional aid programs which use donor grants or MDB loans over limited project lifespans to pay for technical assistance and operational funding. These programs come in all

Table 1.1 *Selected hosting arrangements for project preparation facilities (PPFs)*

Project preparation facility	**Host/manager/sponsor**	**Type of facility**
Infrastructure Project Preparation Facility (IPPF)	European Bank for Reconstruction and Development (EBRD)	Trust funds managed by global multilateral development banks (MDBs)
Global Infrastructure Facility (GIF)	World Bank	
Asia Pacific Project Preparation Facility (AP3F)	Asian Development Bank (AsDB)	Trust funds managed by regional multilateral development banks (MDBs)
NEPAD Infrastructure Project Preparation Facility (IPPF)	African Development Bank (AfDB)	
Project Development and Support Facility (PDSF)	Development Bank of Southern Africa (DBSA)	PPFs managed by national development banks
Estruturadora Brasileira de Projetos (EBP)	Brazilian Development Bank (BNDES)	
Project Preparation and Development Facility (PPDF)	Southern Africa Development Community (SADC)	PPFs hosted by African Regional Economic Communities (RECs)
Project Preparation and Development Unit (PPDU)	The Economic Community of West African States (ECOWAS)	
Project Preparation Implementation Unit (PPIU)	Common Market for Eastern and Southern Africa (COMESA)	
Nigeria Infrastructure Advisory Facility (NIAF)	U.K. Department for International Development (DFID)[a]	Donor-funded PPFs outsourced to private consultants
Private Infrastructure Development Group (PIDG)	Multiple bilateral donors	
Power Africa	U.S. Agency for International Development (USAID)	

Note: [a] DFID was merged into the Foreign, Commonwealth & Development Office (FCDO) on September 2, 2020.
Source: Compiled by the author.

shapes and sizes: the 2017 program by the European Bank for Reconstruction and Development (EBRD) to support Egypt's PPP Unit over three years ($2.3 million); the 2020 program by the Asian Development Bank (AsDB) to support the Bangladesh Infrastructure Finance Fund over five years ($50 million); and the 2012 program by the World Bank to strengthen Kenya's PPP unit and legal-regulatory framework, eventually extended to ten years ($90 million, including over $55 million for the preparation of PPP projects).

1.5 PROJECT PREPARATION FACILITIES: OPERATIONS AND IMPACTS

While PPP advocacy is now a mission shared by hundreds of facilities, agencies, and programs operating in the developing world, research on their operations and impacts has been limited because of the wide variety of facilities and programs, confusion about terminology, and lack of transparency regarding their operations. As with "PPP," there is no single, widely accepted definition of "PPF," "PDF," or "PPP unit" and very few publicly available evaluations of these entities other than promotional materials that they prepare and distribute to maintain support from donors.

Most of the best-known research studies of PPFs have focused on facilities active in particular regions (CEPA 2012; ASI 2014; Fioravanti et al. 2019). A 2012 survey of PPFs focused on the preparation of infrastructure projects in Africa identified 67 potential sources of funding for infrastructure project preparation, including facilities hosted by MDBs and donors, as well as government PPP units (CEPA 2012).[5] A 2018 global survey of PPFs offering support for the preparation of clean energy infrastructure projects, mostly targeting private investment, identified 150 facilities (ODI 2018). But this survey also found a lack of comparable metrics that could be used in evaluating the performance of these PPFs and very little publicly available data that could be used in evaluation. Information about the scale of resources available to each PPF was only available for approximately one-third of the total number. The survey concluded that, even though it was almost impossible to precisely judge the performance of individual PPFs, "Taken together, PPFs fall short of their potential positive impact, given the scale of the challenge" (ODI 2018, 6).

Another 2018 survey, sponsored by the Sustainable Development Investment Partnership (SDIP) in collaboration with the United States Trade and Development Administration (USTDA) and South Africa's Development Bank of Southern Africa (DBSA), identified and contacted 136 infrastructure PPFs in Africa and Asia. But responses to survey questions were received from only 47 of the facilities (SDIP et al. 2018). Nevertheless, the survey appeared to show that for these responding PPFs a significant amount of capital was available to support project preparation—$2.35 billion as of 2017, of which $800 million was earmarked exclusively for preparation support in Africa and $140 million in Asia. Other information tends to confirm that available funding for preparation is quite substantial. The online database for the Private

[5] The survey eventually narrowed its scope to a subset of 15 entities because of problems accessing information, questions about scope and focus, and a decision to exclude government units and funds.

Infrastructure Development Group (PIDG), one of the oldest and largest of the donor-funded PPFs, reports that from 2002 to the end of 2019, the program had committed about $4 billion to the preparation and financing of 286 projects, mostly in least-developed countries (LDCs) and low-income countries (LICs) (PIDG 2019b).

Very few evaluations of governmental PPP units or PDFs in developing countries have been published despite the large numbers of these facilities and the substantial amounts of funding involved. Most existing studies focus on the governmental regulatory functions of PPP units (PPIAF 2007; Lemma 2013; Boardman and Hellowell 2016). Part of the performance measurement problem results from the fact that "PPP units" vary so widely in function and focus (Burger and Hawkesworth 2011; EPEC 2014). But after nearly two decades of proliferation in regions like sub-Saharan Africa, there is little evidence that PPP units facilitate successful PPP programs: "... there is very little quantitative evidence of the value of centralized PPP coordination units ..." (Lemma 2013). The World Bank's survey of PPP legal-regulatory frameworks concluded that "In fact, formation of a PPP unit is not, in itself, a sufficient condition for the success of a PPP program" (World Bank 2020).

Despite all of these performance measurement problems, one thing is now abundantly clear about the current institutional landscape of PPP advocacy. Although a huge amount of funding is dedicated to PPP advocacy in developing countries, these activities are showing very few signs of success. Of course, it would be unfair to expect PPFs, PPP units, PDFs, or related programs and facilities to be able to effect near-term reductions in the massive infrastructure investment gap in the developing world. But directly addressing that gap is not necessarily the primary objective of most of these facilities and programs. Instead, most of this preparation work is undertaken with the expectation that if government officials and private investors are presented with examples of successful, commercially sustainable infrastructure projects involving private investment, they will be convinced to undertake further projects on their own, at their own expense. This is why PPFs are so important for PPP advocacy. The "demonstration effects" of successful PPF-supported PPPs are expected to show how such projects can be done successfully, and thereby incentivize project replication.

But the available project data cited earlier in this introduction confirm that this kind of PPP market development has not emerged over the last 30 years. In response to this failure, the development community has scaled up its use of capital subsidies and guarantees to help attract private operators and investors to these projects. In the early years of PPP advocacy, subsidy funding was intended for use only to prepare projects that ultimately would be sustainable without subsidies or guarantees. Reducing the use of subsidy support for infrastructure investment was a principal justification for the promotion of private participation in the 1980s and 1990s. But it quickly became clear that private infrastructure projects could not be sustainable in poor countries without substantial forms of financial support—even if the projects were prepared by PPFs employing international experts. Subsidies provided by PPP advocates like donors and development banks began to play a larger role in the preparation and financing of PPPs, although this scale-up has been obscured somewhat by the use of imprecise terminology like "blended finance" (OECD 2017). The use of guarantees also quickly ramped up. The 47 PPFs responding to the SDIP survey mentioned above reported that they had access to $1.57 billion in project guarantees.

However, research now shows that the expanded use of subsidies to facilitate private investment is doing very little to solve infrastructure problems in developing countries. A 2019 study by the Overseas Development Institute (ODI) found that the global use of blended finance for major projects by the largest MDBs and DFIs has consistently ignored low-income countries and generated low levels of leveraged private investment (Attridge and Engen 2019).

1.6 THE PARADOX OF PPP ADVOCACY

Despite overwhelming evidence to the contrary, the development community continues to doggedly maintain its expectation that PPPs can and will provide widespread solutions to infrastructure service delivery problems in poor countries, including challenges associated with SDGs and climate change. Regional studies of infrastructure investment show that in middle-income countries, like those in Latin America, it is sometimes possible for PPPs to generate benefits over costs (Fay et al. 2017). Isolated pilot projects are occasionally possible in smaller, poorer countries if private sector risks are mitigated with subsidized preparation, concessional financing, guarantees from multilateral development banks (MDBs), and payments to private partners in hard currency. But this kind of project track record hardly justifies the allocation by development organizations of billions of dollars to pay for policy advice and transaction support for projects that contribute less than about 5 percent of infrastructure investment in a region like sub-Saharan Africa.

What accounts for the willingness to divert that kind of funding away from work on more traditional sector reforms, designed to improve things like management of own-source revenues generated by taxes and user fees, oversight of utility operations, and more effective use of conventional forms of public investment in infrastructure financed by bonds or bank loans? If 95 percent of infrastructure investment in Africa is financed and managed by the public sector, even small efficiency improvements in that process would likely be more cost-effective and have longer-term, more sustainable benefits than struggling to achieve financial closure for a handful of complicated, costly, and non-replicable PPPs.

One explanation for the unshakable preference for PPPs over traditional sector reforms was offered in a 2015 World Bank working paper by Michael Klein, who had by then retired after a successful career at the top levels of the World Bank Group. Klein's paper appears to be a reassessment of his earlier views, cited above, regarding the "revolution" in infrastructure finance that occurred in the 1990s with private provision supplanting the "... hitherto dominant public sector model" (Klein 2003, v). In the 2015 paper Klein admitted that no revolution had taken place, nor could one be expected: "The general picture is one of waves of enthusiasm for PPPs followed by some disenchantment and consolidation. Different countries were caught up in the waves at different times" (Klein 2015, 5).

Klein's revised view in 2015 was that such cycles reflect a constantly recurring effort by governments to seek convenient solutions to problems that are more basic and mostly of their own making: "When governments run into fiscal troubles, they often look again for public-private partnerships ..." (Abstract). In fact, argued Klein, the evidence suggests that well-run public firms tend to match the performance of private firms in regulated sectors (13). Klein concluded that "There is no 'killer' rationale for public-private partnerships" (Abstract). In other words, the real reason why PPPs continue to re-emerge as proposed solutions is the desire by governments to find explanations for their problems, other than admit failure in effectively managing their own affairs.

Professor Klein may have been too modest in his reluctance to acknowledge his own role, and that of the World Bank Group, in the rollercoaster popularity of PPPs. Structural adjustment lending programs, led by the World Bank and International Monetary Fund (IMF) during the 1980s and 1990s, gave birth to modern PPP concepts. Under Klein's direction, the Bank published some of its first and most influential recommendations regarding the benefits of PPPs and the best ways to develop infrastructure concessions and other kinds of PPPs in developing countries (Kerf et al. 1998; Klein 1998a, 1998b; Klein and Hadjimichael 2003). If anyone purported to offer "killer" rationales for PPPs in developing countries, it was precisely Klein and his World Bank Group colleagues, abetted by supporters in the wider development community.

This book explores an alternative hypothesis to explain the recurring popularity of PPPs in developing countries, one that attempts to more fully account for the political economy factors in this popularity, especially the role of development institutions like the World Bank in promoting the use of PPP mechanisms. While acknowledging that governments of developing countries along with the private sector have helped to popularize PPPs, this book focuses on the PPP advocacy activities of the World Bank Group and other members of the development community, often carried out through the creation and funding of the PPFs, PDFs, PPP units, and similar programs and facilities described in the previous section. Over the years, new terminology and revisionist history—like Professor Klein's 2015 working paper—have to some extent obscured the origins and ongoing nature of this PPP advocacy. But its history is nevertheless reasonably clear in policy papers, annual reports, project documents, and program evaluations published by the World Bank and other major development institutions.

As introduced earlier, the hypothesis explored here is that after a brief initial surge in the use of PPPs due to structural adjustment lending programs in the mid-1990s, the PPP concept was promoted as a potentially powerful mechanism for exploiting the power of the private sector to solve economic problems. By the end of the 1990s, structural adjustment lending was coming to an official end, as was the related use of privatization programs. But PPPs survived as a gentler, more user-friendly reflection of the neoclassical views of mainstream economics that had strongly re-emerged in the 1980s and later summarized in the tenets of "Washington Consensus" (Williamson 1989).

From these early days, PPP advocacy has been able to sidestep the evidence-based critique outlined above because it has been led by zealots who have relied on faith and passionate persuasion, rather than evaluation and analysis to promote PPP concepts. Advocates have taken for granted that private finance, mostly in the form of PPPs, is the only realistic infrastructure financing option for poor developing countries, thereby assuming what at some point should have been proven. Confident assumptions of this kind have helped PPP advocates discount the need for objective evaluations of PPP support programs. Instead of rigorous cost-benefit assessments that include estimates of "without the intervention" counterfactuals, PPP advocates have been successful using anecdotal evidence, "success stories," and testimonials by beneficiaries and experts to demonstrate the benefits of PPPs and justify continued funding for efforts to prepare projects.

Several political economy reasons help explain why PPP advocacy has been able to flourish despite the lack of compelling evidence of PPP success in the developing world. Perhaps the most important of these factors has been the creation of a huge ecosystem of facilities and programs dedicated to making PPPs successful in developing countries. This advocacy coalition employs tens of millions of dollars annually to promote the use of PPPs with little rigorous analysis of their costs and benefits or the comparative value of alternative approaches involving traditional public investment.

The coalition members avoid competition but rarely coordinate or collaborate (or conspire), at least not in the way that some civil society critics allege. Instead, they collude, like suppliers in the absence of a competitive market. This is part of what William Easterly called "the cartel of good intentions"—aid organizations repetitively duplicating services in the absence of rigorous evaluation or market pressure from customers which rewards successful aid programs and disciplines unsuccessful ones (Easterly 2009). This collusion helps to diffuse blame when expected long-term impacts of PPP efforts in recipient countries do not materialize as expected. The complicity of coalition members makes it unlikely that they will object to the use of persuasion to convince sometimes skeptical governments of poor countries to commit their own limited resources to the development of PPPs. This despite the fact that resources are taken away from efforts to address more fundamental development problems for which PPPs are mostly unsustainable and often incomplete solutions. Several kinds of attraction, explored in this book, hold the alliance together. But the most powerful cement is probably the common, ideological faith in the power of private market forces to solve infrastructure problems if allowed sufficient freedom from governmental interference.

1.7 THE SCOPE OF THIS BOOK

This book does not argue that PPPs in developing countries can never be successful or should never be attempted, or that all PPPs reaching financial close with the help of PPFs cannot generate development benefits. It is not uncommon to find some stakeholders who are satisfied with the results of infrastructure PPP projects, including public and private partners involved in the projects (along with their respective advisers and consultants), as well as service beneficiaries.

The argument here is that PPPs attract far more attention and resources than is warranted, compared to alternative approaches to infrastructure development. Resources are largely wasted on PPP advocacy, employing thousands of people in single-minded efforts to make PPPs successful. The preparation and financing of PPPs capable of attracting private participation usually require such high levels of subsidization and other kinds of de-risking that the projects would be unable to demonstrate positive value-for-money (VfM) outcomes if compared with traditional public investment alternatives—although almost none of the leading PPFs reviewed in this book attempt these kinds of VfM comparisons involving the PPPs they work on. But even without accurate, transparent VfM analysis of this kind, the subsidization needed for preparation and financing means that these projects are unable to demonstrate commercial viability in a way that encourages non-subsidized replication, the ultimate objective of most PPP advocacy programs and facilities.

In any case, not enough of these subsidized projects have been completed to result in any significant reduction in the infrastructure development needs of developing countries. The use of infrastructure PPPs has never taken root in the poorest kinds of developing countries—LDCs and LICs—despite billions of dollars spent on PPPs in precisely these countries.

This book attempts to explore the nature of this PPP paradox—how it has come about, why it persists, what are its implications for developing countries, and what may be more cost-effective targets for development aid than heavily subsidized PPP projects. The discussion is organized around key themes explored in subsequent chapters:

The Origins of PPP Advocacy. Chapter 2 explores the modern origins of PPP advocacy and in so doing attempts to correct some common misperceptions about these origins. In what way has it been expedient to distinguish PPPs from "privatization," i.e., the divestiture of government assets? Why has PPP advocacy systematically ignored its origins in the "structural adjustment" lending programs implemented by the World Bank Group, International Monetary Fund (IMF), and other development organizations during the 1980s and 1990s?

PPP Lessons of the 1990s: Back to Basics. Chapter 3 discusses some of the refinements to the basic approach to PPPs that were made in the early 2000s by development institutions like the World Bank. The refinements were made as part of efforts to understand the shortcomings of structural adjustment lending programs. How and why did the changing development focus of the World Bank help PPPs avoid the fate suffered by privatization programs after the 1990s? How did this reexamination lead to a slower and more deliberative approach to PPPs by the World Bank?

The Bilateral Donors' Faith in PPPs. Chapter 4 examines how and why bilateral donors began to drive the global PPP agenda in the early 2000s, as the World Bank continued to take a more deliberative approach to the use of these mechanisms. The role of the U.K.'s Department for International Development (DFID) in convincing other donors to support its rapidly growing portfolio of PPFs and related facilities and programs is explored. How did DFID's approach help foster the dominance of faith and persuasion over evaluation and analysis in PPP advocacy?

The Transaction-only Approach. Chapter 5 explains how DFID's faith in PPPs reached its zenith with its support for two of the most powerful and enduring PPFs, IFC PPP Advisory and the Private Infrastructure Development Group (PIDG). These two programs were designed to structure and help finance private investment transactions on behalf of governments in the poorest countries. But their mission was to focus on deals, rather than address reforms needed to fully optimize the benefits of private investment. How successful have these PPFs been in facilitating project replication and sustainable PPP market development?

Using PPP Units to Franchise PPP Advocacy. Chapter 6 shows that while bilateral donors like DFID were directly assisting client governments with PPP transactions, other members of the development community, led by the World Bank, were encouraging governments to take ownership of PPP development by establishing single-purpose government agencies, PPP units, to oversee PPP preparation. Why were dozens of developing countries persuaded to spend scarce resources on the creation and staffing of such units, even though most of these countries had little prospect of establishing active, successful PPP programs?

Regional PPPs on the Global Stage. Chapter 7 argues that beginning with the G8 Gleneagles Summit in 2005, the advocacy of infrastructure PPPs began to take on more of a global character as the international development community began to focus on PPPs generally, and especially regional, "transformational" PPPs as tools to help revive the faltering achievement of development targets like the Millennium Development Goals (MDGs). How important is regional integration and regional infrastructure in Africa, and to what extent have PPPs played a role in regional infrastructure development?

A New Strategy for PPP Advocacy. As explained in Chapter 8, the publication of the *Africa Infrastructure Country Diagnostic* (AICD) by the World Bank in 2010, surprised most of the international development community by estimating that the total annual infrastructure investment gap in Africa was much larger than previous estimates. How and why did various G20 institutions react to the AICD findings? What was the significance of the G20 redefinition of the investment gap as a "project preparation gap" and the G20's recommendations to create new kinds of PPFs?

The Costs and Benefits of the Transaction-only Approach. Chapter 9 is the first of two chapters that seeks to assess what we have learned from PPP advocacy. This chapter focuses on the extent to which the transaction-only approach has been successful, specifically in developing greenfield projects using build–operate–transfer (BOT) contract structures, mostly for power generation and toll roads. This chapter ends with a case study of a recent water BOT in Africa, which assesses the extent to which heavily subsidized projects are likely to generate "demonstration effects" that lead to project replication and the development of market-like behavior.

The Rediscovery of Upstream Project Preparation. Most of the PPFs reviewed in this book were originally created to "scale-up" the use of PPP projects, in the sense of encouraging replication and market development. What market-building lessons can be learned from South Africa's successful, but short-lived, renewable energy independent power producer (IPP) program, profiled in Chapter 10? How did South Africa's program influence the IFC's Scaling Solar program and anticipate the IFC's the much larger organizational changes that have occurred recently with the creation of IFC Upstream? How effective are these changes likely to be?

Conclusion: The Future of PPPs. The private sector has largely decided the future of PPPs by insisting on projects with highly secure revenue streams and strong forms of private sector risk mitigation, including greenfield, wholesale,

BOT projects. But the demonstration effects of these projects will likely encourage little replication and market-like behavior, especially for projects outside of subsectors like power generation and toll roads. A key question posed by Chapter 11 is how soon will donors and MDBs who support PPP advocacy free themselves of misconceptions regarding PPPs, and begin to consider lower cost, more sustainable alternative methods for mobilizing and managing infrastructure investment?

Postscript: Revisiting the Seven Deadly Sins of Donors. What one expert has called the "persuadability" of bilateral donors is a confounding characteristic that underpins the PPP paradox explored in this book: Why does donor support for PPPs remain so strong despite overwhelming evidence that PPPs have not met expectations? Chapter 12 uses the well-known paper by Nancy Birdsall, "Seven Deadly Sins: Reflections on Donor Failings" (2005), as a helpful guide in understanding the various dimensions of donor persuadability as it relates to PPPs. That Birdsall's discussion is still so relevant today, nearly two decades after publication, suggests that donor faith in PPPs will be difficult to change because it has never had much to do with actual PPP project performance.

PART I

The origins of PPP advocacy

2. Structural adjustment: from privatization to PPPs

2.1 INTRODUCTION

This chapter investigates the origins of public–private partnership (PPP) advocacy. Who were the first advocates and how did they come to so strongly believe that infrastructure investment in poor countries was an issue that could be effectively addressed with PPPs? Answering these questions requires correction of several misperceptions about the modern origins of PPPs and PPP advocacy in the 1980s and 1990s. First, the claim is frequently made that PPP mechanisms have a long history of frequent and successful use, in some accounts dating back hundreds of years (e.g., World Bank 2004; PPIAF 2009). Second, a claim made even more vigorously by governments and their development partners is that infrastructure PPPs are fundamentally different from "privatization" in the sense of transfer to private ownership. Classifying PPPs as a form of privatization is a "misconception," according to the official "PPP reference guide" produced by several multilateral development banks (MDBs) (World Bank et al. 2014).

Both of these claims obscure important facts regarding the origins of modern PPPs, how and why these mechanisms are used today, and how they perform. The use of the term "public–private partnership," and the current debate about the use of these mechanisms, stems from their introduction during the policy-based lending activities of the World Bank, the International Monetary Fund (IMF), and other development institutions in the 1980s and 1990s. The privatization of state-owned enterprises (SOEs) was a key prescription of the "structural adjustment" lending operations implemented by these development institutions. PPPs were considered one form of privatization intended to deal with particular kinds of SOE problems. At the time, PPPs were routinely referred to in this way by both development institutions and their government clients.

The promotion of PPPs and other forms of privatization was a reaction to the frustrating failures of earlier efforts that targeted more desirable SOE reforms not involving private participation. The abrupt shift to privatization as a major theme of development work was fueled by an emerging ideological commitment to “market-friendly policies,” which set the tone for the promotion of private participation that continues today. That commitment led to a dominance of PPP advocacy over analytical approaches that assessed the practicality, value for money, and costs and benefits of doing PPPs in particular situations. The history of structural adjustment has been widely documented, but its role in giving birth to PPP advocacy is less well known. That role is the subject of this chapter.

2.2 THE NEED TO REFORM STATE-OWNED ENTERPRISES (SOES)

In the early 1980s, the IMF and the World Bank launched their policy-based “structural adjustment” lending programs. This was a response to a series of economic crises in the global South during the late 1970s, including an oil crisis, debt crisis, multiple economic depressions, and economic stagnation. Starting with Latin America (Mexico in late 1982) and sub-Saharan Africa (Nigeria in late 1985), the IMF and World Bank recommended these policy-based lending programs for the majority of developing country clients experiencing economic crises, making available large resource injections in exchange for government commitments to “adjust” the structure of their economies, to improve their international competitiveness, and restore their balance of payments.

Adjustment requirements included austerity spending measures and rigorous reforms to, and reduction of, the public sector’s role in the economy. In most cases, the dominant form of that government role involved SOEs. Consequently, SOE reform was a key element of almost every adjustment operation (Nellis 2005), and became a key element of the Bretton Woods institutions’ general response to the economic problems mentioned above. Government ownership of “commercial enterprises” was widely viewed as limiting economic growth in developing countries because it led to government interference in the form of price controls, foreign exchange rationing, distorted trade regimes, and restricted financial markets.

When the World Bank, IMF, and other development agencies referred to “state-owned enterprises” or “public enterprises” they generally meant government entities that were expected to earn most of their revenue from the sale of goods and services. Beyond that single defining characteristic, the term was used broadly to mean “… all industrial and commercial firms, mines, utilities, transport companies, and financial intermediaries controlled to some extent by government” (Shirley 1983, 2). Most had some form of operational, financial, or governance separation from general-purpose government, but a separate legal identity was not an essential characteristic. Utilities, organized as government departments, sometimes famously operated with more autonomy than many SOEs, as conventionally defined (Shirley 1983, 3).

Although some SOEs were well managed, many experienced problems that were attributable to a conflicting mix of socio-political and commercial objectives. The mix resulted in a range of problems: managers without the autonomy to take necessary commercial decisions; over-spending; below-cost pricing (justified as socially necessary); failures to fully collect customer service payments; supervision by boards of directors who protected the interests of parent ministries rather than their SOEs; and generally poor monitoring, reporting, and follow-up. Much of this was related to the incompetence of untrained SOE managers, many of whom obtained their positions through personal or political connections.

The role of SOEs in African manufacturing reflected the size of the problem. In the 1970s, the SOE share of manufacturing output in industrialized countries was typically only a few percent, often zero. But in the developing world, the SOE share of manufacturing was in the 30–70 percent range, 15 times the share in industrialized countries (Schmitz 1996). Very few of these SOEs generated revenues sufficient to cover operating costs, depreciation, and capital investment. Most consistently experienced net losses, existed in a perpetual state of negative net worth, and were kept functioning with taxpayer subsidies or the proceeds of excessive government borrowing backed by tax revenues rather than their own operating surpluses.

Of course, SOEs have long existed in industrialized economies. Public utilities have been widely used to supply a variety of infrastructure services, including water and sanitation, electricity, and transport. While not always highly profitable enterprises, their operating principles tend to be more commercial and their subsidies much lower than in developing countries. In the U.S. for example, private and public utilities access the nation's municipal and corporate bond markets to finance power generation, railroads, canals, roads, bridges, water and sanitation systems, and other kinds of public infrastructure. By the 1980s, the U.S. municipal bond market had already become one of the most powerful capital allocation mechanisms in the world, and a mechanism that some developing countries were actively trying to replicate (Leigland 1997). By the end of the 1980s, the U.S. municipal bond market was dominated by over 7,000 corporate enterprises owned by state and local governments, which made up a huge amalgamation of largely autonomous SOEs, most of which were created with the intended purpose of competing for private capital in the municipal bond market (Leigland 1994). By accessing the bond market in this way, these SOEs became subject to the "discipline of the market," formalized in legal covenants that were enforced by bondholders and bond issue trustees and monitored by government regulators, credit rating agencies, and others.

In Western Europe, banks played a larger role than capital markets in channeling private capital into infrastructure investments by local governments and SOEs (De Fiore and Uhlig 2005). The banking approach to infrastructure lending was illustrated by the growth of the Dexia Group, which by the time it became a casualty of the 2011 European sovereign debt crisis had established itself as the premier pan-European specialized municipal lender with equity positions in many other municipal banks throughout Europe, Africa, and Asia. Municipal banks in Europe provided intermediation and monitoring functions that were similar to those carried out by capital markets in the U.S., and in so doing also enforced a form of competitive market discipline that incentivized commercial behavior (Peterson 2003).

This experience in industrialized countries underscored the fact that the nature of enterprise ownership—whether public or private—made little or no difference in terms of whether enterprise debt was attractive to private investors. Instead of ownership, the important characteristics were some degree of autonomy from political interference and an operational strategy aimed at the generation of profit or at least cost coverage through the sale of services. "Commercialization," "competition," and "corporatization" were some of the key terms used to describe the original objectives of SOE reform under structural adjustment. Taken to an extreme, pursuing these objectives could mean conversion from a publicly owned or government-operated entity into a profit-oriented private corporation or company. But the experience in industrialized countries suggested that some form of operational and financial separation from parent government, combined with a commercial business orientation, could be enough to incentivize SOEs to compete for access to private savings (intermediated by banks or capital markets) rather than continue depending exclusively on taxpayer subsidies. Some SOEs would be unable to become efficient enough to compete in this way and would likely go out of business. But as surviving enterprises became better managed and more commercially competitive, they would be better able to access private domestic capital markets for their investment needs and in turn this process would facilitate the growth and maturation of those markets and the reduction of pressure on central government budgets and taxpayers to provide subsidies.

Evan as structural adjustment became more aggressive at the end of the 1980s, many development professional continued to see corporatization and commercialization as the preferred path toward the kind of SOE reform in developing countries that would lead eventually to sustainable infrastructure finance. Miguel Schloss, the World Bank's Division Chief for Corporate and Budget Planning, argued that "The ability to mobilize private savings for the financing of electric power will be a critical factor in this decade" (Schloss 1990, 5). Anthony Churchill, Director of the World Bank's Industry and Energy Department, introduced a 1990 report on private finance in the power sector by noting that "The overarching objective is to develop capital markets" (Churchill 1990, 2).

2.3 THE FAILURE OF PERFORMANCE AGREEMENTS

The promotion of competition, commercialization, and corporatization as a way of subjecting SOEs to market forces and competitive pressures was in keeping with the neoclassical views of mainstream economics, re-emerging in the 1980s, and was consistent with the popular ideological conservatism championed by Ronald Reagan and Margaret Thatcher. The fall of the Berlin Wall in 1989 helped to validate the dominant role of market forces as a means for ensuring growth and productivity, something that the ineffective reform efforts of the 1970s had been unable to accomplish. Economic growth and poverty reduction had been the original twin objectives of the World Bank. But, with Robert McNamara's departure as president of the Bank in 1981, economic growth became the primary objective of World Bank development efforts (Yusuf et al. 2009). The faith in the power of market forces was such that economic growth was expected to lead to poverty reduction without the need to emphasize targeted pro-poor policies and interventions that had been widely recommended earlier.

Structural adjustment lending in the 1980s reflected a new, aggressive effort to push forward with corporatization and commercialization of SOEs. This vigorous promotion of market-based economic reforms and the pursuit of growth strategies using multilateral development bank (MDB) lending as an incentive became a controversial element of structural adjustment programs. The Bank and other development partners viewed this approach as warranted to partially make up for their own history of passive acquiescence in the face of domestic policy mistakes that were largely responsible for the mismanagement of SOEs in the 1970s. These development organizations were well aware of their own contributions to the situation, especially as they had continued to lend to these governments in support of these badly managed SOEs. They had justified this lending on the basis that client governments needed time to sort through improvements to SOE planning, pricing, and operations. The combination of financing and advice was then expected to gradually transform SOEs into more commercial and creditworthy operations, able to access financing on their own.

In the early 1980s, hastened by the spreading debt crisis, SOE performance was rapidly deteriorating. While some governments were at the time resisting reform efforts, it was also evident that Bank personnel were not enforcing performance targets incorporated into loan covenants. To access concessional or near-concessional finance, governments had committed to change policies on pricing, investments, institutional development, methods of governance, etc. But most of these changes never occurred. SOE operations continued to be plagued by conflicting objectives and lack of managerial accountability. Under structural adjustment, the World Bank's objective was to prioritize its work with government clients committed to reforms and to be more forceful in following up to ensure that agreed structural changes were indeed carried out. Bank sector strategies eventually referred to this as "commitment lending," a significant departure from business as usual: "Above all, the Bank will not continue to finance power projects where poorly-performing and highly-polluting utilities and their governments are unwilling to carry out fundamental structural reforms that significantly improve the way they are doing business" (World Bank 1993, 72). All of this meant scaling up the Bank's role as an advocate of specific structural reforms determined to be in the best interests of clients. Under the pressure to accelerate reform, this kind of advocacy began to replace efforts to help clients choose from among reform options based on evidence regarding relative effectiveness.

The first major type of specific SOE reform advocated under structural adjustment in the 1980s was an effort to recreate the kind of relationship that existed between SOEs and parent governments in industrialized countries. These relationships maintained government ownership while guaranteeing operational autonomy as long as the enterprise exhibited a commercial business orientation and did not depend heavily on subsidy support. To achieve this in a developing country context, the World Bank insisted on the use of formal but non-legal performance agreements between SOE owners (usually government sector ministries or departments) and managers, which were intended to subject SOEs to market-like pressures. Performance agreements, usually made a condition of Bank loans, were meant to preserve a level of enterprise independence while providing SOE managers with incentives to behave "commercially," which primarily meant achieving more cost recovery in their operations and competing for access to finance.

The incentives were not expected to result directly from market competition, but from rewards (or penalties) for SOE managers and government owners honoring performance commitments formalized in written agreements. Rewards for managers included things like salary increases and promotions. The agreements called on government owners to maintain some SOE operational autonomy by not intervening in day-to-day enterprise management. A World Bank report to its executive directors after the first year of structural adjustment implementation gave an update on the Bank's recommendation that the Senegalese government sign a "program contract" to improve the commercial performance of its SOEs (World Bank 1981).

Such agreements quickly became the principal SOE adjustment tool during the 1980s (Gomez-Ibanez 2007). By the end of the decade, hundreds of performance agreements had been signed in developing countries, and hundreds more were in preparation. A variety of different names were used for these agreements, including program contracts, contract plans, memoranda of understanding, statements of corporate intent, performance contracts, performance agreements, etc.

But by the end of the 1980s World Bank evaluators were already seeing signs that these agreements were not dramatically improving SOE performance (Nellis 1989). The agreements worked best with commercial enterprises owned by governments, but already operating in market environments and subject to competitive market pressures. Financial targets for such enterprises were relatively simple, and easy to agree on and monitor. Managerial autonomy was largely acceptable to government owners. However, for infrastructure SOEs operating in non-competitive markets, like government utilities providing water and power services, all of this was more difficult. Governments consistently failed to meet many if not most of their obligations under these performance agreements, particularly promises regarding equity injections, managerial autonomy, work force reductions, and even settlement by government agencies of payment obligations to water and electricity utilities (perhaps the most common problem).

By the beginning of the 1990s, there was a growing realization that the problem with performance agreements was that they reflected the interests and expectations of development partners, more than the actual signatories. Both government owners of SOEs and SOE managers derived benefits from SOE behavior which had little to do with the financial performance of the organizations. Moreover, the performance agreements were not legally enforceable contracts and did not offer enough incentives to effectively encourage either party to fulfill commitments. As a result, they often became distractions from the need for more substantial reforms.

Performance agreements continued to be used, particularly in West Africa, until the mid-1990s, but then largely disappeared. By the early 1990s, World Bank researchers had already confirmed what earlier studies had suggested—that performance agreements were not effective in improving the performance of targeted enterprises (Sherif 1993; World Bank 1994a). The Bank's Public Sector Management Division continued to evaluate such agreements during the 1990s, culminating in an econometric evaluation of 500 performance agreements in China. The country had hundreds of thousands of SOEs by 1989, 88 percent of which were under performance agreements. The China study found that, on average, the agreements failed to improve SOE performance and may have worsened it (Shirley and Xu 2001). Already by 1994, Chinese officials had anticipated such conclusions and had mostly ended the widespread use of performance agreements.

Eventually, the 1980s were viewed by many in the World Bank as a "lost decade" in terms of reforms in developing countries, in large part because so little progress was made with SOE performance improvement (World Bank 1995). For example, the Bank's review of structural adjustment performance in Africa during the last half of the 1980s concluded that interventions like performance agreements, along with other efforts to reform SOEs, had failed: "The general assessment, despite a few encouraging stories [...] is that the efforts at reform have been disappointing overall. Few 'rehabilitated' public enterprises have made significant and lasting improvements, and many are being rehabilitated for a second or third time" (World Bank 1994a, 109).

Consequently, the need to deal with SOEs took on a new urgency with the growing recognition that the problems extended beyond the inefficiencies and losses associated with the operations of potentially commercial enterprises like hotels, factories, and farms. It was increasingly clear that so-called "strategic enterprises" were "... the major causes of losses and economic distortions" (World Bank 1994a, 102). These were the utilities, telecommunications companies, transport parastatals, heavy industries, agricultural marketing boards, etc., with huge, ongoing operating losses. The losses meant that these SOEs failed to invest enough to keep pace with improving technology and expanding populations, often because governments kept prices low in misguided efforts to make goods and services affordable to the poor (when it was the non-poor who usually benefited most from the under-pricing). Governments continued to make this problem worse in the 1980s by transferring taxpayer funds to these SOEs in efforts to subsidize operations and investments: "Another worrisome trend is the ongoing, large annual investment in these public enterprises (often financed in part by donor funds), even though they are generating low or negative returns" (World Bank 1994a, 109).

2.4 A NEW GAME PLAN: PRIVATIZATION

After the disappointing results of performance agreements in the 1980s, it seemed that the preferred model for financing infrastructure used in industrialized countries—i.e., borrowing by commercialized public enterprises from competitive capital markets or banks—was more remote than ever. Two obstacles stood out:

- First, many of the SOEs in regions like Africa were technically bankrupt or close to it. Few demonstrated anything like the kind of financial performance required to attract private debt or equity necessary to meet the investment needs of the 1990s.
- Second, functioning domestic capital markets were still essentially non-existent. In Africa, none had the size or activity levels necessary to supply needed levels of investment. By 1990, for example, none of the World Bank's power utility clients had successfully raised money in

> domestic capital markets (Schloss 1990). All of these SOEs still relied on subsidies funded through tax revenues (or loans from development partners) to finance most infrastructure investment. None were accessing private savings via banks or bond markets, based on commercial performance.

Both of these impediments needed to be dealt with. For many World Bank economists, financial sector reform and capital market development still represented key long-term objectives, but little progress had been made during the 1980s in reforming and developing these markets. The problem was compounded by the increasingly urgent need for investment in critical infrastructure sectors like power. World Bank policymakers like Miguel Schloss began to call for "a new game plan" to finance power utilities and other strategic enterprises (Schloss 1990, 6). Schloss recognized that, although critically important for infrastructure finance over the long term, "… in the short term, resorting to domestic capital markets offers no solution […] Direct private sector financing is a more promising option" (6). By "direct" financing, he was referring to funding provided directly to an SOE by private investors, without intermediation by capital markets or banks.

This was an endorsement of "privatization" as a tool for reforming SOEs. Private ownership or control of SOEs, it was argued, could facilitate access to private investment capital in the absence of capital markets or robust banking systems. Schloss noted two generic forms of private sector engagement: (i) transfer of ownership of an *entire* public entity, such as a power utility; and (ii) private sector ownership or operations of *parts* of a utility, meaning the use of leases, management contracts, and concessions to enable private control of one or more elements of utility operation. Schloss noted that "privatisation" was often misrepresented: "Privatisation does not necessarily mean the outright sale of a power utility […] In fact, one of the most useful forms of privatisation is to establish a long-term concession arrangement …" (8).

The real benefits of these arrangements came not so much from generating revenues from sales or leases, but from interrupting the flow of taxpayer funding to SOEs and incentivizing the SOEs to take advantage of private technical and managerial skills to begin to compete on their own account for private capital. Changing ownership or control was a means to an end, not an end in itself. As Schloss argued, "Competition rather than ownership is the key" (8). If performance agreements had been effective in motivating SOEs to compete for the private capital needed to fund their own investments, as SOEs did in the U.S., changes in ownership would not be necessary.

However, it was also clear that this use of privatization to improve SOE competitiveness meant less of a focus on the development and use of the domestic capital market financing models used in the U.S. or Europe. In developing countries, the capital sourced via privatization would mostly come directly from foreign rather than domestic sources. Because this would result in direct access to foreign capital, without intermediation via local banks or markets, domestic capital market development would not necessarily result from privatization.

Because of this, senior World Bank officials were of the view that special efforts needed to be made to ensure that to the extent possible, privatization would facilitate capital market development, rather than retard it. For example, they argued that as capital markets matured, divestiture could eventually be done via sales of listed securities. World Bank Director Anthony Churchill introduced a Bank publication on build–operate–transfer (BOT) projects in the power sector (referred to then as build–own–operate–transfer or BOOT projects), reminding readers that capital market development *still* represented the development priority:[1]

> So, BOOT should be thought of as part of an initial strategy to develop this capital market, not as a final objective. Setting up a BOOT scheme and getting it working is very nice. It does not, however, really solve too many problems, unless there is follow through in developing domestic capital markets rather than in attracting more and more foreign money, of which there simply is not enough. The developing countries are going to have to raise most of their capital requirements locally, and BOOT schemes are one way of developing the local capital market. (Churchill 1990, 3)

Yet Churchill, like many of his colleagues, acknowledged that although BOT projects might help develop capital markets, that kind of impact would be limited. Churchill hoped that the reliance on BOT projects for investment would be a "temporary measure" (2).[2]

Officially, there was never a World Bank policy attempt to justify privatization, rather than competition, as an end-in-itself. World Bank guidance dictated that in order to determine when and how privatization should be prioritized, SOE problems should be assessed on a project-by-project basis, with likely solutions identified and evaluated, and efforts made to achieve some level of commercialization and competition, as well as other key sector

---

1 For definitions of BOT and BOO, and other kinds of PPPs, see Box 2.1 below.

2 There clearly were internal debates on this issue, reflected in the 1989 World Development Report. The report recognized that "it is often argued" that ownership does not matter as much as the independence and accountability of management, and the extent of competition. "In practice, however, the form of ownership goes a long way to determine the environment within which management operates" (World Bank 1989, 89).

reforms. For example, in its 1993 power sector policy statement, the Bank outlined a basic approach to SOE reform, involving a simple prioritization of basic reforms considered necessary, with a recommendation that efforts to achieve commercialization and competition, facilitated by market-friendly regulation, be undertaken first, before any actual attempts at privatization (World Bank 1993).

A decade later, the Bank's own internal evaluations found that although recommendations regarding this basic sequence had been strongly and clearly communicated, the 1993 statement was not accompanied by any strategic or operational guidance on how to achieve an overall reform sequence of that kind: "… while the 1993 Policy enunciated what to do, it was not accompanied by a strategy on how to do it, because of the limited experience worldwide with implementing such policies" (Manibog et al. 2003, vi). There was some recognition of this problem in the 1993 policy document, but it assumed that staff would "learn by doing."

The need to quickly roll out structural adjustment measures, plus the lack of operational guidance from the Bank for staff interventions and prescriptions, meant that the practical results of structural adjustment programs were often quite different from what was intended at a policy level. In practice, privatization deals eventually became ends in themselves rather than means to an end as was intended in World Bank sector policies in the early 1990s. Transactions involving private participation were gradually accepted as proxies for the achievement of commercialization rather than measures that might result and benefit from commercialization (Manibog et al. 2003). For World Bank staff, concluding a privatization transaction was a convenient indicator that sector reform was advancing and structural adjustment performance targets were being met.

Under these conditions, privatization quickly took on a life of its own. From the late 1980s to the early 1990s, SOE privatization focused almost exclusively on commercial and manufacturing enterprises that operated in competitive markets and required little regulation. The full menu of divestiture options was used for government-owned hotels, agribusinesses, airlines, mines, oil refineries, etc. African privatization programs quickly started implementation in Senegal, Niger, Kenya, Ghana, Côte d'Ivoire, and Guinea. During the 1980s, the World Bank averaged five loans per year in Africa which explicitly required privatization. By the mid-1990s, the annual number of such loans had tripled to 15 (Nellis 2005).

2.5 THE EMERGENCE OF PPPS

In contrast to today's popular distinction between privatization and PPPs, Schloss's broad definition of "privatisation" included PPP arrangements like concessions, leases, and management contracts, as well as more conventional forms of privatization involving change in ownership. This was a common understanding in the World Bank Group during the 1980s and 1990s. The difference between the sale of an SOE to a private purchaser and the transfer of control to a private manager was considered merely a matter of degree. During this period, concessions, leases, etc., were not yet widely referred to as "public–private partnerships." Instead, a variety of sometimes awkward terminology was used, all ways of indicating that private participation took the form of private control rather than private ownership:

- "Privatization of management" or "non-ownership privatization" (Kikeri et al. 1992; Husain and Faruqee 1994).
- "Non-asset divestiture" or "divestiture of management functions" (World Bank 1994a).
- "Temporary privatizations" or "privatization through indirect means" (Campbell-White and Bhatia 1998).
- "Privatization through contracting out" (de Luca 1998).

The World Bank's 1994 World Development Report popularized the term, "public–private partnership" ("PPP") for these arrangements and introduced them to a global development audience (World Bank 1994b). Use of this term was given another important boost in 1997, when the new Labour Government in the UK rebranded its "Private Finance Initiative" as "public–private partnerships" (Hellowell 2010). Today, a variety of contracting mechanisms are normally categorized as PPPs (Box 2.1).

BOX 2.1 BASIC TYPES OF PUBLIC–PRIVATE PARTNERSHIPS (PPPS)

Brownfield PPPs: a private entity takes over the management of an existing government-owned enterprise and also assumes significant risk for performance and sometimes for investments needed to extend, complete, or rehabilitate the enterprise facilities. Examples include:

- *Build, rehabilitate, operate, and transfer (BROT):* a private developer finances and builds an add-on to an existing government-owned facility or rehabilitates existing facility assets, then operates and maintains the facility at its own risk for a long-term contract period, after which the facility is returned to government control. Often referred to as "concessions."

- *Lease contracts:* a private entity leases a government-owned facility for a specified period (short- to medium-term), usually paying a rental fee to the government owner, but retains system revenues over and above the rental fee; the government retains responsibility for investments.
- *Management contracts:* the government owner contracts with a private entity to manage a facility for a specified (short-term) period, paying a fixed management fee, sometimes supplemented with performance-based success fees; the government retains responsibility for investments.

Greenfield PPPs: a private entity builds and operates a new facility for a period of time, and under conditions, specified in a contract. Examples include:

- *Build, operate, and transfer (BOT):* a private sponsor finances and builds a new facility at its own risk, operates the facility at its own risk, and then transfers the facility to the government at the end of a long-term contract period. The government usually provides revenue guarantees through long-term take-or-pay contracts for bulk supply facilities or minimum revenue guarantees.
- *Build, own, and operate (BOO):* a private sponsor finances and builds a new facility at its own risk, then owns and operates the facility at its own risk. The government usually provides revenue guarantees through long-term take-or-pay contracts for bulk supply facilities or minimum traffic revenue guarantees.

Source: Adapted from World Bank (2022).

Under structural adjustment lending programs PPPs generally served several, sometimes related, purposes:

First, they could be used to "privatize" SOEs that governments refused to sell because the enterprises were profitable, difficult to sell, or otherwise considered strategic. Development partners like the World Bank were dismayed at the large number of enterprises that developing country governments wanted to continue owning because of "strategic" considerations. These were the same "strategic firms" identified in the early 1980s, which often were the major causes of losses and economic distortions. Governments could at times be convinced to use privatization modalities for these kinds of enterprises, but only if the modalities were limited to private control without changes in ownership (World Bank 1994a). The Bank and other development partners believed that private management would significantly improve operational efficiency even if ownership remained with government.

Second, PPP options were also often seen as first steps toward a full transition to private ownership (Manibog et al. 2003). Early World Bank reviews of privatization frequently made this claim: "… contracts, leases, and other ways of privatizing management are a step in the right direction: they are beneficial in their own right, and they launch a transition to full privatization" (Kikeri et al. 1992, 6). But very little evidence was ever presented that such transitions had occurred with any frequency.

Third, if nothing else, such mechanisms were expected to solve the fundamental problem with performance agreements: specifically, the frequency with which governments reneged on commitments made in such agreements (Shirley 1995). With PPPs, government promises regarding managerial autonomy, equity injections, work force reductions, etc., were legally binding contractual obligations. Theoretically, either of the parties to the contract could appeal to courts of law to enforce compliance with contractual terms (although such legal actions were rarely implemented because they were found to be quite difficult and expensive).

Some kinds of PPPs had already been widely used internationally in the private sector before they were recommended as part of structural adjustment programs. For example, management contracts quickly became highly recommended as a practical way to privatize small commercial enterprises. Such contracts had enjoyed decades of successful use in the private sector, most notably in the hotel industry, as documented in a World Bank study in the late 1980s that strongly endorsed the use of such contracts (Hegstad and Newport 1987). When the privatization of commercial enterprises started in developing countries in the 1980s, dozens of government-owned hotels were quickly "privatized" via management contracts.

Governments of developing countries were also familiar with leases and concessions, but mostly in situations in which such agreements were used to develop natural resource projects in mining, petroleum, agribusiness, and forestry. Governments derived significant revenues from these arrangements. But leases and concessions involved a considerable degree of private sector control over government assets. Because projects like utility concessions did not offer significant, immediate increases in government revenues, they never became as popular with government officials as leases or concessions for natural resource projects.

Surveys of SOE privatization in the 1980s indicated that PPPs were already being used for commercial enterprises, although far less frequently than ownership change (Candoy-Sekse 1988). The privatization of infrastructure began to accelerate in the 1990s, as DFIs and MDBs continued promoting enterprise sales, but also started facilitating the use of PPP mechanisms more frequently. Concessions, leases, management contracts, and eventually BOT or BOO contracts were becoming more widely accepted methods for attracting private investment and management.

In the case of state-owned utilities in non-competitive markets like water and electricity supply, there was serious consideration by donors and MDBs of encouraging ownership transfer, or at least partial transfer. However, it was clear that in low-income or least-developed countries (LDCs), actual ownership sale of a non-competitive utility would require major sector legal and regulatory reforms. Reforms might include the creation of planning and regulatory frameworks that could distinguish potentially competitive from non-competitive activities, establishment of tariff regimes, clarification of service goals, and development of cost minimization targets. Some kind of regulatory agency would be needed to implement the process, and governments would need to maintain commitments to refrain from market interference. There was even some discussion in the World Bank in the early 1990s about the possibility that a completely unregulated monopoly utility operating under private ownership might still be a better option than government-owned and managed service provision (Bradburd 1992). But by the mid-1990s, these considerations were abandoned as impractical and non-competitive utilities were targeted mostly for PPP solutions.

In 1996 and 1997 infrastructure concessions became the fastest growing form of PPP. They involved contractual arrangements in which a private entity would agree to take over the management of an SOE for a given period, and assume significant investment risk. Under these contracts, private partners rehabilitated existing infrastructure assets and, in some cases, built additions to existing facilities, but all assets remained under government ownership. Such contracts were highly recommended by development partners as an ideal solution to many of the problems facing infrastructure utilities in poor countries. The World Bank promoted concessions as "The way to privatize infrastructure sector monopolies" (Guislain and Kerf 1995).

By the mid-1990s, PPPs were being used as privatization tools far more frequently than had been the case a decade earlier (Nellis 2005). Sometimes these tools were used alongside performance agreements and asset sales. But the number and variety of SOE sales and liquidations were still far more numerous under structural adjustment, demonstrating that ownership changes still dominated most of the reform programs. A World Bank survey published just before the Asian financial crisis in 1997 found that although over 200 brownfield PPPs had been concluded by that time, this amounted to only 8 percent of total SOE privatizations. This was considered a disappointing result, and expectations were that much more would be done with infrastructure PPPs by the end of that decade (Sarbib 1997). The 1997 Asian financial crisis resulted in a sharp decline in efforts to privatize infrastructure because so many existing transactions collapsed or required renegotiation. It was not until about

2005 that private infrastructure investments began to slowly trend upward again, driven by PPPs.

BOT and BOO projects were also hard hit by the Asian crisis, especially independent power producer (IPP) projects that had begun to proliferate in Asia. Initially, because they were complex and expensive to develop, these projects were slow to gain popularity in the developing world and often seemed inappropriate for the poorest countries. They were not often classified together with more popular PPP forms like leases, concessions, and management contracts. But BOT or BOO projects were inherently attractive to governments because they did not affect existing service delivery assets; nor did they allow private involvement in utility management or tariff setting. When Anthony Churchill was writing about BOTs in 1990, these contracts were being used almost exclusively in Europe and North America, particularly for power and transport. In 1990, fourteen BOT projects were under consideration in the Bank, most of them involving electricity generation (Churchill 1990).

But the World Bank was still carefully considering its involvement with BOTs, and in fact was not yet completely convinced that these privatization modalities would be useful under structural adjustment. A 1990 World Bank working paper was one of the first Bank publications to consider BOTs as a "privatization technique" for use in developing countries (Augenblick and Custer 1990). Some Bank managers like Churchill were cautiously supportive, particularly in respect of the power sector. But a comprehensive 1992 Bank review of lessons learned in 180 privatization operations did not include BOTs because they raised "... a different and complex set of issues" from those associated with other forms of privatization, including concessions and management contracts (Kikeri et al. 1992, 79).

Churchill's hope that BOTs would be a "temporary measure" clearly reflected a miscalculation regarding the powerful attraction of these types of projects. He thought they would be needed only until banking systems and capital markets could be developed to provide larger scale, less expensive, and more sustainable sources of private infrastructure finance. However, generous contractual terms and risk mitigation mechanisms quickly enabled BOT and BOO projects to dominate all private infrastructure investment in developing countries, and not just for the power sector where BOT or BOO models made IPP projects so lucrative for private investors and operators.

The first African IPP project investment took place in 1994 in Côte d'Ivoire, involving a BOT contract. That project was quickly followed by projects in Kenya, Mauritius, Senegal, Tanzania, and Ghana. In Asia by 1997, countries like Indonesia, Malaysia, Philippines, and Thailand already had large numbers of IPPs underway. By the late 1990s BOT and BOO projects were generating far more private investment in infrastructure than all other forms of private investment combined, and that trend has continued to the present day. While the Asian financial crisis slowed the spread of BOT and BOO projects like IPP projects, these types of projects recovered after the crisis more quickly than was the case for concessions and leases because of the BOT potential for private profits and the private sector's insistence on risk mitigation mentioned above. (See Chapter 9 for a more extensive discussion of these projects.)

Privatization in all of its varieties became a dominant World Bank SOE reform tool under structural adjustment, even though privatization was never officially endorsed as an end in itself. Between 1990 and 2001, over 2,100 private infrastructure projects worth $426 billion were financed in developing countries, about 40 percent of this investment was in the power sector (World Bank 2022). So while World Bank officials like Churchill hoped that privatization would be a temporary solution, investment via banks or capital markets has never become a functional alternative.

2.6 PERSUASION VS. ANALYSIS UNDER STRUCTURAL ADJUSTMENT

The rapid roll-out of privatization, including the use of PPPs, was not facilitated by rigorous analyses or evaluations demonstrating the extent to which privatization was a cost-effective solution. The conditionalities associated with most World Bank adjustment loans began to reflect the tenets of "Washington Consensus," articulated by John Williamson in 1989. Williamson's list became an authoritative if unofficial shorthand guide to recommended market-oriented development prescriptions, including privatization of SOEs (World Bank 2005). And the value of those prescriptions in the 1990s was largely taken for granted as the World Bank began to experience what officials later admitted was a "euphoria over privatization" (World Bank 2005).

A reliance on persuasion over analysis in privatization advocacy resulted from a tendency in the World Bank and other development institutions to use simple, easily understood messaging regarding the "received wisdom" underpinning what the Bank determined to be the prevailing development orthodoxy. The annual World Development Reports (WDRs) produced by the Bank starting in 1978, articulated these messages in a fashion that Bank staff could use to communicate with client governments worldwide. Joseph Stiglitz, senior vice-president and chief economist at the World Bank from 1997 to 2000, later admitted that these messages were usually of the "one-size-fits-all," cookie-cutter variety (Yusuf et al. 2009). The need to support these public messages recommending privatization and PPPs with compelling evidence seemed largely unnecessary. By the end of the 1980s, confidence in market-based development had by then spread widely among economists and development professionals. Advocacy and persuasion seemed like priorities as opposed to analysis and evaluation.

In fact, because of the pressure to rapidly roll-out of structural adjustment lending programs there was little time to carry out any kind of meaningful analysis and evaluation. The rapid scale-up of privatization projects in the 1990s meant that privatization options were being selected primarily based on negotiations with government counterparts rather than as a result of value-for-money analysis. Operations were initiated before lessons were learned from previous efforts, and in any case not much information was available from previous projects because of widespread failure to set performance targets. When performance targets were set, they were often inappropriate or too ambitious (Castalia Strategic Advisors 2005). This lack of information was also due to the fact that privatization programs were often inadequately monitored and evaluated, leading to situations where new programs could not be justified based on empirical evidence of past benefits (Campbell-White and Bhatia 1998). From 1991 to 2002, little monitoring took place to assess the fiscal impact of privatization, creating an inability to anticipate the outcomes of these activities (Buchs 2003). The World Bank's internal evaluation of its power sector work in the 1990s found that suitable systems for project monitoring and evaluation had not been established, making it difficult to understand the country factors under-pinning the success or failure of projects (Manibog et al. 2003). A fundamental lack of data made the overall retrospective evaluations of privatization efforts extremely difficult to do once structural adjustment lending programs had ended (Estache 2005).

In 1989, World Bank analyst John Nellis noted that "… the Bank has not proven to be particularly adept at advising governments on the timing or detailed mechanics of privatization ventures" (Nellis 1989). When Nellis looked back 15 years later he found that "Detailed data on what took place in the 1990s must exist in the World Bank project and African country records; but no summations, similar to those cited for the earlier period, are readily available" (Nellis 2005, 38). He concluded that although theoretical justifications were plentiful, the shift from previous reforms like performance agreements to widespread privatization had been "a leap of faith" (3).

Without more analysis and compelling justifications, this faith was not necessarily something that many of the Bank's client governments wanted to embrace. The Bank underestimated the political complexity and sensitivity of structural adjustment reforms like privatization, and as a result miscalculated the time required for reforms to mature before it made sense to push forward with privatization: "… this technocratic view did not give adequate weight to the political economy of reform and proved too optimistic" (Manibog et al. 2003, xvii).

Governments, especially in Africa, were simply not convinced that various forms of privatization were necessary. But they often acquiesced under the weight of persuasion from development partners, because of the need to access funding:

> … most African leaders were not persuaded that the emphasis on private initiative was applicable and appropriate in their settings. But the dire financial circumstances in which they found themselves had increased their reliance on donors in general and the IFIs [international financial institutions] in particular. African governments felt they had little choice but to go along with policies requested and required by their financiers. They could marginally amend the content and scale and slow the pace of the implementation of policies, and they could employ passive non-compliance to dilute their impact—but only in the rarest of cases could they and did they explicitly reject them. (Nellis 2005, 37)

2.7 OUTSOURCED PREPARATION OF PPPS

This lack of operational guidance and the growing importance of persuasion over analysis in interactions with government clients resulted in a variety of unintended consequences as the World Bank and other development partners scaled up the recommendations for structural adjustment reforms affecting infrastructure utilities in the early 1990s. With PPPs, Bank staff entered territory that was even more unfamiliar to them than asset divestiture had been. The publication of the World Bank's 1994 World Development Report set a policy direction that endorsed PPPs for infrastructure SOEs (World Bank 1994b). After that, under the direction of Michael Klein (appointed in 1993 as the Bank's Senior Manager, Private Participation in Infrastructure) Bank staff began to publish guidance materials on concessions and other kinds of PPPs (e.g., Kerf et al. 1998). But the justifications for PPPs, techniques for project structuring, and monitoring and evaluation procedures were no better developed for these projects than they had been for asset divestiture privatization projects at the end of the 1980s. The emergence of PPPs in the 1990s meant that Bank staff needed to continue "learning by doing." The scale-up of PPP projects had all the characteristics of another "leap of faith."

Some of the over-confidence regarding the ability to develop sustainable PPPs may have resulted from the fact that the project finance principles underlying long-term infrastructure PPPs were already well developed in industrialized countries long before the PPP boom began in the developing world. Project finance was being used on investment projects in the 1970s, particularly after the viability of the approach was demonstrated in pioneering projects like British Petroleum's North Sea Forties oil field project in 1972 (De Lemos et al. 2000). But this success in developed countries may have been part of the problem. PPPs in developing countries were being done in legal, regulatory, and policy environments that were under-developed and in any case not tailored for PPPs. Consequently these PPPs were being done in conditions radically different from those in industrialized countries. This meant that serious project mistakes could happen if project teams were overly optimistic in assuming that risk levels were remotely close to standards in industrialized economies. There were few relevant and reliable PPP models or precedents to go by as these projects began to spread in the developing world in the 1990s.

This fundamental inexperience with a mechanism that had suddenly become a central element of development policy, combined with several other characteristics of the structural adjustment programs of the 1990s, gave rise to serious challenges for some of the early PPPs. One feature was the perceived need for speed in advancing PPPs to financial closure. Another was the need to keep preparation costs as low as possible to avoid slowing down preparation and risk disincentivizing counterpart government support for the use of PPPs.

A convenient, and seemingly logical, way to meet these challenges was to take advantage of the problem-solving power of market forces by requiring potential private partners to prepare these PPP projects as part of their normal due diligence preparation for project tenders. The recommendation to do a PPP reflected the development partners' faith in the ability of the private sector to solve government service delivery problems. Private companies were considered experts in operating commercial enterprises so it was assumed that they were best placed to design and structure PPPs. Potential private partners would thus be incentivized to effectively carry out preparation if it was clear that should a project ultimately fail, it would be at the sole cost of the contracted private partner.

This reasoning of course ignored the fact that governments initially needed independent, objective assessments of the condition of existing assets, as well as the need for new assets, in order to be able to identify realistic objectives for proposed PPPs and evaluate project tenders. By leaving such assessments to the private bidders who spent differing amounts of time and resources on respective feasibility studies and asset reviews, such bids were often difficult to evaluate much less compare. Alternatively, such bids were based on incomplete or inaccurate judgments regarding infrastructure investment needs. Sometimes the intense competitive pressures to win projects incentivized these bidders to reduce preparation costs to unrealistic levels in order to win project tenders. Frequently, the winning bidder hoped that they would be able to identify problems and renegotiate the contract after a short period of implementation. Without independent assessments being done by or on behalf of governments in preparing these PPPs, bidders and government officials often had different opinions about how much investment was needed to turn service delivery into a commercial operation.

A notable early and well-documented example of problems resulting from outsourced PPP project preparation was the Buenos Aires water concession signed in December 1992. This was one of the first large brownfield concessions, and was part of a structural adjustment effort led by the World Bank to "commercialize" Argentina's water sector (World Bank 1990). Because of a perceived need to accelerate the procurement process, very little pre-bid information on the condition of the service system was supplied to bidders by the government, and officials refused to take any responsibility for the quality or accuracy of the information that was provided. The winning bidder used the first four pages of its proposal to describe the lack of information made available for bidding purposes (Alcazar et al. 2000). The final Buenos Aires water concession agreement required the operator to assume all information risks and stated that "... claims based on defects of information provided will not be allowed" (Aguas Argentinas S.A. Concession Contract 1993). In fact, the project company eventually did make such claims, based on what it said was new information about the poor condition of the assets. A series of contract renegotiations followed before the contract was prematurely canceled in 2006.

The Buenos Aires water concession experience was not an isolated case of preparation problems. A similar sequence of events transpired in South Africa in the late 1990s, although the World Bank was not directly involved. The Buenos Aires approach of incentivizing bidders to gather basic information, assess project feasibility, and accept all related project risks was intentionally copied by two municipal governments, to reduce the cost and increase the speed of preparing South Africa's first two long-term water concessions in the towns of Dolphin Coast and Nelspruit (later renamed Mbombela).

The largest of these PPPs was the Mbombela concession that reached closure in 1999. The city's advisers were well aware of the Buenos Aires approach to project preparation. Indeed, that project was used as a case study by the Development Bank of Southern Africa (DBSA) in its internal training for staff engaged in the early stages of developing the Mbombela project (Kotze et al. 2000). Some information about existing system assets and operating performance was provided to bidders in a request for proposals (RFP) and in a project data room. The RFP also specified levels of services that the concession was required to achieve in the different residential areas. But bidders were advised not to assume that the municipality's information was necessarily thorough or correct. This caution was underscored by a warning that the eventual contract would have to be entered into on a "*voetstoots*" basis, an Afrikaans legal term meaning, "... without guarantee or warranty; and at the buyer's risk."

As with the Buenos Aires water concession, this meant that the municipality was taking no responsibility for "latent defects" in the system. Therefore, the municipality took no responsibility for the "... nature, condition, fitness of purpose, merchantability or suitability of any existing asset" (Nelspruit TLC 1999). This was intended to be a way of incentivizing the bidders to do more than "reasonably thorough" investigations into project feasibility as part of the bid process.[3]

This approach to project preparation had several far-reaching consequences for the Mbombela project, which were similar to problems faced by other earlier concessions:

- It meant that the town did not supply bidders with a detailed project overview that inventoried and assessed the condition of all assets, organization structures, procedures, and other aspects of the existing service provision system. Project databases and asset registers were not complete at the time of bidding. Even the list of assets to be transferred to the concessionaire was only made available to the preferred bidder, so could not be used in preparing bids.
- Although the RFP contained detailed levels of service required for the different residential areas, these levels were not based on an accurate assessment of willingness and ability to pay—reflecting the biggest failure of the contract. The RFP indicated that the municipality would accept no liability for customer non-payment (Nelspruit TLC 1996, Sect. 17.1.2), which the concessionaire would have to deal with using contract-based rules for service cut-offs. Non-payment quickly became a serious project issue during implementation, but the use of what by South African standards were harsh service cut-off provisions (cut-offs made 14 days after written notice of non-payment), eventually exacerbated popular opposition to the project and nearly collapsed the contract in 2003.
- An unintended consequence of this approach to project preparation was long delays in procurement decision-making. Bidders needed more time to do their own due diligence because very little information was provided in bid documents. The announcement of a preferred bidder followed RFP issuance by almost a year. Contract negotiations took much longer than expected because many risks associated with the operation of the existing system were still not clear and risk allocation needed to be negotiated as risks were defined in laborious meetings between municipal officials and the preferred bidder.

---

3 A new South African Consumer Protection Act, passed in 2012, prohibited the use of "voetstoets" clauses in sales agreements, requiring the seller to inform the buyer of the condition of the property, including any defects (whether latent or obvious). The buyer would then be able to make an informed purchasing decision. Any excluded defects found after the purchase were to remain the responsibility of the seller.

This aggressive approach to PPP contracting—forcing private partners to take responsibility for anything that went wrong—was a common feature of early brownfield concessions. But few private concessionaires were prepared to suffer even moderate financial losses because assets had latent defects or customers would not pay their bills. If such problems emerged, most operators would threaten to default on the agreement to force renegotiation or let the contract collapse and exploit contract termination clauses usually allowing for various kinds of financial restitution. In both Mbombela and Dolphin Coast, contract disputes and renegotiations, similar to those that occurred in the Buenos Aires case, followed the signing of the contracts in 1999. Substantial efforts by the government and development partners helped the South African contracts weather these early challenges and the contracts continued operating. But lessons regarding the difficulties experienced in these two cases were not lost on other South African municipalities and no other PPPs of this kind have ever been attempted in South Africa's municipal water sector.

2.8 CONCLUSIONS

Privatization activities under structural adjustment began as a means to an end, rather than an end in itself. The original objective was to create efficiently functioning, competitive state-owned enterprises that could raise their own capital from banks or capital markets for investment, rather than continuing to depend for survival on taxpayer subsidies. Privatization was not the first choice solution for reaching this objective. The World Bank and other development partners spent most of the 1980s trying to improve SOEs without changing the ownership of these enterprises, by using performance agreements and technical assistance. The intention was to approximate the role played by SOEs in industrialized countries like the United States where enterprises owned by state and local governments (public authorities, special districts, etc.) raised money for investment in the municipal bond market, as long as they operated in a commercial manner and were considered creditworthy by investors.

But this first choice solution was not able to work fast enough to help address an emerging debt crisis and other problems in the developing world. Performance agreements and similar measures proved to be ineffective. Capital markets and banking systems were too slow to mature. Direct private investment, mostly involving foreign investors, was viewed by World Bank policymakers like Churchill and Schloss as necessary, although not ideal. Development institutions like the World Bank concluded that the only practical way of attracting private investment was to transfer control of SOE operations to investors via ownership change or legally enforceable contracts in cases where governments could not or would not relinquish ownership—hence the adoption of PPPs.

Because privatization was not supposed to be an end in itself, MDB policy statements initially prioritized efforts to improve the competitiveness of SOEs, via corporatization, cost-reflective tariffs, etc., *before* privatization would be considered. It was assumed that these efforts would increase the chances that entities could operate efficiently and might forestall the need to sell enterprises if implemented successfully. But as later evaluations confirmed, these policy statements calling for sequencing of reforms were not accompanied by operational guidance demonstrating how best to do all of this. Privatization transactions became ends in themselves, proxies for the achievement of deeper sector reforms that should have been done first.

By the late 1990s, structural adjustment came under attack as a doctrinaire "one size fits all" approach to development. Critics accused development institutions of advocating privatization too quickly and inflexibly, and badly underestimating its social costs. Poverty continued to rise and economic growth had not dramatically improved. Because of these negative effects, deep resentment grew in many of the countries where government officials felt they had been strong-armed into unpopular structural reform measures. Academicians and civil society groups criticized structural adjustment in books, articles, and reports. In 1999 the World Bank and IMF replaced "structural adjustment loans" with "Poverty Reduction Support Credits," largely in reaction to criticism that structural adjustment was not paying enough attention to poverty-related issues (Easterly 2007b).

By the end of the 1990s, the frequency of structural adjustment operations, particularly privatizations, was in rapid decline, leaving many SOEs still under government ownership and control by the early 2000s. In a subsequent re-examination of the value of structural adjustment, the lessons learned by the development community focused more on the manner in which measures like privatization were implemented than on privatization itself. Confidence in the efficacy of market-based policies and approaches still dominated development thinking. The sharp rise in PPP activity in the mid-1990s, largely driven by structural adjustment pressures, seemed to suggest that PPPs were potentially powerful, workable solutions because in some cases they had successfully attracted private sector support.

PPPs were thus able to survive the end of structural adjustment when more conventional forms of privatization had by then been largely abandoned. This survival is attributable to the continuing belief in the power of the private sector to solve economic development problems, and the effort to re-brand PPPs as something other than "privatization." This rebranding process began almost immediately following the end of structural adjustment.

The next chapter argues that PPPs might have suffered the same fate as privatization. However, when the development focus of the World Bank shifted in the late 1990s from economic growth to poverty alleviation, PPPs were identified as a useful tool in this new strategic approach, because of their presumed ability to improve service delivery, particularly in providing services for the poor. But particularly in the World Bank, officials needed a better understanding of PPPs before launching once again into lending programs recommending these kinds of policy changes. This in turn triggered a "back to basics" movement in the Bank and some other development partners in the early 2000s. This movement and the lessons learned are explored in the next chapter.

3. Lessons of the 1990s: back to PPP basics

3.1 INTRODUCTION

Structural adjustment lending programs of the World Bank and International Monetary Fund (IMF) lost momentum in the early 2000s as donors, development finance institutions (DFIs), and multilateral development banks (MDBs) began to realize that the benefits from privatization, along with other forms of adjustment incentivized with loans, were smaller than expected and not as equitably distributed as hoped (Gomez-Ibanez 2007). The strategy of using privatization to reduce the restrictions on economic growth caused by mismanaged state-owned enterprises (SOEs) lost much of its support. Unlike asset divestiture, interest in public–private partnerships (PPPs) was sustained after the end of adjustment operations even though PPPs originated as a form of privatization under structural adjustment. This was because PPPs remained consistent with the prevailing market-based development ideology, but also because PPPs seemed to offer practical private sector assistance in pursuing an objective that was re-emerging as a key development target in organizations like the World Bank: poverty reduction.

But this sustained interest in PPPs did not result in large numbers of completed projects as the developing world recovered after the Asian financial crisis. It would take 13 years for PPP-related infrastructure investment to exceed its 1997 peak in real terms. To help PPPs regain momentum, development experts in institutions like the World Bank needed to better understand the lessons of the 1990s—why did the use of these projects diminish so quickly with the Asian crisis; what project risks had materialized during that period; how could such risks be better mitigated going forward; to what extent were infrastructure PPPs cost effective; and how could client governments be persuaded regarding what still seemed to be the compelling benefits of PPPs?

World Bank researchers concluded that factors "extraneous" to the transactions, like infrastructure service pricing and other legal and regulatory considerations, were important in enabling the sustainability of PPPs. World Bank policy in the 1990s had recommended addressing these factors before PPPs and other forms of privatization were implemented, but this was often not done for reasons explored in the last chapter. The World Bank's 2002 private sector development strategy proposed a "back to basics" approach, with more work to better understand these factors. But the results of this effort were mixed, and few PPPs resulted in the 2000s directly from World Bank assistance.

3.2 PPPS AND POVERTY REDUCTION

In 1995, James Wolfensohn became World Bank president. He initiated efforts to rebuild the Bank's frayed relationships with civil society organizations and expand the influence within the Bank of social scientists other than economists (Yusuf et al. 2009). Joseph Stiglitz, already a Washington Consensus skeptic, became the Bank's chief economist in 1997. By the end of the decade, "sustainable development" and poverty reduction once again balanced economic growth as a key objective in the World Bank's corporate strategy. This reflected a shift from structural adjustment's focus on reducing restrictions on growth as a primary development objective, which had been expected to lead almost automatically to a host of socio-economic benefits, including poverty reduction. The reassessment of structural adjustment led to the realization that such benefits were not necessarily automatic. "Sustainable development" reflected a stronger focus on more flexible reform strategies, some of which involved directly targeting poverty reduction (Yusuf et al. 2009).

The international agreement on Millennium Development Goals (MDGs) in 2000 accelerated the pro-poor momentum in the development community. In 2002, the Bank formally expanded its use of Poverty Reduction Strategy Papers (PRSPs) as tools to plan pro-poor reform efforts over which counterpart governments theoretically would have more responsibility and control. The re-emergence of poverty reduction development objectives, important in the Bank before the onset of structural adjustment in the 1980s, shifted the Bank's attention away from a single-minded focus on economic growth and quickly reduced the pressure on Bank operations to continue the desperate pursuit of state-owned enterprise (SOE) privatizations as a way of rapidly reducing interference by client governments in their economies.

Various World Bank studies and reports published in the early 2000s indicated that a change had taken place in the objectives of development operations, but not a fundamental change in the basic means of achieving objectives. The principal goal of the Bank's work pivoted to include a strong emphasis on poverty reduction rather than the almost exclusive focus on economic growth that characterized the 1980s and 1990s. But the Bank's new private sector development strategy continued to extoll the benefits of private participation, including PPPs—but now in terms of their role in poverty reduction (World Bank 2002b). Basic services provided by PPPs, like telecommunications, electricity, transport, and water, were seen as "empowering" the poor by creating

"… the conditions for sustainable improvement of livelihoods" (i). And unlike economic growth, which during the 1990s proved difficult to influence, basic services—and thus poverty reduction—could be addressed directly. To do this the World Bank and other development partners remained confident that unfettered market forces were the best means of facilitating achievement of these objectives.

Most of the World Bank references to "privatization" in the early 2000s continued to apply the term to both "asset divestiture" as well as what were increasingly referred to as "PPPs"—contractual mechanisms like leases and concessions which involved private finance and management, but did not involve ownership change. All these mechanisms were said to coexist on the "spectrum of privatization" (26). But the policy shift toward more of a focus on service provision was beginning to drive a distinction between these two forms of privatization, with "privatization" increasingly reserved for asset divestiture, and "public–private partnerships" used for other forms of private participation.

The distinction was necessary if PPPs were to flourish—by the early 2000s, asset divestiture had a damaged reputation and, in any case, had not proved to be a particularly effective tool for improving infrastructure service delivery or in building new infrastructure assets. In contrast, PPPs could be used for existing infrastructure service systems, referred to as "brownfield" projects, or could focus on building new assets, as in the case of "greenfield" projects, like independent power producer (IPP) projects in Asia which had quickly become popular in the mid-1990s. With all forms of PPPs, the ongoing contractual relationship between public and private partners could, theoretically, help ensure a continuing pro-poor service delivery focus, which would be more difficult to do with a fully divested service delivery system under private ownership.

The distinction between PPPs and privatization was maintained in several ways. References to "privatization" (like "structural adjustment") simply disappeared from the World Bank lexicon, replaced with references to "private sector provision" or "private participation in infrastructure" (PPI). These terms referred to wide array of project types, including full and partial divestiture, PPPs, as well as non-PPP private arrangements like merchant projects and asset rentals. Combining all of these private mechanisms in this way caused some readers to assume that a much more dramatic shift from public to private service provision had taken place in the 1990s than was the case. The impacts of the brief 1997 surge in "private participation in infrastructure" registered by the World Bank's Private Participation in Infrastructure (PPI) Database were often exaggerated in later accounts promoting the use of PPPs (Box 3.1).

Of course, it is clear now that there never was rapid and widespread shift of infrastructure service provision to the private sector in developing countries. Public provision never relinquished its dominant position to the private sector. The brief 1997 spike in private provision was driven by policy-based, structural adjustment lending programs of development institutions like the World Bank and the IMF, with over a quarter of the private participation investments resulting from SOE asset divestitures. Most of these projects were implemented more to reduce the limitations on economic growth caused by mismanaged and heavily indebted SOEs than to improve service delivery.

BOX 3.1 CLAIMS OF PRE-1997 GROWTH IN PPP USE

- "Recent trends in providing essential services point to the potential of public-private partnerships [...] Large cities are moving to private sector provision" (World Bank 1999, 10).
- "Overall private sector provision of infrastructure rose tremendously during the 1990s in all sectors in all regions" (World Bank 2002a, 151).
- The shift to private sector provision by governments around the world "... has expanded the provision of infrastructure services through improvements in efficiency and increases in investments" (166).
- "Private participation in infrastructure (PPI) schemes have been introduced in over 150 countries during the 1990s, often driven by fiscal constraints and efforts to improve efficiency" (World Bank 2002b, 42).
- "The 1990s saw a revolution as governments in developing countries adopted the new paradigm of private provision of infrastructure services" (Harris 2003, 5).
- "Over the past decade, private participation has grown significantly in water, sanitation, and electricity in different forms and across many regions ..." (World Bank 2004, 165).

Source: Compiled by the author.

But the kind of hyperbole illustrated in Box 3.1 quickly became a hallmark of PPP advocacy—exaggerated claims of PPP success in the absence of compelling evidence. The World Bank's PPI Database facilitated this exaggeration by inflating the size and number of private investments. The database records private investment commitments in projects at the time of financial close, so does not capture projects that never reach commercial operation for a variety of reasons. The database figures also registers total project investment commitments that combine the investments made by both private and public parties to these transactions. In the case of PPPs, a private party need only have a 20 percent participation in the project for the project's total (public plus private) investment to be counted by the database as "private participation." To be counted as privatized infrastructure assets, private parties need own only 5 percent of the project equity. Investments by public entities and SOEs in foreign jurisdictions are classified as private. The database also includes under "private participation," projects that are not public–private in nature, but are "strategically supported" by governments or SOEs, without any public sector ownership.

Also important for PPP advocacy was the absence of any reliable way to measure total infrastructure investment, so no way to tell if increases in private investment registered by the PPI Database were "spectacular" relative to increased total investment. Comprehensive pictures of infrastructure investment in developing countries only started taking shape at the end of the 2000s when experts began to collect fiscal data to make possible detailed examinations of regional spending on infrastructure. One of the first of these regional studies was the *Africa Infrastructure Country Diagnostic* (AICD). Published in 2010, AICD (discussed later in this chapter) found that the private sector accounted for about 29 percent of all infrastructure investment in sub-Saharan Africa (SSA), but 77 percent of that investment was in telecommunications, a sector with no significant funding gap (Foster and Briceño-Garmendia 2010). Most of that private telecom investment was in the form of commercial investment, not involving contractual risk sharing arrangements with governments, so was not included in the World Bank's PPI Database.

Other regional and global studies of infrastructure investment followed AICD (Andres et al. 2013; AsDB 2017; Fay et al. 2017, 2019). Methodologies and data sources differed among the studies, but none of them estimated the private share of global infrastructure investment in developing countries to be outside the range of 5–15 percent. If a new infrastructure investment "paradigm" achieved rapid and widespread acceptance in 1997, there was no sign of it when regional investment profiles were developed in the late 2000s.

3.3 THE NEED FOR A MORE DELIBERATIVE APPROACH TO PPPS

By the early 2000s, two themes dominated the World Bank's work on PPPs. First, PPPs were being widely recommended for pro-poor infrastructure service delivery, largely based on what seemed like the rapid growth in PPP use in the mid-1990s. Second, development experts in institutions like the World Bank were also trying to better understand what had gone wrong after 1997, resulting in the inability of PPP projects to quickly regain momentum after the Asian financial crisis. By the early 2000s, something was still going wrong in this market despite what seemed like clear potential benefits of PPPs, because in developing countries these projects continued to show no sign of sustainable recovery (and would not start to do so until about 2005): "… the increase in private provision during the 1990s, although large by historical standards, has been smaller than might be possible. By 1999 total private investment in infrastructure provision in the developing world had fallen significantly from its peak in 1997 …" (World Bank 2002a, 151).

The 2000–2001 World Development Report (WDR) repeated traditional Bank warnings about government interference in the economies of developing countries and endorsed the use of PPPs to supply infrastructure services, but warned that "… the right policies and regulations" needed to be established ahead of time (World Bank 2000, 87). The WDR implied that in the 1990s, factors seemingly "extraneous" to the transactions were too frequently not considered and dealt with. These factors included: "… governance structures, macroeconomic and structural factors, the competitiveness of the market, social sustainability, regulatory regimes, corporate and commercial law, financial sector reforms, and the state of business accounting" (World Bank 1999, 18).

For project finance professionals, these extraneous project factors came to be known collectively as the "upstream enabling environment" for projects, as opposed to "downstream" project activities like structuring and negotiating PPP contracts. The World Bank's 2002 private sector development strategy recommended preparing the foundations for private participation with market-friendly policies to commercialize relevant sectors, including things like cost-recovery consumer price regulation: "This experience demonstrates the importance of sound policy reform before introducing private participation in infrastructure. As in the case of privatization in competitive sectors, the establishment of a competitive market structure appears to be the best way to obtain efficiency benefits from privatization" (World Bank 2002b, 42).

The key was in taking a more deliberative approach to projects and avoiding "indiscriminate privatization," an allusion to privatizations undertaken as part of structural adjustment borrowing programs (i). For PPPs in non-competitive sectors, this called for careful efforts to identify "… structural changes needed in advance of privatization" (World Bank 2002a, 152). In some cases, where private providers could not supply essential services to poor customers because the PPP project was not commercially viable, subsidies for the private providers might be justified. As the 2004 WDR concluded, "Overall, the impact of private sector participation is best leveraged within a broader reform context …" (World Bank 2004, 170).

Concerns about the need for better upstream as well as downstream preparation increased in the early 2000s as some of the early PPP projects began to experience operational problems. These were projects that were originally considered to be successful in the sense that transactions had reached financial closure—investment was mobilized, construction had started, and in many cases operations had begun. But for the first time in the history of the PPP mechanism, in-depth research studies by respected World Bank economists began to raise questions about the operational sustainability of such projects. Among other things, the studies suggested that although project preparation had resulted in financially closed projects, it had also apparently missed some of the key "extraneous" factors that limited the potential for long-term commercial success.

The preliminary results of a study by World Bank economist Luis Guasch were cited in the 2002 WDR (World Bank 2002a).[1] Guasch found high rates of PPP contract renegotiation after only a few years of operation. Using a sample of brownfield and greenfield PPPs in Latin America, the study concluded that projects in that region registered a high incidence of renegotiation, about 42 percent, coming on average after only 2.2 years of operation. The results of renegotiation tended to favor operators, mostly with improvements to cash flows and profitability via compromises such as permitted delays in investment obligations (69 percent), reductions in investment obligations (62 percent), tariff increases (62 percent), and increased pass through to tariffs of cost items (59 percent). This suggested that PPP cash flow problems often were severe, generating stresses that many operators and investors had to live with over the long term, unless they could prompt renegotiation.

Another widely cited study, led by World Bank economist Sophie Sirtaine, examined the profitability of PPP projects in Latin America during the late 1990s using a sample that included brownfield and greenfield infrastructure PPPs (Sirtaine et al. 2004). This study suggested that, on average, projects demonstrated profitability only after about 10 years. Up to that point, project shareholders earned negative returns on their investments, even when adding in management fees, estimated accumulated capital gains, and investment markups. The study further found that 40 percent of the sampled concessions seemed not to have the potential to ever become profitable, with that proportion increasing to 50 percent for concessions in the energy and transport sectors. Indeed, Sirtaine estimated that over the history of these projects, on average they were unable to generate sufficient annual operating income after taxes to cover all of their financial obligations. Only by adding in "indirect forms of dividends" like investment mark-ups, transfer fees, and payments for capital appreciation paid at the end of the contract period could these concessions generate reasonable compensation for their private partners. The study suggested that, at a minimum, these PPPs faced constant cash flow problems over at least the first decade of their existence. Again, financial closure had been reached, but sustainability had been compromised by extraneous project factors that had not been correctly assessed during project preparation.

---

1 The full study was published two years later (Guasch 2004).

3.4 BACK TO PPP BASICS

The World Bank's 2002 private sector development strategy conceded that although there seemed to be evidence that private participation in infrastructure service provision could result in substantial socioeconomic benefits, precisely how to achieve those benefits was not yet clear. The growing number of studies, like those by Guasch and Sirtaine, which questioned the sustainability of PPPs, suggested that the legal, regulatory, policy, and institutional environments within which these projects operated, were more complicated and riskier than previously thought. So, the World Bank's 2002 strategy proposed more careful "upstream" project preparation, plus a kind of internal World Bank research program to more fully understand key extraneous upstream project factors that might affect long-term success (World Bank 2002b).

This was not so much a change in policy, but more of a "back to basics" approach to PPPs. As discussed in the last chapter, official World Bank guidance in the early 1990s called for SOE problems to be assessed on a project-by-project basis before deciding on privatization options. The World Bank's 1993 power sector policy had recommended that market-based reforms to achieve commercialization and competition precede attempts at privatization in the sector. But an assessment by the Bank's Independent Evaluation Group (IEG) a decade later found that this policy was rarely implemented at the operational level. The policy had not included any strategic or operational guidance on how to achieve an overall reform package of the recommended kind (Manibog et al. 2003, vi). As a result, privatizations had become proxies for the achievement of commercialization rather than projects that might result and benefit from commercialization done first.

The World Bank's 2002 private sector development strategy made more of an effort to operationalize this "back to basics" approach by launching an effort to better understand extraneous project factors. Investment climate surveys to assess the key obstacles to private investment were championed by Nicholas Stern, who succeeded Stiglitz as the Bank's chief economist in 2000. Such surveys "… are to be part of systematic and regular analysis in preparation of country strategies …" (World Bank 2002b, iv). More work was needed to find new and more effective approaches to sector regulation: "Beyond improving existing approaches, it is also proposed to develop principles for regulatory regimes that reflect emerging best practice …" (v). Output-based aid was identified as a promising subsidy approach to facilitate PPP commercial viability, especially when poor customers were involved, but "More experience is needed to assess how useful output-based aid can be …" (vi).

As for developing PPPs, the strategy acknowledged that "… compared to privatization in competitive sectors, like manufacture or agriculture, the introduction of private participation in infrastructure has been less easy to manage and presents more risks" (42). The strategy recommended that "In non-competitive markets, case by case decisions are required to assess whether public or private provision may be preferable ..." (iii).

With the Asian crisis and the end of structural adjustment, and the absence of any remaining enthusiasm for asset divestiture, the World Bank and other development institutions maintained their faith in market-based policies and were prepared to continue supporting private participation in infrastructure. But as the foregoing sections suggest, the mistakes of the 1990s confirmed that a more deliberative approach to projects was called for, an approach that gave higher priority to upstream issues like commercialization, corporatization, and improved regulation as preconditions for private participation, as well as a much more thorough approach to project preparation.

3.4.1 "Getting Prices Right"

The World Bank's private sector strategy was clear regarding the need to focus on the upstream environment to ensure the sustainability of PPPs. But the operational details of preparing the way for PPPs with "market-friendly policies to commercialize sectors" were not at all clear. As PPP advocacy scaled up in the early 2000s, there was no better example of the confusion about how the upstream project environment should be reformed to support PPPs than the debate regarding the regulatory arrangements for the pricing of infrastructure services—how to "get prices right" for electricity, water, or other services so that market mechanisms could better perform their allocative functions and appropriately reward private investment in infrastructure.

The Asian crisis had prompted a good deal of attention to the problem of setting end-user prices, especially in the power sector. Asian countries like Indonesia, Malaysia, Philippines, and Thailand led the world in the use of privately financed independent power producer (IPP) projects in the 1990s. From 1990 to 1997, these countries accounted for 60 percent of all such projects in the developing world, but when the Asian financial crisis began to impact these economies in 1997, currencies suffered major devaluations and gross domestic product (GDP) dropped sharply across the region, as did power demand (Klein 1999).

Even though IPP projects were structured as BOT projects that left responsibility for the retail sale of electricity exclusively to government utilities that purchased the power on a wholesale basis from IPP projects, the end-user price for power became everyone's problem when the Asian crisis began. Utility revenues began to sharply decline, making it more difficult for utilities to meet commitments to IPPs and this led governments to put pressure the IPP projects to help with solutions. Among the most negatively affected projects were those that had power purchase agreements (PPAs) with government utilities whose revenues were already well below cost levels because of government reluctance to raise consumer prices to cost-recovery levels. These governments were unwilling to treat their utilities as private companies, subject to default and bankruptcy procedures. This left the governments with the obligations to make good on their sovereign commitments to back utility payments in full.

Legally, the IPP projects and their investors were supposed to have been insulated from market risk, and end-users (or taxpayers) were supposed to bear the full risk, even though they were the hardest hit in the crisis and least able to diversify this risk. But as the crisis unfolded, governments often simply refused to live up to their sovereign commitments to pay power producers because the revenues from the sale of power to end-users were so far below costs. Governments pressured IPPs to either accept lower payments or renegotiate off-take agreements to allow utilities to take less available power. Private operators and investors were forced to accept restructured contracts, faced financial difficulties, and sometimes experienced bankruptcy as a result.

Customer tariffs were even more important for brownfield concessions, the preferred way to privatize utilities in the World Bank's view (Guislain and Kerf 1995). In these projects, private concessionaires invested in system assets and managed retail utility operations. In the classic form of concession, like the Buenos Aires and Mbombela projects described in the last chapter, private concessionaires collected revenues from end-users and used the money to cover the costs of operations and maintenance (O&M), financing costs, plus their profits. So these projects were directly dependent on end-user payments for their viability. If end-user tariffs were not set at cost-recovery levels, the concession could not be commercially sustainable unless the public partner topped-up the concessionaire's revenues, which they were obligated to do pursuant to the original concession contract.

But for almost all the World Bank's client countries in the 1990s (developing or former socialist countries), tariff revenues from basic infrastructure services fell far short of covering costs. Often these gaps were even larger than they needed to be for pro-poor reasons because governments commonly depressed end-user prices even for affluent households and businesses in the interests of stimulating economic activity and maintaining political support from influential constituencies. The Asian financial crisis exacerbated these revenue short-falls, requiring public partners or government owners to dramatically increase their top-up funding, which they were reluctant to do in many cases. In cases where this did not happen, contracts had to be renegotiated or collapsed. This vulnerability of classic concessions to underpricing of end-user services by government regulators is one of the main reasons why these kinds of contracts quickly fell out of favor with the private sector after the Asian crisis (Leigland 2018).

In these ways, the Asian financial crisis underscored the importance of customer pricing for the long-term commercial sustainability of both greenfield and brownfield PPPs: "Establishing credible regulatory systems is one of the most important factors affecting private investment in infrastructure" (World Bank 2002a, 154). However, the best way to organize sector price regulation had already long been a matter of considerable debate beginning in the early 1990s as structural adjustment programs turned toward PPP recommendations. That debate continued well into the 2000s.

In the World Bank, there was a consensus that private investors would not be attracted to privately managed infrastructure projects unless tariff setting, the core regulatory activity, could be insulated from political interference. The World Bank's 1993 power sector policy paper encouraged the creation of independent regulatory commissions that would set prices that were fair to both consumers and investors. But private investors along with some academics argued that simply establishing regulatory agencies with superficial trappings of independence and general tariff-setting principles could do more harm than good. Such "independent" regulators could easily abuse their discretion and set tariffs in a way that would benefit consumers at the expense of investors.

These critics argued that "regulation by contract" would be more conducive to private investment than "independent regulation." "Regulation by contract," an approach successfully used most notably in the French water sector, meant that a regulatory agency was not needed because the PPP contract could cover all important regulatory issues, including customer pricing, with disputes handled by courts without the need for intervention by government regulators. The World Bank's 1994 *World Development Report*, which strongly promoted the use of infrastructure PPPs like concessions and leases, argued that such arrangements "… do not require the establishment of independent regulatory bodies because regulatory procedures are specified in the underlying contract" (World Bank 1994b, 10).

Similar arguments were made for other features of PPPs that supposedly reduced the need for new regulatory institutions. Repeated tendering of PPP contracts would allow frequent adjustments to contracts as needed. PPP advocates also argued that in most situations the restraint of private partners could be relied on when it came to regulatory issues: "Self-regulation also may play an important role: most concessionaires are concerned with protecting their reputation (or their shareholders') in the market" (Guislain and Kerf 1995).

Governments of developing countries tended to have very mixed views on regulation. On the one hand, allowing a private (and often foreign) company to use pre-agreed contract formulas to increase tariff levels was often politically unacceptable, because it might seem to stakeholders that the private company, rather than government, was making tariff decisions. On the other hand, a completely independent regulator, guided only by general tariff-setting principles, also presented governments with significant political risks, particularly because the regulator might adopt what was perceived to be the World Bank's preferred approach of allowing supply and demand to function as efficiently as possible in setting prices. And that meant, in the interests of private investors, tariffs would be set at levels that "... allow full cost recovery and ensure the investor a reasonable rate of return ..." (World Bank 2002a, 151).

But, as noted above, governments commonly depressed end-user prices for social as well as political reasons. The last thing politicians and government officials in these countries wanted was any kind of noticeable movement in the direction of full cost recovery for services like water, sanitation, electricity, or transport. Even in cases where purportedly "independent" regulatory agencies had been created, regulators were highly sensitive to being blamed for higher prices that might delay improvements in service quality or quantity. As the World Bank admitted in the early 2000s when it reassessed its work on infrastructure tariff regulation, when faced with political sensitivities, "... a regulatory commission can almost always find creative but plausible reasons to rationalize small or no increases in tariffs" (Bakovic et al. 2003, 13).

Although the importance of price regulation for PPP sustainability was clear, the best way of structuring regulatory functions remained unclear as PPPs started to recover in the mid-2000s. How could regulation be implemented in such a way that both consumers and private investors would benefit? "Regulation by contract" and "independent regulatory bodies" continued to vie for best-practice supremacy, but by the early 2000s, it was recognized that neither of these alternatives had worked effectively. World Bank energy experts admitted that the Bank had been "naïve" in assuming that the formal elements of independence plus general tariff setting principles would somehow result in tariffs set at levels that would benefit both investors and consumers (Bakovic et al. 2003, 12). On the other hand, a contract could not substitute for a regulatory body, because too many regulatory decisions could not be specified in advance, and too many elements of the tariff setting process needed to be frequently reset by technical experts.

In fact, there were few real-world examples of either of these alternatives operating in their pure forms: "... in actual operational work, Bank task managers rarely proposed an independent regulatory commission as a 'stand-alone' option" (Bakovic et al. 2003, 12). A more sophisticated World Bank policy position on regulation eventually emerged in the 2000s, which combined independent regulatory commissions with pre-specified tariff-setting formulas, a kind of regulation-by-contract implemented by an independent regulator (Bakovic et al. 2003). But this approach proved to be complicated and no easier to implement. The issue of service pricing has never been resolved in a way that has significantly increased the use of PPPs by effectively balancing the interests of investors and end-users.

3.4.2 Understanding PPP Costs and Risks

The impact of the Asian financial crisis on Asian IPP projects underscored the fact that tariff setting for PPPs was difficult to do in a way that satisfied both public and private partners. But the IPP project problems also highlighted a related, but more profound fact about PPPs: governments often misunderstood their obligations pursuant to these contracts and the risks they assumed as project owners when entering into these agreements. PPP advocates in institutions like the World Bank needed to explain these purposes and risks in order to help create more sustainable projects, but do so in a way that would not make it even more difficult to convince client governments of the value of these mechanisms. The ultimate inability to do this effectively is one of the reasons why so many government officials in the developing world still have exaggerated expectations of what PPPs can do.

The misunderstanding, evidenced in the Asian IPP projects, was summarized in the World Bank's private sector development strategy: "In a number of cases, governments pursued private infrastructure ventures to avoid extra fiscal burdens [...] Such schemes amounted to a large degree to expensive off-balance sheet borrowing by governments" (World Bank 2002b, 42). Michael Klein described the issue more succinctly a few years earlier in his review of financial crisis impacts on Asian IPP projects: "Private investors can finance a project and assume specified risks, but only consumers or taxpayers can pay at the end of the day" (Klein 1999, 20).

But many government officials mistakenly believed that PPPs offered a new source of funding for infrastructure, which did not need to be repaid from public sources. Officials often correctly understood some of the basic facts of PPPs: that pursuant to a PPP contract with a government, a private commercial entity would accept responsibility for raising necessary investment finance, spending that money on construction or rehabilitation of service delivery infrastructure assets, and operating the service system for a long enough period to recover the costs (and profits) associated with financing, constructing, and operating the system. This meant that a government would not have to borrow on its own account from banks, capital markets, or development partners, because a private company would be responsible for all borrowing (as well as having to contribute its own equity in many cases). Thus, pursuant to most government accounting requirements, the finance needed for PPP investments would not be reflected as obligations in government accounts and budgets.

To many government officials, this mechanism appeared to be a way to shift service delivery investment and operational responsibilities completely into the hands of private service providers. But this was the essential misunderstanding. Contrary to the notion that PPPs offered new sources of infrastructure funding for which governments would not be responsible for repaying, the essential PPP advantage usually involved financing flexibility, which was quite different:

1. The full cost of any PPP project is ultimately covered by tax revenues or end-user tariffs, just as with any public investment project. A PPP typically provides a financing advantage over public projects by changing the timing of the government expenditures. Instead of a large upfront government investment of capital, a PPP allows a government to spread out payment over the life of the contract. Like a new home owner's housing mortgage, a PPP usually allows more manageable annual payments but as a result the total size of those payments is far higher than an upfront payment covering total project cost.
2. Other advantages, like efficiency gains, can result from private service provision. And these gains can be important in developing countries. It is theoretically possible for such gains to compensate for the increased total size of future payments to the private provider necessitated by the usually higher cost of private finance. But a key lesson of PPP experience has been that efficiency gains that are high enough to achieve this kind of compensation, are often not possible in poor countries.
3. The illusion that PPPs somehow create access to new sources of funding has been created by situations in which PPPs create "fiscal space," meaning that budgetary resources required for infrastructure spending are freed for use on other priorities. This can happen in countries where fiscal reporting and accounting rules allow PPP commitments to be excluded from deficit or debt totals, and therefore circumvent hard budget limits on spending. This allows infrastructure to be financed "off budget," thereby avoiding situations where the government budget is pushed beyond legal borrowing limits. But evolving public sector accounting norms, led by best-practice reforms in countries like the UK, increasingly recognize the equivalence of PPP obligations and other public liabilities, as well as the importance of contingent government liabilities that materialize in cases of contract collapse. As a result, the "off budget" advantage of PPPs has been disappearing and some high-profile PPP programs have been discontinued, like the U.K.'s pioneering Private Finance Initiative (PFI), terminated by the government in 2018.
4. Increased fiscal space can also be created by PPPs financed in full by end-user charges (i.e., without recourse to government budgets). User fees are a source of revenue for funding PPPs, as long as government departments or SOEs are willing to forego the revenue that they would normally receive from their provision of infrastructure services. Among PPP advocates, it has traditionally been argued that charging customers cost-reflective tariffs for infrastructure services is politically easier pur-

suant to a PPP project than a conventional public investment project. But the PPP experience of financing infrastructure with end-user charges has proved to be no less controversial, often involving disputes about tariff levels that are necessary for commercial viability of a PPP but onerous for customers. Consequently, PPPs financed exclusively by end-user charges are now rare in the developing world (this is discussed in more detail in Chapter 9).

The developing world's experience with PPPs since the end of structural adjustment has provided a long list of lessons learned about the limitations of a mechanism that was promoted in the 1990s as an ideal solution to infrastructure investment and management problems. The 1997 Asian financial crisis triggered a steep decline in the use of PPPs by demonstrating among other things that the private sector could not always be expected to take on and mitigate all of the commercial risks associated with infrastructure service provision. Even when private partners were willing to manage project risks, they did not always do this effectively. But, most importantly, as academic researchers began to focus on PPPs in the late 2000s, they quickly confirmed that the idea of free money generated by PPPs was indeed a myth: "Of course, governments do not avoid paying for projects by using a PPP: they just pay later (and sometimes considerably more when computed in terms of net present cost)" (Boardman and Vining 2012, 125).

During the Asian crisis, the World Bank and other development institutions began trying to help government clients understand these PPP realities, without further discouraging the use of these mechanisms at a time when PPP enthusiasm was already quickly diminishing. The World Bank offered detailed advice on how to monitor and manage government liabilities and risks associated with PPPs "... to protect governments from unknowingly entering into commitments that might jeopardize future budgets" (Irwin et al. 1997, 1). An extensive body of technical literature eventually developed around this topic (e.g., Irwin et al. 2018), but much of it was difficult for non-specialist readers to understand. Many other PPP advocates, particularly those associated with transaction-focused project preparation facilities (PPFs) made less of an effort to explain risk and liability issues to counterparts (see the discussion in Chapter 5).

3.5 AICD: UNDERSTANDING THE INFRASTRUCTURE INVESTMENT GAP

Through the first decade of the 2000s, the World Bank continued to take this more deliberative approach to PPPs. The World Bank's mandate has always been to work with sovereign borrowers, so its natural focus was more on upstream reforms than downstream transactions, which were more the province of the other two members of the World Bank Group (WBG), the International finance Corporation (IFC) and the Multilateral Investment Guarantee Agency (MIGA). In keeping with this focus the Bank continued to investigate the conditions necessary for successful private investment deals as recommended in the 2002 private sector development strategy.

By the end of the decade, the Bank had a better understanding of the infrastructure investment gap in Africa and more confirmation of the need to take a deliberative approach to private investment as a way to close that gap. This understanding was considerably enhanced by the *Africa Infrastructure Country Diagnostic* (AICD) (Foster and Briceño-Garmendia 2010). AICD was the first of two major infrastructure research studies commissioned by the G8 at the Gleneagles Summit in 2005. The second study was the *Programme for Infrastructure Development in Africa* (PIDA), prepared by the AfDB. Both studies were designed to generate comprehensive information that more precisely than ever before would calculate the infrastructure financing needs in Africa and identify ways in which those needs might be met.

AICD was a study of the infrastructure investment needs of individual African countries (AfDB's PIDA study, covering regional infrastructure requirements, is discussed later in Chapter 7). AICD was a massive effort, involving hundreds of experts and millions of dollars in funding contributed to a specially created multi-donor trust fund by the likes of DFID, Agence Française de Développement (AFD), the European Commission, and Germany's development bank (KfW). Draft AICD publications were released to stakeholders in 2008 and 2009, followed by the flagship report in 2010. The library of publicly available outputs eventually consisted of dozens of sector reports, working papers, and books, as well as the AICD database which was subsequently transferred to the African Development Bank.

The first and best-known phase of AICD focused on 24 countries that together accounted for 85 percent of GDP, population, and infrastructure aid flows of SSA. AICD estimated the annual infrastructure spending needs in SSA for the 10-year period leading up to 2015. These needs were based on what was required to: (i) address the region's infrastructure backlog; (ii) keep pace with the demands of economic growth; and (iii) achieve several key social targets for broader infrastructure access. In the case of water and sanitation, for example, AICD took as its target the achievement of the MDG objectives related to water (Foster and Briceño-Garmendia 2010). Along with estimates of the infrastructure investment gaps, AICD also expressed opinions about the most cost-effective methods for closing those gaps, based on inputs from the hundreds of experts and governments officials consulted during the study.

Table 3.1 *Sources of annual financial flows to SSA infrastructure, 2009*

Sources	Capital investment	Operations & maintenance	Totals
Public sector	9.3	20.4	29.7
Non-OECD financiers	2.4	–	2.4
Development partners	3.7	–	3.7
Private sector	7.3	–	7.3
Private households	2.1	–	2.1
Totals	24.8	20.4	45.2

Note: Figures in US$ billions.
Source: Foster and Briceño-Garmendia (2010).

The AICD study reached conclusions about the size of the investment gap that had not been widely anticipated in the development community:

- The first unexpected conclusion was that the public sector was already contributing a very large share of infrastructure investment in SSA. In respect of all categories of infrastructure, spending by the public sector accounted for almost 40 percent of total capital investment (capex) (Table 3.1). This was in addition to public funding provided for O&M. The combination of public sector O&M expenditure ($20.4 billion) and public sector capex ($9.3 billion) accounted for almost two-thirds of all current annual spending on infrastructure in Africa ($29.7 billion out of a total of $45.2 billion).
- A second surprising conclusion was AICD's estimate of the total amount needed for SSA to reach relatively modest service delivery levels. AICD determined that the amount, $93.3 billion, was almost 2.5 times larger than previous estimates. Existing total capital investment in SSA from all sources, $24.8 billion, plus the $20.4 billion a year spent by governments on O&M, accounted for less than half of the total needed, leaving an annual gap of $48 billion. The report documented how far behind other developing country regions SSA had fallen since the 1970s. AICD acknowledged that the challenge was immense—finding the $48 billion needed to meet the AICD targets would require annual expenditures equal to about 15 percent of SSA's GDP with as much as 34 percent of GDP required in fragile, low-income African states.
- A third unexpected conclusion was the report's attribution of responsibility for lack of investment. AICD highlighted what amounted to poor investment planning and prioritization by most of the entities involved in infrastructure investment in SSA, but especially the development partners providing official development assistance (ODA) and the governments themselves. This was evident in the sectoral breakdown of existing investment flows (Figure

3.1). AICD found that the private sector accounted for an impressive level of infrastructure investment in SSA, contributing about 29 percent of total capex—about a quarter less than the African public sector, but more than the combined flows of ODA and investments from non-OECD countries like China, India, and so on. But 78 percent of that private investment went into telecommunications, the only sector where AICD found no funding gap. The energy sector, which represented 61 percent of the total funding gap, attracted only 7 percent of private investment. Water and sanitation, representing 30 percent of the funding gap, attracted little or nothing from the private sector, other than substantial contributions from private households. Governments and their development partners were spending more than half of their money on transportation, where the investment gap was only 4 percent.

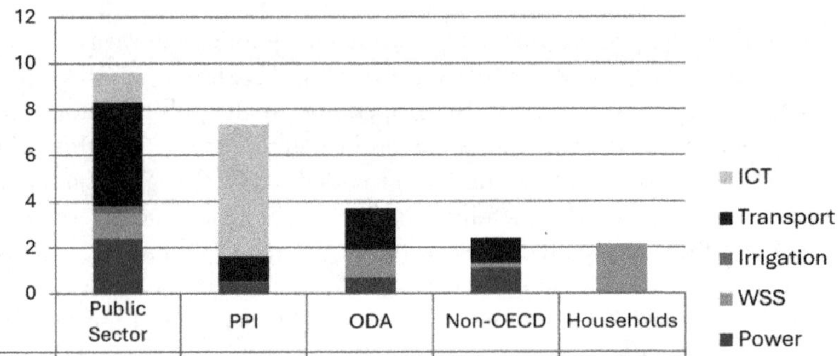

	Public Sector	PPI	ODA	Non-OECD	Households
ICT	1.3	5.7	0	0	0
Transport	4.5	1.1	1.8	1.1	0
Irrigation	0.3	0	0	0	0
WSS	1.1	0.02	1.2	0.2	2.13
Power	2.4	0.5	0.7	1.1	0

Note: US$ billions.
Source: Foster and Briceño-Garmendia (2010).

Figure 3.1 Sources of infrastructure investment in SSA, by sector, 2009

AICD's recommendations for closing the massive infrastructure investment gap that it had identified were also unexpected in several ways. The study proposed no single, simple strategy for closing the gap. It did not offer the easily understood, private sector-friendly messaging of earlier World Bank flagship documents, like the World Development Reports or the series of high profile reports on economic policy research published during the 1990s.[2] Instead, a collection of tactics was proposed to incrementally close the investment gap, with some tactics more practical and politically acceptable than others.

The first of these tactics had nothing to do with seeking new sources of investment financing. AICD made a strong case for starting with efforts to reduce the inefficiencies that plagued infrastructure service provision in SSA. This meant a focus on existing infrastructure rather than the construction of new assets. It included efforts to address things like poor budget execution, mismanagement of state-owned enterprises, and end-user tariffs that did not recover service delivery costs (Box 3.2). AICD estimated that the $48 billion annual investment gap could be reduced by $16–17 billion if such efficiency measures were widely introduced.

BOX 3.2 SSA'S INFRASTRUCTURE EFFICIENCY GAP, 2009

✓ Public sector budget execution ratios only 65%
✓ Widespread inefficiency of operations:

- Utilities recover only 70–90% of billings
- Utilities lose 20–35% of production in distribution
- Utilities over-staffed by 50% or more
- About one-third of infrastructure assets are in need of rehabilitation due to lack of preventive maintenance

✓ User charges fail to fully recover costs:

- Utilities recover only 60–70% of costs

✓ Public funds are not always well allocated:

- Apparent over-spending in some areas, under-spending in others

Source: Foster and Briceño-Garmendia (2010).

2 For a critique of flagship reports published during the World Bank's structural adjustment lending period, such as *Bureaucrats in Business* (1995), see Bayliss and Fine (1998).

Another financing tactic suggested by AICD was to increase the size of investment projects to achieve economies of scale and deal with the fact that SSA's economic geography created special challenges for infrastructure development. The bulk of these countries had small populations, low overall population density, and small economies. Many of the countries were land-locked and had poor access to major trade or transport routes. Many countries lacked connectivity via regional information and communications technology (ICT). All of this contributed to the extremely high prices paid in these countries for various infrastructure services. Most of these countries were too small to supply these services on a cost-effective basis. But if larger projects could be undertaken, which could supply services like water or power on a regional, multi-country basis, these services could become much more affordable. Therefore, AICD concluded that regional economic integration held the key to reducing infrastructure costs by allowing countries to capture scale economies and manage regional public goods effectively. But AICD also noted that the complexity of such projects made them "costly and time-consuming to prepare" (Foster and Briceño-Garmendia 2010, 144). (Chapter 7 discusses the costs and benefits of large regional infrastructure projects.)

After reducing inefficiencies associated with existing infrastructure, and re-prioritizing projects by sector and size, AICD estimated that an annual investment gap of $31 billion would remain. Huge amounts of new investment would still be urgently needed to meet service delivery targets. Here again, AICD offered no simple solutions, but rather a combination of tactics, including more and better targeted donor support, and more government finance from taxes and user fees in middle-income countries. AICD also mentioned the possibility that a practical approach to these problems would be to extend timelines for achieving service delivery improvements and consider second-best solutions. The one major new source of finance proposed by AICD was a $50 billion African stimulus package that could be capitalized by G20 countries to finance economic regeneration in Africa's poorest countries. Such a package "... would have the largest short-term impact on GDP growth," and ultimately would be in the self-interest of financing countries because it would help sustain African demand for their exports (25).

AICD's lukewarm endorsement of PPPs as a solution to infrastructure finance needs in Africa, might have also been an unexpected conclusion of the study, at least from the perspective of the World Bank's rapidly growing internal PPP constituency. But in most respects the endorsement was consistent with the Bank's "deliberative" approach to PPPs, which had taken shape earlier in the decade. AICD noted that the experience with private participation in Africa had produced "... very heterogeneous results [...] The numerous concessions (and related contractual forms) covering railways, power and water distribution have not delivered significant investment" (13). AICD concluded that "The recognition that the private sector will never be a ubiquitous service provider has come with the realization that state-owned enterprises are here to stay" (17). As a result of this fact, argued AICD, there was a need to "recommit" to the reform of existing SOEs, even revisiting the possibility of using performance agreements to incentivize SOE efficiencies. This of course was an echo of the arguments for SOE performance agreements made in the 1970s and 1980s, before privatization became the preferred option for dealing with SOEs.

Echoing the World Bank's caution regarding PPPs, AICD was careful to point out that the lesson from the experience with private participation in Africa was "... not that the approach should be discarded, but that it should be applied selectively and carefully ..." (116). Among other things, this meant paying attention to upstream factors that enable downstream transactions:

> Of course, one cannot deny the problems in African private participation, or that many of them can be attributed, in all sectors, to institutional deficiencies. Poor sectoral planning, vague or absent sector policies, and long-standing weak financial and operational performance in the utilities helped create the crises of demand and insecurity that led to rushed decisions. (116)

3.6 EVALUATING THE DELIBERATIVE APPROACH TO PPPS

The pursuit of this more deliberative approach to PPPs in World Bank operations was based on the assumption that Bank research on upstream project factors would support efforts by Bank staff to "learn by doing," and PPP projects eventually would be forthcoming. But the Bank found that the deliberative approach resulted in very few PPPs.

The 2015 IEG evaluation of the Bank's PPP activities from 2002–2012 found that upstream policy reforms took up so much of the Bank's project time that actual PPP transactions typically happened only as the Bank project engagements ended, if at all. The main reasons for the Bank's inability to achieve anticipated transactions were the unexpected complexity of needed project designs and overly optimistic timeframes. Bank PPP engagements often began by focusing on needed reforms to enabling environments but set timeframes that failed to acknowledge "... the complexity and political nature of such processes" (IEG 2015, 95).

IEG found that it was almost impossible to evaluate the Bank's PPP performance because Bank project completion reports usually were prepared before recommended PPP structures were clear, and well before any data was available on PPP results in terms of improved access to service, efficiency of service provision, and quality of services. Project completion reports "... contain little information about actual PPP success" (97). IEG pointed out that this lack of information on PPP project implementation also made it difficult to assess the quality of the upstream reform work implemented to prepare the projects.

In the meantime, PPP investment in the developing world was clearly trending upward again by the end of the 2000s, but not because of reforms in the upstream legal, regulatory, and institutional environment for projects. The private sector quickly developed strategies for mitigating private partner risks associated with service pricing and other upstream factors. Market recovery was occurring because governments and development partners were acceding to private sector demands for risk mitigation and more favorable risk/return ratios.

IPP projects, for example, had suffered high-profile losses during the Asian crisis, but rapidly recovered and soon became by far the most popular single type of infrastructure PPP. The recovery was mainly due to strengthened security and credit enhancement arrangements (such as third-party guarantees), generous PPA terms that created opportunities to achieve required rates of return, and the improved insulation of IPPs from problems associated with customer tariff setting and non-payment (Eberhard et al. 2016). The urgent need for more power generation in most developing countries meant that PPP market recovery, although limited, rode the wave of IPP projects meeting these requirements.

On the other hand, as a result of other lessons learned during the Asian crisis the private sector also began to avoid projects posing the highest levels of risk exposure, like brownfield concessions that depended for commercial viability directly on end-user revenues (Leigland 2018). After 2000, brownfield concessions for water or electricity supply played only minor roles in the global PPP market in developing countries, despite their characterization by the World Bank in the 1990s as the ideal mechanism for privatizing monopoly infrastructure utilities.

3.7 CONCLUSIONS

After the experiences with PPPs in the 1990s and early 2000s, the World Bank and other major MDBs and donors still firmly supported the use of private participation as a market-based mechanism for solving infrastructure problems. But it was also becoming clear that the upstream legal and regulatory environment was crucial for the sustainability of PPPs. Lack of attention to upstream factors, seemingly "extraneous" to the transactions themselves, had contributed to the fragility of some PPPs during the Asian financial crisis, helping to account for the sharp decline in PPP-related investment starting in 1998. Attention to such factors had been recommended in World Bank policy statements, even during structural adjustment lending programs in the 1990s.

But very little guidance had been provided on precisely how to deal with those factors.

The World Bank's 2002 private sector strategy proposed renewed attention to extraneous project factors as part of a more deliberative approach to PPPs. But the strategic and operational details of what needed to be done to reform that upstream environment in preparation for PPPs remained unclear. Infrastructure price regulation was an example of a critical upstream area where it was extremely difficult to identify broadly applicable best practice measures.

The 2010 publication of the AICD study presented PPP advocates with new questions and challenges. The global PPP market in developing countries was beginning to grow once again, but AICD found a much larger infrastructure investment gap in Africa than had been previously assumed, and raised questions about the ability of PPPs to help close that gap. AICD offered a strong endorsement of efforts to improve sector operating efficiencies and SOE governance, in addition to cautious efforts to use private participation in efforts to mobilize infrastructure investment.

The World Bank remained a PPP advocate, offering vocal support for PPPs and hosting several multi-donor trust funds designed to help socialize Bank staff regarding the use of PPPs so that such projects could be mainstreamed in Bank lending operations. But the Bank's deliberative approach to PPPs meant that it facilitated very few project closures or sustainable projects. As the next chapter argues, not everyone in the development community was comfortable with the slow roll-out of PPPs in the 2000s. This discomfort led to a more transaction-focused effort by bilateral donors to help with PPPs during the decade.

PART II

Bilateral donors drive the PPP agenda

4. DFID assumes the leadership of PPP advocacy

4.1 INTRODUCTION

In his 2008 study of public policy advocates and their common reluctance to submit to rigorous program evaluation, Lant Pritchett described advocates who mobilize funding for public or non-profit activities as the "entrepreneurs" of international development: "… advocates are the men and women with the passion, concern, and vision to make new things happen […] Without advocates pushing to address issues and for innovative instruments—new programs, policies, treatments—the public and non-profit sectors would be stagnant" (Pritchett 2008, 124).

The most successful advocates tend to be those that Pritchett referred to as "true believers"—single-problem, single-solution advocates who strongly believe that they know the importance of both a particular problem that needs to be addressed as a priority, as well as the most effective solution for that problem. For true believers, program evaluations are rarely useful and therefore infrequently agreed to "… because evaluations do not increase advocates' knowledge about program efficacy (as they already know) and yet they risk cutting political support" (124). Since true believers think that they understand which problems require action as well as the efficacy of their preferred instruments to redress these problems, their main goal is to increase total expenditure on the preferred instrument. To accomplish this, they usually try to "persuade," by disseminating "… non-rigorous claims about the efficacy of the program," rather than risking rigorous evaluations (125). Pritchett calls this the "strategic ignorance of advocates," a widespread phenomenon in the development community, including the World Bank (Pritchett's employer at the time).

It was not difficult to find bilateral donors willing to support public–private partnership (PPP) advocacy during the 2000s. Donors eventually funded many of the advocacy programs and project preparation facilities (PPFs) launched during this period, including the pioneering PPP-oriented trust fund programs hosted by the World Bank Group. This was the heyday of what William Easterly has called the "ideology of development," the desire to find the "one correct answer" to development questions, "… a definitive, complete answer to the tragedy of world poverty and inequality" (Easterly 2007a). PPP advocacy was able to exploit what Pritchett called the "persuadability" of potential supporters because of the prevailing popularity of doctrinaire abstractions, like "market-friendly policies," "getting prices right," "trickle down economics," "people-centered development," "private participation in infrastructure," etc.

Some bilateral donors were so persuaded regarding the value of PPPs that they resisted the idea that it was necessary to take a more deliberative approach to PPPs after the Asian financial crisis and the end of structural adjustment. Several of these donors did not want to delay the development of PPP projects until all of the upstream legal and regulatory reforms were in place to support projects. Such donors pushed for more rapid progress on PPPs in order to recapture the momentum of the mid-1990s. One way to achieve such progress was to develop projects in parallel with efforts to reform the upstream legal and regulatory environments and, when possible, push project transactions more aggressively as a way to incentivize upstream reforms. This position reflected a remarkably strong faith in the ability of PPPs to generate "demonstration effects" that would dramatically exhibit the problem-solving power of market-based private sector participation in infrastructure and encourage project replication.

No donor was more confident in this regard, or played a stronger role as a PPP "true believer" in the 2000s, than the U.K.'s Department for International Development (DFID). Perhaps emboldened by the early successes of U.K.'s domestic PPP program, known as the Private Finance Initiative (PFI), DFID used a large development budget to rapidly launch and support a collection of PPFs advocating PPPs in developing countries, particularly in Africa. DFID's emphasis was on facilities and programs focused on completing transactions.

4.2 THE U.K.'S EXPERIENCE WITH PRIVATE PARTICIPATION

Structural adjustment efforts to privatize infrastructure utilities using mechanisms soon to be widely known as "public–private partnerships," were paralleled by the simultaneous emergence of PPPs in industrialized economies like the U.K. There seems to be no strong evidence that privatization under structural adjustment had direct connections with the U.K.'s PFI. But the ideological faith in the power of markets was similarly robust in both cases. As one senior World Bank economist put it: "Theorizing and policy making triggered by political and economic exigencies in the United Kingdom, the United States, and a few other Western industrial countries quickly spilled over into the advice given to developing countries, with the World Bank leading the charge" (Yusuf et al. 2009).

In the U.K. at least, the faith in "market-oriented" development policies seemed to be dramatically confirmed by the successes of the domestic PFI program. In the 1980s, the U.K. government began to roll out its private finance policy for infrastructure projects. In 1992, the Conservative government launched the PFI program. A PFI road program was initiated in 1994 and the Public Private Partnership Programme (4Ps) was created in 1996 to extend PFI concepts to local government. PFI had limited successes with transport and prison projects. But after a Labour government assumed office in 1997 and changes were made to PFI policies and procedures, a Treasury Taskforce was established to promote what were now officially referred to as "public–private partnerships" (PPPs). In 1997–98, transactions with a capital value of £2.3 billion were signed, a dramatic increase in the number and total value of projects (Hellowell 2010).

In order to address further refinements needed by the PFI program and promote the continued expansion of PFI, Partnerships U.K. (PUK) was created in 1999 as a government program staffed with private sector professionals. But a year later, a collection of private companies purchased a majority ownership share in PUK so that going forward it was owned by financiers and active players in the PFI industry (Hellowell 2010). With PUK's support and encouragement, the use of private finance continued to grow. In 2006, transactions with a total capital value of over £7 billion were signed, but after 2008 deal flow began to diminish as changes to government accounting rules made these projects more difficult to justify (Winch et al. 2012). The PFI program was eventually terminated by the government in 2018.

PPPs under the PFI program were somewhat different from the ones most heavily promoted at least initially by development institutions pursuant to structural adjustment programs. Under PFI, end-users did not pay directly to private providers for infrastructure services. Providers were reimbursed by the relevant public sector agency through a unitary charge for facility availability and service provision. So, under PFI the retail side of service provision remained with government entities. Under structural adjustment the intention was to move the government out of service provision as much as possible. Plus, many of the governments targeted by structural adjustment were not collecting enough in taxes and user fees to be able to pay service providers. So whenever feasible, service providers would be paid directly by end-users, as was the case with brownfield concessions that combined capital investment, operations and maintenance (O&M), and retail service management. However, as both the public and private sectors became more experienced with PPPs in developing countries, greenfield build–operate–transfer (BOT) projects that left retail service management to government utilities became much more popular, especially because they sharply reduced private partner project risks. So, beginning in the 2000s, the difference narrowed between PFI-type projects in the U.K. and PPPs that were most popular with the private sector in developing countries.

Despite some distinctions in types of projects, PFI project successes in the 1990s and early 2000s seemed to confirm the wisdom of the market-oriented approach of structural adjustment. PFI also had a strong influence directly on some developing countries, like South Africa, which copied the PFI focus on greenfield BOT projects and tried to duplicate the PFI legal and regulatory approach to PPP development (Winch et al. 2012). Perhaps most importantly, by the end of the 1990s, DFID arguably became the strongest donor advocate of infrastructure PPP programs in developing countries, and that role continued over most of the next two decades.

4.3 PROMOTING THE CONCEPT OF PRIVATE INVESTMENT: DFID'S PSI PORTFOLIO

Beginning under the newly elected Labour government in 1997, DFID used a robust development budget and a collection of broad policy statements to start building a portfolio of PPFs designed to promote what DFID referred to as "private sector infrastructure" (PSI), and thereby counter the effects of the Asian crisis in depressing the PPP market in developing countries (DFID 1997, 2000, 2002, 2006). From 1999 to 2007, DFID helped establish 13 PPFs to which it allocated over \$377 million in funding. By 2007, DFID claimed that its support had leveraged an additional \$537 million in funding from other sources (Table 4.1).

DFID's PSI portfolio initially tried to balance an emphasis on upstream enabling environment reforms, led by the World Bank trust funds like PPIAF and GPOBA, with a focus on structuring downstream transactions, eventually led by the PIDG facilities. But over time, the need to analyze infrastructure shortcomings in target countries and prepare projects with upstream legal, policy, and regulatory reforms was de-emphasized in favor of a push to simply complete as many downstream transactions as possible. It was assumed that broader reforms, to the extent they were necessary, were being adequately addressed by PPIAF and other programs, or would begin to happen without outside help as government officials recognized the benefits generated by completed PPPs. In any case, advocates like DFID strongly believed that structuring and negotiating transactions required a completely different kind of specialized expertise than that needed for sector reforms, and that such expertise was found almost exclusively in the private sector rather than in institutions like the World Bank. For PPP structuring to be done competently, it could not be distracted by efforts to reform sector policies or regulations, which trust funds like PPIAF, GPOBA, ESMAP, and WSP were already demonstrating could be a long-term process.

Table 4.1 *DFID-supported PSI research and transaction facilities, 2007*

Facilities/Programs		DFID Funding Start Date	Funding as of 2007 - US$m		
			DFID	Other Sources	Total
Public-Private Infrastructure Advisory Facility	PPIAF	1999	77.4	66.9	144.3
Community-Led Infrastructure Finance Facility	CLIFF	2002	12.2	6.3	18.5
Private Infrastructure Development Group:	PIDG				
- Emerging Africa Infrastructure Fund	EAIF	2002	60.0	305.0	365.0
- Infrastructure Development Collaboration Partnership (IFC)	DevCo	2003	31.7	18.0	49.7
- Technical Assistance Facility	TAF	2003	5.3	10.4	15.7
- GuarantCo	-	2004	25.0	48.0	73.0
- InfraCo[a]	-	2005	10.0	10.0	20.0
- Asian Private infrastructure Financing Facility[b]	AsPIFF	2007	60.5	0.0	60.5
Global Partnership on Output-Based Aid	GPOBA	2003	51.5	63.6	115.1
Slum Upgrading Facility	SUF	2003	10.0	8.8	18.8
Water and Sanitation for the Urban Poor	WSUP	2004	7.9	0.5	8.4
Energy Sector Management Assistance Program-Small & Medium Enterprise	ESMAP-SME	2005	12.7	0.0	12.7
Water & Sanitation Program - Domestic Private Sector Participation Initiative	WSP-DPSP	2005	13.0	0.0	13.0
Total			377.2	537.5	914.7

Notes: Figures shown are in US$ millions; [a] later renamed InfraCo-Africa; [b] later renamed InfraCo-Asia.
Source: WSP (2008).

A 2008 independent evaluation of DFID's PSI portfolio broadly categorised its various PPFs into four groups (WSP 2008):

- Four Facilities (DevCo, SUF, WSUP, TAF) provided advisory support for preparation of PSI transactions, for example, by analyzing the financial, technical, and economic feasibility of projects.
- Two Facilities (InfraCo and AsPIFF) participated in project development by acting as principals in structuring potential PSI transactions.
- Four Facilities (CLIFF, EAIF, GPOBA, GuarantCo) financed investment in PSI transactions, through grants, loans, or guarantees.[1]

1 GPOBA is counted twice on this list because it provided advice to governments as well as financing for subsidy programs.

- Four Facilities (PPIAF, ESMAP, GPOBA, the Water & Sanitation Program), all multi-donor trust fund programs hosted by the World Bank, facilitated transactions by advising governments on PPP policies and instruments, capacity building, and dissemination of best practice.

The large number of DFID-supported PSI facilities, their governance structures, and targeted clients reflected the fact that the purpose of DFID's PSI portfolio was mostly advocacy, the promotion of a concept already assumed to be valid, rather than analysis or evaluation of that concept. None of these facilities were created to do comparative evaluations of PPPs versus other modalities of infrastructure investment. They were created to demonstrate how PPPs could be designed and structured in ways that would lead to the financial closure of transactions. Each facility or program targeted stakeholders whom DFID considered to be necessary participants in broadening the use of PPPs in developing countries. These main stakeholder groups, and DFID's strategies for influencing them, are reviewed in the following sections.

4.3.1 World Bank Group, Donors, Public Sector

In the early 2000s, these were viewed as the PPP stakeholders requiring the most motivation, and initially at least DFID allocated most of its funding for this purpose. The World Bank Group was of course extremely influential in the developing world, with considerable ability to effectively promote the idea of private participation, as demonstrated during the 1980s and 1990s with privatization activities under structural adjustment. But after the Asian financial crisis, the World Bank was taking a more deliberative approach to PPPs, emphasizing the need for more analysis and preparation before going forward with projects. And in any case the Bank's core business was lending to, and reforming, government institutions rather than supporting individual transactions involving private investors and sponsors. The Bank's sister institution in the World Bank Group (WBG), the International Finance Corporation (IFC), had a private sector focus and was already advising on private investment deals, but focused largely on middle-income countries to ensure successful, sustainable transactions, and recovery of IFC's own transaction costs. So, poverty reduction was less of an IFC priority than it was for donors like DFID.

By the end of the 1990s, a widely used method by bilateral donors to incentivize the World Bank Group to support a particular development theme or activity in multiple client countries was to make funding available to specialized trust funds staffed and managed by the World Bank (or in a smaller number of cases, the IFC). The funding would be ear-marked for specific purposes identified by participating donors, approved for individual activities by a trust fund secretariat staffed by dedicated WBG personnel but answerable to the donors. Trust fund resources would be spent on activities managed by specially accredited staff from across the Bank and IFC, usually in connection with larger WBG programs. In 2011, the World Bank's Independent Evaluation Group (IEG) documented the dramatic growth in Bank-managed single- and multi-donor trust funds beginning in 2000. By the time of its review, IEG counted 1,075 active trust funds supported by 205 donors (IEG 2011, vi).

The perceived benefit of multi-donor trust funds to a donor like DFID was that they could facilitate policy coherence among participating donors and bring together what would otherwise be piecemeal aid contributions. Policy coherence with the WBG itself was also seen as an important benefit: because trust fund activities were managed by WBG staff, the donor expectation was that the kinds of activities focused on by the trust fund—in this case, PPPs—would be mainstreamed across the WBG over time as Bank staff learned more about the work and became more comfortable with it. The IEG evaluation in 2011 noted that it was common for donors to use trust funds in this way, in attempts to influence Bank policy priorities.

DFID was instrumental in setting up the PPIAF and GPOBA trust funds, whose primary purpose was to advise governments on PPP-related legal-regulatory reforms and subsidy programs, respectively. By the mid-2000s, PPIAF had as many as 15 donors contributing simultaneously. ESMAP (focusing on energy) and the Water & Sanitation Program (focusing on water) were already-existing trust funds to which DFID made special contributions to create dedicated funding windows specifically for activities focusing on private participation. DevCo was also a new trust fund created by DFID to channel funding to IFC PPP Advisory, in order to reduce IFC's costs of working in countries that were less developed than normal IFC clients. All of these multi-donor trust funds worked primarily with government counterparts rather than with private sector entities, so this meant that another important stakeholder group for infrastructure PPPs (governments of developing countries) was attended to by these trust fund activities.

4.3.2 The Private Sector

DFID addressed the private sector constituency for PPPs by creating and providing substantial amounts of seed capital to the Private Infrastructure Development Group (PIDG). PIDG eventually consisted of five facilities that focused on different aspects of transactions involving private participation—long-term project development (InfraCo Africa and InfraCo Asia), local currency financing and guarantees (GuarantCo), foreign currency finance (EAIF), and various aspects of project preparation requiring unusually large amounts of concessional funding (TAF). PIDG used a private corporate governance model, based on a single, multi-donor trust fund managed by a private financial services company in London. PIDG's intended message to the private sector was that infrastructure investment transactions involving private participation could be done on a commercial basis, even in the poorest countries. So, the private sector constituency consisted of private firms that the PIDG facilities worked with to complete private financing transactions, as well as other firms, potentially interested in working in the countries where PIDG was active, who presumably would be influenced by the demonstration effects created by successful PIDG transactions (PIDG is discussed in more detail in Chapter 5).

4.3.3 Community and Not-for-Profit Institutions

Civil society groups like non-governmental organizations (NGOs) and community-based organizations (CBOs) represented another key constituency for PPPs, because they could be important participants in pro-poor infrastructure financing at the local level, plus the civil society community produced perhaps the most formidable and consistently negative criticism of large-scale infrastructure PPPs in developing countries. DFID funded three programs that each operated in a relatively small number of countries and in only one or two specific sub-sectors of infrastructure. All three were strongly focused on pro-poor benefits and depended on participation of multiple local actors, like NGOs and CBOs, for successful activities:

- CLIFF used funding from DFID, the Swedish International Development Agency (Sida), and the Norwegian Agency for Development Cooperation (NORAD) to make loans available to CBOs and NGOs to finance housing, water, and sanitation in India, Kenya, and the Philippines. The World Bank's Cities Alliance trust fund channeled donor funding to CLIFF and helped manage the program.
- SUF used funding from the same donors, also channeled via Cities Alliance, to make grants to local governments, CBOs, and NGOs for housing and urban infrastructure in a variety of low- and middle-income countries. The SUF secretariat was hosted by UN Habitat.
- WSUP used funding from DFID, Germany's *Kreditanstalt für Wiederaufbau* (KfW), and the German Federal Ministry for Economic Cooperation and Development (BMZ) to make grants available to local governments, CBOs, NGOs, and the private sector for the preparation of projects in water and sanitation, again in a variety of low- and middle-income countries. WSUP was established as a U.K.-registered not-for-profit company.

4.4 PERSUASION VS. ANALYSIS IN THE DONOR APPROACH

DFID's commitment to infrastructure PPPs in the 2000s was a remarkably large, comprehensive effort rolled out quickly to target all the key stakeholders that DFID thought needed encouragement to recapture the enthusiasm for PPPs, which had diminished after the Asian financial crisis. But the independent review of this program in 2008 found that this effort depended on a considerable amount of faith, like that which drove the push into privatization under structural adjustment in the 1990s (WSP 2008). The review noted that the policy documents published by DFID beginning in the late 1990s, which it used to justify its approach to "private participation in infrastructure" (PPI), established "... a very broad strategic framework; but with little specific reference to PPI" (iii). At the time of the review in 2008, DFID had still not published a PPI strategy (iv).

The review also pointed out that DFID was exercising very little strategic direction and oversight of these facilities. This shortcoming was exacerbated by "little quantitative evidence" used to assess the development impact of the facilities. Plus, the lack of comparable data distinguishing operational and administrative costs made it impossible to evaluate the cost-effectiveness of these programs: "This highlights a number of weaknesses in DFID's operational data" (vi). Nor did DFID have a strategic vision for the future of these facilities: "DFID has not published an explicit strategy regarding the continuation or disengagement of support for the Facilities in the Portfolio" (vii).

The review suggested that part of DFID's problem could be attributed to "staffing constraints" affecting the division nominally overseeing these facilities but noted that DFID seemed to consider these constraints "partially compensated for" by the creation of the PIDG facilities. The PIDG project management unit "provides outsourced capacity" for the DFID team, although that PIDG unit was itself under-funded and had little or nothing to do with the other programs or facilities in DFID's PSI portfolio. In DFID's formal response to the review, it argued that "Current governance arrangements reflect a conscious decision of DFID to delegate responsibility for implementation to qualified professionals ..." (x).

DFID's aggressive approach to the roll-out of these PSI facilities, sharply contrasted with, and was perhaps partly a response to, the World Bank's more deliberative approach to PPPs. But DFID's approach exhibited the same kind of faith regarding the power of markets and private sector experts to efficiently invest in and operate infrastructure services which drove many of the excesses of privatization under structural adjustment. DFID's creation of this portfolio of facilities represented a foregone conclusion about the value of PPPs—donor funding was earmarked exclusively for the promotion of PPP best practices, not for comparative evaluation of PPPs and alternative instruments.

Researchers evaluating the performance of the U.K.'s PFI program in 2012 concluded that an approach similar to that used by DFID risked employing PPPs in situations where they were not appropriate solutions: "Making private finance the only option for public procurement can lead to rampant strategic misrepresentation [...] Private finance can only ever be one of a number of procurement options for public infrastructure" (Winch et al. 2012, 123–124).

With DFID's apparent lack of internal expertise, its delegation of implementation and strategic direction to private sector "professionals," and the lack of meaningful performance evaluation, its PSI portfolio was operating largely without oversight or strategic direction. DFID had no way to confirm that the facilities were primarily pursuing development objectives rather than other interests. Again, this lack of oversight mimicked weaknesses in the U.K.'s PFI program, attributed by researchers to the influx of private sector experts into government policymaking positions (Hellowell 2010, 311), and the use of private sector professionals as both advisers on and evaluators of PFI projects (Shaoul et al. 2007). At a minimum, these kinds of experts and the firms they represented "... have a vested interest in the further development of the use of private finance ..." (Winch et al. 2012, 120).

The independent review of DFID's PSI portfolio noted undertakings by DFID officials regarding their intentions to formalize exit strategies for these facilities. But such strategies were never prepared. CLIFF and SUF were eventually discontinued because of their small sizes, slow activity rates, and limited generation of benefits. DFID never developed explicit exit strategies for the largest facilities like PIDG, DevCo, PPIAF, and GPOBA (although eventually DFID abruptly stopped funding the latter two). The need to make subsidies time-bound is widely recognized as essential to avoid the waste of resources, lack of innovation, and market distortion. Without exit strategies, these DFID-supported facilities faced no reckoning regarding cost-effectiveness or overall achievements. The facilities learned to count on the routine renewal of donor funding commitments as long as activity levels remained relatively stable.

The use of the multi-donor trust fund mechanism to govern facilities inside the World Bank (PPIAF, GPOBA, ESMAP, etc.) did not produce the kind of policy coherence intended by either the World Bank or donors like DFID. From the Bank's perspective, the trust funds often were not doing enough to support Bank policies. The 2011 IEG evaluation of the Bank's trust funds found that "... the trust funds themselves are not well integrated into the Bank's country assistance strategies or the consultations around them, which makes it more difficult to ensure their alignment and coordination with overall aid at the country level" (IEG 2011, viii). IEG's review concluded that

> Trust funds have not been a consistently effective way of providing financing. They do not necessarily integrate well with countries' own programs, nor do they foster coordination on the ground with other sources of aid [...] Notably, many trust funds of global scope involve insufficient recipient participation in the design of their objectives and modalities, and lack clear outcome objectives. (vi)

A major reason for the inability of trust funds to integrate into the Bank's country assistance strategies was that trust funds were allowed to bypass the performance-based assistance allocation system used for countries qualifying for Bank funding allocated to the International Development Association (IDA), the concessional grants and loans available for the poorest developing countries. IDA used two performance-based country rating systems to help allocate core assistance activities: Country Policy and Institutional Assessment (CPIA) ratings and the World Bank's worldwide governance indicators. But trust funds were not required to use these ratings in their selection of projects and activities, so World Bank judgments regarding the policy performance and institutional capacity of aid recipients could be disregarded in trust fund decisions about where to spend donor money.

Donors also eventually lost some of their enthusiasm for PPP-oriented trust funds in the World Bank. From the perspective of these donors, trust funds were not having enough of an impact on Bank policies and behavior. Trust funds were required to seek approval for country-specific activities from World Bank country or regional directors, but even when country directors approved trust fund activities it did not mean that these activities were considered development priorities for the WBG. Trust fund activities were managed by Bank personnel who were often reluctant to collaborate with donor programs or country offices, even those established by their own contributing donors. More importantly, trust fund grants were also often used to support Bank lending programs, rather than specific trust fund priorities.

In general, the trust funds did little to socialize World Bank staff regarding the use of PPPs or mainstream these kinds of projects across the Bank lending portfolio. But in spite of the IEG's concerns about trust funds, donor proposals to create and capitalize new trust funds were rarely rejected because of the need for the Bank to maintain strong relationships with governments involved in periodic WBG capital replenishment efforts.

With very little compelling justification, DFID created and contributed seed funding to a small but influential industry of semi-autonomous PPFs devoted to promoting the use of infrastructure PPPs in developing countries. Some of these facilities continue to operate today with donor funding. They comprise the core of a kind of informal PPP advocacy coalition that lobbies for the use of PPPs without analyzing the comparative value of alternative approaches. As such, these facilities represent the continuing dominance of PPP advocacy and persuasion over analysis and evaluation. They have helped to maintain an unrealistically high level of enthusiasm for PPPs in poor countries, and that enthusiasm has helped distract from efforts to address more fundamental development problems.

The concluding sections of this chapter discuss in more detail two of the most important multi-donor trust funds set up and funded by DFID and other donors to lead PPP advocacy within the WBG.

4.5 PUBLIC–PRIVATE INFRASTRUCTURE ADVISORY FACILITY (PPIAF)

In 1999, DFID led efforts to establish PPIAF, the first of the major PPFs in DFID's PSI portfolio. Initially, PPIAF was a partnership between DFID, the government of Japan, and the World Bank. It was established as a multi-donor trust fund managed by the Bank, and soon attracted other donor members. The creation of PPIAF was a response to the sharp decline in private sector investment flows into developing country infrastructure beginning with the Asian financial crisis in 1997.

PPIAF's ostensible mission was to focus on the upstream legal-regulatory enabling environment, which World Bank officials recognized as an import target of reform before private investment flows in developing countries could be re-started. Among other things, this meant that PPIAF was expected to concentrate its work on government counterparts and leave to other facilities and programs the responsibility for downstream work on actual transactions and work with prospective private partners.

PPIAF was given a broad mandate to provide technical assistance in support of the creation of enabling environments conducive to infrastructure PPPs, including assisting developing country governments in formulating strategies for private participation, designing and implementing effective legal and regulatory frameworks, and building relevant institutional capacity. PPIAF was expected to codify and disseminate best practice through the publication of case studies and toolkits and the sponsorship and management of workshops and conferences.

Bilateral donors led by DFID were easily persuaded to provide operational funding for this work. In two years, the donor membership had grown to include Canada, France, Germany, the Netherlands, Norway, Sweden, and Switzerland, as well as the Asian Development Bank and the United Nations Development Program. During financial year 2001, PPIAF allocated $19 million in funding—roughly half of it sourced from DFID—for 74 activities in more than 39 countries (World Bank 2002b, 57). By 2010, PPIAF had attracted funding from 17 different donors.

But the ultimate strategic objective of donor support for PPIAF was more complicated than working on upstream policies, laws, and regulations. Donors like DFID were keen to recruit the World Bank and its massive financial and technical resources in the effort to do more PPP projects. For donors, the advantage of setting up a capacity building activity like this as a World Bank trust fund was in the possibility of mainstreaming the use of PPPs across the World Bank's huge program portfolio. The mainstreaming could happen via the PPIAF knowledge products and toolkits that Bank staff would help to prepare and disseminate to Bank clients.

Bilateral donors like DFID understood that the World Bank's public sector focus and close country ties gave it unmatched leverage to influence client countries' policy reform agendas. The Bank's sister institutions, the IFC and the Multilateral Investment Guarantee Agency (MIGA), did much more to support specific transactions with finance and guarantees, but did not have the close, long-term relations or opportunities for in-depth policy dialogue possessed by the Bank. The World Bank also routinely dealt with less developed countries than did the IFC, again making it a better partner for donors focused on poverty reduction.

So the World Bank was an ideal partner in donor efforts to rebuild the waning enthusiasm for PPPs. But bilateral donors were concerned that the recovery of private infrastructure investment after the Asian financial crisis, especially in poor countries, might be delayed because of Bank staff incentives that prioritized the design and management of public sector lending operations. Bank staff might also be spending too much time deliberating about the upstream enabling environment issues that were most important for the downstream success of transactions or simply avoiding the delays and complexity associated with efforts to develop PPPs as part of their work.

Establishing PPIAF in the World Bank therefore was a way to increase Bank interest in PPPs. It took advantage of the fact that PPIAF's focus on the PPP enabling environment resonated with Bank analysts and policymakers responsible for the organization's policy and strategy documents published in the early 2000s. The trust fund business model helped because the facility was managed by Bank staff, plus every grant approved by PPIAF, for training, regulatory reform, or upstream project preparation, needed to be applied for and managed by a non-PPIAF World Bank Group staff member acting as the activity's "task team leader." For PPIAF activities in specific countries, each grant also required approval by the relevant World Bank country director, or a regional director. PPIAF could not disburse grants for activities not directly sponsored in this way by WBG staff. So, if PPIAF was successful in scaling-up its grant activities, it meant that World Bank staff members were directly involved and presumably developing their PPP-related skills with each PPIAF engagement.

PPIAF did scale-up its activities quickly and by the time of the independent review of DFID's PSI portfolio published in 2008, PPIAF accounted for 72 percent of all DFID-funded technical assistance interventions targeted at improvements in the enabling environment for private infrastructure investment. But a focus on PPPs was never mainstreamed across World Bank activities as DFID and like-minded donors hoped. This was partly because of reasons associated with trust fund mechanisms mentioned in earlier sections. But it was also because compared with IFC client countries, the enabling environments in the Bank's client countries needed more work, capacity levels and government commitments were lower, and competent local project sponsors were fewer. The need for upstream preparation in these countries was greater. But Bank staff typically had lower levels of transaction-type skills and experience than their IFC counterparts. Of course, it was conceivable that Bank and IFC staff could collaborate on PPP transaction work, but the differences in clients, business models, and staff incentives kept this from happening in any kind of routine, meaningful fashion. Bank resident country teams were also particularly sensitive to local political economy suspicions regarding PPPs for essential services. And in some cases, country directors were reluctant to sanction PPP-related activities in their client countries, because of concern that such work might distract from the country team's core work promoting sovereign-backed borrowing.

In general, many Bank staff members did indeed use some PPIAF grants and knowledge resources to address legal-regulatory weaknesses that might hold back PPPs. However, as with other trust funds, many of PPIAF's activities were carried out in support of conventional World Bank projects, in which PPPs played relatively small roles. This was confirmed by a 2013 internal IEG evaluation of World Bank Group PPP work from 2002 to 2012 (IEG 2015, 38). Almost all PPIAF's funding was used for upstream capacity strengthening, consensus building, or sector reforms, typically through workshops, seminars, advice, or studies. But because PPIAF was prohibited from working with private sector actors on deals, and the upstream work had little if any connection to downstream transactions, the upstream work was usually not directly relevant for actual deals and therefore had little effect in terms of incentivizing specific transactions. PPIAF's performance was never supposed to have been measured in terms of numbers of completed PPP transactions, but the trust fund's inability to show even indirect connections to financially closed deals eventually began to cost it support among donors like DFID.

By 2011, the IEG was questioning whether trust funds had meaningful effects on the Bank's policies or projects (IEG 2011, vi). At roughly the same time, PPIAF donors were growing concerned about the relationship between

PPIAF and the World Bank, worried that the Bank was not being sufficiently influenced by the trust fund and had in fact captured the trust fund resources for its own purposes. In 2012, the PPIAF donor council insisted that for the first time a new PPIAF program manager be recruited from outside the WBG. But this only made it more difficult for the trust fund to exercise influence inside the Bank. Donor funding for PPIAF was becoming increasingly erratic and in 2018, after 18 years of continuous support, DFID abruptly stopped contributing to PPIAF's trust fund. As of 2019, PPIAF reported $187.7 million in total donor funding received since 1999. DFID was listed as the largest single contributor, accounting for about 48 percent of this total. But after DFID's departure, the trust fund's funding and activity level have not recovered and its influence inside and outside the World Bank has diminished considerably compared with its role in the mid-2000s.

4.6 GLOBAL PARTNERSHIP ON OUTPUT-BASED AID (GPOBA)

GPOBA was a second major DFID–World Bank collaboration designed to meet PPP challenges in a way that could be mainstreamed across the WBG. Again, reflecting the World Bank's more cautious and less doctrinaire approach to PPPs in the 2000s, background research for the Bank's 2002 private sector strategy recognized the need in many cases for subsidies to at least partially cover infrastructure service delivery costs in poor areas and help make private service provision more commercially sustainable (Brook and Smith 2001). Subsidy payments made directly to private firms were somewhat controversial. In the 1990s, private participation was introduced as an alternative to the over-subsidization of SOEs. Private service providers operating on commercial principles were not supposed to need subsidies if tariffs were properly set at cost-recovery levels.

But the new World Bank approach proposed in the 2000s recognized that many pro-poor PPPs simply could not be done on a fully commercial basis. In such situations, subsidies were justified if they could be tied to the achievement of actual outputs, rather than inputs as with traditional aid projects. This meant that subsidy payments could only be made after improved access to service was confirmed (e.g., the delivery of potable water to households), rather than to finance inputs that might or might not eventually lead to better or more abundant services (e.g., the construction of a water pipeline or treatment plant). The output-based nature of these payments could help justify a subsidy paid to a private company because the subsidy was associated with a shift of service delivery performance risk to the private company. It was assumed that profits could be kept at "normal levels" if private providers competed for the right to supply services.

The 2002 World Bank private sector strategy was sensitive to the optics of "giving away" public money to reduce the capital costs of profit-making private companies for projects in poor countries. In keeping with the Bank's new, more cautious approach to PPPs, the strategy acknowledged that more research was needed to fully understand how best to implement output-based aid schemes and proposed that the WBG attempt to "play an important role in supporting progress in this area" (World Bank 2002b, 64). In 2003, the World Bank, with encouragement and financial support from DFID, provided an institutional home for this effort by launching the Global Partnership on Output-based Aid (GPOBA). GPOBA was a World Bank-managed multi-donor trust fund designed to guide Bank staff and clients in the design and management of output-based aid (OBA) programs, monitor and assess their effectiveness, and provide limited amounts of donor financing for pilot subsidy programs. GPOBA used multiple "windows" to provide application-driven technical assistance (Windows 1 and 2) and subsidy funding (Window 3). Created as a sister facility to PPIAF, GPOBA used a similar management structure led by a multi-donor governing council, and modeled much of its documentation and guidance, including application forms, on PPIAF versions.

Like PPIAF, GPOBA also scaled-up quickly and proved to be highly successful in attracting funding contributions from other donors after DFID's initial vote of confidence and significant financial commitment. A variety of evaluations conducted by GPOBA and others subsequently confirmed that OBA schemes could generate pro-poor benefits. But by the end of the 2000s, it was also clear that OBA involved significant costs and limitations as well. Some evaluations pointed to the high transaction costs associated with the justification and design of such subsidy schemes. Implementation was also complicated and expensive—the achievement of outputs needed to be independently verified before subsidies could be disbursed. OBA schemes could also be complex, beginning with carefully designed and managed competitive procurement, and later administering multiple payments contingent on the confirmed achievement of multiple outputs (Mumssen et al. 2010). Despite considerable effort by GPOBA to set up OBA operations that would eventually be fully financed and managed by client governments, the level of expertise required for this work meant that most large-scale OBA schemes required on-going support from GPOBA staff or similar experts from other development organizations.

Perhaps the most significant limitation of OBA schemes was the need for service providers to pre-finance investments, for which they were reimbursed only after output achievements were independently verified. The pre-financing requirement significantly limited the effectiveness of OBA in catalyzing private investment. Many local commercial lenders in low-income countries were unfamiliar with project finance lending and in any case reluctant to treat contingent OBA subsidies as security for loans (Kumar et al. 2010). Local private sector lenders or investors also sometimes viewed the verification process with suspicion, concerned that output audits, especially when arranged by host governments, might be biased or poorly done. There was concern that audits might need to be repeated, and in any case might take longer than expected, potentially delaying subsidy payments.

The contingent nature of OBA subsidies tended to limit the size of the projects. The 2002 World Bank private sector strategy noted that most of the existing examples of successful OBA schemes involved "small domestic service providers" (World Bank 2002b, 61). Meanwhile, the overall World Bank Group portfolio continued to be dominated by projects involving large investments in subsectors such as mining, railways, and ports. A 2009 mid-term review of OBA schemes noted that access to finance was a common problem for OBA projects involving significant investments. As a result, OBA "… can be used only selectively and cannot be utilized for projects financing large upstream investments" (IDA 2009, 5). "Upstream" in this case referred to large projects with long construction periods required before projects became operational. Contractors on such projects expecting to be reimbursed for their pre-financed investments would have wait for considerable periods of time before audits could confirm output performance and reimbursements made. For large projects, this was not an attractive arrangement and most of the OBA projects identified in the 2009 review were small, involving extensions to existing infrastructure networks. The overall OBA share in WBG project volumes remained very low over the review period. The review acknowledged that mainstreaming the use of OBA in the World Bank Group had been slower than expected.

Beginning in 2010, GPOBA initiated a process of transforming itself into a "center of excellence" with a primary mission of providing technical assistance in the design of OBA facilities and disseminating best-practice lessons learned regarding the most cost-effective ways of designing, implementing, and evaluating OBA schemes. The objective of this expanded technical assistance role was to more aggressively mainstream the OBA concept in the WBG and other institutions. By the end of 2010, GPOBA's subsidy funding was mostly limited to projects developed by the IFC (which was also becoming the main source of GPOBA subsidy money) and the facility was no longer accepting applications for subsidy funding from sources outside the WBG.

A decade after the mid-term review cited above, GPOBA had significantly expanded its activities, but OBA was still not mainstreamed across the work of the World Bank as envisioned in the Bank's 2002 private sector strategy. The World Bank Group's OBA portfolio never expanded beyond small projects aimed at increasing household access to basic services. Meanwhile, the overall WBG portfolio continued to be made up mostly of large capital-intensive projects that were not well suited to OBA support. After 2015, DFID stopped funding GPOBA, leaving just one active donor contributing to the program budget. In early 2019, GPOBA again revised its mission, changing its name to the Global Partnership for Results-Based Approaches (GPRBA). The name change was part of a rebranding effort to focus the facility on a wider range of financing mechanisms with performance-based characteristics. As of 2019, GPRBA reported $348 million in total donor funding received since 2003. DFID was listed as the largest single contributor, accounting for about a third of this total. Notably, IFC also contributed almost $98 million to this total, with its last contribution coming in 2011. Most of GPOBA's funding was used for capital subsidies, with much smaller amounts used for technical assistance and knowledge management.

4.7 CONCLUSIONS

Beginning in the late 1990s, DFID played a catalytic role in global efforts to regain the PPP momentum that seemingly had been lost with the Asian financial crisis and widespread disillusionment with structural adjustment. Using a substantial budget from the U.K. government and a considerable measure of confidence likely built to some extent on the early successes of the U.K.'s domestic PFI program, DFID quickly established and funded a variety of programs and facilities extolling the benefits of private participation in infrastructure, most of them operating as PPFs. Like many others in the development community at the time, DFID's confidence in the problem-solving power of market-oriented policies was so strong that its private infrastructure portfolio was stacked with programs and facilities without theories of change, performance monitoring frameworks, or exit strategies. These facilities focused exclusively on PPPs and private investment, without considering alternative approaches, or even attempting the basic kinds of value-for-money comparative analysis that the PFI program had pioneered for domestic U.K. PPPs.

PPIAF, a multi-donor trust fund managed by the World Bank, was the first major beneficiary of DFID's PPP-related support and continued to receive large amounts of funding from DFID and eventually other donors for many years. But already by the early 2000s, it was clear that the results produced by PPIAF and other DFID-supported trust funds like GPOBA would not necessarily include completed PPP transactions. PPIAF and GPOBA focused on upstream legal, regulatory, and policy issues and capacity building. Neither program made much progress in identifying specific upstream reforms which should be implemented in particular kinds of countries to lead directly to downstream PPP project completion. This lack of authoritative guidance slowed the expected "mainstreaming" of PPPs in the World Bank. PPIAF and GPOBA grants were popular with World Bank staff but were used mainly to support conventional Bank lending programs that might include small numbers of PPPs but usually only as secondary project objectives.

While PPIAF and GPOBA attended to upstream legal and regulatory issues, DFID saw the need to directly provide deal-making support to downstream transactions, to achieve quick, dramatic, and measurable results. DFID got the approach that it wanted, if not all the results, by channeling funding to IFC's PPP Transaction Advisory and creating the Private Infrastructure Development Group (PIDG), the subjects of the next chapter.

5. Project preparation facilities: the transaction-only approach

5.1 INTRODUCTION

The retreat from policy-based structural adjustment lending by multilateral development banks (MDBs) and the Asian financial crisis fueled a sharp drop in private investment in infrastructure in developing countries beginning in the late 1990s. The World Bank, in the soul-searching aftermath of its unsuccessful structural adjustment lending programs, advocated a more deliberative approach to public–private partnerships (PPPs), recognizing the importance for downstream transactions of dealing with upstream factors seemingly "extraneous" to the transactions themselves—legal and regulatory reforms, needed capacity building, policy rationalization, etc. The Public–Private Infrastructure Advisory Facility (PPIAF) was established as a World Bank-managed trust fund in 1999 to deal with upstream issues, and it ramped up activities quickly. But the intention was never that PPIAF would work on specific transactions and after a few years of operations it was clear that downstream transactions were not going to result immediately from PPIAF's upstream reform recommendations.

The U.K.'s Department for International Development (DFID) and a collection of other donors, many of whom by the early 2000s also supported PPIAF, were eager to recapture what seemed in retrospect to be the PPP momentum of the mid-1990s when, for a few years at least, projects seems to be replicating in developing countries. Replicating successful projects and ultimately creating efficiently functioning and competitive markets for projects of this kind was the ultimate goal of PPP advocates beginning in the 1990s. This goal was clearly stated in the World Bank's first private sector development strategy (World Bank 2002b). Replication was important because although one-off infrastructure PPPs might have positive impacts locally, they would do little to help close the massive infrastructure investment gap in developing countries unless they could inspire others to try to copy the model employed and scale-up its use.

A group of donors informally led by DFID eventually concluded that although upstream reforms were important, it was also possible to more quickly to re-start project replication by directly engaging in downstream transaction structuring. The feasibility of using donor funding to carry out transaction work, with little or no attention to what the World Bank was calling "extraneous" factors critical for project success, was based on the assumption that transactions carefully selected, prepared, and structured by experts, could reach financial closure prior to or in parallel with upstream reform work facilitated by PPIAF and other advisory programs. There was also a related belief, long shared by donors and later more fully articulated by the International Finance Corporation (IFC), that successful PPPs could "… stimulate reform upstream …" (IEG 2015, 81).

The motivation behind this approach was the apparent belief that, among all of the ways in which project replication and market development could be facilitated, one of the most powerful was the ability of successful PPPs to generate "demonstration effects." Already by the early 2000s, demonstration effects were widely recognized as a mechanism leading to replication. But other mechanisms were recognized as well. The World Bank's private sector development strategy stressed that some of the "extraneous" factors mentioned above, like reformed policies, laws, and regulations were also powerful factors facilitating replication. In keeping with the Bank's deliberative approach, that strategy made clear that regulatory reform needed to be in place most of the time for pioneering PPPs to trigger wider replication (World Bank 2002b). So, in this view, demonstration effects were necessary but often not the most critical factors factor in precipitating replication.

There was no rigorous research available in the early 2000s to help answer the question of which mechanisms were the most powerful or even essential in promoting project replication. The U.K.'s dramatic surge in private infrastructure investment via the government's Private Finance Initiative (PFI) program in the late 1990s, suggested that successful transactions could spur imitation, although that happened in a developed legal and regulatory environment and a well-established market-based economy. But the idea of funding facilities and programs that focused exclusively on project preparation was particularly appealing to bilateral donors who did not have the resources or convening power of the World Bank. Being able to work on transaction mechanics while spending minimal amounts of time and money on longer-term upstream activities like sector reforms, technical assistance, or capacity building meant the available funding could be concentrated on paying for financial engineering skills rather than the much wider set of consulting and training skills needed to deal with upstream reforms.

Whatever the merits of the transaction-only approach, its success has been undeniable at least in terms of attracting funding support, especially from bilateral donors. The 2000s saw the emergence and proliferation of project preparation facilities (PPFs) using this approach. An early survey of PPFs defined them as special purpose facilities created by bilateral and multilateral donors to "… help take infrastructure projects to financial closure," thereby helping to "… improve the flow of 'bankable' projects" (ICA 2006a, 2). That survey identified 27 PPFs active in Africa. A follow-up survey six years later identified 67 PPFs (CEPA 2012). Six years after that, various surveys were recognizing hundreds of different kinds of PPFs active in developing countries (SDIP et al. 2018; ODI 2018). The operational strategies of these PPFs routinely emphasized their focus on "demonstration effects," "first movers," "pioneering projects," and "catalytic effects."

DFID was one of the strongest donor advocates of the transaction-only approach, used by most of the facilities and programs making up this growing global population of PPFs. This chapter explores DFID's support for two of the earliest, largest, longest-lasting, and most influential of these PPFs, IFC's PPP Transaction Advisory and the Private Infrastructure Development Group (PIDG). The performance of these PPFs illustrates the challenges of trying to precipitate PPP replication in poor countries.

5.2 IFC PPP ADVISORY

5.2.1 The Transaction-only Approach

By the late 1990s, the transaction-only approach was already taking shape within IFC Advisory Services (AS), with the early organizational iterations (under a variety of different names) of what is now generally known as "IFC Public–Private Partnership (PPP) Transaction Advisory" (henceforth "IFC PPP Advisory"). By the early 2000s, this was a unit of the IFC that acted as a PPF, working directly on infrastructure PPP transactions, largely bypassing legal-regulatory reforms or other upstream issues not directly and immediately related to downstream deals. IFC PPP Advisory rapidly expanded its activities in the 2000s with help from DFID and other donors who appreciated the program's deal-making style and desire for quick, dramatic, and measurable results. The approach was consistent with, and may have influenced, DFID's belief that demonstration effects of successful projects could incentivize replication and ultimately lead rather than follow upstream legal-regulatory reforms.

Unlike PPIAF and the Global Partnership on Output-based Aid (GPOBA), IFC PPP Advisory was created as an operational part of its parent organization's corporate structure rather than a separate trust fund facility managed with direct donor involvement. It was designed to cover most of the costs of its work primarily from fees paid by government clients, as well as from success fees paid by private companies selected as preferred bidders via project tenders. Funding provided by donors like DFID has helped partially cover IFC

PPP Advisory's costs of project development work in "frontier economies" that were not fully able to meet IFC fee requirements. IFC PPP Advisory has also occasionally benefited indirectly from donor funding in the form of project-specific grants from PPIAF, GPOBA, and other WBG-managed multi-donor trust funds.

IFC PPP Advisory, and the Advisory Services (AS) platform of which it is a part, are distinct from the larger IFC Investment Services (IS), which specializes in lending mostly to private enterprises or financial institutions on near-commercial terms.[1] These transactions can include PPPs, merchant projects, divestitures, etc. But IFC PPP Advisory and IFC Investment have not traditionally worked together on deals. Until recent changes in IFC policy (see Chapter 10) IFC PPP Advisory was prohibited for conflict-of-interest reasons from structuring transactions on behalf of, or "steering" projects toward, IFC Investment. This restriction was enforced by requiring advisory teams to exit projects at "commercial closure," meaning that all project agreements were signed by public and private partners, with financing ("financial closure") yet to be fully arranged. The reasoning was that this early departure by IFC PPP Advisory meant that they would be unable to influence financing decisions in favor of IFC Investment.

The World Bank's 2002 private sector development strategy recognized the importance of IFC's work in generating demonstration effects, and justified that focus by saying that it was complemented by the World Bank's focus on upstream reform issues:

> The broad division of labor in the WBG with regard to PSD is as follows. IBRD/IDA [the World Bank] focus on investment climate and related institution building, improvements of governance, legal and regulatory systems, financial sector policies and public financing. IFC pursues demonstration projects that promote the credibility of government policies, provides additional financial services in local markets and provides political risk protection to co-financiers. (World Bank 2002b, 65)

5.2.2 The Evolution of IFC Advisory Services

By the end of the 1990s, IFC managed several types of advisory services. In keeping with the structural adjustment priorities of the World Bank Group, IFC's Private Sector Advisory Services (PSAS), a joint IFC–World Bank department managed by IFC, had prioritized privatization transactions starting

---

[1] Other development finance institutions (DFIs) that invest principally in the private sector include the Netherlands Development Finance Company (FMO), the German Investment and Development Corporation (DEG), Proparco, and the Norwegian Investment Fund for Developing Countries (Norfund).

in 1996, particularly transactions involving state-owned enterprises. Other kinds of advisory work were done by IFC departments and programs, including the Foreign Investment Advisory Service (FIAS), which began in 1985 to help governments attract foreign direct investment. IFC advisory programs also focused on SME project development and privatization activities in the former Soviet Union. IFC's Technical Assistance Trust funds (TATF) program, initiated in 1988, collected money from donors and made it available to the various IFC advisory and technical assistance efforts. Through financial year 2002, the IFC reported that cumulative donor contributions to the TATF had reached $673 million (IFC 2002).

IFC PPP Advisory gradually took on a distinct identity during the 2000s, with different names for the organizational unit providing these services and different advisory priorities. By 2007, advice to support infrastructure PPPs had become a business line distinct from support for other kinds of private participation like privatization. In 2010, in the aftermath of the global financial crisis, IFC attracted over $181 million in new donor commitments to support the five business lines of advisory services, of which one was infrastructure. By then, 29 donors had contributed to IFC's PPP advisory work in 86 countries. In 2010, the Infrastructure Advice business line was renamed the "Public–Private Partnership (PPP) Transaction Advisory" business line (IFC 2010). Any mention of "privatization" had largely disappeared from IFC annual reports by 2010.

IFC PPP Advisory's approach to project development has evolved into what has become a standardized, disciplined process involving several phases. A first phase typically involves interactions with potential government clients regarding project opportunities, as well as finalization of a project concept note reviewed and approval internally by IFC management. This phase ends when government clients agree to formally request IFC help in structuring a PPP described in the concept note, by signing a financial advisory services agreement (FASA) that defines mutual responsibilities, sets a retainer fee structure for payments to IFC, and describes details of the expected PPP transaction.

Among other things, FASAs helps commit government partners to important aspects of the PPP tender process, like the structure of the expected transaction and the role of the IFC team in acting as the government's lead transaction adviser. FASAs also signal IFC's appointment on a non-competitive basis, which in many countries requires an exception to official government procurement rules requiring competitive tendering of such services. IFC is prohibited from tendering for such work because a tender exercise involving multiple bidders is prima facie evidence that a competitive market for such services exists and therefore IFC's assistance is not required.

After the FASA is signed, IFC team members prepare option reports and recommendations on PPP transaction structure. During this phase, the IFC team often begins market soundings and a dialogue with potential investors that continues throughout the PPP preparation process. This market research provides a sense of how the PPP terms and conditions can be structured to facilitate a transaction that successfully attracts private sector interest. A final phase involves IFC help in organizing and managing a competitive tender process, which if successful results in selection of a preferred bidder, contract negotiations, and commercial closure. A condition of the contract award usually is a success fee payment to IFC by the preferred bidder to help cover transaction costs. Before recent policy changes, IFC PPP Advisory normally exited the process at commercial close—the winning bidder was left to secure financing for the project to reach financial closure.

5.3 IFC: THE QUESTION OF REPLICATION

IFC PPP Advisory quickly scaled up its work in the 2000s, expanding its staff, organizing them into field-based regional teams, and attracting funding from donors like DFID to help it focus more of its work in low-income countries. Senior IFC management also strongly supported the PPF's activities even though it rarely led directly to projects for IFC Investment. This support was based on the conviction that the facility was successfully generating demonstration effects that would lead to PPP project replication and ultimately would at least indirectly support IFC Investment's business. In its evaluation of the WBG's work on PPPs during the 2000s, almost all of it implemented by the IFC, the WBG's Independent Evaluation Group (IEG) claimed that this work generated powerful demonstration effects that encouraged project replication as well as upstream reforms: "Bank Group-supported transactions often created a market for PPPs through their demonstration effects and, at times, helped shape the regulatory environment. Demonstration and replication effects of individual PPPs may be as important as the actual transaction" (IEG 2015, 143).

But a close examination of this work suggests that it struggled to demonstrate in any compelling fashion that the development and implementation of PPPs can be accomplished on a commercially viable basis in low-income countries. The low-income country (LIC) focus has been an important part of this work, with funding support from donor partners. In 2003, DFID helped create and began contributing to DevCo, a multi-donor trust fund managed by the Private Infrastructure Development Group (PIDG), which has channeled funding to pay for IFC PPP Advisory costs in low-income countries for over 20 years (see the discussion of DevCo later in this chapter). Some PPPs have been completed in these countries with this subsidy support, but the overall demonstration effect has been to show that, without subsidies and a development partner like IFC, infrastructure PPPs are difficult if not impossible in these countries.

IFC's own track record tends to confirm this. By 2012, the largest regional share of DevCo's trust fund's global resources had gone to sub-Saharan Africa (SSA), but IEG found that globally, more than 59 percent of successful IFC PPPs (projects reaching commercial closure) had been in middle-income countries. IEG concluded that IFC PPP Advisory was operating successfully mostly in medium-risk countries, that is, in countries with an *Institutional Investor* Country Credit Rating (IICCR) of between 30 and 45.[2] This average country risk rating was only slightly higher than for conventional IFC Investment projects. In other words, to achieve its performance targets, IFC PPP Advisory was focusing on more developed PPP markets where legal and regulatory environments conducive to PPPs usually were already in place and did not require significant amounts of additional upstream work. Meeting quantitative project targets on an annual basis required that the team avoid spending large amounts of time and money to complete projects. This meant, ideally, reaching agreement with clients on FASAs as quickly as possible, then moving directly from FASA to commercial closure—the actual transaction work—in 24–30 months.

IFC experience quickly demonstrated that these time frames could not be met if extensive upstream, or pre-FASA, work was needed for things like legal and regulatory reforms or project conceptualization and justification. Of the 105 IFC PPP Advisory transactions reviewed by IEG in 2015, about one-third involved some preparation prior to the actual transaction, but this was all transaction-related work rather than improvements to the "extraneous" upstream legal and regulatory factors identified as important in the World Bank's 2002 private sector strategy. IEG concluded that "These upstream efforts were clearly the minority of IFC advisory work, which largely focuses on getting transaction closed" (IEG 2015, 85). The inability or unwillingness to take responsibility for upstream preparation work guaranteed that most of IFC PPP Advisory's successful PPP transactions would be in middle-income countries (MICs).

Other basic characteristics of IFC PPP Advisory's methodology and performance, like closure success rates and preparation costs, have severely limited

---

2 *Institutional Investor*'s Country Credit Ratings are based on information provided by economists and sovereign-risk analysts at global banks and money management and securities firms. The respondents grade each country on a scale of 0 to 100, with 100 representing the least likelihood of default. Respondents' responses are weighted according to their institutions' global exposure.

any demonstration effects the program might have generated in either MICs or LICs:

- First, the advisory team has been unable achieve high enough project "hit rates" for the projects to have replication effects, even if upstream project preparation is minimized and the work focuses on middle-income countries. "Hit rates" for IFC PPP Advisory projects—the percentage of assisted projects reaching commercial closure—have routinely been far lower than what would be considered commercially acceptable. Anecdotal evidence suggests that the percentage of concept notes resulting in signed FASAs has been 30–40 percent. The IEG review confirmed that the percentage of FASAs resulting in commercially closed projects has been approximately 50 percent. In other words, only about 15–20 percent of IFC's PPP concept notes result in commercially closed projects. Reasons for these low hit rates include disagreements between IFC and government clients about project structures (for example, when a government client decides ultimately to reject a PPP solution), the reluctance of government clients to pay fees to the IFC, government decisions not to appoint IFC on a non-competitive basis, or simply the inability to identify or structure a commercially viable PPP project.
- Second, the low hit rates and the relatively large amounts of time needed to go from FASA to commercial closure (24–30 months on average)—even without any substantial upstream preparation work—have meant that the overall cost of this preparation is considerable, much more than would be acceptable for fully commercial projects. The extent to which IFC originally thought that IFC PPP Advisory work eventually would fully cover its costs is not clear. The approach makes use of upfront fees and retainer fees paid by government clients, and success fees paid by the winning bidders. These fees ensure the commitment of the government client and allow IFC to argue that it does not knowingly distort the market through provision of subsidized services. The agreed fees are almost always paid. But as the IEG review concluded in 2015, these fees "... do not cover a significant proportion of IFC's costs: the largest share (about 50 percent) comes from donor contributions" (IEG 2015, 83).
- Third, IFC PPP Advisory involvement in a project represents a level of expert assistance that can rarely be replicated without the resources and convening power of a development finance institution (DFI) like IFC. The IEG 2015 review of World Bank Group PPP activities noted that although IFC PPP Advisory was prohibited from competing for advisory work, it often worked in situations in which "Other consultants can do the same job" (85). So tenders for this work were theoretically possible in many cases. But the involvement of IFC PPP Advisory generated benefits

> that other consultants were rarely able to duplicate: "… IFC's name and reputation for transparency and competitive bidding help to kick start pioneering PPP projects and attract sufficient numbers of bidders" (85). So the possibility of replicating the kinds of PPPs that IFC helps to bring to tender—without IFC involvement—is remote.

More clarity on the development benefits and demonstration effects generated by these PPPs is not possible because IFC makes public very little information about this kind of performance. IFC does not publicly disclose things like the percentage of commercially closed PPPs that go on to reach financial closure, or the performance track record of these projects as they move through implementation. The IEG review found that IFC documented activities only up to commercial closure "… with very little evidence beyond and into the actual lifetime of a PPP" (84). IFC claims to have strengthened their monitoring of projects after their teams exit, but there is no publicly available evidence of this. As with most facilities and programs established to promote the use of PPPs, the IFC attempts to persuade donors and clients regarding the value of PPPs without referring to the results of rigorous monitoring and evaluation to substantiate such claims.

In 2007, IFC took steps to strengthen its PPP project development performance in the poorest countries by creating InfraVentures, a facility designed to provide project preparation support directly to potential private partners in PPP transactions. This was a $100 million trust fund with a five-year lifespan approved by the IFC board to support upstream PPP development in power, utilities, and transport in the poorest countries—those eligible for loans from the World Bank's International Development Association (IDA) (IFC 2007). Essentially, InfraVentures was designed to work directly with prospective private partners to bring PPP deals to the financing stage, unlike IFC PPP Advisory which works with public partners. For each project, InfraVentures could fund up to $4 million of project development expenses at an early stage, typically 20–30 percent of the total amount required for preparation. But these were not grants. In return for its support, InfraVentures would take an equity stake in the project after financial closure. InfraVentures funding could be allocated for studies covering economic, social, technical, and environmental topics, management of stakeholder relationships, financial modeling, legal expenses, and standard feasibility studies. The idea was that with this kind of early support, InfraVentures could help structure PPP projects to reduce risk and increase bankability. In theory, this would accelerate project development and reduce the time to financial closure.

But InfraVentures built its pipeline very slowly. The development of individual projects took longer than anticipated, three to five years, as opposed to initial estimates of two to three years. By 2013, InfraVentures had engaged on only 25 projects, with an average commitment of $2.2 million per project (IEG 2015). Of these, none had yet reached financial closure. Nevertheless, in 2013 the IFC board agreed to extend the fund's lifespan. The fund size was increased to $150 million, with the upper limit on individual allocations increased to $8 million. The first two InfraVentures financial closures occurred in 2014, seven years after the IFC Board had approved the program. Recent IFC policy and organizational changes affecting InfraVentures are discussed in Chapter 10.

For donors like DFID, eager to recapture the PPP momentum of the mid-1990s, IFC PPP Advisory served as a model for a transaction-only approach to PPP project development that seemed capable of generating demonstration effects leading to project replication. This suited the interests of donors who were already contributing to upstream reform programs like PPIAF, and wanted a way to more directly drive actual PPP transactions. But IFC PPP Advisory was slow to complete deals and its projects were not encouraging much replication or market development in LICs. Rather than question the potential of the transaction-only approach, much less the viability of PPPs in poor countries, DFID wanted a way to structure more transactions and achieve faster results in the poorest countries. They found it by designing and funding a transaction-only PPF managed and staffed by private sector experts, which could work directly with both public and private counterparts and provide a wide variety of preparation services and bespoke investment products.

5.4 THE PRIVATE INFRASTRUCTURE DEVELOPMENT GROUP (PIDG)

5.4.1 DFID's Flagship PPF

The Private Infrastructure Development Group (PIDG) was DFID's solution to the problems that seemed to be limiting the performance of IFC PPP Advisory. After starting operations with DFID support in 2002, the PIDG program quickly became the leading recipient of DFID funding targeted at facilitating private investment in infrastructure in developing countries. In five years, PIDG had a secretariat and six facilities in place: two facilities focused on project preparation from project concept to financial close (InfraCo Africa and InfraCo Asia); two facilities providing downstream transaction financing and guarantees (the Emerging Africa Infrastructure Fund, or EAIF, and GuarantCo); one facility supplying the others with technical assistance grants and capital subsidies for unusual or unusually expensive project preparation work (Technical Assistance Facility); and a PIDG-managed trust fund ("DevCo") that channeled donor funding to IFC PPP Advisory for some of its own projects in LICs. By 2007, seven donors recruited by DFID were funding PIDG.

At the time of the 2008 independent review of DFID's Private Sector Infrastructure (PSI) portfolio (discussed in Chapter 4), the PIDG facilities had already received over half of all DFID funding provided to the 13 programs in the portfolio and about 50 percent more than the total received by PPIAF and GPOBA (WSP 2008). Six years later, the total donor funding received by PIDG had almost doubled to over $1 billion. Several donors, led by DFID and the Dutch Directorate-General for International Cooperation (DGIS), continued for many years to actively provide funding for the program. PIDG's annual reports confirm that from 2002 to the end of 2019, the organization had prepared and financed 286 projects using about $4 billion in funding.[3]

5.4.2 PIDG's Original Business Strategy

The fundamental ambitions behind PIDG's transaction-only approach to PPP preparation were summarized in a 2003 "consultation document" prepared by PIDG and sanctioned by DFID to solicit support from donors and other stakeholders for the creation of what became PIDG's flagship facility, InfraCo Africa (PIDG 2003).[4] These ambitions reflect the extraordinary strength of donor faith at the time regarding the potential of a transaction-only approach to generate demonstration effects that would lead ultimately to project replication in poor countries. Most of these ambitions proved to be unrealistic, not because of any lack of effort on the part of PIDG, but because of the failures of everyone involved to understand the shortcomings of the underlying PPP mechanisms and the weaknesses of a transaction-only approach.

Upstream reforms underway

PIDG's proposal to donors was that a transaction-only approach was possible because upstream enabling environment issues limiting private participation in infrastructure were already adequately being addressed by existing programs like the Private Sector Advisory Services (PSAS, a joint IFC–World Bank program created in the mid-1990s to assist with SOE privatization), and PPIAF,

---

3 Funding sources were said to include contributions by PIDG donor members (about 70 percent from DFID), debt financing, contingent capital, U.K.-backed promissory notes, as well as expectations of future donor transfers based on existing commitments.

4 When this document was prepared, the proposed facility was called "DevCo." But that name was later used for a trust fund used by DFID to channel funding to IFC PPP Advisory.

which DFID helped establish a few years earlier. The consultation document noted that additional funding was needed for this work but added that, even if better funded, general advisory support of this kind was not enough—"more is needed" to stimulate substantial increases in privately financed infrastructure (PIDG 2003, 1). "More" meant the ability "… to structure financeable infrastructure opportunity in developing countries" (1).

The belief that upstream enabling environment issues affecting PPPs were being addressed to an extent that would justify a major new focus on downstream transaction work proved to be the first of many overly ambitious assumptions underlying the PIDG approach. This was one of the lessons from the experiences with PPPs and other forms of privatization in the 1990s, which prompted the World Bank to take a more deliberative approach to PPPs in the early 2000s. Development institutions like the World Bank found the legal and regulatory problems inhibiting PPPs and their development impacts to be far more entrenched and obstructive than assumed by DFID when PIDG was established. The difficulties associated with the upstream preparation of PPPs were already clearly outlined in the World Bank's private sector development strategy (World Bank 2002b).

Enabling environment programs cited in the 2003 PIDG document, like PSAS and PPIAF, were actively spending their donor funding on grant-funded operations, but their sustainable impacts on the upstream environment for PPPs were not apparent. PSAS was one of many efforts by the World Bank Group to address upstream problems and was soon replaced by other programs. PPIAF's work was disconnected from transactions, or any interactions with the private sector, and was mostly used by World Bank staff in the preparation of normal Bank lending activities, as documented in the IEG review of World Bank Group (WBG) PPP activities (IEG 2015). PPIAF long struggled to document cases in which its studies of PPP legal and regulatory frameworks led to actual reforms, much less downstream projects. DFID stopped funding PPIAF in 2018.

Multiple project opportunities

The PIDG consultation document (2003) claimed that enough potentially successful private investment projects existed in LICs, and their return on investment was likely high enough, to justify the creation of a donor-capitalized PIDG facility that would fund "pre-investment" transaction preparation activities as well as investments and guarantees (4). The consultation document claimed that a PIDG project development facility of this kind (eventually called InfraCo) would need to take projects only to financial close, after which they could be sold to private sector operators and investors. In some developing countries, "weak fundamentals" like small markets or lack of purchasing power might contribute to low levels of private investment, but "... the potential for economic projects ..." existed in many other countries (4).

The consultation document argued that governments of developing countries could be persuaded to hand over the responsibility for preparing these projects to PIDG facilities like InfraCo. This hand-over would be similar to that which was said to take place in sectors like oil and gas mining, where governments allowed private companies to "prospect and develop the resource" (4). Because such "prospecting" required private sector skills not found in the public sector, governments would be willing to relinquish control over project preparation on condition that if a "prospected" project successfully reached financial closure, the government would share in the financial benefits.

PIDG's operating experience quickly confirmed that the approach it proposed taking to identify project opportunities betrayed a misunderstanding regarding realities on the ground and capabilities of private sector experts. The pre-investment preparation activities needed for successful transactions of this kind were not at all similar to those needed in a sector like oil and gas mining. Potentially profitable infrastructure projects are not hidden from sight like underground gas reserves. They do not necessarily require private sector skills to "prospect and develop the resource" because other observers would likely misunderstand the private investment potential.

By the time all of the PIDG facilities began functioning in mid-2000s, regions like SSA were being constantly surveyed for viable project opportunities by public officials, private investors, DFIs, MDBs, and donors. Governments were rarely willing to simply turn over potential projects to developers like PIDG, especially given the enabling environment advice from entities like PPIAF that governments should develop their own projects using best-practice legal and regulatory frameworks and government-managed PPP units (see the discussion of this in the next chapter). The project drought that confronted PIDG as soon as it began operations, meant that the InfraCos (InfraCo Africa and eventually InfraCo Asia) would find few projects to develop and would need to rely on directly negotiated projects developed by others, or on complex and unwieldly projects that most private developers would avoid (and would never replicate) because the projects could not be done on a full cost-recovery basis.

Private sector expertise

The consultation document (2003) argued that all of the PIDG facilities would need to recruit and retain private sector experts, and to do that successfully these experts would need to be remunerated in line with competitive private sector standards, including substantial success fees in some cases (8). These experts would ensure that the PIDG facilities acted as "honest brokers," because they would be able to understand and appreciate the commercial interests of private investors and therefore be able to appropriately balance them with the developmental priorities of governments (6).

Staffing and managing PIDG companies with private sector experts maximized the transaction-only focus of the facilities, but arguably did little to promote development priorities. In what became a constant struggle to identify project opportunities, the facilities simply moved from country to country, selecting projects opportunistically with little sense of strategic purpose beyond the compulsion to close transactions. The founding chairman of both EAIF and InfraCo Africa eventually admitted that PIDG's approach to projects was opportunistic: "... seeking out viable opportunities case by case wherever they can be found [...] There is relatively little dialogue with host governments about their infrastructure priorities and which of their investments they see as potentially suitable for private investment" (Palmer 2014, 16).

PIDG's business model also meant keeping donors at arm's length to avoid too much emphasis on donors' non-commercial development priorities. Donors weighed in on PIDG operations in meetings held once or twice a year but were repeatedly told that facility managers and boards were "best placed" to take necessary financing and development risk-taking decisions: "An important challenge in the PIDG approach is to actually make sure that the donors are hands-off in their approach" (PIDG 2008, 36). One of the important lessons learned by PIDG's first program manager was to "Make clear from the outset that it is the company's board and not the donors who hold the responsibility for project selection" (Hodges 2009, 3).

Cost recovery

The consultation document argued that even though the use of private sector experts would be expensive, the cost of this work would be fully recovered, along with modest profits, by competitively auctioning off these prepared projects to private investors at, or just prior to, financial close (5). Surplus revenue beyond cost recovery would be reinvested in future projects—each of the PIDG facilities would generate revenues sufficient to sustain their on-going activities after initial donor capitalization. PIDG facilities would "never" undertake actual project ownership or operation because this might suggest the possibility that PIDG was not developing commercially sustainable projects. Through the planned auctions, the private sector would take on these roles of owner or operator for well-prepared projects (6).

DFID correctly anticipated that other PIDG donors would be uncomfortable with the private sector style remuneration arrangements used for PIDG managers and staff. But DFID argued that the commercial orientation of PIDG would solve the optical problem of paying for expensive private sector staff with public sector money. Because the PIDG facilities were expected to at least cover their costs of developing projects, PIDG would soon be able to revolve the initial donor contributions and become, in effect, self-financing. Donors would no longer need to deal with the problem of funding "highly remunerative" private sector-like compensation. So, the ability of PIDG facilities to eventually cover the costs of their work was critical in justifying the use of expensive private sector experts.

However, the much lower than expected number of commercial project opportunities meant that the costs of preparing available projects was higher than expected and there were not enough successful project closures to pay for the preparation of unsuccessful ones. Nor would auctioning off such projects to private investors just prior to financial close be a practical way to recover such costs. Auctions were far too time- and labor-intensive for a transaction-focused program like PIDG, eager for its facilities to move on to the next deal. In any case, when private developers are not directly involved in project preparation, they are often reluctant to invest until the project has an operating track record and even then may not be comfortable covering all of the project costs incurred by others.

The two InfraCos, like the other PIDG facilities, faced a challenge that was almost insurmountable: They had to achieve project successes in the poorest countries, where project preparation was particularly expensive and time consuming and private sector interest was low. But facilities were nevertheless expected to achieve these successes while covering their costs, which were driven even higher by the private sector-style salaries and success fees paid to PIDG staff, board members, and consultants. The financing facilities, like EAIF and GuarantCo, had less of a challenge because they worked downstream, closer to financial close. They did not need to spend much of their own operating capital developing projects. But the InfraCos were expected to play much more substantial upstream roles in early stage project development. However, already by the mid-2000s, most potentially commercial infrastructure project opportunities even in low-income countries had attracted the attention of public and private developers and financiers of all kinds. The InfraCos had to expend much more time and operating capital than anticipated to find or create early-stage project opportunities.

Collaboration with PPIAF and GPOBA

DFID assumed that PIDG would work in coordination with the other facilities funded by the U.K. government—especially PPIAF, GPOBA, and IFC PPP Advisory (particularly IFC PPP Advisory activities funded by DFID's contributions to the DevCo trust fund). PPIAF would address upstream problems with legal-regulatory enabling environments in poor countries. GPOBA would add a subsidy dimension to PPP projects, reflecting the fact that PPPs benefiting poor people were not as commercially robust as hoped for in the 1990s. IFC PPP Advisory would use PIDG's DevCo funding sourced from

DFID to structure PPP transactions in mostly low-income countries, something that IFC's normal cost-coverage requirements restricted them from doing. As per their mandates, the three World Bank trust funds would work primarily with public sector counterparts, using World Bank or IFC personnel. PIDG facilities would work primarily with private sector partners using their private sector experts, but would have the flexibility to work as necessary with public or private counterparts. Both PPIAF and GPOBA were persuaded to sign Memoranda of Understanding (MOUs) naming them as "affiliate" PIDG facilities. PIDG was even encouraged to submit grant applications to GPOBA to access output-based aid (OBA) subsidies for PIDG projects. The stage was set by DFID for collaboration by all of these U.K.-supported facilities and programs to work together in scaling up the use of PPPs.

But meaningful collaboration failed to materialize. PPIAF could not work on specific downstream transactions, or interact with the private sector, and all of its funding allocations were required to be endorsed and managed by World Bank task managers and approved by World Bank country directors. So PPIAF had no way to respond to PIDG requests for assistance or collaboration and no way to channel funding to PIDG projects. GPOBA had similar restrictions and ultimately rejected all of the PIDG applications for OBA support. Reasons given for rejections included failure to meet World Bank safeguard requirements and the fact that subsidy requests vastly exceeded GPOBA limits on grant size relative to overall project costs. After a few years, any formal relationship between PIDG, PPIAF, and GPOBA had disappeared and the PIDG affiliate status of PPIAF and GPOBA was forgotten.

5.4.3 Adjustments to the Strategy

The 2008 independent review of DFID's private sector infrastructure portfolio anticipated some of PIDG's future problems. The review found that GuarantCo (established in 2003) and InfraCo (established in 2005) "… have yet to establish a track record of completed transactions" (WSP 2008, 44). InfraCo's board assured evaluators that "… a self-sustaining business with an appropriate mix of commercial and 'high development intensity' projects can be reached within 2–3 years" (44). Achieving such an objective was important for PIDG, because InfraCo was in many respects the flagship PIDG facility—its success would confirm that private investment in infrastructure, including the costs of project preparation and financing, could be done on a commercial, cost-recovery basis in the poorest developing countries. But InfraCo continued to struggle. Its first two project closures were achieved later in 2008. By 2015, after a decade of operation, it had closed (or sold) only nine projects, while spending over $68 million in donor funding on preparation (PIDG 2015).

The business strategies of the PIDG facilities eventually evolved in ways that better reflected the realities of developing and financing PPPs in poor countries.

Narrowing types of targeted projects

Under pressure to ramp up project numbers, the PIDG facilities quickly gravitated to the types of private investment projects requiring the least amount of time and money to prepare, the least amount of risk to private partners, and the least amount of resistance from governments. These were grid-connected power generation projects, done as independent power producer (IPP) projects using build–operate–transfer (BOT) or build–own–operate (BOO) contracting structures. Like almost all the PIDG projects, these IPP projects were directly negotiated, in the sense that private sponsors were not selected via competitive tendering. Of the nine InfraCo projects reaching closure or sale by 2015, six were directly negotiated IPP projects. For PIDG by 2015, 53 percent of all historical spending commitments on traditional kinds of infrastructure (energy, telecoms, transport, water and sanitation) was on directly negotiated IPP projects (PIDG 2015). By the time the COVID-19 pandemic started in 2020, power generation IPP projects made up the largest share of PIDG's general portfolio (Figure 5.1).

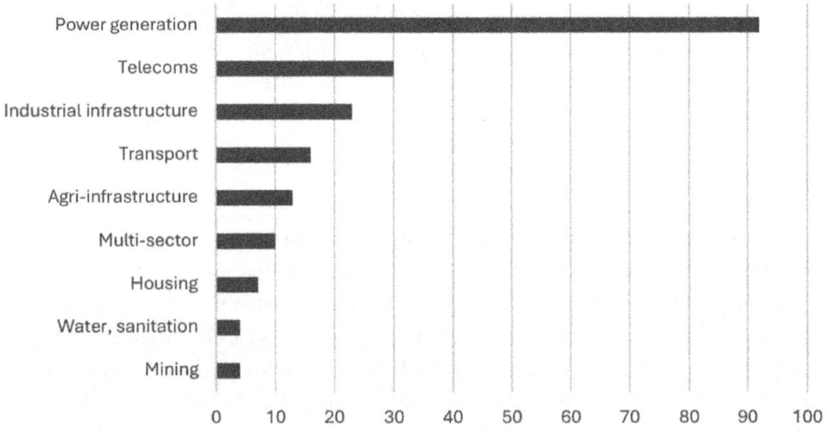

Note: Numbers of projects by sector; projects involving private participation in infrastructure developed by four PIDG companies: InfraCo Africa, InfraCo Asia, EAIF, and GuarantCo.
Source: PIDG (2019b).

Figure 5.1 PIDG projects in LICs and LMICs, 2003–2019

Brownfield project solutions like concessions and management contracts, mentioned in the 2003 consultation document, never made up a large proportion of PIDG projects. This was because such projects were difficult to structure, required close collaboration with governments, and involved mostly rehabilitation rather than larger capital investments needed for BOT projects like IPP projects. PIDG management justified a shift away from the original focus on brownfield projects by arguing that BOT projects were more difficult and more necessary than brownfield concessions in the developing world (Palmer 2014). This was generally assumed to be the case in industrialized countries, but the logic has never applied strongly in the developing world. After the Asian financial crisis the private sector became much more interested in greenfield projects like IPPs in developing countries than brownfield concessions (Leigland 2018). (This private sector shift from brownfield to greenfield projects is discussed in more detail in Chapter 9.)

PIDG's emphasis on directly negotiated IPP projects became essential in bolstering the PIDG portfolio numbers of financially closed projects. Compared to most other kinds of PPPs, IPP projects were less complicated to do and less fragile, because their sustainability did not necessarily depend on expensive or time-consuming sector reforms. The responsibility for improving the efficiency of government-owned utility power off-takers remained with governments. Responsibility for grid extensions and new end-user connections also typically remained with the government. The pro-poor impacts of grid-connected IPP projects were often minimal because of existing distribution inefficiencies and tariff inequities, and because most of the inhabitants of developing countries officially classified by their governments as "poor" were not connected to power distribution grids.

Broadening the definition of "infrastructure"

Another way of improving PIDG's project performance involved broadening the definition of "infrastructure" in ways that suited the capabilities of the different facilities. The boards of the different PIDG facilities gradually expanded DFID's original definition of "infrastructure" to add types of eligible projects which helped them meet project targets (Table 5.1). EAIF and GuarantCo added mining, agriculture, and "industrial infrastructure" (steel mills, fertilizer plants, petrochemical processing facilities, aluminum manufacturing plants, cement plants, etc.). InfraCo Africa, making the slowest progress toward project targets, was the most innovative in expanding its menu of authorized project options, adding housing, mining, agriculture, bulk storage, logistics,

Table 5.1 *PIDG eligible investments, 2009*

Sectors	Facilities: EAIF	GuarantCo	InfraCo	DevCo (IFC)
Water/sanitation	x	x	x	x
Power/energy	x	x	x	x
Transport	x	x	x	x
Telecom	x	x	x	x
Solid waste	x	–	–	x
Housing	–	–	x	x
Mining[a]	x	x	x	–
Agribusines	x	x	x	–
Infra components[b]	x	x	-	–
Urban infrastructure	–	x	x	–
Bulk storage/logistics	–	–	x	–
Oil transport, distribution, storage	–	–	x	–
Industrial	–	–	x	–
Agro-tourism	–	–	x	–

Notes: [a] related infrastructure with third party access; [b] cement, steel, etc.
Source: Author's compilation based on a survey of PIDG facility websites in 2009.

oil transport and storage, other kinds of industrial infrastructure, and tourism.[5] Broadening the definition of infrastructure in this way also helped improve performance against other development metrics of interest to PIDG donors. In its 2013 annual report PIDG claimed its facilitation of private investment in a Nigerian fertilizer plant meant that over 1.2 million people were "… provided with new/improved infrastructure," and investment in a Nigerian steel mill meant that 7.5 million people benefited in the same way (PIDG 2013, 103). By the time of PIDG's 2015 annual report, these non-traditional kinds of infrastructure made up 25 percent of total historical spending commitments (PIDG 2015).

Redefining commercial projects like cement plants and tourist resorts as "infrastructure" had another knock-on advantage for the PIDG facilities in terms of accelerating achievement of performance targets—more freedom to

5 IFC PPP Advisory, bound by WBG definitional restrictions, included housing as the only non-traditional type of infrastructure in its menu of allowable project sectors.

avoid complicated PPP project structures. Since the end of the 1990s, the focus on "private participation in infrastructure" had meant PPPs—risk-sharing contracts between public and private partners for the investment in and delivery of public services. The struggle to find ways of designing, structuring, and negotiating PPPs that would have sustainable impacts on poverty reduction preoccupied DFID, the World Bank, and other members of the development community after the Asian financial crisis abruptly brought an end to the PPP boom in developing countries in the late 1990s. Redefining infrastructure to include commercial investment in fertilizer and cement plants meant that, for these kinds of projects at least, complicated PPP structures and lengthy negotiations with government counterparts were not necessary, the improvement of essential service provision was not a target, and poverty reduction was not a priority. Commercial projects could also completely circumvent government investment planning and least-cost prioritization processes. This definitional shift did not go unnoticed by PIDG donors, some of whom strongly questioned it, most notably in a 2010 Sida-funded evaluation of PIDG (GRM International AB 2010). The study noted with concern PIDG's efforts to attract new donors and add "… more financially sustainable projects in its portfolio" (25).

Redefining target countries

The Sida-funded evaluation also questioned other steps taken by PIDG to redefine its mission in a way that resulted in improved performance optics. One approach that benefited all the facilities involved adjusting the definition of PIDG-eligible countries. The original PIDG mission statement allowed the facilities to work only in "low-income" and "least-developed" countries, as defined by the Development Assistance Committee (DAC) of the Organisation for Economic Co-operation and Development (OECD). Until 2007, the PIDG facilities followed this requirement with only a few exceptions (PIDG 2008). But the Sida-funded evaluation found that the country requirement had been relaxed, noting that the original PIDG mission of providing aid to the most financially difficult countries "has been weakened" (GRM International AB 2010, 25).

By 2012, PIDG had also added post-conflict states to its list of allowable countries and reported that two-thirds of new projects were in low-income and least-developed countries (PIDG 2012). The process of softening the country focus of PIDG continued. The PIDG Annual Review 2020 reported that the percentage of projects in low-income and least-developed countries since 2002 had dropped to 44 percent. The percentage in fragile and conflict-affected states had dropped to just over 50 percent (PIDG 2020).

Avoiding competitive tendering

As the pressure on PIDG to produce project numbers increased, the different facilities began to abandoned their "financier/developer of last resort" objectives in the interest of taking at least partial credit for projects already in development by other public or private partners. This in turn made it impractical for PIDG to accede to growing international pressures to require competitive tendering for private investment projects. This was because most of the projects supported by the PIDG facilities already involved private partners, most of whom had arranged their participation via direct negotiation rather than competition. Requiring that all PIDG projects be tendered would likely have reduced costs to government owners and rate payers and led to projects less likely to require renegotiation after financial close. These were reasons why tendering was strongly endorsed by development partners and taken up by many governments, particularly in the power sector where PIDG was most active (IEA 2017; Kruger and Eberhard 2018; Kenny 2020).

By the early 2000s, IFC PPP Advisory was already requiring government PPP auctions for all the PPPs on which they worked as advisors. South Africa's Renewable Energy IPP Procurement Program (REIPPPP) used auctions to demonstrate dramatic project cost reductions. Donors and MDBs imitated REIPPPP's competitive tendering with programs like IFC's Scaling Solar and the multi-donor GET-FiT program, and confirmed the cost-reduction potential of tendering. But for PIDG, an insistence on tendering would have meant unwinding existing public–private relationships and slowing down the project development process as well as PIDG's achievement of its performance targets. So, despite the spread of auctions for infrastructure projects across the developing world, PIDG opted not to take this approach, occasionally supporting a preferred bidder after a tender process, but only on an opportunistic, ad hoc basis.

Incentivization

In a further effort to incentivize creative project origination and development, the InfraCo board tried to take advantage of the private sector orientation of their project staff by offering large financial incentives to encourage more developmental InfraCo projects. They began to classify some projects as high development value (HDV), meaning projects that were "… expected to have a particularly significant direct impact on poorer communities and individuals, in water and sanitation, renewable energy, and agriculture-related infrastructure" (InfraCo 2007, 29).[6] To incentivize InfraCo to do more of these projects, the InfraCo Board offered InfraCo's management contractor a minimum

[6] InfraCo Asia used the term, "high development opportunity."

$1 million success fee for each project completion of this kind. Perhaps not surprisingly, the number of projects designated "high development value" grew rapidly. By 2011, InfraCo Africa listed 11 HDV projects in its pipeline. However, the use private sector-style incentives to optimize development outcomes risked unintended consequences. Evaluation consultants pointed out that the potential development costs and success fees associated with these projects "... at times exceed the maximum income InfraCo can realize for these projects" (Castalia Strategic Advisors 2011a, 26).

What was left unsaid in the consultant comments on the use of success fees was that it would be remarkable if a $1 million success fee for projects of uncertain commercial viability did not distort project selection, with possible targeting of projects requiring far more time and money to develop than would ever be possible for normal private sector projects. Such projects would typically not have any positive demonstration effects because their replication by private developers would be so unlikely.

Cost recovery abandoned

Another significant adjustment in PIDG's business strategy reflected a profound lesson learned about PPPs in poor countries. This was PIDG's quiet abandonment of cost recovery as its original prime objective. PIDG was established to demonstrate that sustainable private infrastructure investment in the poorest developing countries could be done on a commercial, cost-recovery basis. However, by 2015, none of the PIDG facilities had recovered their project development costs. The PIDG financing facilities (GuarantCo and EAIF) were making some progress toward cost recovery, based largely on their ability to participate in projects already prepared for financing, usually with other financiers involved. But the two InfraCos were not making progress toward becoming "self-sustaining" businesses in the sense of full cost recovery, as this characterization was originally understood in PIDG and as the InfraCo Africa board promised DFID evaluators in 2008.

The inability to recover costs resulted from preparation that took longer and was more expensive than expected, and a lack of interest among private sector actors in purchasing projects that PIDG had prepared. Part of the reason for the high costs of preparation was the high costs of PIDG's management and staff (including private sector salaries and $1 million success fees). Successful project auctions were supposed to cover these costs and eventually relieve PIDG donors of the burden created by the recurring need to pay for these staff costs. But as the cost-recovery objective was abandoned, PIDG's donors were told that high staff costs were a natural cost of doing this kind of business. A 2008 PIDG "lessons learned" paper pointed out that donors would simply need to become comfortable with the situation: "It is thus important for donor organisations looking to work with the private sector to recognise the relatively high cost of the remuneration packages that would be needed ...” (PIDG 2008, 42).

Relaxed rules on project ownership

The inability to auction projects to private investors just prior to financial close as promised in the 2003 consultation document, meant that PIDG also had to abandon its pledge that the InfraCos would “... never undertake actual project investment or operation” (PIDG 2003, 6). PIDG made that pledge to prospective donors because of the concern that the ability to own projects they developed might reduce the incentive for the InfraCos to facilitate private sector ownership of and investment in these projects—the achievements that were supposed to be measures of PIDG success. Continued PIDG ownership of projects that could not find private investors might allow non-commercial projects to reach “financial closure” and therefore to be counted inappropriately as PIDG project successes.

Despite these concerns, after a decade of operation and continual struggle by the two InfraCos to bring projects to financial close, it had become clear that some projects required continued ownership, investment, and often operation by PIDG companies like the InfraCos before they could attract private investors—if private investors could ever be interested in these projects. PIDG eventually amended its rules to allow the InfraCos to own some projects indefinitely. These arrangements were formalized in 2014 with the creation of InfraCo Africa Investments Ltd. and InfraCo Asia Investments Ltd. which would own and invest in projects prepared by InfraCo Africa and InfraCo Asia. Both InfraCos immediately developed small project ownership portfolios where they parked projects that they had been unable to sell.

5.5 ASSESSING PIDG PERFORMANCE

Pritchett’s 2008 study of the political economy of program evaluation, cited several times earlier, underscores the importance to program advocates of avoiding rigorous evaluations that have the potential to jeopardize program funding (Pritchett 2008). Among other things, this suggests that PPFs promoting the use of PPPs in the developing world, but struggling to complete significant numbers of projects, are typically very careful about the type and extent of performance information that they collect and make public.

PIDG was no exception to this. The first program manager of PIDG reported that over the first decade of PIDG operations the various performance evaluations of the PIDG facilities triggered heated discussions with donors who demanded better explanations for why some of the facilities were so slow to make progress (Hodges 2009). A 2014 review of DFID’s oversight of PIDG by the U.K. National Audit Office (NAO) also raised serious questions about the performance information released by PIDG. The NAO acknowledged that although PIDG was beginning to report substantial numbers of project beneficiaries and investments, it could provide no compelling evidence of value-for-money: "… DFID lacks sufficiently robust information to demonstrate that investment in PIDG is the best option" (U.K. NAO 2014, 10). The NAO review concluded that DFID was not exercising enough oversight of PIDG strategy or operations and could not fully justify the level of U.K. investment in PIDG.

Like most PPFs, PIDG faced a complex measurement challenge. First, it could not meet the NAO's value-for-money challenge because the PIDG facilities did not have the budgets or the expertise to carry out compelling evaluations of their private investment solutions compared with various kinds of public and private investment alternatives. "Value-for-money" assessments were not done by the PIDG facilities.

Second, PIDG could not demonstrate that the total investment it generated was significant in terms of addressing the infrastructure investment challenge in the poorest developing countries. At first glance, PIDG's investment numbers seemed large—by 2022 PIDG claimed to have "mobilized" $37 billion over 20 years of operation. But already by 2010, the AICD study estimated that the *annual* investment requirement of SSA countries was over $93 billion. A decade later, that investment requirement had grown significantly. PIDG was making little progress in closing the investment gap.

Third, like other PPFs, PIDG could try to show that its work was valuable with evidence that it was generating demonstration effects resulting in market development, with more projects prepared and financed by others than would have been the case without PIDG's pioneering examples. This was in fact something that PIDG claimed: "The need for infrastructure in these countries is huge and cannot be met by one organisation alone. Therefore our focus will remain on demonstrating to others the commercial viability of our projects" (PIDG 2012, 5).

But again, like most donor-funded PPFs, although PIDG has made repeated claims that it generates demonstration effects, it has made almost no effort to document such effects in terms of project replication or market building. The few studies of this kind funded by PIDG have either been non-rigorous reviews using anecdotal evidence and small convenience samples of projects (Lion's Head 2018) or studies that diplomatically question the existence of such effects, and as a result quickly disappear from the PIDG website (Spratt and Collins 2012). Moreover, when the PIDG facilities effectively admitted that they could not recover the costs of developing projects, the organization abandoned what would have been its most powerful means of encouraging project replication by private developers, sponsors, and investors, all of whom must do projects on a cost-recovery basis.

Table 5.2 provides a performance snapshot of the four core PIDG facilities at the end of 2021, summarizing some of the limited information available from the organization's online database (the database appears not to have been updated since 2022). This review suggests several basic conclusions about PIDG performance:

- The performance of the two InfraCos, the PIDG flagship companies, has been particularly disappointing, especially given how long they have each been in operation. Between them, they achieved 36 financial closures, with 20 of those done as IPP projects. So, by 2021, these two companies had averaged a little over one financial closure per year over their lifespans, despite receiving a total of nearly $483 million in total donor funding over that period (PIDG 2021).[7]
- By far the most successful PIDG company, EAIF has the least risky business model, making hard-currency debt available to projects developed and mostly financed by others.

5.6 CONCLUSIONS

IFC PPP Advisory and the various PIDG facilities have been extraordinarily successful PPFs in navigating the pitfalls of trying to develop infrastructure PPPs in developing countries, if measured by their consistent ability to attract money from outsiders to continue, and in some respects even grow, their operations. As discussed later in Chapter 10, IFC PPP Advisory is now being absorbed into a much larger organization-wide effort by the IFC to focus on project preparation. That effort has attempted to incorporate lessons from the two decades of PPP Advisory's operations and is trying to address the shortcomings of the transaction-only approach. In 2018, PIDG transformed itself into a limited liability company, dramatically reducing the role of donors in its operations, and allowing the organization to more freely operate like a private sector financier, focusing on whatever it chooses to define as "infrastructure" or "development benefits."

But these two PPFs have achieved very little in terms of encouraging replication of their projects or wider PPP market development. They have not been able to confirm that PPPs can be done on a commercial basis in LICs. The thesis of this book is that PPPs probably cannot be scaled up in poor countries because they cannot be done without the help of donors and DFIs, much less

7 There was no indication in the database of how much, and for which projects, performance bonuses of as much as $1 million per project were paid to InfraCo staff for completing "high development value" projects.

Table 5.2 *PIDG company performance data, December 31, 2021*

PIDG companies	Years of operation	No. of financial closures	Closures per year	Donor allocations (US$ millions)	PIDG financial commitments (US$ millions)		Predicted investment (US$ millions)	Actual investment (US$ millions)
					Total	Per project		
EAIF	20	90	4.5	395	1,964	21.8	25,558	15,946
GuarantCo	18	56	3.1	323	1,199	21.4	6,032	3,473
InfraCo Africa	17	20	1.2	296	116	5.8	1,299	1,110
InfraCo Asia	15	16	1.1	187	81	5.1	743	461
Totals	20	182	9.1	1,201	2,227	12.2	33,632	20,990

Source: PIDG (2021).

commercially. But it seems even less likely that a transaction-only approach to preparation can help in encouraging the spread of these projects in the developing world. The key assumptions about PPPs in PIDG's 2003 "consultation document" were all largely incorrect, as PIDG operations confirmed almost immediately.

By the late 2000s, a series of development challenges seemed to suggest that PPPs were needed more than ever. PIDG, PPIAF, GPOBA, IFC PPP Advisory, and other PPFs continued operating, but were doing just enough to maintain their own access to donor funding. Not enough projects resulted from this work for these PPFs to be considered leaders of the PPP agenda, the role that DFID expected would be played by the PPFs in its Private Sector Infrastructure portfolio. Something more was needed to effectively drive PPP advocacy. Governments of developing countries needed to become more convinced of the value of PPPs, and more technical and financial resources were needed to help these governments realize that value. All of this required more commitment to PPP advocacy on the part of the largest and most influential international development organizations. The "globalization" of PPP advocacy is explored in the next chapter.

PART III

The globalization of PPP advocacy

6. Franchising PPP advocacy: PPP units

6.1 INTRODUCTION

The aggressive advocacy of public–private partnerships (PPPs) led by the U.K.'s Department for International Development (DFID) was successful to the extent that it persuaded donors and multilateral development banks (MDBs) to support transaction-only project preparation facilities (PPFs) like IFC PPP Advisory and the Private Infrastructure Development Group (PIDG). But another group of supporters assembled around the more deliberative approach to PPP advocacy favored by the World Bank and other international organizations like the International Monetary Fund (IMF), the Organisation for Economic Co-operation and Development (OECD), etc. This approach involved persuading governments of developing countries regarding the value of PPPs and the need to spend their own resources on amendments to regulations, policies, and procedures, and the creation of new government institutions in order to facilitate such projects. Ironically, this more deliberative approach to PPP advocacy occasionally came into conflict with the transaction-focused approach of the DFID-funded programs. This was because PPP legal-regulatory frameworks tend to frustrate the entrepreneurial tendencies of transaction-focused PPFs like PIDG by requiring specific "best practice" sequences of governmental actions before PPPs can be approved. These actions include things like least-cost sector planning, project identification and prioritization, prefeasibility and feasibility studies, value-for-money analysis, the competitive tendering of projects, etc. Historically, PIDG facilities have avoided projects in environments where such requirements are strictly enforced. IFC PPP Advisory has typically requested exemptions from most rules of this kind if they complicate or slow the project preparation process.

The creation of laws, regulations, and institutions to support PPPs in developing countries has also been successful in the sense that many governments have been convinced to adopt these elements of PPP "best practice." And the exercise has created a large international cadre of civil servants whose employment is linked to PPP project development, evaluation, or implementation. These civil servants now constitute an influential share of the global population of what Lant Pritchett called the "true believers" and "core supporters," who passionately advocate a particular solution (PPPs) to a priority problem (infrastructure investment) (Pritchett 2008). But this effort to enable PPP projects on a much wider scale than possible with the help of transaction-only PPFs has been far less successful than hoped, as this chapter explains.

6.2 PPP UNITS: GOVERNMENTS TAKE OWNERSHIP OF PPP PROJECT DEVELOPMENT

One of the "best practice" measures most frequently recommended as a way to facilitate sustainable PPPs is the creation of a governmental "PPP unit." This recommendation stems from a reality documented in the 2015 evaluation of the World Bank's PPP activities by its Independent Evaluation Group (IEG), which found high rates of delay and failure to complete PPP transactions. The World Bank's deliberative approach to PPPs, reflected in its 2002 private sector development strategy, recommended preceding transactions with attention to the policies, procedures, and laws necessary to make projects sustainable. But very few World Bank projects were able to effect enabling environment changes, plus complete PPP projects, in the four- to five-year lifespan of a typical Bank development project.

One of the tactics used by the World Bank and other development partners to deal with this situation was to encourage the creation by governments of official agencies that would take forward PPP projects after World Bank assistance had ended, or in the absence of outside assistance. The World Bank, often using grant funding from the Public–Private Infrastructure Advisory Facility (PPIAF), would assist client governments in the design, establishment, and funding of "PPP units" that would assume a combination of responsibilities. These might include driving the upstream reform process, developing PPP capacity in line departments, providing downstream transaction assistance to complete PPP projects, evaluating and recommending approval of PPPs, etc. The World Bank's *African Infrastructure Country Diagnostic* (AICD) study recommended the creation of "... a specialist national agency dealing with privatization" that could develop governmental PPP policies and identify appropriate forms of private participation (Foster and Briceño-Garmendia 2010, 209).

Because such units are typically incentivized to focus only on PPP projects without evaluating public sector investment alternatives, they naturally become PPP advocates in the governments where they are established. But more importantly, the act of creating a PPP unit, involving changes to laws and organizational structures, the allocation of budget resources, and the recruitment or reassignment of staff, represents a serious government commitment to the proposition that PPPs are realistic, cost-effective solutions to infrastructure investment and management problems. In effect, development partners like the

World Bank have "franchised" PPP advocacy by convincing governments to create such units.

By the mid-2000s, PPP units were already widely used in OECD countries, and strongly recommended by the European Commission (2003) and the United Nations (2007). OECD reported that 17 of its 29 member countries had created such units by 2009; all but three of them created before 2006 (OECD 2010, 3). Most of these units were established in countries with active PPP programs. The specific functions of the units varied, but their focus was mostly on assisting with government management of expanding pipelines of actual projects. The OECD defined them as "dedicated units" created by or with government support "… to enhance the capacity of government to successfully manage the risks associated with a growing number and value of public–private partnerships" (3).

The United Nations described PPP units as part of the evolution of a country's PPP program, with dedicated units commonly established in an intermediate stage of program development after an initial stage in which the government carries out the upstream actions needed for a PPP program to begin making progress: defining the policy framework, testing legal viability, identifying a PPP project pipeline, developing basic concepts to guide PPP project evaluation and procurement processes, applying lessons from earlier PPP transactions to later ones, and building a national PPP marketplace (UN 2007, 7).

In developing countries, expectations for PPP units tended to be even more ambitious. In low-income countries (LICs) for example, PPP units were almost always created in the absence of active PPP programs. Such units were much more frequently intended to drive the upstream reforms as well as downstream development of projects, to act as agents of change within these governments to take on the complicated list of legal, regulatory, policy, institutional, and procedural reforms necessary for governments to take effective advantage of PPPs, but beyond the ability of development partners to effectuate.

A wide variety of development partners helped to create PPP units all over the developing world, including the European Investment Bank (EIB), the European Bank for Reconstruction and Development (EBRD), the Asian Development Bank (AsDB), and the U.S. Agency for International Development (USAID). The World Bank used PPIAF funding to create or build PPP capacity in a wide variety of countries like Jordan, Haiti, Egypt, and Bangladesh. PPIAF's website claims that it has helped establish over a dozen units in Africa where, from the mid-2000s to 2020, 35 countries created PPP units (or in several cases, passed legislation authorizing the creation of such units, but as of 2020 had not yet established units) (Figure 6.1). The 2020 World Bank survey of PPP legal and regulatory frameworks in 140, mostly developing, countries found that 84 percent had established dedicated PPP units (World Bank 2020).

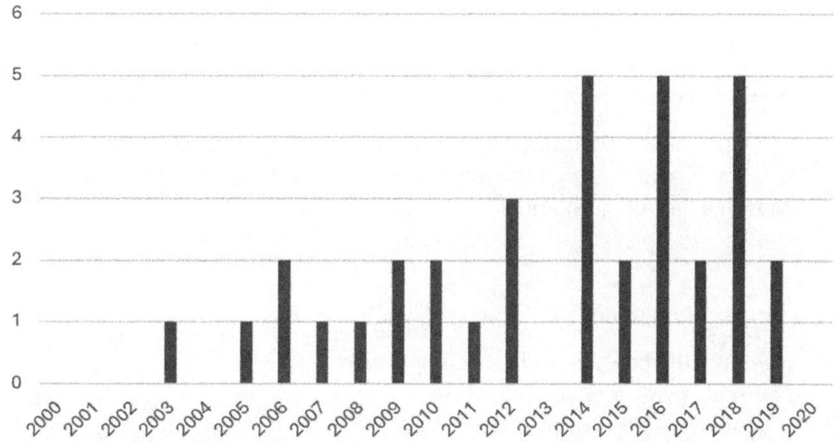

Source: World Bank (2020).

Figure 6.1 PPP units created annually in SSA, 2000–2020

In Africa, these units are known by a variety of names: the PPP Unit (Uganda); the Directorate of Public Private Partnerships (Kenya); the Support Council for the Realization of Partnership Contracts (Cameroon); the National Steering Committee for Public–Private Partnerships (Cote d'Ivoire); the Public Private Partnership Commission (Malawi); the PPP Department (Zambia), and so on. The numerous variations in PPP unit focus, function, organizational set-up, funding, staffing, etc., reflect the huge task of helping PPP projects gain traction in these countries and the fact that key obstacles are perceived differently in different countries (Box 6.1).

6.3 BENEFITS AND COSTS

PPP units are widely perceived to be beneficial, even necessary, for the success of a country's PPP program (Lemma 2013). PPP units often represent the first step in a government's efforts to establish PPP-friendly legal and regulatory frameworks (World Bank 2020). But recommendations to create PPP units in developing countries are almost never justified with rigorous evaluation or analysis. Little best-practice guidance exists regarding how such units should be designed or even what their responsibilities should be. And nearly two decades after PPP units began proliferating in regions like sub-Saharan Africa (SSA), there is little evidence that such units facilitate successful PPP projects, much less programs involving multiple projects.

BOX 6.1 PPP UNITS IN DEVELOPING COUNTRIES, SELECTED DESIGN OPTIONS

1. Project focus

- Infrastructure and/or non-infrastructure (agriculture, tourism, etc.)
- Economic and/or social infrastructure (schools, hospitals, etc.)
- National and/or sub-national projects
- PPPs and/or privatization (asset sales)

2. Primary functions

- Regulate the process of developing projects
- Facilitate project development
- Financial support for projects
- PPP capacity building
- PPP promotion
- Monitor implementation
- Manage PPP procurement

3. Organizational set-up

- Within government structure
- Semi-autonomous unit set up as a government-owned company outside of regular government structure (with its own government-appointed Board of Directors (BOD))
- Separate corporate entity with a completely independent BOD

4. Staffing

- Employment methods: secondments, contracts, permanent hires
- Skills: project management, financial engineering, technical sector knowledge
- Recruitment: from the civil service or private sector

5. Funding sources

- Contributions from general government budget
- Contributions from departmental / enterprise operational budgets
- Success fees paid by private partners at the time of contract closure
- Donor funding

Source: Compiled by the author.

Because these units vary so widely in function and focus, researchers have found it difficult to even agree on how to measure their value (Burger and Hawkesworth 2011; EPEC 2014). But counting the small numbers of PPP projects completed, or similar basic metrics, do not seem to demonstrate anything regarding PPP unit value or performance: "There is very little quantitative evidence of the value of centralized PPP coordination units ..." (Lemma 2013). The World Bank's survey of PPP legal-regulatory frameworks concluded that "In fact, formation of a PPP unit is not, in itself, a sufficient condition for the success of a PPP program" (World Bank 2020). The only frequently cited tangible benefit of such units seems to be that they demonstrate government commitment to PPPs. An early study of PPPs concluded that "… the private sector is more concerned to see an established PPP unit within the client organisation …" as an indication of the government's ability to effectively negotiate and manage PPP projects (Ahadzi and Bowles 2004, 976).

Most PPP units in the developing world do have a role in recommending PPP policies and procedures, but very few can drive reform processes in these areas. Units almost never have the leadership, stature, or expertise that would warrant that kind of influence. In low-income countries governments can rarely afford to employ the kinds of experts whose advice is of significant value to public or private sector project proponents. Heads of state, ministers, politicians, etc., take key decisions on policies and legal and regulatory reforms, not lower-level civil servants. In situations where top politicians do not support the PPP program, where procurement of infrastructure and capital works is not transparent and competitive, and where the machinery of government is chronically uncoordinated, PPP units are unlikely to dramatically increase the number of PPPs successfully reaching financial closure.

Most PPP units are not given the authority even to require compliance with their recommendations regarding specific projects, much less high-level policies. Lemma found that "The majority of the PPP Units reviewed in the literature do not play a particularly important role in approving or rejecting PPP programmes or projects" (Lemma 2013, 1). The World Bank's 2020 survey of PPP legal and regulatory frameworks in 140 countries found that only just over 40 percent "Approve, provide an opinion, or participate in an approval process" (World Bank 2020). But most units with approval powers were in OECD countries.

In the minority of cases where PPP units are given the authority to set up and implement procedural frameworks for ex ante evaluation and approval of proposed projects, they sometimes disappoint stakeholders by slowing deal flow. Government officials in developing countries typically expect such units to accelerate the process of getting PPPs to completion. But such units often produce exactly the opposite result—the deal flow slows because of the perceived need to carefully apply standardized procedures in project development. Better prepared projects should be more sustainable, and that may off-set lengthy preparation periods to some degree. But this logic rarely satisfies government officials who have invested in the creation and operation of PPP units with the expectation that this will help get projects done as quickly as possible (see the case study below of South Africa's PPP Unit).

When PPP units are given responsibility for PPP project selection and procurement, other problems can result. The World Bank notes that this kind of authority may discourage line ministries, normally responsible for infrastructure projects, if they are asked to engage in the contract management phase without a strong level of participation in the selection process (World Bank 2020).

The focus of most PPP units in developing countries is on information dissemination and promotion of PPPs. This limited role results from the fact that the ways in which most of these units are set up and staffed restricts more direct involvement in PPP projects. There is little reason to assume that PPP units will be better able than other government agencies to attract or develop the technical expertise needed to recommend policies or support individual projects. One of the earliest studies of these units, sponsored by PPIAF (2007), noted that PPP units are often established due to frustration with the inability of existing institutions to move PPP programs forward. But these units often end up sharing the same organizational, operational, and staffing shortcomings as the departments they are supposed to assist. The PPIAF study concluded that the most often cited obstacles to PPPs in poor countries have almost nothing to do with problems that a PPP unit is likely to solve, or even address.

Governments sometimes try to anticipate PPP unit staffing problems by recruiting expensive experts, only to find that this approach is not sustainable. Sometimes experts can be seconded to PPP units from private sector firms or recruited for limited periods with the help of donor funding. But these kinds of experts typically cannot be retained long enough to transfer significant levels of professional skills to regular staff (and if they do, regular staff members tend to leave for higher-paying jobs). In most cases, PPP units need effective project managers rather than financial experts or transaction advisors, but these also tend to be in short supply in poor countries.

PPP units often limit their own credibility and effectiveness by taking on too many primary functions, some of which lead to conflicts of interest. Regulation of project development conflicts with facilitation of transaction closure. Developer or facilitator roles conflict with roles as ex post monitor or evaluator. Ethical barriers are sometimes erected to block the exchange of information between sections or departments within PPP units, but the effectiveness of such separation is often questionable, undermining a unit's credibility with line departments (see the case study below of Nigeria's PPP unit).

6.4 EX ANTE PROJECT ANALYSIS: THE U.K. EXPERIENCE

If PPP unit functions are limited to activities like PPP promotion and capacity building, units run the risk of acting exclusively as PPP advocates, encouraging the use of PPPs in all situations, including those where other infrastructure solutions might be more appropriate. The OECD warned against this in some of its earliest publications on PPP units, saying that "Establishing a dedicated unit may imply an implicit approval of PPP as a policy tool and weaken the case for other viable procurement methods" (OECD 2010, 29).

Most PPP units may not have the authority to approve projects, but many are expected to do more than just promote PPPs by carrying out one or more types of ex ante project analysis to confirm that a PPP is a cost-effective solution to an infrastructure problem. Implementing analytical approaches for doing this has long been a role given to PPP units. In 2008, a joint statement by the 21 finance ministers of the Asia-Pacific Economic Cooperation (APEC) countries recommended that dedicated PPP units manage PPP risks by establishing robust quantitative and qualitative methods to identify and assess projects (APEC 2008).

Perhaps the most influential type of ex ante PPP project analysis, and one of the most widely employed by PPP units around the world, involves the use of "public sector comparators" (PSCs). PSC analysis was pioneered as part of the U.K.'s PFI program in the 1990s, and later adopted by PPP units in OECD countries like Australia, Canada, the Netherlands, and in developing countries like South Africa. The PSC method was meant to objectively assess the need for private participation compared with traditional public investment approaches. Its quantitative approach has been used in many countries to counter criticism from those unconvinced by theoretical arguments in favor of private participation. The PSC method does this by allowing a quantitative comparison between a PPP reference project and a public sector comparator project designed to deliver the same services. The PSC is a risk-adjusted financial model of the hypothetical public sector project. It estimates the total costs to the government of achieving the targeted outputs, assuming that the project is handled as a normal public investment project, with reasonably foreseeable efficiency improvements.

In the United Kingdom and Australia, the use of this method in the early 2000s quickly led to recognition that it had problems and that in a significant number of cases it had become an expensive way of endorsing the choice of private participation. Much of the PSC analysis depends on subjective judgment, and small adjustments for risk or in discount rates can have dramatic effects on cost estimates. Because of this, many U.K. experts were unsurprised when a parliamentary committee discovered cases involving "… manipulation of the underlying calculations and erroneous interpretation of the results" (U.K. House of Commons, Committee of Public Accounts 2003, 7). A U.K. Audit Commission report concluded that "… the PSC has lost the confidence of many people, and risks being seen more as a hoop to jump through on the way to government funding than a valuable exercise that can help ensure better VfM [value for money]" (U.K. Audit Commission 2003, 37).

In response to criticisms like these, in 2004 the U.K. Treasury initiated changes in the PSC method to counter "optimism bias," with cost estimates based on actual historical costs, a stronger role for qualitative analysis, and more open-mindedness toward conventional public procurement. These efforts by the U.K. Treasury to tighten guidelines for ex ante VfM analysis improved the rigor of the approach, but at the same time made it more difficult to develop compelling ex ante arguments for individual PFI projects. The difficulty was in making the basic ex ante case to justify the projects—demonstrating in a compelling fashion that the benefits to be gained from additionality, risk transfer, and improved decision-making would outweigh the costs associated with private financing, expert transaction advice, lack of contract flexibility, etc.

In the U.K., the need for effective ex ante VfM analysis of PPP projects increased as PFI began to face other challenges in the late 2000s. The global financial crisis created difficulties in raising finance for PFI projects. Many of the viable opportunities for larger greenfield projects had already been taken up earlier in the decade, leaving brownfield projects that were generally less attractive for private finance. The U.K.'s 2009 shift to new accounting rules affecting these projects made them less likely to be considered "off balance sheet" investments and more likely to be counted against permitted levels of public sector debt, making the projects less attractive to government agencies. The flow of PFI transactions peaked in 2006 and started to decline more rapidly after 2008. By late 2010, the U.K.'s market for private finance of public infrastructure was largely inactive. In 2018, the U.K. government ended the PFI program. A major cause of PFI's inability to sustain its success was the inability to justify projects on an ex ante basis. As one expert concluded: "Private finance can deliver considerable benefits for the provision of public infrastructure in appropriate conditions but it can be difficult to establish with confidence any value for money in the investment appraisal" (Winch et al. 2012, 123).

6.5 EX ANTE ANALYSIS IN DEVELOPING COUNTRIES

The U.K.'s experience with PSCs illustrates the many difficulties that PPP units face in using this kind of analysis effectively. Those difficulties are even more challenging in developing countries:

- *Lack of historical data.* Even industrial countries have little objective data on which to base cost estimates. Without such data, calculating with any accuracy the running costs of a project over 25–30 years is almost impossible. There have also been difficulties in standardizing methods for determining the "normal way" in which the public sector implements a project, and the "reasonably" foreseeable efficiency improvements that public officials might make.
- *High costs of modeling.* The financial modeling required for PSCs and PPP reference projects can be enormously expensive and time consuming. This is a particular problem in developing countries where government agencies have modest budgets for PPP project development, and few local consulting firms have the expertise to carry out sophisticated VfM analyses. Even in South Africa, with perhaps the deepest private consulting sector in Africa, National Treasury's PPP Unit found that PSC analysis of PPPs quickly became dominated by a few large consulting firms.
- *No realistic public sector alternatives.* The PSC may be hypothetical, but it must refer to a project that could be implemented if private financing was unavailable. If no public funding is available, as is the case in most low-income countries, the PSC is largely irrelevant. Early in the development of Australia's PPP program, the Fitzgerald report recommended against carrying out the PSC comparison where public sector provision "is not a reasonable option" (Fitzgerald 2004, 31).

Despite these and many other well-documented shortcomings, requirements to use ex ante PPP project assessment procedures like VfM are now commonplace in the developing world. But PPP units in developing countries typically lack the technical skills and financial resources to use these techniques effectively, and the various problems and limitations of the techniques described above present challenges that are beyond the technical capacity of most PPP units in developing countries to solve. What this means is that in most developing countries, although various kinds of ex ante PPP project assessments are required by applicable legal-regulatory frameworks, methodologies for implementing those procedures are typically not specified. The World Bank's global survey of 140 PPP legal and regulatory frameworks found that roughly three-quarters of the governments required some form of ex ante project analysis, usually including VfM analysis, but only half of these governments specified methodologies needed to ensure effective and consistent implementation. Most of the governments without methodologies were in low-income or lower middle-income countries.

Across Africa, the World Bank survey found that 33 of 39 countries required VfM analysis for PPPs, but only six of these countries specified a methodology. Table 6.1 reports on a random selection of five African countries included in the World Bank survey regarding their use of nine of the ex ante analytical procedures that constitute best practice (according to the Bank's large panel of international experts). Except for environmental and social impact assessments (#8 and #9), almost none of the assessment procedures have associated methodologies specified. All but one of these countries require some form of value-for-money assessment (#4), but none of these countries specify methodologies. In other words, these governments require different kinds of ex ante analysis, but have no standardized technical approaches for implementing those analyses. There is no guarantee that best practices are used in these analyses, and no assurance that the same methodology will be used consistently, meaning that analytical results cannot be assessed on a comparative basis. The use of these techniques also exhibits relatively low levels of what the World Bank survey calls "de facto regulatory compliance," meaning that although required, in many cases no real attempt is made to implement the techniques and no effort is routinely made to hold violators of these rules accountable.

6.6 THREE PPP UNIT CASE STUDIES

6.6.1 South Africa's PPP Unit

The expectation has been that PPP units deploying state-of-the-art procedures and methodologies can accelerate the development of beneficial PPPs in developing countries. But the actual experience with such units suggests that a rigorous process of documenting PPP benefits can complicate and slow the project development process to such an extent that a PPP program loses momentum and begins to stall, even in middle-income countries where PPPs in some sectors are possible. The experience of South Africa's PPP Unit offers a perspective on this issue.

The South Africa unit, which was established in 2000, was one of the first and most influential PPP units in Africa. As noted in PPIAF's early study of PPP units, the first models for the design of such units were the "privatization agencies" established during the MDB policy-based lending programs of the 1980s and 1990s to manage privatization of state-owned enterprises (SOEs) (PPIAF 2007). But South Africa had no structural adjustment program in the 1980s and 1990s. Prior to the end of the apartheid government in 1994, the

Table 6.1 *Procedure vs. methodology in ex ante PPP project analysis, five SSA countries, 2020*

PPP procedures & methodologies	Cameroon	Cote d'Ivoire	Kenya	Uganda	Zambia
1. Socio-economic analysis (C/B analysis):	Yes	Yes	Yes	Yes	Yes
Specific Methodology?	NO	NO	NO	NO	NO
2. Fiscal affordability assessment (including contingent liabilities):	Yes	No	Yes	Yes	Yes
Specific Methodology?	NO	NO	NO	NO	NO
3. Risk identification & allocation:	Yes	No	Yes	Yes	Yes
Specific Methodology?	NO	NO	NO	NO	NO
4. Comparative assessment—PPP vs. non-PPP:	Yes	No	Yes	Yes	Yes
Specific Methodology?	NO	NO	NO	NO	NO
5. Financial viability & bankability assessment:	Yes	Yes	Yes	Yes	Yes
Specific Methodology?	NO	NO	NO	NO	NO

PPP procedures & methodologies	Cameroon	Cote d'Ivoire	Kenya	Uganda	Zambia
6. Market sounding (likely market interest):	No	No	Yes	Yes	No
Specific Methodology?	NO	NO	NO	NO	NO
7. Environmental impact assessment (plus community consultation):	Yes	Yes	Yes	Yes	Yes
Specific Methodology?	Yes	NO	Yes	Yes	Yes
8. Social impact assessment (plus community consultation):	Yes	Yes	No	Yes	Yes
Specific Methodology?	Yes	NO	NO	Yes	Yes

Source: Adapted from World Bank (2020).

government was isolated by international sanctions and did not receive support from development institutions like the World Bank. So by the end of apartheid in 1994, South Africa had no privatization program and no privatization agency that could be used as a model for a PPP program.

However, several early PPP project successes triggered consideration of a government-administered PPP unit. The first and largest of these projects to reach completion as a PPP was a 30-year concession awarded in 1997 to a private company to upgrade, construct, operate, and maintain a toll road from Pretoria to Maputo. Two years later, two 30-year water concessions were signed with private international water companies. The largest of these was located near the border with Mozambique, at the eastern end of the Maputo Corridor.

However, by the time the water concessions were signed in 1999, municipal-level PPPs had already attracted strong anti-privatization criticism from South African civil society groups and organized labor. Some senior Treasury officials also had doubts about the practicality and socio-economic benefits of private participation in the country's infrastructure service delivery. The early PPP successes seemed to suggest that such projects would proliferate, so National Treasury officials saw a need to exercise strong quality control over project selection and development, particularly at the sub-national level.

In 2000 the government created a PPP Unit as a sub-division of the Budget Office within the National Treasury. A principal source of inspiration for the design of the unit was the U.K.'s PFI program. PFI's centralized project oversight unit, Partnerships U.K. (PUK), was staffed with project finance experts who developed and enforced the use of standardized PPP contracts and evaluated PFI projects on a VfM basis before they were launched in the market. The PUK emphasis was on quality control and consistency of approach in relation to issues such as VfM and affordability.

The South African Treasury's PPP Unit, like PUK, was structured primarily to regulate the development of projects rather than advise on or facilitate project development. Thousands of pages of National Treasury PPP guidelines were eventually issued, calling for over two dozen project preparation steps, as well as a series of National Treasury approvals of the process. But there had apparently been no realistic attempt to estimate the likely costs and benefits of such a unit, especially one using the elaborate PFI-style operating procedures and regulations. Also not assessed was the likely effect of such a process on the existing pipeline of relatively small sub-national PPPs. The benefits of the unit and its procedures were simply assumed.

The entire process, including the use of "public sector comparators," was quickly judged by the private sector to be too lengthy, complex, expensive, highly over-regulated, and responsible for dramatically slowing PPP deal flow (Castalia Strategic Advisors 2007). The PPP Unit itself admitted that its required VfM studies at the municipal level averaged about 30 months (Levinsohn and Reardon 2007). PPP project development in South Africa eventually stagnated; PPPs at the local government level completely stopped making progress. The experience of South Africa's PPP Unit seems consistent with the findings of several researchers, confirming that complicated frameworks for regulating the development of PPP projects can significantly slow the process of moving projects to financial close (Zhang and Kumaraswamy 2001; Chan et al. 2010).

South Africa continued to use PSC analysis long after the U.K. and Australia took more nuanced approaches to its application. In South Africa, the analysis was expensive and time-consuming, difficult for civil servants to understand or manage, and could be implemented effectively only by large consulting firms. Despite its effects in slowing down and complicating PPP project development, the PPP Unit's approach quickly became widely recognized in Africa as best practice for regulating PPP project development. Treasury's PPP guidance material was used by other governments in Africa as they set up their own PPP units (Lemma 2013). But in 2013, after years of PPP stagnation in the South Africa, the PPP Unit was moved from Treasury's Budget Office and absorbed by the Government Technical Advisory Centre (GTAC), where it was given a new role as provider of PPP advice (GTAC 2015). The unit's regulatory functions were left behind in the National Treasury. In effect, most of the original PPP unit was transformed from a development process regulator to a project facilitator.

A 2021 World Bank-funded evaluation of South Africa's PPP legal and regulatory framework confirmed that the country's PPP deal flow had largely stopped, with only two local government transactions completed since the issuance of regulations tailored specifically for municipal-level deals in 2005. Lack of technical capacity at different levels of government, including the PPP Unit, plus the accumulation of overlapping laws and regulations, all contributed to an overwhelmingly negative view of PPPs by government officials, particularly at the local level: "The current perception of PPPs within the municipal sphere as confirmed by stakeholder feedback [...] is that they are time-consuming, complicated, laborious and expensive as compared to traditional government procurement" (CPCS 2021, 17). In order to remedy this situation, the World Bank-funded study recommended massive new expenditures on capacity building and institutional reorganization.

Even if it is possible to streamline South Africa's PPP legal and regulatory framework and build more capacity in the PPP unit, South Africa will still face a fundamental challenge to infrastructure PPPs, especially at the sub-national level. Annual municipal audit reports by the government's Auditor General demonstrate that over the last decade the financial condition of the country's sub-national governments has sharply deteriorated. This has occurred as a result of unprofessional management, over-spending, under-collection of rates and taxes, over-pricing of services, poor service delivery, and massive amounts of wasted and unaccounted-for funds—most of which is never recovered (South Africa Auditor General 2021). By 2020, less than 10 percent of the nation's 257 municipalities were regularly receiving unqualified audit opinions, and less than 20 percent were estimated to be in good financial health. Based on the Auditor General's widely reported conclusion that "accountability failures" were not being addressed at the local level, it is no surprise that potential private partners have shown no enthusiasm for PPPs at the sub-national level in South Africa (de Villiers 2021).

6.6.2 Zambia's PPP Department

The creation of PPP units has been widely recommended in Africa as a way of focusing government attention on legal and regulatory reforms needed to facilitate PPPs, and as centers for the development and use of guidelines and evaluation procedures needed to ensure that projects generate appropriate levels of value for money. But is the creation and maintenance of a PPP unit cost-effective in a low-income country with a minimal PPP track record and little likelihood of developing robust project pipelines? Is the creation of such a unit in a low-income country likely to make a difference in the number of successful PPPs implemented in the country? The experience of Zambia's PPP unit (now known as a "PPP Department") suggests answers to these questions.

The creation of a Zambian PPP unit was largely due to the reform momentum that existed in the aftermath of the country's policy-based, structural adjustment borrowing program. The need for structural adjustment in Zambia, in the view of development partners, was caused by the proliferation of SOEs in the 1970s and 1980s which triggered dramatic increases in deficit financing. From 1968 to 1988 Zambia's fiscal deficit increased by almost 90 times. In 1984, Zambia was the most indebted country in the world relative to its gross domestic product (GDP). The principal source of the deficit was subsidy support for SOEs (AfDB 2000). By the end of the 1980s, the government was coming under considerable pressure from the IMF and World Bank to launch a structural adjustment program centered on SOE privatization. To facilitate the process, in 1992 the parliament passed the Privatization Act which established the Zambia Privatization Agency (ZPA) as the lead institution responsible for the divestiture of state-owned enterprises.

ZPA and its management of the privatization process was strongly supported by the World Bank and a host of other development partners. In 1992 and 1993 the Bank supplied balance of payment credits conditioned on policy reform and privatization. During the 1990s, ZPA also received support from a variety of bilateral donors. This support was mainly in the form of technical advice to assist ZPA in the evaluation of companies to be privatized and the training of personnel. Support from development partners helped ZPA quickly begin activities, eventually selling off 270 SOEs. By 1996 the World Bank called ZPA's program "... the most successful privatization program to date and the experience there offers many examples of best practice" (Shirley 1995).

Privatization was a condition for debt relief, so as the program proceeded, several debt relief initiatives slowed the growth of the country's sovereign debt burden, until Zambia reached the "Completion Point" of the Heavily Indebted Poor Countries (HIPC) initiative in April 2005. The debt write-off triggered government expectations of major new investments in various sectors of the economy. To facilitate the investment process, the Zambia Development Agency (ZDA) began operating in 2007. The ZDA was a merger of the Zambia Privatization Agency, and several other agencies and boards concerned with investment. In 2009, the Zambian parliament passed the PPP Act, formalizing a policy framework for the implementation of PPPs which covered stakeholder roles, protection of public interest, value for money, and service quality. Along with the 2008 Public Procurement Act, this body of legislation constituted a legal, regulatory, and institutional framework for most types of PPPs.[1]

The PPP Act created a PPP Unit authorized to conceptualize, identify, coordinate with contracting authorities, promote participation of the private sector in PPP projects, and ensure the proper implementation, management, enforcement, and monitoring of agreements. A PPP Technical Committee was created by the Act as a diverse group of specialists to provide technical input and recommendations to both the PPP Unit and a PPP Council, established as the policymaking body with the final authority to award PPP projects to private sector companies. The Council comprises five ministers (including the Minister of Finance as the chair) and three experts from the private sector.

According to the World Bank, Zambia's basic PPP legal and regulatory framework, including the design of its PPP unit, ranks highly in SSA in terms of consistency with international best practice (World Bank 2020). However, other than several electricity generation projects (not governed by the PPP Law), as of 2021 no infrastructure PPPs had reached financial closure in Zambia since the creation of the PPP Unit in 2009. Various reasons have been cited to account for this poor PPP performance:

- Various reviews have noted that regulations and guidance promised in the legislation have not yet been issued, and that this lack of clarity likely undermined the implementation of the legal framework. In 2014, during

---

1 Independent power producer (IPP) electricity generation projects in Zambia are covered by a separate body of legislation and procedures.

its brief tenure as the institutional home of the PPP Unit, ZDA noted that PPP regulations, guidelines, manuals, and standardized bidding documents had never been prepared, as called for in the 2009 law. ZDA indicated an intention to begin preparing these documents, but the process apparently stopped when the PPP Unit was moved to the State House in late 2015.

- A report issued in September 2017 by a committee of the National Assembly that reviewed the draft amendment to the PPP Act was critical of the fact that the institutional entities in the PPP framework were staffed almost exclusively by civil servants with very little actual PPP experience or technical capacity (Republic of Zambia 2017). The committee recommended the recruitment of more full-time experts to fill these roles, changing the PPP unit into an independent government agency rather than a department under a ministry, and the preparation of detailed guidelines on how the PPP tender and contracting processes should be implemented. In general, the committee felt that the legislation reflected too much of an emphasis on regulation of PPPs, and too little attention to the need to promote these kinds of projects. However, by 2024 the committee's recommendations had not been implemented.
- The government also has a long history of difficult relations with the private sector. A management contract to supply water in the Copperbelt region signed with French water company, SAUR Services, in 2001 was terminated early in 2005 because the government alleged that SAUR was not demonstrating VfM compared with publicly owned water utilities (the claim was strongly disputed by SAUR). Other concerns about transparency in the PPP process have been raised in news accounts, which have also highlighted instances of government administrations failing to honor agreements made by previous administrations, as occurred with President Michael Sata's government regarding agreements made by the previous government of President Rupiah Banda. Perhaps the most notable example was the abrupt cancellation of a $120 million railway concession funded in 2003 by three South African banks: Sanlam, Old Mutual, and Nedbank (EIU 2015).
- Domestically, the PPP program has inherited some of the criticism directed at the privatization program, which rapidly accelerated with the sale of the Zambia Consolidated Copper Mines between 1997 and 2000. Although celebrated by the World Bank and the IMF as the crowning achievement of Zambia's structural adjustment program, local critics found the copper mine sales and other divestitures to be one-sided transactions benefiting private investors, with the privatized mines poorly regulated, free to carry out illegal operations, consistently demonstrating disregard for workers and local businesses, and failing to protect social infrastructure (Fraser and Lungu 2009). Other critics claimed that the privatization program

facilitated the corrupt acquisition of government assets by investors linked to the ruling party (Craig 2000).

The government has taken several steps to strengthen the PPP unit's performance. Among other things the location of the unit has been shifted several times since 2009 in efforts to improve its management. Moving the PPP unit into the State House (under direct presidential control) in 2015 was described as a way of reducing the "bureaucratic" character of the unit. But critics worried that the move would reduce the independence of the unit as well. In May 2016, Cabinet approved an amendment to the PPP Act in order to establish the PPP Unit as a Statutory Body in line with the recommendation by the President. The Bill was supposed to have been presented to Parliament for consideration in 2017, but the effort was eventually abandoned. A 2018 PPP Amendment Act moved the PPP Unit to the Ministry of Finance and changed its name to the "PPP Department." But the 2018 act also eliminated some of the functions of the PPP Department and the PPP Council, raising questions about whether the government wanted the PPP process managed by technical experts or politicians.

Although there have been flaws in the government's legal-regulatory framework for PPPs and in the capacity of the PPP unit, these are probably not the main reasons why the government has been so unsuccessful with PPPs. As is the case in South Africa, the most important reasons in Zambia have little or nothing to do with PPP units or laws and procedures. Two more basic reasons stand out.

First, as a low-income country with one of the world's lowest per capita incomes, Zambia was never a likely candidate to do enough infrastructure PPPs to justify the creation of a PPP unit. The "success" of an SOE privatization program in the view of a development partner like the World Bank is not a reliable predictor of PPP program success. A PPP program requires service delivery projects that are stable, profitable, long-term commercial arrangements for which governments retain ownership responsibility over 20–30 years. In the 1990s, Zambia had many near-bankrupt SOEs to sell to the private sector at bargain prices, but has never had many commercial, sustainable PPP project opportunities.

A second factor militating against Zambia's PPP success is the fact that the government's poor record of fiscal management makes it an unattractive partner in PPP contracts, as is now the case with sub-national governments in South Africa. In November 2020, the government defaulted on interest payments for a $1 billion Eurobond issue. COVID-19 played a role in the default, but weaknesses in public financial management were also cited by rating agencies as principal causes of the problem. At the same time, the government's power utility, Zesco, began delaying payments to IPP bulk power suppliers. By the end of 2021, Zesco's debts had reached $3.5 billion due to a combination of liabilities to IPPs, long-running disputes with mining companies, and depreciation of the local currency (African Energy 2021). Even if the national government is willing and able to provide sovereign guarantees for PPP projects, the guarantee will likely not be acceptable to private investors for some time to come. The recent track record of Zesco's non-payment to IPPs also severely damages Zambia's reputation as a reliable public partner in PPP transactions.

6.6.3 Nigeria's Infrastructure Concession Regulatory Commission (ICRC)

PPP units exist in many different forms and carry out a variety of different functions. Presumably, the design of a PPP unit and decisions about its role and location in a governmental structure require careful consideration if such a unit is to have an optimal impact in terms of facilitating successful PPPs. To what extent is expert advice available to developing countries regarding these issues? What is the track record of development partners when it comes to advising on the creation of PPP units that are intended to have positive impacts on PPP project development? The World Bank's involvement in Nigeria's efforts to create a PPP unit provides one perspective on these issues.

In the 1970s and 1980s, Nigeria's oil revenues enabled the federal government to develop and build infrastructure, which was perceived as the sole responsibility of the public sector. Almost all infrastructure assets were owned, managed, operated, and maintained on a monopoly basis with public sector funding. But by the time that Olusegun Obasanjo was elected president in 1999 after 15 years of military rule, the country's infrastructure services were in disrepair because of economic mismanagement, poor maintenance, a fast-growing population, and stagnating oil revenues. Under Obasanjo, the federal government embarked on an ambitious commercialization and privatization program to reduce its liabilities and harness the investment potential and expertise of the private sector. This program was set out initially in a 1988 decree establishing the Technical Committee on Privatization and Commercialization and then through the Public Enterprises Act of 1999, which established the National Council on Privatization and the Bureau of Public Enterprises (BPE) to lead privatization efforts. The privatization and commercialization program registered multiple achievements. Between 1999 and 2006, 116 enterprises were privatized, including the sale of telecommunications companies and 24 port terminal concessions. In 2010, the government began unbundling the Power Holding Company of Nigeria into 18 companies responsible for power generation, transmission, and distribution in anticipation of an extensive privatization program that was later implemented in the sector, most of it managed by BPE.

The World Bank was a major development partner during this period, advising the government on power sector reforms and directly assisting with privatization of ports and telecoms. Initially, Bank support took the form of the $115 million Privatization Support Project in 2002, which provided funding to BPE to hire consultants and transaction advisors for many of the privatization transactions. However, the Bank's Independent Evaluation Group (IEG) later found that World Bank staff had been frustrated by their limited ability to influence outcomes of the privatization sales (IEG 2008). The privatization of NITEL, the state-owned fixed-line telephone company, was disappointing to Bank staff after their advice regarding bidder qualifications was ignored. In the power sector, BPE invited expressions of interest (EOIs) for the privatization of power distribution companies, and more than 200 responses were received. However, the process remained stalled for an extended period because the EOIs were solicited without adequate preparation, again contrary to Bank advice.

Later IEG reviews concluded that the World Bank and IFC had missed opportunities to proactively collaborate on the tailoring of strategies for infrastructure privatization and public–private partnerships. Infrastructure PPPs were very slow to begin development despite the government's support for other forms of privatization (IEG 2008). IEG's 2005 review of the Bank's Nigeria program found that its work on privatization and private sector development (PSD) was "unsatisfactory," despite the achievement of some commercial enterprise sales. The 2008 IEG review found that "The Bank program does not add up to a coherent strategy for PSD. Both the Bank's analytic work and lending for PSD have been opportunistic" (71).

In 2011, the World Bank tried to strengthen and focus its support for Nigeria's infrastructure PPPs by approving the Public–Private Partnership Program, a six-year, two-phase program worth $315 million. The program's two main components included PPP capacity building for key ministries, departments, and agencies (collectively referred to as "MDAs") and substantial support to the Infrastructure Concession Regulatory Commission (ICRC), which acted as the government's executing agency for the program, at the request of the Bank. The overall development objective of the program was to increase private investment in core Nigerian infrastructure sectors. Achievement of this objective would be measured by (i) a minimum of three PPP projects taken to financial close; and (ii) a minimum $1 billion increase in private investment realized in the PPP market during the life of the program (out of the total $5.13 billion identified in MDA PPP pipelines at the time of program approval by the World Bank).

Phase 1 of the program, worth $115 million, was designed to focus on preparation of the upstream foundations for PPP investment and consisted only of provision of technical assistance, goods, and services. Phase 2, worth

$200 million, was expected to focus on establishing a financing mechanism to address the lack of local finance for PPP transactions through the provision of a credit line. The second phase would be triggered by successful completion of capacity building and project preparation that would take up most of the first phase. Ultimately, however, Phase 2 was never approved and the government eventually requested cancellation of all but $17.6 million of the $315 million loan. No completed PPPs were credited to the program after the original six years of implementation plus a six-month extension. By selecting the ICRC as its principal government counterpart for the Public–Private Partnership Program, the World Bank effectively set ICRC on a path to become the Nigerian government's "PPP unit." But ICRC was a somewhat surprising—and risky—choice that strongly contributed to the program's failures, for several reasons.

First, ICRC was a new entity and had no experience with development projects. The commission only became officially operational at the end of 2008. By the time the World Bank program was being designed in 2009, ICRC had only a handful of employees. BPE was a more logical choice to lead a program like this at the time. It had already been operating for a decade, had completed dozens of privatization projects and several PPP concessions, including the 24 successful port terminal transactions mentioned above. But after ten years of privatization work, BPE had attracted criticism from inside and outside the government. The Bank had been frustrated when its advice on power sector and telecommunications privatizations was ignored. BPE also operated in an intensively competitive government environment, with the large and complex network of federal MDAs constantly jockeying for power and access to resources. The Bank's appraisal document for the Public–Private Partnership Program noted that many of BPE's PPP projects had been politically and commercially controversial, with some of the high-profile deals failing to reach closure. The Bank concluded that the challenge of coordinating MDAs and their private sector counterparts in privatization projects had proved difficult for BPE: "The task required close cooperation with the line ministries but frequently triggered conflicts with ministries that resisted the BPE role. This, in turn, created problems in terms of outreach to the private sector" (World Bank 2011c, 18). Bypassing BPE, the World Bank team gambled that ICRC could engage skilled technical staff and build MDA relationships quickly enough to lead the implementation of the Bank's new $315 million PPP program.

A second reason why ICRC was a risky choice as the government's executing agency for the new World Bank program was that the Infrastructure Concession Regulatory Commission Act, which created the ICRC, was vague and confusing. But it was clear in stating that the purpose of ICRC was limited to the regulation of contract compliance *after* concession contracts were signed. No role in project preparation was indicated in the legislation. Only two specific ICRC responsibilities were defined in the act: (1) "... take custody of every concession agreement ..." and monitor compliance with the contract; and (2) "... ensure efficient execution ..." of these agreements.

The act did go on to say that ICRC had the authority to "... make, alter and revoke rules and regulations for carrying on the functions of the Commission." It might also be directed by the President to carry out special functions. This language gave comfort to the World Bank designers of the Public–Private Partnership Program that ICRC could draft necessary legislation and regulations to craft a legitimate role for itself in regulating the development of PPP projects. Unfortunately for the World Bank program, ICRC could not act quickly enough to effect needed legal or regulatory changes to achieve legitimacy among the MDAs who were expected to turn leadership of their PPP development activities over to the ICRC. In fact, no new PPP legislation was approved during the lifespan of the program. The MDAs responsible for originating the pipelines of PPP projects, on the basis of which the Bank program was approved, immediately resisted ICRC's commanding role in the program, many seeing that role as an illegitimate assumption of power, contrary to the legislation establishing ICRC.

Once the World Bank board approved the new PPP program, the PPP transactions that had been selected for the project pipeline were not moved forward by the line ministries, nor were they replaced by other transactions later. As noted above, no completed PPPs were attributed to the Bank program. On June 30, 2018, the program closed without a single completed PPP. The Bank's Implementation Completion Report (ICR), issued in March 2019, identified the key problems:

> The key underlying factors that affected efficiency in the operation are lack of ownership by the MDAs, lack of acceptance of the ICRC in a coordinating/facilitating/regulating role by the MDAs and other stakeholders leading to critical problems in coordination, unrealistic time lines in the design of the operation, changes due to restructuring, changes in the credit amount due to credit cancellation, and lack of PPP and/or infrastructure expertise within the task team during implementation. (World Bank 2019b, 23–24)

The Bank's failed program did, however, have one enduring legacy—the entrenchment of the ICRC as Nigeria's de facto "PPP unit." When the Ministry of Finance eventually shifted execution of the World Bank program from ICRC to the ministry's Technical Services Department, the ministry began considering what to do about ICRC. By 2016, ICRC was already claiming to be the government's official PPP unit, despite unresolved issues about its legitimate role and authority (Nwangwu 2016). The situation has never been resolved and ICRC has successfully filled the resulting legal and regulatory vacuum with its own proactive efforts to establish a powerful role for itself. Nigeria's official response to the World Bank's 2020 global survey of PPP legal and regulatory frameworks lists the ICRC's now extensive list of responsibilities:

> … responsible for formulation of PPP policies, regulating PPPs and is a gatekeeping/approving authority for PPP procurements. It also issues guidelines on PPP policies, processes and procedures (including those for concessions), and acts as a national center of expertise in PPP (including the PPP Resource Centre with the PPP Toolkit), promotion and procurement […] It provides technical support in implementing PPPs and also oversees PPP implementation […] It works closely with MDAs to identify potential PPP projects, and acts as the interface with the private sector to promote communication on national policies and programmes. (World Bank 2020)

So, the conflict of interest resulting from ICRC's roles as both facilitator and regulator has never been resolved. Soon after ICRC's World Bank support ended, ICRC exacerbated that conflict of interest by requiring MDAs to pay fees for ICRC's ex ante PPP-related evaluations and ex-post monitoring work. This was apparently a way to finance ICRC operations. It is not unheard of for PPP units to charge other units of government for their services, especially in OECD countries. But where such a model is used, PPP units typically try to manage the conflicts between revenue generation and the need to ensure quality control of projects: "The impact on the perception of the credibility of the PPP Unit with the rest of government and with the market must be managed together with the risk of creating incentives not to use PPP Unit support (because it has to be paid for)" (EPEC 2014, 10).

In ICRC's case, its efforts to manage these perceptions seem not to have been completely effective. Evaluators of a DFID-funded infrastructure support program in Nigeria reported that by 2015, ICRC was circulating a "charge sheet" indicating that MDAs were expected to pay N12.5 million ($62,500 at the time) for ICRC approval of PPP Business Case, and 1–10 percent of total PPP project costs to be paid annually over the lifetime of project implementation for ICRC monitoring of contract compliance (NIAF 2015). Some of the MDAs involved in the DFID program attributed their inability to move forward with infrastructure PPPs to the size and nature of ICRC fee requirements.

6.7 CONCLUSIONS

The creation of PPP units in developing countries, along with the development of supporting legal and regulatory frameworks, represents a different approach to PPP advocacy from that championed by DFID in the 2000s with its emphasis on transaction-oriented PPFs like PIDG and IFC PPP Advisory. PPFs race to find any kind of viable PPP to complete on behalf of client governments, taking over the development process as much as possible from counterpart officials to increase the chances of realizing sustainable projects in a timely fashion. This is done in the expectation that isolated, one-off project successes will generate demonstration effects capable of inspiring replication and eventual scale-up.

The PPP unit approach reflects some of the lessons learned in the 2000s from the failures of policy-based structural adjustment programs, which recognized the need to consider a much wider range of seemingly "extraneous" project success factors than just the mechanics of a transaction. In effect, the PPP unit approach represents an effort to move the PPF function inside government, under the control of government officials, so they can take ownership of, and better address, this wider range of success factors as part of project development and at the same time build their own knowledge and capacity to continue doing projects.

Many of the same donors contributed to both approaches, as in the case of donors like DFID, SECO, Sida, and others who simultaneously supported both PIDG and PPIAF. These donors assumed that the two approaches were complementary, encouraged by assurances from the programs themselves that they were cooperating as "affiliates." But except for their shared advocacy of PPPs, the programs could hardly have been more different. Head-to-head encounters in the field were marked by competition and conflict as PPIAF's efforts to set up PPP units and establish government ownership of project development ran directly counter to PIDG's efforts to assume control of the project development process and circumvent government rules that would slow down or complicate their entrepreneurial approach.

But creating PPP units has been no more successful in scaling up the use of PPPs than the transaction-only approach of PPFs like PIDG. As government agencies staffed mostly with civil servants, PPP units rarely have enough technical expertise or decision-making leverage to drive forward PPP programs. The units are subject to the same performance limitations that routinely affect all mid-level government agencies in these countries—such limitations are, of course, a basic reason why PPPs are considered necessary in the first place. Most of these units have been unable to adapt so-called best practice project evaluation techniques to their skill sets or project situations, and it is now no longer even clear what "best practice" means after the U.K.'s disappointing experience using PSCs as a key element of VfM analysis. Finally, in the poorest developing countries, there are too few commercial or near-commercial project opportunities for PPP units to justify large budgets or highly trained staff. PPP units in countries like Zambia, simply have nothing to do.

However, the emphasis on PPP units has benefitted PPP advocacy in another important way. The investment in a PPP unit and a PPP legal-regulatory framework signals a significant government commitment to pursue PPPs. And once such an investment is made, responsible officials are reluctant to reconsider the value or practicality of PPPs compared with traditional forms of public investment. If PPPs are not forthcoming, it is seen as a problem with the PPP unit or legal framework. As in the case of South Africa, the widespread failure to roll out PPPs must be remedied by even greater investments in PPP units and frameworks. More importantly, other, more cost-effective ways of extending or improving infrastructure services do not get the full attention they deserve. Meanwhile, the proliferation of PPP units means a steadily growing coalition of PPP true believers and core supporters whose livelihoods depend on the use of PPPs to solve infrastructure problems in developing countries.

7. PPPs on a global stage: regional projects

7.1 INTRODUCTION

Beginning in the mid-2000s, public–private partnership (PPP) advocacy entered a new phase as global development issues began to emerge, which seemed well beyond the capacity of development partners to address with direct forms of official development assistance (ODA). The Millennium Development Goals (MDGs), approved in September 2000, took what one critic has called a non-prioritized, "do everything" approach (Easterly 2009), and as a result created a massive global development financing challenge. A 2002 World Bank study found that a doubling of aid flows would be required for the simultaneous achievement of multiple MDGs. To fully meet this kind of challenge a substantial increase in investment would be needed, and the development community began to take a closer look at the possibility of accessing private finance.

These efforts paralleled, but were largely separate from, PPP work already underway by World Bank trust funds, the International Finance Corporation (IFC), and the Private Infrastructure Development Group (PIDG). And to some extent this new level of international attention represented a recognition that these existing PPP programs were not producing large enough results fast enough. Existing project development facilities (PDFs) were demonstrating that small, isolated, heavily subsidized PPPs could be done successfully, mostly in middle-income countries if enough money and effort was applied. But these projects were selected opportunistically, largely without reference to sector needs or reform priorities. The slowly growing population of national PPP units, spawned by multi-donor programs like the Public–Private Infrastructure Advisory Facility (PPIAF), still generally lacked capacity and, if anything, were slowing down project development with complicated, unclear, and often under-developed regulations and procedures.

By 2004, there was no evidence of PPPs having appreciable positive impacts on infrastructure services in poor countries. PPP projects were not being widely replicated; PPP markets were not expanding. The level of private investment in the infrastructure of developing countries was barely above the

2002 level, the lowest point in a decade. Donors and multilateral development banks (MDBs) were becoming desperate to find ways to re-ignite the PPP trend that seemed to show so much promise in the mid-1990s, before the Asian financial crisis brought an abrupt end to PPP enthusiasm after 1997.

In 2005, another dimension of these emerging development challenges came into focus for the global development community, the possibility of addressing issues like MDG achievement and climate change reduction with regional infrastructure projects rather than just national ones. This was especially important in Africa, with its many small, poor, landlocked countries, where regional infrastructure solutions often appeared to be, theoretically at least, more cost-effective than national ones. Regional integration issues of all kinds were already in discussion across the African continent, but a series of developments beginning in 2005 brought these issues to the attention of the international community. Infrastructure PPPs were eventually seen as one of the best ways to respond to these new challenges and this fueled a new wave of PPP advocacy, this time at the regional and international levels, providing PPPs with a kind of global endorsement that they had not enjoyed to that point. But if individual governments were encountering problems completing sustainable infrastructure PPPs under normal circumstances, regional or multi-country PPPs took project development and financing challenges to much higher levels of difficulty. As this chapter explains, even the involvement of the international development community helped very little in improving the flow of PPP transactions.

7.2 THE G8 GLENEAGLES SUMMIT

Two major events in 2005 sharpened the development community's focus on the need to take a regional approach to infrastructure investment especially in Africa, the likelihood that private finance would be needed for regional project investment, and the role that PPPs would be required to play in arranging and managing much of that investment if regional projects were going to be successful:

- First, in July 2005 the G8's annual summit at Gleneagles, Scotland, covered issues such as climate change and terrorism. But much of the discussion focused on lagging economic development in Africa: slow progress toward achievement of the MDGs, the need for sovereign debt relief to allow more public investment in infrastructure, and ways of removing impediments to investment by the private sector in African countries.
- Second, in September 2005, the United Nations World Summit in New York was convened to assess the progress made in achieving the MDGs, five years after the goals were agreed on. The summit confirmed the impor-

tance of the goals but noted a dramatic lack of progress attributable in large part to a lack of finance.

Many of the priorities discussed at the Gleneagles Summit had first emerged during the 2001 G8 meeting at which African leaders presented new plans for the continent's development. At the 2002 Kananaskis Summit in Canada, African leaders presented the New Partnership for Africa's Development (NEPAD), which had been established in 2001 by the Organisation of African Unity (OAU). NEPAD prepared and published a pioneering list of priority regional infrastructure projects in Africa, known as the "Short Term Action Plan" (STAP). STAP was endorsed by Africa's Regional Economic Communities (RECs), as well as the African Union and the African Development Bank (AfDB). The G8 responded positively to NEPAD in its G8 Africa Action Plan. African issues remained at the center of G8 discussions at the summits in 2003 and 2004.

By the time of the 2005 G8 summit in Gleneagles, the widely agreed on general development direction to take in Africa was defined in the MDGs, NEPAD's STAP, and the G8 Africa Action Plan. And this direction was endorsed by other industrialized country governments, African governments, African regional organizations, international multilateral organizations, as well as many civil society organizations. But the key unanswered question was what needed to be done to ensure the availability of the resources required to finance the pursuit of objectives like the MDGs and STAP.

As a way to structure the discussion at the G8's Gleneagles Summit, two substantial reports were released in 2005. The first one was *Investing in Development: A Practical Plan to Achieve the Millennium Development Goals*, prepared by a team led by Jeffrey Sachs (United Nations Millennium Project 2005). The second was *Our Common Interests*, prepared by a team appointed by British Prime Minister Tony Blair (Commission for Africa 2005). Both reports advocated major new efforts by the international community to assist with African development, but neither report recommended a dramatic expansion in the use of PPPs.

The report by the United Nations Millennium Project emphasized the need for large increases in official development assistance (ODA) but noted the positive role that the private sector could play in supporting the MDGs: "In some situations, it can also help support service delivery through public-private partnerships" (United Nations Millennium Project 2005, 18). This report also stressed the need for a regional approach to MDG achievement: "The Millennium Development Goals cannot be achieved solely through country-level investments, debt relief, and trade reform. National strategies need to link with one another and with international coordination mechanisms to provide regional and global public goods" (47).

The Commission for Africa report emphasized the central importance of infrastructure in development and highlighted the role that the private sector could play in financing key infrastructure assets. Acknowledging the recent poor performance of PPPs in developing countries, the report noted that it was a "policy mistake" to assume that the private sector would finance most of this investment (Commission for Africa 2005, 233). But the private sector's role was nevertheless important and needed to be promoted using a "pragmatic approach" that built on existing programs like PPIAF, PIDG, and IFC PPP Advisory (235). The need for regional infrastructure projects was also emphasized, and the NEPAD STAP was repeatedly cited as an authoritative listing of regional infrastructure project priorities in Africa.

The G8 members at Gleneagles pledged support for increased investment in Africa, but the magnitude of the investment needed in infrastructure was still unclear, as evidenced in the various estimates cited in the two preparatory reports mentioned above. Consequently, the G8 requested separate research studies by the World Bank and African Development Bank (AfDB) to more precisely estimate infrastructure investment needs. The World Bank focused on infrastructure at the country level, agreeing to start work on what became the *Africa Infrastructure Country Diagnostic* (AICD), issued in 2010. AfDB, in partnership with the African Union and NEPAD, agreed to focus on regional infrastructure investment needs. This led to the *Programme for Infrastructure Development in Africa* (PIDA), approved by the African heads of state in early 2012. PIDA was an assessment of infrastructure investment needs with regional or cross-border implications, meant to parallel the AICD study of individual country investment needs prepared by the World Bank.

7.3 REGIONAL INFRASTRUCTURE ISSUES IN AFRICA

By 2005, regional integration had already long been a priority in Africa. In 1991, the adoption of the Abuja Treaty established a timetable for the creation of a pan-African economic community by 2025, which was expected to reduce the high internal and external barriers to trade, transport, and communication plaguing the continent. A continuing focus on the importance of regional integration spawned a complex network of regional and sub-regional organizations designed to work across borders on essential issues. These organizations included power pools, transport corridor authorities, river basin authorities, as well as Regional Economic Communities (RECs) recognized by the Commission for Africa as the "building blocks" of the African Union. RECs are regional groupings of African states, originally proposed by the Abuja Treaty as the basis for the eventual continental integration mentioned above. But RECS proliferated rapidly, becoming involved in efforts to coordinate the interests of AU member states in areas such as peace and security, trade, governance, and infrastructure. By 2005, African RECs and sub-regional organizations constituted a vast, overlapping population of multi-country entities already much more numerous than the eight regional communities officially approved by the AU (Figure 7.1). By the early 2000s, many of these entities had developed their own lists of priority infrastructure projects and strategies for implementing them.

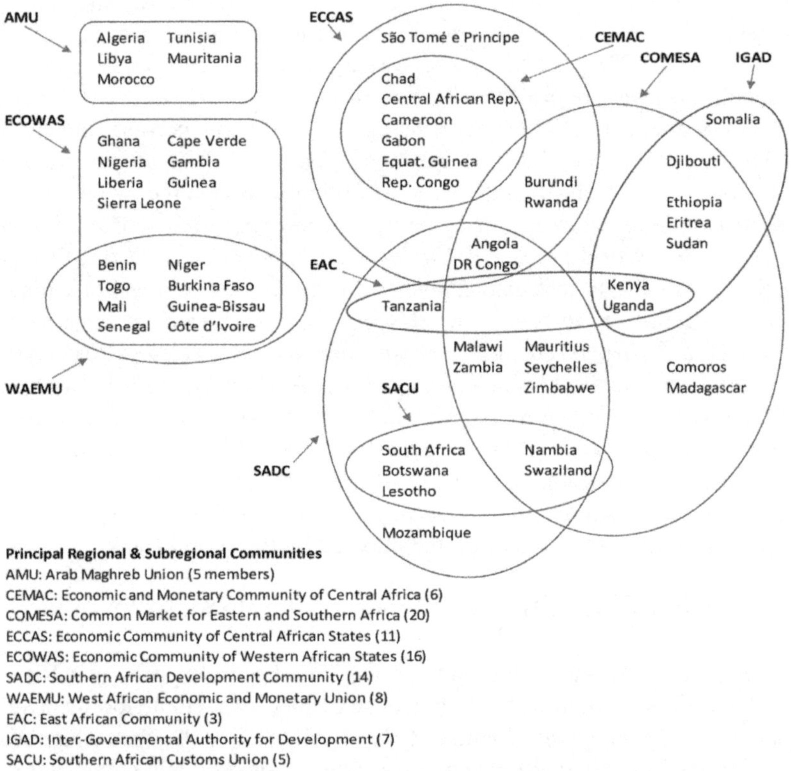

Source: Adapted from Commission for Africa (2005).

Figure 7.1 *African regional and sub-regional economic communities, 2005*

In order to exercise some control and coordination over the activities of these entities, especially in areas like regional infrastructure planning, continent-wide bodies like the African Development Bank (AfDB) the African Union (AU), and the United Nations Economic Commission for Africa (UNECA) began playing more prominent roles in regional development planning efforts and representing regional African interests in meetings with the G8 and United Nations. NEPAD was the continent-wide body that quickly became the authoritative leader of African regional infrastructure planning efforts by the time of the Gleneagles Summit, with NEPAD's STAP taking center stage in the G8 discussions. The STAP was an effort to consolidate and prioritize regional infrastructure projects and related activities, to achieve a workable list that everyone, theoretically at least, could agree on.

In 2002, the OAU was replaced by a successor organization, the AU, led by the African Union Commission (AUC). The AU began immediately to consolidate its position as the apex continent-wide regional coordinating body.[1] The G8's request at Gleneagles for a study of regional infrastructure needs represented an opportunity for the AU, with AfDB's help, to update and extend STAP, and take ownership of the result, which became PIDA.

The effort to plan and implement regional infrastructure projects in Africa sometimes takes on the appearance of a struggle for influence or access to resources. In some cases, RECs or other regional bodies have tried to assume leadership roles in the prioritization and implementation of regional projects, or in interactions with international development finance institutions (DFIs). But African national governments jealously protect their sovereignty and are reluctant to allow interference in national strategic decision-making by outsiders. In many cases, this reluctance arises from security concerns—the unwillingness to share ownership and control of strategic assets with neighboring countries. In other cases, national officials are willing to proceed with cross-border projects but are unwilling to cede project planning or management responsibilities to regional planning bodies that are thought to lack expertise in project finance much less the ability to coordinate and monitor project progress. This has been especially true of the many African national governments that have created their own specialized project preparation and oversight agencies, like PPP units and project development funds.

The disputes about control over projects sometimes obscure what continues to be a fundamental problem, the profound need for a regional approach to certain kinds of infrastructure investment because of the small size and land-locked location of so many African economies. Nothing better illustrated

---

[1] In 2010, the AUC also began a process of integrating NEPAD into the African Union structure, seen by the AUC as the rightful home for a regional African entity like NEPAD. The NEPAD Secretariat was replaced by "The NEPAD Planning and Coordinating Agency" (NPCA), and most of NPCA was moved to the AU headquarters in Addis. In 2018, NPCA was given a broader role as the lead AU technical advisory facility for member states and renamed "The African Union Development Agency—NEPAD" (AUDA–NEPAD).

this than challenges in the power sector, particularly Africa's lack of electricity generating capacity. At the time of the Gleneagles Summit, the need for more electricity generation was already massive and growing rapidly in sub-Saharan Africa (SSA). The thermal and especially hydro resources necessary to produce needed power were available, but generally not under development. Two years before the PIDA study was published, the AICD study had already made a compelling case for regional infrastructure projects as an outcome of its review of the infrastructure needs of individual African countries. The AICD study pointed out that SSA accounted for 10 percent of the world's economically feasible hydropower potential, but only about 7 percent of SSA's potential was being exploited.

Africa had been unable to make full use of this potential largely because most of the exploitable hydro resources were located in countries like the Democratic Republic of Congo (DRC), Ethiopia, and Guinea, which could not justify the exploitation of such resources based on their own national needs and were far removed from industrial centers with the demand for that kind of supply. A country like Ethiopia was exploiting these resources for its own needs. Accordingly, the projects did not involve transmission lines or off-take agreements necessary for them to serve regional purposes.

Because such projects were done for national purposes, they were relatively small and this created other problems for infrastructure investment. By 2010, the average size of African independent power producer (IPP) projects in a sample of 38 mostly thermal projects was 91 MW (Eberhard and Gratwick 2010). It is not impossible to find international companies willing to take on such projects, but the size makes these projects relatively unattractive compared with opportunities in other developing country regions. Too much must be spent on project preparation compared with the ultimate financial returns and the risks that must be managed.

The most cost-effective exploitation of regional hydropower resources would require the countries with power development potential to become exporters of power and others to become importers. AICD estimated that as many as 16 SSA countries would be economically better off if they imported more than 50 percent of their power needs. But this meant that many African countries would have to reconcile themselves to a situation in which they were not responsible for their own energy security, a situation with which most of these governments were uncomfortable.

Any kind of large infrastructure project involving more than one country owner is exceptionally difficult to do, anywhere in the world. And such projects involving private sector participation involve a further level of complexity. These projects raise difficult questions about who should develop such projects, who borrows to finance them (and under what conditions), who benefits from the projects, who administers them, etc. All of these problems can be solved, but large, regional PPP projects are not common anywhere. These were the kinds of issues that the PIDA study was expected to address.

7.4 FROM NEPAD'S STAP TO THE AU'S PIDA

NEPAD's STAP, originally issued in 2002, identified 40 regional investment projects, about half of which were classified as regional transport projects. A key objective of STAP was to attract private investors to these projects. But progress on the STAP projects was consistently disappointing over the years. A considerable number of STAP projects were abandoned as unsuccessful or simply stopped making progress. The final independent STAP evaluation in 2010 confirmed that regional entities had accumulated almost no information on many of the projects and could not even provide an official list of STAP projects because of all the changes to the list since 2002 (CRISIL 2010). In the view of many potential private investors and development partners, STAP developed a reputation as being primarily a wish list of projects proposed by RECs for political reasons.

PIDA began life after the Gleneagles G8 Summit as the "Medium to Long-Term Strategic Framework" (MLTSF)—essentially an updating and extension of the "Short-term Action Plan." To help ensure that the study was an objective economic and financial assessment, MLTSF was supported with substantial amounts of funding provided by donors and MDBs—over $11 million according to the AfDB.[2] DFID also established and funded a peer review committee of outside experts to provide quality control of the study findings. But for MLTSF to earn official African endorsement from the AU, the apex regional institution, it needed to maintain support from the stakeholder organizations that made up the system of regional government organizations in Africa illustrated in Figure 7.1. Most of these stakeholder organizations had their own ideas about which investment projects to prioritize. By 2007, some of these stakeholders, particularly the RECs, felt that their priority projects were not being adequately recognized by the MLTSF consultants. The consulting team was abruptly replaced, and the work started again. This time the name of the expected end-product was changed to the *Programme for Infrastructure Development in Africa* (PIDA).[3]

---

2 See https://www.afdb.org/en/topics-and-sectors/initiatives-partnerships/programme-for-infrastructure-development-in-africa-pida.

3 Interview with Dr. Rosalind H. Thomas. In 2007, Dr. Thomas was AfDB's Director for NEPAD and Regional Integration (ONRI) and responsible for overseeing the MLTSF.

The key output of PIDA work was the Priority Action Plan (PAP), expected to be justified by an extensive body of research and economic forecasting much like the many reports and studies issued in support of the World Bank's AICD study. PAP was basically a list of infrastructure projects endorsed by the AU and eligible for whatever support was available from African regional institutions or the international development community. The ideal PIDA project involved infrastructure investment that would pay for itself over time from end-user revenues, with high-quality assets making possible service delivery levels at least as advanced as the AICD targets. This meant using private investment and avoiding government borrowing whenever possible, and not accepting second-best infrastructure service solutions unless necessary. The original terms of reference for the PIDA study emphasized the importance of the private sector for the achievement of PIDA objectives: "... it should be noted that an explicit aim of PIDA is the mobilization of private sector participation in infrastructure development" (AU et al. 2009, 6).

However, as with STAP, the prioritized PIDA projects were very slow to roll out. The PAP included 51 cross-border programs, consisting of 400 individual regional infrastructure projects. Most of the projects were in the transport sector, followed by the information and communication technology (ICT), and energy sectors. Water projects comprised only 3 percent of the total. By 2019, almost half of the ICT projects had been completed, driven almost exclusively by private, commercial interests. But only 6 percent of the projects in the energy sector were operational, 19 percent of the projects in transport, and 11 percent of projects in water.

Although much better resourced than STAP, PIDA exhibited many of the same shortcomings that plagued the earlier planning process. One problem with STAP had been that it included too many projects seemingly chosen for political reasons. This was the "wish list" criticism mentioned above, with many projects appearing to have no particular social or economic justification for development, at least nothing disclosed publically. Many of the STAP projects were being promoted by RECs with little attention to whether financiers (public or private) considered them to be viable.

PIDA seems not to have done a much better job in establishing the credibility of its project selection process with investors, development partners, and national governments. The PIDA project list, prepared with millions of dollars of donor funding, was supposed to have resulted from a careful economic cost–benefit prioritization of potential projects. But the quality of that background analysis was difficult to judge. The details of PIDA's long-term economic forecasts and its sectoral studies—thousands of pages of analysis prepared by French consulting firm SOFRECO—have never been made fully available for review by outsiders, although some of these reports, a fraction of the original analysis, were eventually posted on the PIDA website. Based on a "study synthesis" and a preliminary list of projects, the African Heads of State approved the PIDA program in January 2012 (AUC et al. 2012).

To the extent that projects identified in the PIDA Priority Action Plan were practical and realistic, they were mostly projects already in some stage of development by national governments and their development partners. For most of these projects, recommendations regarding PPP options were already too late, because most had been developed as public projects. In cases where public money for investment eventually was found to be unavailable, and private options needed to be considered retroactively, most of the prior preparation did not meet private sector requirements and needed to be repeated at considerable expense. Despite prioritizing private investment in regional projects, NEPAD and AUC officials responsible for the PIDA program have never made public any information on the extent to which private investment has played a role in PIDA projects.

A fundamental STAP problem, which PIDA could do little to solve, was that regional or cross-border projects depend heavily on the intentions and capabilities of the national governments involved. For large projects, private partners insist on dealing with sovereign governments, not supranational entities. Regional organizations like RECs cannot borrow on their own account to finance infrastructure, and do not own or control projects of this kind. And because every large infrastructure project in Africa involves support from DFIs, the funding restrictions applied by these institutions to "regional projects" are also extremely important. Like the private sector, these institutions tend to favor relationships with sovereign governments, and they typically define regional projects in ways that emphasize leading roles for the individual sovereign governments involved. In the case of PIDA, as with STAP, national governments continued to display a marked lack of enthusiasm for regional projects.

7.5 QUESTIONS ABOUT THE VIABILITY OF REGIONAL PPP PROJECTS

7.5.1 The Fragility of Megaprojects

PIDA, like STAP, faced questions about the fundamental viability of large, regional PPP projects. Arguments in favor of such projects usually point to the advantages of economies of scale and scope. This "bigger is better" argument is also consistent with some popular theories of economic development, which argue that big development challenges like poverty alleviation, energy scarcity, and urbanization can only be solved by "big push" solutions involving large projects and large amounts of aid (Sachs 2006). However, these "transformational" projects frequently exhibit the size and complexity that make them vulnerable to what Bent Flyvbjerg has referred to as the "iron law of megaprojects" (Flyvbjerg 2014). According to Flyvbjerg, 90 percent of projects costing over one billion dollars end up "over budget, over time, over and over again." This is a problem for all large projects, not just PPPs, but Flyvbjerg points out that "Private capital is no panacea for the ills in megaproject management, to be sure; in some cases, private capital may even make things worse ..." (20). Part of the reason for this is that the complexities of large PPPs—with multiple players, complicated and lengthy contract negotiations, high transaction costs, forecasting uncertainties, etc.—lead to what Flyvbjerg and some of his colleagues have referred to as a low "investment fragility threshold," a dangerous vulnerability of the projects to become unsustainable due to the impact of random events (Ansar et al. 2017).

The private sector has long been aware of the risks associated with regional projects simply due to their size. In 2009, international rating agency Fitch Ratings summed up these reasons in a special report, "Large Projects, Giant Risks?" (Fitch Ratings 2009). Some of the lessons discussed in the paper included the following:

- Large infrastructure projects require popular support and political clarity (especially regarding comprehensive costs) for approval, funding, and implementation to be carried out in an uninterrupted, non-controversial fashion.
- Risk allocation and governance are critical factors for the success of infrastructure projects, but large regional projects typically entail an even larger and more complex set of risks generated by public and private stakeholders with overlapping and conflicting interests.
- Typically, there is very little cross-border harmonization of the legal-regulatory enabling frameworks needed for regional projects to reach financial close. And many African countries have unclear or under-developed policies, plans, procedures, and regulations for preparing, structuring, and overseeing PPI projects.
- The conceptualization and planning of large projects are particularly lengthy and complex exercises. This complexity entails uncertainty, which in turn requires contractual and financial flexibility—things that are not often found in tightly engineered PPP contracts.
- Large projects usually involve extraordinary construction constraints that must be carefully managed in terms of technical, contractual, and managerial arrangements.
- Cross-border projects are highly sensitive to geopolitics, a type of risk that is particularly difficult to manage.

- Reasonably accurate demand forecasting for infrastructure projects is always difficult, but it is especially difficult—and quite hazardous—for large regional projects.

With large, transformational projects, economies-of-scale are also cited as a factor that should help increase the value for money of spending on project preparation, with each dollar spent on preparation generating more value because the regional projects are so much larger than conventional projects. But even assuming some economies of scale, the costs of preparing large transformational PPP projects are staggering. The average total cost of the 14 regional power sector projects in the first phase of the PIDA Priority Action Plan was $2.9 billion (AUC et al. 2012). Standard rules of thumb suggest that preparing each project of that size could require as much as $430 million in total development costs, with roughly one-third of that being the responsibility of the respective governments and development partners.

An additional problem for PIDA was a reputational one. It invited comparison with its sister study, the AICD report, which was prepared by the World Bank (discussed in Chapter 3). Both studies were commissioned at the 2005 G8 Summit. But AICD was much faster to secure funding and roll out, with key elements of its flagship report circulated to stakeholders in 2008, almost four years before only a short summary of the PIDA study was first available. AICD had an innovative structure and style and supported its conclusions with dozens of background publications released by the World Bank along with the complete study database. As noted above, PIDA's background data has never been fully released.

Perhaps more importantly, not all of the AICD and PIDA findings could be easily reconciled. AICD was consistent with PIDA in terms of findings regarding the importance of infrastructure, the massive amount of investment that was required in SSA, the considerable degree to which Africa governments were already investing in their infrastructure networks, and the logic behind claims that large projects with regional impacts could theoretically capture economies of scale and reduce end-user prices in a region with so many small, land-locked countries.

But some of AICD well-argued findings represented implicit challenges to PIDA and its supporters: that policy and administrative inefficiencies were costing the continent $17 billion annually, government-determined sector investment priorities were misallocating huge amounts of resources, and rehabilitation and maintenance of existing infrastructure should be prioritized over building new assets. Other AICD findings that were clearly inconsistent with the PIDA approach included claims that PPPs might have limited value for African infrastructure, a G20 stimulus package might be a better way to finance new infrastructure in SSA than to expect too much from the private sector, and second-best infrastructure solutions might ultimately be needed in the interests of benefiting the largest numbers of Africans in the least amount of time.

7.5.2 The Regional PPP Track Record

The global track record of large cross-border infrastructure projects involving private participation reflects the kinds of challenges described above. Such projects have not played the kind of regional or transformational role hoped for by AICD, PIDA, and the G20. Such projects have been far less successful than smaller and simpler PPP projects, particularly in low-income countries, where cross-border projects have been almost non-existent. As of 2021, the World Bank's private participation in infrastructure (PPI) database had recorded only 14 cross-border infrastructure PPP projects in developing countries since 1996 (Tables 7.1a–7.1d). Five of these projects were gas pipelines and three were power generation projects (IPP projects).

Table 7.1a Cross-border PPPs: sub-Saharan Africa, 1995–2021

Year	Countries	Income group	Project name
1995	Burkina Faso	LIC	Abidjan–Ouagadougou Railway
	Cote d'Ivoire	LMIC	
1997	Mozambique	LIC	N4 Toll Road: Mozambique–South Africa
	South Africa	UMIC	
2003	Mali	LIC	Dakar–Bamako Railway
	Senegal	LMIC	
2003	Mozambique	LIC	Mozambique–South Africa Gas Pipeline
	South Africa	UMIC	
2005	Nigeria	LMIC	West African Gas Pipeline Company Ltd.
	Togo	LIC	
	Benin	LIC	
	Ghana	LMIC	
2006	Kenya	LMIC	Kenya–Uganda Railways
	Uganda	LIC	
2011	South Africa	UMIC	Beitbridge Border Post
	Zimbabwe	LIC	

Notes: LIC = low-income country; LMIC = lower middle-income country; UMIC = upper middle-income country.
Source: World Bank (2022).

Table 7.1b *Cross-border PPPs: East Asia and the Pacific, 1995–2021*

Year	Countries	Income group	Project name
1995	Myanmar	LMIC	Yardana Gas Pipeline
	Thailand	UMIC	
1996	Lao PDR	LMIC	Houay Ho Hydro Power Project
	Thailand	UMIC	
1996	Lao PDR	LMIC	Theun Hinboun Hydro Power Plant I
	Thailand	UMIC	
1997	Myanmar	LMIC	Yetagun Gas Pipeline
	Thailand	UMIC	

Notes: LMIC = lower middle-income country; UMIC = upper middle-income country.
Source: World Bank (2022).

Table 7.1c *Cross-border PPPs: Europe and Central Asia, 1995–2021*

Year	Countries	Income group	Project name
2001	Russian Fed.	UMIC	Blue Stream Gas Pipeline
	Turkey	UMIC	
2011	Georgia	LMIC	Georgia Urban Enerji Ltd. (hydropower plant)
	Turkey	UMIC	

Notes: UMIC = upper middle-income country; LMIC = lower middle-income country.
Source: World Bank (2022).

Table 7.1d *Cross-border PPPs: Latin America and Caribbean, 1995–2021*

Year	Countries	Income group	Project name
1996	Argentina	UMIC	Santo Tome: Sao Borja Toll Bridge
	Brazil	UMIC	
1998	Bolivia	LMIC	Bolivian Brazilian Gas pipeline
	Brazil	UMIC	
2000	Argentina	UMIC	Companhia de Interconexao Energetica (electricity transmission)
	Brazil	UMIC	

Notes: LMIC = lower middle-income country; UMIC = upper middle-income country.
Source: World Bank (2022).

Africa has registered more cross-border PPPs than any other region, perhaps because some of these projects demonstrate the high level of innovation often necessary on the part of participating governments and development partners to make regional PPP projects successful:

- Regional projects are often hindered by the inability to harmonize the legal and regulatory frameworks for participating governments. The Kenya–Uganda rail concession solved this problem by structuring the concession as two separate, but coordinated, national projects. This involved separate concession contracts in each country, supported by two separate MDB support packages, as well as two different local incorporations of the same operating company. However, both Kenya and Uganda prematurely terminated their contracts with the private operator in mid-2017.
- The development of regional PPP projects has also often been hindered by different levels of interest or motivation on the part of participating governments—one government may have a strong interest in a project, while other government partners do not. The South Africa–Mozambique Maputo toll road PPP avoided this problem in 1996 due to the enthusiastic support for the project from the presidents of both countries, Nelson Mandela and Joaquim Chissano. The corridor links South Africa's industrialized heartland, the Gauteng province, via Mpumalanga province in the east, to the Mozambican port of Maputo. This arguably is the only successful regional spatial development corridor in Africa—perhaps because of the strong degree of mutual interest and cooperation at the highest levels of the two governments.
- Regional PPPs are often so large that the complicated and expensive process of structuring a project finance transaction discourages development efforts (see the case study of Inga III in the next section). The West African Gas Pipeline solved this problem by using a special purpose vehicle (SPV) jointly owned by private companies and the participating governments. The resulting PPP was structured using "corporate finance" (rather than "project finance") with the participating governments supplying equity and shareholder loans, rather than borrowing exclusively from expensive outside sources.
- The Beitbridge "one-stop" border post represents the kind of small regional project that is needed in many developing countries, particularly in Africa, to facilitate cross-border trade and travel. These projects are technically uncomplicated and can generate large economic benefits. The fact that there is only a single one-stop border post in Tables 7.1a–7.1d reflects the fact that even small cross-border PPPs of this nature face significant challenges in terms of multi-country collaboration and bureaucratic coordination.

Ultimately, of course, a key reason why so few regional PPPs have been done in developing countries is that regional infrastructure projects often do not necessarily need to be developed as PPPs at all. They can be wholly financed and operated by governments or financed by the private sector on a "merchant" basis, meaning that the assets are built, operated, and owned by a private company at its own risk, without a government commitment, formalized in a PPP contract, to buy the services. The private owner of a merchant project negotiates sales agreements with any government or private sector customers willing to buy the services. In the telecommunication sector, fiber optic cable projects that sell ICT services to multiple governments or private customers have become quite common, but are no longer classified by the World Bank as PPPs (and therefore are not included in the Tables).

7.6 CASE STUDY: INGA III AND THE CHALLENGES OF REGIONAL PROJECTS

One potentially transformational PPP that has long been on almost every list of priority regional projects, including PIDA's, is Inga III. In 2003, Inga III was conceived as the third and largest power project in the Inga basin of the Congo River in the Democratic Republic of Congo (DRC). At that time, the project was expected to generate 3,500 MW and cost $5 billion, including transmission system investments of $1.5 billion. Inga III illustrates many of the characteristics that make huge regional projects completely different from normal national projects, and exceptionally difficult to finance, even if private investors can be attracted to such projects. These characteristics include the following:

- *Private involvement*: At 3,500 MW Inga III would be by far the largest energy project with private sector participation ever attempted in Africa. Private sector participation in such a project is a requirement rather than an option. A project the size of Inga III would require funding from a variety of private and public sources, as well as an IPP operating structure, the normal PPP arrangement for power generating projects of this kind.
- *Cost and complexity*: A financing plan for Inga III was commissioned by the World Bank in 2009 (BNP Paribas 2009). The consultants found that the total cost of the project had already reached almost $9 billion, a 78 percent increase over initial estimates. The staggering size of the project meant that nothing more than a massively complex financing structure would be needed to cover project costs. The consultants recommended a financing plan involving $6.6 billion provided by four MDBs, six DFIs, export credit agencies, Chinese policy banks, and commercial banks. In addition, over $2.2 billion in equity financing would have to come from

independent power producers; vendors; and engineering, procurement, construction (EPC) contractors; as well as the DRC government, which would have to source loans for its share.

- *Timing*: The consultants estimated that it would take 12 years to complete construction of Inga III. The problem with this duration was that the other countries that must agree to purchase the power from the plant before financiers would commit funding to the project, may or may not still want or need that power after such a long construction period. The consultants concluded that it would be "… extremely challenging to commit the off-takers for such a long period on a take-or-pay basis […] no one can foresee what price countries or private users will be willing to pay in 12 years for power" (BNP Paribas 2009, 90).
- *Preparation tasks*: Before it could reach financial close, a massive amount of preparation would be required for a project of this size, located in a country like the DRC. In addition to normal preparation including feasibility studies, project structuring, and funding syndication, a variety of "upstream" reforms would be necessary. These would include the cross-border harmonization of legal-regulatory frameworks, as well as a good deal of work in the DRC to reduce project risks caused by weak government policies and procedures. Among other things, the consultants found that the DRC had "… no specific legislation and no single set of procedures for the award of a concession in a form suitable to the project" (BNP Paribas 2009, 49). Unless changed, this situation would require project sponsors to obtain rights and authorizations from a large variety of governmental and local authorities in order to implement the project. But such authorizations likely would be granted in different ways for different time periods, increasing political risks for private investors, as well as the possibility of corruption.
- *Preparation costs*: Partly because of the expertise required for the large amount of preparation work mentioned above, preparation would be hugely expensive for a project of this size. The AfDB estimated that preparation costs for large infrastructure projects can reach 10–15 percent of project capital costs (AfDB 2013a). The World Bank calculated that the preparation costs for the Nam Theun 2 hydropower project in Lao PDR (total investment: $1.4 billion) amounted to $124 million at project close in 2005, or 9 percent of total project investment.[4] Because this kind of preparation work happens before financial close, money is not yet available from

[4] At the time of signing in 2005, NT2 was the world's largest private sector cross-border power project financing and the largest private sector hydroelectric project financing.

> project lenders to pay for it. Private partners are reluctant to pay for such preparation because of the possibility the project will not reach financial close. Some grant money is available from donors and early-stage preparation loans from MDBs, but nothing like the $1 billion that would likely be needed to prepare a project like Inga III.

Perhaps the biggest challenge associated with Inga III has been to determine who is responsible for preparing a regional project like this, located in a country like DRC, with four or five other countries that have strong interests in accessing the power from such a project, in some cases, a stronger interest than the DRC's. In 2003, DRC's power utility joined with four others in southern Africa—the likely off-takers of Inga III power—to create the Western Power Corridor Company (Westcor Pty Ltd.), to develop the project. Westcor agreed to finance technical pre-feasibility and feasibility studies, as well as an environmental impact assessment. But the individual country shareholdings in Westcor were never more than $100,000 each, and Westcor never raised the financing needed to pay for a technical feasibility study or environmental impact assessment.

As project development under Westcor slowed, the DRC government was approached by BHP Billiton with an offer to locate an aluminum smelter in the country if they could construct Inga III as a 2,500 MW plant, at a total cost of $3.5 billion, which would also supply electricity to the smelter. The DRC accepted BHP Billiton's offer in 2010 and declared Inga III to be no longer a regional project. At that time, the chief executive of the DRC's National Electricity Society announced that Westcor was dissolved (Independent Online 2010).

But BHP Billiton also quickly withdrew from the project and the government announced that Inga III was once again a regional project. In May 2013, the government began seeking financiers to invest in what had become a $12 billion, 4,800 MW project. Following an announcement that South Africa had committed to buying 2,300 MW of Inga III electricity, in June 2013 the DRC signed agreements with the AfDB to design a process for implementing the hydropower project (AfDB 2013b). A team led by Electricité de France completed a $15 million project design with AfDB financing. Although no lenders had yet made firm commitments to invest in the project, three international consortia (from China, Spain, and South Korea) expressed interest in implementing the project.

In 2014, the World Bank committed $73 million to finance environmental, institutional, social, and technical studies for supporting infrastructure related to Inga III (World Bank 2014). As a condition for receiving a grant from the World Bank's International Development Association (IDA), the government agreed to create a semi-autonomous development authority to act as a kind of independent PPP unit specifically for the Inga project, combining financial resources and expertise to ensure that responsible best practice was followed in the development of the project. The grant was approved, work started, but the government did not establish the development authority as agreed with the World Bank—the country's president had decided to take personal control of the project. In September 2016, the World Bank canceled its grant support to Inga III, with only about 6 percent of the total preparation funding disbursed. Most of the studies had not been completed and many had not been started (World Bank 2016).

In October 2018, the DRC government awarded Inga III development rights to a consortium involving two groups, a consortium led by China Three Gorges, and another headed by Spain's Actividades de Construccion y Servicios (ACS). At the time, the project was described as an 11,000 MW hydropower project, expected to cost $14 billion with construction lasting eight years. But the joint consortium was never formally established and details about how the project would be managed were not finalized. At the end of 2019, ACS announced its withdrawal from the project, citing disagreements regarding project ownership shares (M'Bida and Maussion 2020). Complicating matters further, the DRC president indicated his preference for a smaller project, no larger than 4,800 MW.

In June 2021, the DRC government announced that Fortescue Metals Group of Australia would develop the Grand Inga hydroelectric power project, involving a much larger dam in the Inga basin, of which Inga III would be a 4,800 MW subsidiary facility. But Fortescue admitted that no formal binding agreement with the DRC had been concluded. A Memorandum of Understanding (MOU) signed by Fortescue and the DRC government in September 2020 was reviewed by Reuters. In the MOU, Fortescue acknowledged "… the existing potential rights held on Inga III by third parties […] In the event that, for any reason, such rights to develop Inga III become available, the government of the DRC undertakes to secure for Fortescue Future Industries an exclusive first option to develop Inga III" (Reuters 2020).

Also in 2021, a research study was published by the non-governmental organization, International Rivers. It concluded that the cost to the South African government of its Inga III power off-take commitment (2,300 MW)—essential for the commercial viability of the project—would be prohibitively expensive for Eskom, South Africa's struggling national power utility (TMP Systems 2021). Power supplied would likely be three times more expensive than the current cost of energy production in South Africa and generate a host of negative social consequences. The study was widely reported on in the South African press.

7.7 THE GLOBAL FINANCIAL CRISIS AND THE NEED TO RETHINK PPP FINANCE

As the AICD and PIDA studies were nearing completion in the late 2000s, the recovery of the global PPP market in developing countries appeared to be well underway—2007 was the first year in which investment commitments to PPP projects in developing countries exceeded the record level of 1997, at least in nominal value. But the global financial crisis beginning in mid-2007 and lasting until early 2009, posed new threats to the use of PPPs in developing countries, and a particular threat to the prospects for large, transformational regional PPPs in developing country regions like Africa. The crisis, and the changes it left behind in the global structure of international finance, helped account for why so few regional infrastructure PPPs, like those on the PIDA PAP list, have reached financial closure.

7.7.1 The Project Finance Liquidity Machine

The threat was the result of a breakdown in the project finance dynamic that had facilitated the growth in PPP investment in developing as well as developed countries over the 2003–07 period—the first signs of PPP market recovery since the Asian financial crisis. In just six years the international project finance market grew by four or five times, depending on the measure used (Abadie 2008). Much of the growth in the global market was driven by huge increases in liquidity generated mostly in industrialized economies. Changing banking practices accounted for some of this liquidity growth. Project finance banks shifted from "originate and hold" to "originate and distribute" strategies: they would book project loans and then quickly distribute them into the market through syndication, securitization, secondary market sales, and other techniques. The emergence of a secondary market in loans (in contrast to secondary markets that already existed for securities such as bonds) was facilitated in Western Europe by the rapidly growing use of credit ratings on loans. These ratings made investors more comfortable about buying project loans while knowing little about the borrowers or the underlying projects.

These methods of distribution created space in the originators' balance sheets for new lending and helped banks make money without retaining loans in their portfolios. The resulting increase in liquidity generated tremendous competition among lenders, driving down the price of loans and giving borrowers the upper hand in negotiations. Most of this excess liquidity for project finance was generated in developed markets and helped fuel the large private investment programs in Western Europe. In the United Kingdom, the government's Private Finance Initiative reached record levels of investment. But not all the liquidity could be absorbed in these markets, and some spilled over into developing countries. Much of it went to Eastern Europe, where Western European lenders were quick to take advantage of the need for project finance for public–private partnerships and privatization in infrastructure, reforms driven by European Union accession. The surge in project finance liquidity also benefited Latin America, with a long tradition of using international credit ratings to access project finance from international banks and bond markets.

Larger projects in poorer regions like Africa also benefited. Banks in Africa were less tightly integrated into the global banking networks than those in East Asia or Latin America. Apart from a few in South Africa, they had little long-term money available at affordable interest rates for infrastructure investment. And the few capital markets that existed in the region were shallow. But the huge amount of international project finance liquidity that grew over the 2002–07 period meant that international lenders occasionally had space in their balance sheets for riskier loans in emerging markets, and some larger African projects benefited directly. In other cases, the spill-over was more indirect: local or regional African banks borrowed from these international banks or from international capital markets to raise financing needed to make loans to PPP projects or used credit lines from international banks to back lending to large African projects.

This project finance liquidity began to dry up when the mechanism for distributing it shut down with the financial crisis beginning in 2007. The interbank borrowing market was the main mechanism used by international banks to raise money for project finance, and that market was disrupted as the subprime mortgage crisis began to raise doubts about the ability of banks to repay their own debts. The distribution of project finance slowed dramatically. The underlying mechanism for generating this liquidity also collapsed. By early 2009 the "originate and distribute" model was no longer working because originators could no longer distribute project loans into the market. The secondary market for this debt collapsed because credit ratings of loans lost credibility.

Excess liquidity was no longer being generated in developed markets nor spilling over into the developing world. Many of the world's leading project finance lenders sharply reduced their activity in the project finance market (Royal Bank of Scotland, Lloyds Banking Group, DEPFA Bank, Fortis, Dexia, Halifax Bank of Scotland). In addition, Basel II banking regulations, issued in 2004, required banks to hold more assets in reserve against the risks of longer-term lending and were already leading to a general repricing of project finance credit risk. Additional international banking regulation in the form of Basel III was issued in 2010 in response to the crisis, making private investment projects even less attractive to the big international project finance banks.

As the crisis continued to unfold, there was concern that some of the changes in the market for project finance would likely affect liquidity and pricing far into the future. The secondary market in project debt that drove liquidity generation at the top of the project finance cascade in developed countries was expected to take years to rebuild. Stricter Basel regulations would also have long-term effects. Investment commitments to PPP projects were expected to drop sharply in 2008 and even more in 2009. Governments and development institutions were understandably concerned about returning as quickly as possible to the investment levels of 2007 and avoiding the kind of "lost decade" of private investment in infrastructure that followed the Asian crisis in 1997 (Leigland and Russell 2009).

7.7.2 The Delayed Market Reaction

Surprisingly, however, PPP investment commitments did not drop as expected in 2008 or 2009. In fact, total commitments increased, and continued to do so until 2013. Among other things, this suggested to some PPP advocates like the authors of the PIDA study that the PPP mechanism had more than survived the global crisis. But that apparent survival was the result of governments and their development partners responding to the crisis with several kinds of short-term ameliorative measures. The most dramatic of these involved the direct provision of some or all the financing for PPP projects, through loans, equity, grants, or guarantees. Developed countries, such as Australia and the United Kingdom, led the way with such measures. The U.K. government attempted to salvage its Private Finance Initiative with an investment fund that provided up to 100 percent of the financing needed for projects to proceed. The financing was intended to be as short term as possible, with the loans refinanced from commercial sources as soon as markets recovered (Farquharson and Encinas 2010).

In developing countries such as Brazil, India, Mexico, and South Africa government-owned DFIs provided funding or guarantees to kick-start PPP projects. In countries without such resources, donors and multilateral development banks attempted to help fill the gap. The IFC created a global fund that substituted donor funding for commercial finance to start new PPP projects and keep existing ones functioning. In other developing countries, donor or multilateral development funding allowed some infrastructure projects to begin using conventional public sector procurement and implementation, with the aim of bringing in private participation when feasible.

Because countries like Brazil and India accounted for such a large share of private investment activity in developing countries, their use of government-owned banks and local public banks to fund large projects meant that global PPP market investment numbers continued to increase through 2008 and into 2009 (Izaguirre 2009). Ushering in what later became widely known as "blended finance," governments in larger middle-income countries continued to replace scarce commercial finance with public money from government budgets or donors, DFIs, and MDBs. In 2015, World Bank data confirmed that 57 percent of PPP funding in IDA countries came from governments, multilaterals, and bilateral institutions, with the balance coming from commercial sources. For all developing country regions in 2015, the percentage was 41 percent from public sources (Chao and Saha 2016).

PPP market growth fueled with funding from governments and development partners disguised what, for PPP advocates, was an uncomfortable reality. The use of PPPs continued to stagnate in the poorest countries that most needed new infrastructure investment. And the kind of market growth that had been achieved in middle-income countries proved to be unsustainable. As soon as a handful of middle-income countries (MICs) like Brazil, China, and India began to reduce their provision of large subsidies for PPPs, the overall market numbers began to decline. The sharp reduction in toll road investments in South Asia, especially India in 2013, and in Latin America in 2015, had major impacts in terms of reducing total private infrastructure investment in developing countries and began to sharply moderate the global market surge that peaked in 2012.

Developing countries and their development partners emerged from the global financial crisis facing several challenges: the governments had unprecedented levels of debt on their balance sheets, plus a desperate need to stimulate their economies to avoid stagnant growth. Regional infrastructure had become even less of a priority for individual sovereign governments than it had been before the crisis, but the imminent publication of both the AICD and PIDA studies would underscore the importance for the global development community of investment in regional infrastructure. These challenges, plus the ongoing PPP advocacy efforts of the ever-growing constituency of true believers and core supporters, suggested that private participation in infrastructure investment and management was needed more than ever.

But the sustained disruption of the global project finance market created another new and very substantial challenge: how to finance needed national and regional PPPs if commercial banks were no longer able to provide necessary levels of project finance. To address this challenge, the development community began to turn its attention to the largest untapped source of private finance that could potentially be used for infrastructure investment—the vast pool of public and private long-term savings controlled by institutional investors like pension funds, insurance companies, and sovereign wealth funds. The effort to access this massive source of finance seemed poised to precipitate what some observers expected to be a "PPP revival" (Alexander 2015; Bayliss and Van Waeyenberge 2017). The reasons why this revival did not happen are discussed in the next chapter.

7.8 PIDA COURSE CORRECTION

The changing landscape of the global project finance market began with the global financial crisis while both the PIDA and AICD studies were in preparation. The AICD study (2010) recognized that the effects of the crisis in Africa would likely be substantial but might not be recognized in Africa for some time. But the study did not suggest that PPPs would be a major solution in infrastructure investment problems in African and proposed the creation of a G20-funded $50 billion African stimulus package to finance economic regeneration in Africa's poorest countries.

The PIDA study (2012) was more optimistic about the impacts of the crisis as well as the role of the private sector:

> Africa commands a powerful position on the world stage. It is seen as a land of opportunity—an emerging destination of choice for many investors and development actors as they look for high-growth markets, despite the ongoing economic turmoil and the lingering effects of the financial crisis and recession. (AUC et al. 2012)

At first, PIDA's optimism seemed warranted. As noted in the section above, total PPP investment commitments continued on their upward path in developing countries through the worst of the crisis, buoyed by government subsidies in large middle-income countries. But in 2013, a year after PIDA was launched, the effects of the crisis on PPPs started to become apparent and the PPP market in developing countries went into decline. The various organizations managing the PIDA process eventually reacted. The duration of the PIDA lifespan was originally expected to extend from 2012 to 2040, but the slow pace of project completions and the almost total absence of private finance finally triggered a 2019 "mid-term review" of the PAP along with a new market demand study. Based on these studies, the AUC and AUDA–NEPAD decided a course correction was needed for PIDA. But instead of re-examining PIDA's focus on PPPs and private investment, the revised plan intensified that focus.

The PIDA secretariat engaged consultants to prepare a second phase of the PIDA Priority Action Plan (PIDA PAP 2) in mid-2019. The revised list of projects was smaller and more focused on infrastructure priorities, with projects jointly proposed by respective RECs and national governments to better ensure cooperation in preparation and oversight. But an essential element of PIDA PAP 2 was a more careful prioritization of projects based on their attractiveness to the private sector: "This need to mobilise more private sector financing for project implementation is key to pave the way for successfully implementing the PIDA PAP 2 projects. Therefore, we can attribute greater weight to the financial attractiveness criterion during the screening exercise" (African Union 2020, 42).

PIDA architects acceded to the prevailing wisdom of the international development community which held that the lack of private investment in infrastructure was a result of failed project preparation rather than any inherent shortcomings in PPP mechanisms or fundamental risk aversion of private investors (see the discussion of this in the next chapter). So, to better ensure that PIDA projects attracted private finance, the AUC and AUDA–NEPAD identified several options for providing PIDA projects with access to resources that could be used for better project preparation.

AUDA–NEPAD already hosted its own PPF, known as the PIDA Service Delivery Mechanism (SDM), which had been created in 2014 to address the lack of capacity for early stage PIDA project preparation at the national and regional levels. SDM attracted very little demand from project proponents, primarily because it insisted on managing the preparation activities it funded (rather than allowing recipient execution), but SDM lacked the necessary expertise to advise on private sector financing options. As a key part of PIDA's revisions to its strategy in 2019, AUDA–NEPAD used funding from development partners to add new tools to improve SDM performance and in some cases create pathways for projects to seek help from other donor-funded PPFs that were assumed to be more proficient in preparing projects for private finance. Tools included a pool of experts available to advise regional and national infrastructure project owners regarding project preparation; a methodology to certify the quality of early-stage preparation in the hopes of attracting further support from donor-funded PPFs; and a network of African business experts to discuss private financing options for high priority PIDA projects.

7.9 CONCLUSIONS

The need for regional infrastructure projects seems beyond question, particularly in Africa where so many countries are too small, poor, and landlocked to be able to meet their infrastructure needs without collective action involving multiple countries. The importance of these kinds of projects is one of the principal areas of agreement between the AICD and PIDA studies.

Unfortunately however, the historical track record of efforts to implement such projects demonstrates very little success. If anything, the track record seems to offer additional evidence that PPPs are not likely to be widely successful in developing countries, particularly low-income countries. STAP achieved very little, and the first phase of PIDA did not do much better, despite a planning and preparation effort supported with massive levels of donor funding. It remains to be seen if the more recent adjustments to the PIDA program will produce intended results.

Some private investors and development partners continue to question the basic PIDA approach, which is still very much a top-down exercise. Projects may be proposed for inclusion in PAP 2 by governments and REC partners, but final decisions are made by PIDA officials and consultants overseen ultimately by AUC. New project selection criteria, including a new sensitivity to social inclusiveness, have received nominal support from RECs and member states in a series of PIDA workshops, and reflect legitimate development priorities. But heavily weighting such criteria in project selection serves mainly to incentivize the selection of projects based on development value rather than their likely commercial sustainability. So, while such projects may be worthwhile, and attract political support, they often cannot attract enough affordable private sector-funding to reach financial closure.

Critical questions about regional projects have never been satisfactorily answered: How should such projects be financed after the changes in project finance caused by the global financial crisis? How should the development of such projects be managed—what should be the relationship between sovereign governments who "own" these projects and the regional governmental entities who feel compelled to take on project leadership roles? What is the optimal role of development partners in such projects? Finally, what is the private sector's ideal role? Private participation of some kind is unavoidable in large regional projects like Inga III. But should these be conventional PPP projects, or more modest and proven forms of private involvement, like EPC contracts or performance-based contracting?

8. A new strategy for PPP advocacy: the project preparation gap

8.1 INTRODUCTION

In 2005, the United Nations World Summit and the Gleneagles G8 Summit put the infrastructure problems of developing countries, particularly African countries, on a global stage. But the precise size and nature of all the problems involved were not yet clear; nor were the most cost-effective solutions. It took another five years and the release of the World Bank's *Africa Infrastructure Country Diagnostic* (2010) for G20's approach to these problems to take shape. Over the period from 2010 to 2013, a variety of policy documents and action plans were issued by G20 working groups and multilateral development banks (MDBs), which outlined an aggressive new phase of public–private partnership (PPP) advocacy.

Both of the reports prepared in advance of the G8's Gleneagles discussion recommended a modest increase in the use of PPPs, a stronger focus on regional projects, and support for regional organizations in Africa like the New Partnership for Africa's Development (NEPAD). But both reports primarily emphasized the need for increased funding from public rather than private sources. The report by the United Nations Millennium Project (2005) noted that the achievement of the Millennium Development Goals (MDGs) was "entirely affordable" if developed countries fulfilled their commitments to provide 0.7 percent of their national income as official development assistance (ODA)—representing a nearly three-fold increase over 2003 levels (xvii).

The Commission for Africa report (2005) spoke approvingly of the "pragmatic approach" to PPP project development taken by the Public–Private Infrastructure Advisory Facility (PPIAF), the Private Infrastructure Development Group (PIDG), and the International Finance Corporation (IFC), but cautioned against repeating the mistakes of the 1980s and 1990s in expecting that PPPs would play a dominant role in infrastructure finance, as privatization was expected to do under policy-based structural adjustment lending programs. The caution was not surprising. In 2005, global PPP investment commitments were still only about 40 percent of the 1997 peak in real terms. The Commission for Africa report estimated sub-Saharan Africa's infrastructure financing needs to be $39 billion per year. Based on that estimate, the report recommended a doubling of infrastructure spending in the region, to be supported by increased donor allocations of $10 billion annually up to 2010. The main donors agreed to this increase and largely met this commitment, with ODA flows to African infrastructure nearly doubling from $4.1 billion in 2004 to $8.1 billion by 2007 (Foster and Briceño-Garmendia 2010, 78).

However, the release of the *Africa Infrastructure Country Diagnostic* (AICD) study, with preliminary findings circulated to stakeholders as early as 2008, changed the nature of this discussion. Using a more rigorous analysis, AICD estimated the total annual infrastructure investment needs in Africa at over $93 billion, almost 2.5 times the Commission for Africa estimate (Foster and Briceño-Garmendia 2010).[1] AICD also estimated that existing spending on infrastructure from all sources amounted to about $45 billion per year, leaving an annual funding gap of $48 billion, mostly for electricity (61 percent) and water and sanitation (30 percent).

The AICD study had a considerable impact on the development community. The G20's MDB Working Group on Infrastructure recognized it as a pioneering achievement and recommended that MDBs "cooperatively expand" the study to other developing country regions using an annual budget of $2–8 million depending on coverage (G20 2011b, 8). The results of the AICD study were widely publicized and, although sometimes misquoted or misunderstood,[2] the fundamental message resonated loudly in both developed and developing countries—even after recent increases in ODA, far too little was being invested in African infrastructure. An annual increase of tens of billions of dollars was needed.

The enormous size of the infrastructure investment gap in Africa prompted a global strategic review of potential solutions to the problem, which led to G20 decisions to opt for an approach that heavily favored PPPs and initiated

---

1 A 2007 update of the analytical model used for the Commission for Africa report produced a revised estimate in the range of $80–90 billion, much closer to the AICD estimate (Yepes 2007).

2 AICD readers often misunderstood the methodology used to arrive at an infrastructure investment gap: the gap was based on the annual investment needed to achieve specified service delivery targets for basic infrastructure sectors over a ten-year period, from 2006 to 2015. Much depended on the sector targets. For example, the AICD target for electricity was very ambitious: the realization of a demand–supply balance in power production by developing 7,000 MW of new generation capacity annually to 2015, as well as a total of 57 million new household connections.

a new phase of PPP advocacy. The approach focused on project preparation and included the creation of a new generation of project preparation facilities (PPFs). But as this chapter explains, this new strategy has not led to more PPPs and has contributed very little to infrastructure investment in developing countries.

8.2 THE NEED FOR A NEW STRATEGY TO INCREASE INFRASTRUCTURE INVESTMENT

Like the two studies done in preparation for Gleneagles, AICD recommended against expecting too much from the private sector (discussed in more detail in Chapter 3). PPP investment commitments had increased substantially in the developing world since 2005, but the global financial crisis suggested that further increases would likely be limited because of the diminishing availability of project finance. AICD recommended efforts to correct policy and administrative inefficiencies to free up more public funding for infrastructure, the prioritization of infrastructure rehabilitation and maintenance to sharply reduce investment needs, and the rationalization of sector investment allocations so that more investment was directed to sectors like electricity and water where it was most needed. Finally, AICD recommended a $50 billion infrastructure investment stimulus package to offset the impact of the global economic crisis on gross domestic product (GDP) growth in Africa.

The report by the United Nations Millennium Project in preparation for the 2005 Gleneagles Summit had quickly dismissed any notion that the ODA needed to reach the MDGs was unaffordable for developed nations, arguing that the amount needed "… will make up only half a percent of rich countries' combined income" (United Nations Millennium Project 2005, 64). But the AICD estimates of investment needs in Africa were enormous compared to previous estimates. Plus, infrastructure investment needs on a global level were also scaled up as researchers began to apply AICD analytical methods to other regions. By 2011, estimates of infrastructure investment needs across the developing world topped $1 trillion for capital costs and $1 trillion for operations and maintenance (Fay et al. 2019).

Another enormous increase in ODA would be needed if development assistance of that kind could have a significant impact on this investment gap. The World Bank Group, the largest multilateral financier of infrastructure in 2010, had an infrastructure budget allocation for the year of $29 billion (World Bank 2011b). And even that amount was under threat in the aftermath of the global financial crisis. As the Bank noted, previous exercises in infrastructure investment planning had been characterized by "… volume scale-up and growing resources …" (9). But by 2010 the investment plans were being updated in a "… very different internal context …" characterized by severe resource constraints (9).

At the same time, the World Bank Group and other multilateral financiers were coming under immense criticism for the situation highlighted by AICD and later surveys. Despite years of "volume scale-up and growing resources" these financiers had allowed a massive infrastructure investment gap to open in the developing world at the same time that an even larger, rapidly growing pool of savings was accumulating in the global economy. In a report prepared for the G24 by the London School of Economics and others,[3] the authors concluded that "The existing architecture is deficient in providing financing on the scale and with the characteristics needed" (Bhattacharya et al. 2012, 6). The report claimed that MDBs were at the heart of this problem because they were cumbersome, costly, excessively risk-averse, unable to assess risk-return profiles or policy risks, and unable to crowd-in private investment when needed: "… they will face capital, governance and other constraints in responding to the scale and urgency of the challenge" (6). MDB efforts to address these problems were acknowledged, but the G24 report went on to recommend the creation of a "… new Development Bank for Infrastructure and Sustainable Development" (6).

Disappointment with the existing MDB institutional architecture was widespread. In 2013 the creation of the New Development Bank was announced by the five countries known as the "BRICS": Brazil, Russia, India, China, and South Africa. In 2014, China led the creation of the Asian Infrastructure Investment Bank (AIIB). At the 2013 G20 Summit, officials announced that they were considering modifications to the mandates of national and international development banks, in order to force these institutions to facilitate more infrastructure investment (Alexander 2013).

Like AICD and the reports prepared for the Gleneagles Summit, the 2012 report prepared for the G24 cautioned against expecting too much from PPPs: "Even before the current financial crisis, PPIs [public–private investments] had proven often difficult to execute and have had limited success" (Bhattacharya et al. 2012, 18). The poor performance of PPPs, especially in low-income countries reflected "… the greater risks, both perceived and real, as well as the underdeveloped nature of local capital markets in those countries" (18).

---

3 The Intergovernmental Group of Twenty-Four on International Monetary Affairs and Development, or The Group of 24 (G-24), is an association of developing countries established in 1971 to coordinate the policy positions of developing countries on international monetary and development finance issues.

8.3 THE PROJECT PREPARATION GAP

PPPs may not have been recommended as priority solutions to infrastructure investment problems by the authors of the Commission for Africa report, the G24 report, or AICD. But the G20 and its MDBs apparently concluded that they had no other feasible financing option to turn to for a rapid scale-up of infrastructure investment than private finance. So, private finance and PPPs became the center of the G20 response to challenges posed by the infrastructure investment gaps described by AICD and similar studies. World Bank management still included true believers who felt that PPPs had never fully realized the potential that seemed so clearly evident in the mid-1990s. Many of the G20 members were also not prepared to give up on using PPPs to finance infrastructure investment in the developing world, even though none of these countries were using PPPs extensively in their own economies, as noted in Chapter 1. In general, the development community, as represented by MDBs and most bilateral donors, still had a strong faith in the power of private sector market forces to drive economic growth, so building a new financing strategy around PPPs would not be too difficult.

By 2010, PPP advocates were also encouraged by what looked like a recovery in the global PPP market in developing countries. As discussed in the last chapter, the use by larger middle-income countries of blended finance to de-risk PPPs with public money was keeping overall PPP investment commitments from falling in response to the global financial crisis. By 2010, PPP investment commitments exceeded the 1997 record total in real terms for the first time. By 2012, these commitments reached what is still their all-time peak, more than 60 percent above the 1997 total (led by Brazil's massive PPP investments in transport and power). Large, regional or "transformational" infrastructure projects, de-risked with "blended finance" provided by governments or donors, and financed by the private sector, seemed like an ideal solution to the urgent need for infrastructure investment. Plus, this was a solution that would not increase the financial burden on donor countries, already under pressure due to the global financial crisis.

The elements of the G20's PPP strategy were drafted in a series of closely coordinated documents:

- In the preparations for the 2010 G20 Seoul Summit, the G20 requested its MDB Working Group on Infrastructure to prepare "... comprehensive infrastructure action plans ..." that would include strategies for facilitating regional infrastructure projects involving private financing (G20 2010, 2).[4]

- Such a strategy was proposed as part of the "Infrastructure Action Plan," submitted by the Working Group a year after the summit. The strategy added that the *Programme for Infrastructure Development in Africa* (PIDA), still several months from official approval by the African heads of state, "… will provide the strategic framework for the prioritization of transformative regional projects going forward" (G20 2011b, 4).[5]
- The Action Plan was heavily influenced by the recommendations to the G20 by the High Level Panel on Infrastructure (G20 2011a) and the World Bank Group's "Infrastructure Strategy Update," which helped shape the basic arguments in the MDB Working Group's Action Plan (World Bank 2011b).

The central theme of this new strategy, articulated in all these documents, was the argument that the infrastructure investment gap in regions like Africa had been allowed to grow so large because private investment had been restricted by poor project preparation. Potential investors did not understand how profitable such projects could be—a "project preparation gap" was to blame for lack of investment rather than a financing gap. The G20's High Level Panel on Infrastructure described the issue in this way:

> Our fundamental belief as HLP is that appropriate funding could be made available for bankable projects in LICs [low-income countries]. The constraint is less one of funding than an insufficient pipeline of bankable projects […] Success in infrastructure investment, especially for Public–Private Partnerships (PPPs) […] is dependent on well-designed projects i.e., on effective project preparation. (G20 2011a, i–ii)

The G20 MDB Working Group's Infrastructure Action Plan noted that "Inadequate financial and technical resources for project preparation—whether for development of PPPs or for regional projects—are a key bot-

---

4 The MDB Working Group on Infrastructure on Infrastructure included the African Development Bank (AfDB), Asian Development Bank (AsDB), European Investment Bank (EIB), Inter-American Development Bank (IDB), Islamic Development Bank (IsDB), and World Bank Group (World Bank Group).

5 The G20 eventually agreed on a "G20 Compact with Africa," the aim of which was to help meet the G20 commitment "… to address key constraints to regional projects and PPPs for transformational infrastructure projects in low income environments" (WBG 2017a, 25). The G20 recognized the AU's Agenda 2063 as "the starting point" for this compact, and PIDA as "a central pillar" of that agenda.

tleneck" (G20 2011b, 3). The World Bank Group's "Infrastructure Strategy Update" noted that "High quality of project preparation and execution is needed to ensure success in PPPs and deliver sustainable outcomes" (World Bank 2011b, 36).

If poor project preparation was a reason for the massive shortfall in infrastructure investment revealed by AICD and other studies, then the G20 and its MDBs had identified something that could be fixed without the need for massive increases in ODA. The problem could be solved without addressing other, less tractable and more unsettling reasons for the investment shortfall, such as the possibility that most infrastructure PPPs were unable to attract private investment because they were not profitable enough to outweigh risks, or the failure of donors and MDBs to allocate enough ODA to the infrastructure sectors most in need of investment, as documented by AICD.

8.4 PPP PROJECT PREPARATION CHALLENGES

The focus on project preparation was of course not new. Similar concerns dominated the World Bank's more deliberative approach to PPPs which emerged as the Bank began to identify lessons learned from the shortcomings of policy-based lending during the 1980s and 1990s (see Chapter 3). At that time, the Bank made the claim that careful, well-funded project preparation, including upstream reforms to the laws, regulations, and procedures, was needed to "enable" successful PPPs. But the Bank and other development institutions struggled to definitively identify the best practice reforms and preparation steps that should be prioritized in the interests of scaling up the use of PPPs. As a result, few PPPs resulted from the Bank's work during the 2000s (IEG 2015). The best sector reforms and preparation steps needed to facilitate PPPs were no clearer in 2010 than they had been a decade earlier.

8.4.1 What Needed to Be Done

The G20 and its working groups faced enormous challenges in trying to explain precisely how projects were going to be prepared in a way that would significantly scale-up the use of PPPs, especially regional projects, to help meet the investment challenges identified by AICD and other studies. In developing countries, particularly low-income countries planning large, urgently needed projects, preparation can be complex and expensive, with costs as high as 10–15 percent (or more) of total project capital costs, much higher than in OECD countries.

One reason for this cost and complexity relates to the wide variety of project preparation tasks typically necessitated in LICs and the correspondingly wide range of technical skills required. Large infrastructure projects involving private finance often need two overlapping phases of preparation work (stylized in Figure 8.1). "Downstream" preparation is a familiar phase of project preparation in developed economies. It involves structuring the project and managing the transaction work that leads to an agreed PPP contract. Private sponsors, borrowers, and commercial lenders expect to pay for their own share of downstream due diligence and transaction costs on projects for which potential bankability seems reasonably clear.

Upstream Preparation	Phase 1:	**Enabling Environment**	Designing enabling legislation Designing regulatory approaches Project relevant institutional reforms Policy reforms Capacity building to support projects Consensus building re projects
	Phase 2:	**Project Definition**	Identification of desired outputs Prioritization vs. other projects Identification of project champions Action planning Pre-feasibility studies
	Phase 3:	**Project Feasibility**	Financial modeling Economic, Social, Technical, and Environmental studies
Downstream Preparation	Phase 4:	**Project Structuring**	Public/private options assessment Project finance Legal structuring
	Phase 5:	**Transaction Support**	Procurement/ contract drafting Financial/ legal negotiations
	Phase 6:	**Post-Signing Support**	Post-signing financial arrangements Monitoring & tariff reviews Renegotiation/ refinancing

Source: Adapted from Leigland and Roberts (2007).

Figure 8.1 Upstream and downstream PPP project preparation

However, "upstream" preparation is often more important, costly, and risky in developing countries, as well as something that private sector sponsors and investors typically will not pay for. This is early-stage work involving preliminary assessments of likely bankability, project-specific improvements to the legal and regulatory enabling environments, and capacity building for government counterparts. This is upstream work to identify and improve the "extraneous" project factors that were identified as so important by the World Bank in the early 2000s. Upstream preparation is critical for PPPs because, unlike most MDB-financed projects, a PPP usually requires a supporting enabling environment to ensure sustained commercial viability (e.g., reasonable quality standards, tariffs set at cost-recovery levels, supporting sector policies and investments).

8.4.2 The Role of Governments

In addition to not knowing precisely what needed to be done to prepare PPPs, the roles of key stakeholders in preparation was unclear as well. Government "owners" of PPP projects are of course required to play a major if not dominant role—more so than with MDB-financed programs and projects because the PPPs represent long-term contractual relationships between governments and private companies, involving substantial financial commitments and contingent liabilities. It is one thing to play a passive role in agreeing to a project designed and implemented by an MDB and financed with near-concessional money. But commercially financed and operated PPPs require much more active engagement by government owners because of the much higher costs and risks involved.

The World Bank Strategy Update noted that "Improving public sector capacity for project preparation should be a priority for most countries, especially those with some experience with PPPs" (World Bank 2011b, 48). But by 2010, experience with PPPs was still almost non-existent in the low-income countries that were the primary targets of the new MDB PPP strategy. As discussed in Chapter 6, the creation of governmental PPP units in Africa had not yet achieved much momentum and the few units that did exist still lacked staff, funding, and operational direction.

The degree to which government officials in Africa misunderstood their responsibility for preparing PPPs became apparent almost immediately in the post-Gleneagles meetings of the Infrastructure Consortium for Africa (ICA). ICA was established by G8 members and the World Bank, with the subsequent addition of African participants, including AfDB, the AUC, and NEPAD. Staffed with a full-time secretariat hosted by AfDB and mostly financed by donors like DFID, ICA's original role was to monitor and evaluate the G8 commitments made at Gleneagles.[6] But it quickly became a forum in which representatives of these organizations strategized, and sometimes argued, regarding ways in which investment in African infrastructure could be increased. Initial ICA discussions centered on what Africa participants

---

[6] The creation of an "independent mechanism" of this kind, "… supported by a small unit within an existing African or international institution," was a recommendation of the Commission for Africa (2005, 381) as a way to monitor and report on progress made after the Gleneagles Summit.

perceived to be a failure of MDBs like the World Bank to facilitate enough financing for projects already identified and prioritized in the NEPAD STAP.

A typical topic for ICA's early meetings was whether G8 countries were doing enough to meet the demands of African infrastructure. In response to these kinds of questions, representatives of MDBs and bilateral donors invariably pointed out that their investment funding was severely limited, and for projects to attract private investment they needed to be demonstrably "bankable"—projects with enough time and money already invested to confirm that they were likely to be viable from the standpoint of a financier (whether public or private). When the ICA participants began to review the various pipelines of African infrastructure projects circulating at the time, such as STAP, the lists revealed many projects supported only by out-of-date engineering studies, with little additional analysis that would be necessary for investment purposes such as detailed demand forecasts, cost–benefit analyses, or sustainability assessments. Many projects on these lists, which might have been desirable socially or economically (or politically), were not clearly bankable either by the private sector or even MDBs like the World Bank, no matter how much of a development priority they seemed to represent.

8.4.3 The Role of MDBs

The role of MDBs in the preparation of PPP projects was also quite complicated. A recurring theme in the G20 infrastructure strategy documents cited above was the need for MDBs to play a more effective role in project preparation. DFIs like the IFC, the Netherlands Development Finance Company (FMO), the German Investment and Development Corporation (DEG), and the Norwegian Investment Fund for Developing Countries (Norfund), had considerable experience with PPPs because they specialized in lending mostly to private companies on near-commercial terms. But the members of the G20 MDB Working Group on Infrastructure (World Bank, Asian Development Bank, African Development Bank, and Islamic Development Bank, etc.) concentrated on lending to governments and this was reflected in their meager PPP track records. The G20 High Level Panel concluded that "… some adjustment to the culture of MDBs will be required, moving from a lending culture to an enabling culture, from an emphasis on balance sheet growth to one on 'crowding in' private sector capital" (G20 2011a, iii). The MDB Working Group's Infrastructure Action Plan noted that the World Bank and the Asian Development Bank were "… finalizing plans to introduce incentivizes for staff to focus on leveraging rather than lending resources and undertake complex catalytic and regional projects" (G20 2011b, 6).

But the World Bank's Infrastructure Strategy Update was forthcoming about the challenges involved in shifting to an "enabling culture" focusing on project preparation rather than just appraising conventional sovereign-backed loans. The Strategy Update acknowledged that preparation was a "specific business" for IFC PPP Advisory, but not so in the World Bank:

> By contrast, in the Bank, there are few incentives to pursue costly, risky and time-intensive PPP projects [...] Moreover, PPPs are a complex business from a technical point of view. This difficulty is further exacerbated by the fact that about 20 different units and groups contribute one way or the other to the PPP agenda. (World Bank 2011b, 28–29)

The Strategy Update went on to outline various initiatives to train and incentivize staff to do more work with PPPs. But questions about how quickly World Bank staff could become "enablers" of privately financed projects rather than "lenders" were already circulating in the development community. Other than the relatively small number of IFC PPP Advisory personnel, most World Bank Group staff had little more actual experience with PPP project preparation than their government clients. In 2006, François Bourguignon, Chief Economist of the World Bank, conjectured that the analytical tools with which Bank staff were most familiar were not particularly useful in the preparation of infrastructure PPP projects. The use of economic cost–benefit analysis, for example, was often overwhelmed by a combination of problems caused by incomplete or inaccurate data, the complexities of mixed public–private funding options, as well as so-called "political economy" issues such as weak governance and the behavioral responses to controversial projects by beneficiaries and bureaucrats (Bourguignon 2006).

Bourguignon speculated that the inability to cope with these problems accounted for the World Bank's declining use of cost-benefit techniques in infrastructure project appraisals since the 1980s. The techniques had become associated with unrealistic evaluations and failed projects and consequently were no longer widely used even on conventional Bank lending projects even though Bank policy required the application of cost–benefit analysis on all its projects at appraisal.

Several years later, an evaluation by the World Bank's Independent Evaluation Group found that the use of cost–benefit analysis had dropped from 70 percent of all projects in 1970 to 25 percent in 2008, largely because of problems with data and the difficulties in quantifying costs and benefits (IEG 2010). The 2012 G24 report prepared by staff from the London School of Economics clearly had some of this background in mind: "MDBs [...] do not have adequate instruments to crowd-in private investment or address

policy risks [...] they are often also unable to adequately assess risk-return profiles ..." (Bhattacharya et al. 2012, 6).

The difficulty in articulating an effective MDB role in PPP project preparation reflects an issue discussed in Chapter 2. Evaluations of the World Bank's power sector work during the structural adjustment programs of the 1990s found that the Bank's 1993 power sector policy presented a basic approach to reform, promoting IPP projects, concessions, and management contracts within a wider context of structural sector reforms. But the policy was not accompanied by specific strategic or operational guidance on how to prioritize and sequence reforms to achieve an overall reform package of the desired kind. World Bank staff were expected to "learn by doing," which the later evaluation found did not happen (Manibog et al. 2003, vi). The reason for the lack of guidance was the fact that there was no consensus about how the upstream project environment should be best reformed to support PPPs.

The discussion in Chapter 3 regarding the different recommendations regarding regulatory arrangements for the pricing of infrastructure services suggests that this lack of consensus continued well into the 2000s. The documents produced in 2010 and 2011 describing the G20's new PPP-centered infrastructure strategy (and the World Bank's infrastructure strategy update) describe what would be done and what objectives would be achieved but included very few operational details. The approach was strongly reminiscent of the "learn by doing" approach under structural adjustment. All of this raised questions about the extent to which most MDBs would be able to directly participate in PPP project preparation.

8.4.4 The Role of Donors

A major question to be answered in developing a compelling global strategy for PPP project preparation was to identify the appropriate role to be played by bilateral donors. As noted in Chapter 4, donors like DFID had begun in the early 2000s to play a strong role in PPP advocacy by financing programs and facilities like PPIAF, GPOBA, PIDG, and IFC PPP Advisory. DFID's efforts created some of the first, largest, and most long-lasting project preparation facilities (PPFs). Donors were the ideal source of grant funding needed to help pay for project preparation, for which governments were not able to pay or not inclined to do so with borrowed money.

In 2006, guided by a series of in-house technical advisors seconded from DFID and funding from PPIAF, the ICA Secretariat hired consultants to prepare and publish a user guide to donor-supported programs and facilities that at the time purported to offer preparation support for African infrastructure projects. The 60-page guide described two-dozen PPFs and supplied contact information (ICA 2006a). The list included IFC PPP Advisory as well as several PIDG facilities, but also identified many lower-profile programs and facilities as well. The global network of such facilities had been expanding precipitously since the 1990s, and the sheer size of this growing population caught ICA participants, including G20 governments and major MDBs, somewhat by surprise. Clearly the role of PPFs was a topic worthy of further investigation as the G20 began to craft its new PPP strategy.

But another unintended consequence of the 2006 guide, which simply listed PPFs without any effort to evaluate them, was to highlight the fact that this network seemed not to be having much of an impact on PPPs in regions like Africa. The network included many small PPFs, mostly offering grants to cover relatively small and specific aspects of the project preparation process. This business model was largely intentional. Most of these facilities were not established to pay for all the costs of preparing a project. Part of the reason for this was practical. If a PPF paid for all of the preparation costs of an individual PPP that failed to reach financial close, the large amount of "lost" funding would be far more difficult to justify to funding donors than a percentage of funding spread across several different projects.

However, there was also a policy reason why most PPFs did not fund 100 percent of preparation costs for PPPs. The strategy used by most of these PPFs was to provide relatively small amounts of funding to catalyze contributions and support from government owners and private partners. Over time, with enough successful demonstration projects of this kind, the expectation was that public and private project partners could be expected to "scale-up" the use of PPPs by paying for the full cost of preparation and doing projects on a fully commercial basis.

However, ICA and its secretariat had little patience for the long-term results of demonstration effects. For the ICA Secretariat, the findings of its first survey of PPFs meant only that to fully fund preparation of privately financed infrastructure investment projects in SSA, funding typically would be needed from several of these PPFs rather than from governments or others. The ICA Secretariat tried to help with the coordination of PPFs by mapping out what they called a "tunnel of funds." This was stylized arrangement of preparation facilities in an idealized project preparation sequence, which was meant to show how such PPFs might work together to cover all the preparation activities needed to fully package prospective investment projects. Figure 8.2 displays one of several "tunnel of funds" sequences considered by ICA Secretariat.

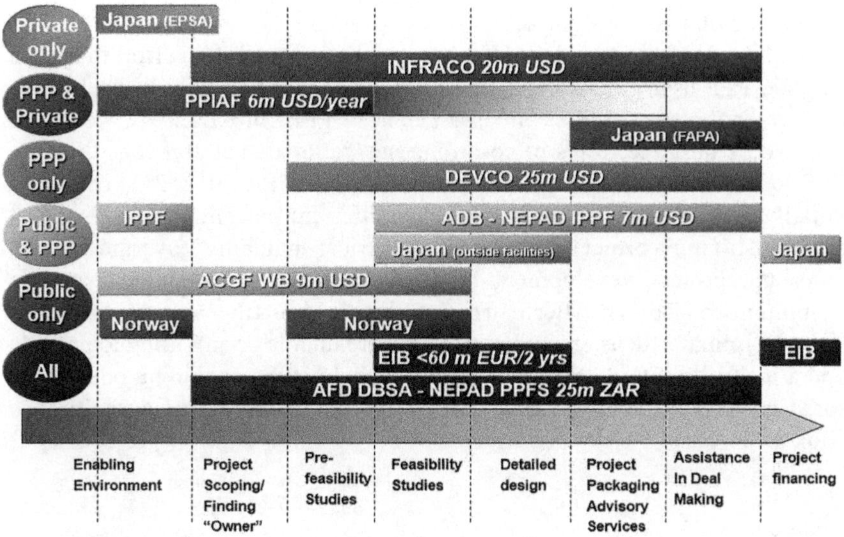

Source: ICA (2006b).

Figure 8.2 ICA's tunnel of funds

8.5 THE G20'S PROJECT PREPARATION STRATEGY: A FOCUS ON PPFS

The response by the G20 and MDBs to the investment needs described by the AICD study in 2010 took a more aggressive "tunnel of funds" approach than the ICA Secretariat had contemplated. The G20 focused on converting the haphazard collection of existing PPFs into a much better resourced and coordinated network of facilities that could take on a much more significant share of preparation work per project and deal with much larger, regional projects when necessary. A draft discussion document prepared by the World Bank in 2011 went a step further in proposing a new, much larger PPF to develop transformational infrastructure projects in Africa. The discussion document suggested that the Bank host and manage the new facility (World Bank 2011a).

This approach was outlined in G20 and MDB documents by 2011. But to add more weight to this PPF-centered argument, in 2012 the G20 Development Working Group requested that ICA further evaluate the performance of African-oriented PPFs. The Working Group was hoping to confirm its assumption that the shortcomings of this network of PPFs were a probable reason why regional, transformational projects with private participation were achieving so few contract closures.

The ICA Secretariat undertook this evaluation as part of an effort to update its 2006 PPF user guide. Consultants who produced the original user guide were re-engaged to produce an assessment of PPFs in Africa, "… to establish, where possible, ways of co-ordinating, rationalising and consolidating PPF activities to improve overall performance" (CEPA 2012, 21). The study initially identified 67 programs and facilities purporting to offer support for infrastructure project preparation in Africa, including government PPP units and project development facilities created by Regional Economic Communities (RECs). After narrowing this field to filter out facilities that lacked a primary focus on preparation or were unable or unwilling to provide operating information, the survey focused on 15 PPFs, including ones sponsored by PIDG, the World Bank, IFC, and other development institutions (Box 8.1).

BOX 8.1 INFRASTRUCTURE PPFS ACTIVE IN SSA, ICA SECRETARIAT SURVEY, 2012

1. The New Partnership for African Development Infrastructure Project Preparation Fund (NEPAD IPPF)
2. New Economic Partnership for Africa's Development Project Preparation and Feasibility Study (NEPAD PPFS)
3. Common Market for Eastern and Southern Africa Project Preparation Implementation Unit (COMESA PPIU)
4. South African Development Community Project Preparation & Development Facility (SADC PPDF)
5. U.S. Agency for International Development Africa Infrastructure Program (USAID AIP)
6. Arab Financing Facility for Infrastructure Technical Assistance Facility (AFFI TAF)
7. The Global Infrastructure Project Development Fund (IFC InfraVentures)
8. Public–Private Infrastructure Advisory Facility (PPIAF—World Bank)
9. The Development Bank of Southern Africa—European Investment Bank Project Development and Support Facility (DBSA–EIB PDSF)

10. African Development Bank African Water Facility (AfDB–AWF)
11. European Union–Africa Infrastructure Trust Fund (EU–AITF)
12. Energy Sector Management Assistance Program (ESMAP—World Bank)
13. PIDG Technical Assistance Facility (PIDG TAF)
14. InfraCo Africa (PIDG)
15. Infrastructure Development Collaboration Partnership Fund (DevCo–IFC–PIDG)

Source: CEPA (2012).

The findings of ICA's 2012 PPF assessment confirmed the assumptions already articulated by the HLP and MDBs about PPF shortcomings, but raised serious questions about the practicality of collaboratively linking together existing PPFs in ICA's "tunnel of funds":

- *Small size but poor prospects for collaboration.* The study concluded that although at first sight it seemed that many project preparation facilities existed to support infrastructure projects in SSA, the amounts of money available to each were relatively small, the focus of most of the facilities (and the range of potential beneficiaries) was narrow, and very few facilities worked with the private sector or helped with early stage project preparation. Perhaps most important, the facilities displayed almost no willingness or ability to coordinate or collaborate with each other. In general, the report recommended consolidating or closing PPFs to make more funding available to the best performing facilities.
- *Poor cost recovery.* The ICA study argued that the main reason for a widespread lack of PPF sustainability was their inability to recover the costs of preparation from successful projects. Most PPFs evaluated in the study used grant funding for all project preparation activities, with no attempt to capture reimbursements even for late-stage support. This not only threatened sustainability of the PPFs, but also created a degree of moral hazard because free resources were unlikely to be treated with the same degree of care as repayable resources. The study explicitly supported the MDB Infrastructure Action Plan argument that PPFs too frequently used grants "... where more recoverable resources should have been used" (CEPA 2012, 76).
- *Lack of upstream focus.* In the view of the ICA consultants, a glaring weakness of most of the PPFs evaluated was the almost total absence of focus on upstream preparation. For example, facilities that were integrated into and managed by MDBs were typically used exclusively by their hosting entities to support projects in later stages of develop-

> ment, close to financial close. Facilities in this category included facilities funded by the European Investment Bank (EIB) and hosted by the Development Bank of Southern Africa (DBSA), as well as the European Commission's European Union–Africa Infrastructure Trust Fund (EU–Africa ITF, the largest of these facilities). Because of pressure from their hosts, these facilities were usually reluctant to support early-stage project development work.

The study concluded with recommendations to scale-up the resources of selected, existing PPFs to enhance their focus on priority regional projects, while closing down smaller, non-viable PPFs. But the report also left open the possibility of a solution more like that proposed by the World Bank's Financial Solutions Unit in the 2011 discussion paper cited above:

> Where these recommendations fail to deliver the desired results within an acceptable timescale, the establishment of a new entity should be considered [...] In our view, a strong case exists for establishing a stand-alone entity, with its own legal personality, focused exclusively on infrastructure preparation [...] This kind of new facility will require African budgetary resources and support from new donors as well as traditional ones. (CEPA 2012, 17)

By 2012, the G20 Working Group had commissioned a study of PPFs in Asia, "Assessment of Project Preparation Facilities in Asia" (ASI 2014). Along with the ICA report on Africa-oriented PPFs, the Working Group had what it called "a substantial evidence base" for its recommendations regarding infrastructure project preparation, most of which were already anticipated in the MDB Infrastructure Action Plan and other reports.

A third study commissioned by the G20 Working Group, "Misperception of Risk and Return in Low Income Countries," was an assessment of investment risks and returns in low-income countries (LICs) (Roland Berger 2012). The study purported to offer strong justification for the G20's position, fundamental to the G20 focus on project preparation, which maintained that inadequate preparation was a principal reason why infrastructure investment in LICs was so limited. The study concluded that inadequate preparation resulted in the systematic over-estimation of project risks in LICs. Accurate assessment of project risks, along with efforts to strengthen the upstream project environment, were said to be particularly important considering the G20's effort to target institutional investors estimated by OECD to hold over $65 trillion in assets at the end of 2009 (Della Croce et al. 2011). These investors had never demonstrated much interest in infrastructure because of their risk-averse approaches to investment. However, without substantial increases in ODA, access to additional "non-traditional" sources of finance like that controlled by pension funds, insurance companies, and sovereign wealth funds was essential for large transformational infrastructure projects to be possible and infrastructure needs, like those estimated by AICD, addressed.[7]

8.6 THE DEVELOPMENT COMMUNITY'S RESPONSE: A COMPETITION FOR PPF RESOURCES

G20 discussions emphasizing the need for MDBs to take the lead on the preparation of regional infrastruture projects triggered a competition for PPF resources similar to one that occurred in Africa after the publication of the NEPAD STAP agenda in the early 2000s. Beginning in 2013, regional and international MDBs hurried to design and set up new and improved PPFs, along the lines of the G20 discussions, so that these new entities could attract significant shares of the large amounts of additional preparation funding being discussed. A 2018 survey of 10 MDBs found that all of them established at least one PPF, and half had two or more (EBRD 2019). Over 80 percent of these PPFs had been established since 2015. Box 8.2 presents a selection of high-profile MDB approaches to project preparation formulated in the wake of the 2011 G20 Infrastructure Action Plan.

BOX 8.2 SELECTED INFRASTRUCTURE PROJECT PREPARATION & FINANCE FACILITIES CREATED SINCE 2012

- Africa50—2013 (AfDB)
- Asia Pacific Project Preparation Facility (AP3F)—2014 (AsDB)
- Global Infrastructure Hub (GIH)—2014 (G20)
- Global Infrastructure Facility (GIF)—2015 (WB)
- Infrastructure Project Preparation Facility (IPPF)—2015 (EBRD)
- IDA Private Sector Window—2017 (World Bank Group)

Source: Compiled by the author.

---

[7] This case for the over-estimation of project risks was not supported by a more extensive follow-up study conducted jointly by the Organisation for Economic Co-operation and Development (OECD) and the World Bank Group. The subsequent study, requested by the G20 Development Working Group in 2014, concluded that the general lack of quantitative data available on the risk and return characteristics of infrastructure projects in LICs meant that it was not possible to draw definitive conclusions about whether or not risks were being misperceived (OECD and World Bank Group 2015).

8.6.1 Africa50

Africa50 was the first, and in some ways the most ambitious example of this new generation of PPFs. It was established on a unilateral basis by the AfDB without the prior blessing of the G20, unlike most of the later PPFs created by MDBs (although G20 reports later endorsed Africa50). The ICA evaluation of PPFs, conducted under the supervision of the AfDB-hosted ICA Secretariat, had recommended the creation of a new "super PPF" only after consideration was given to transforming an existing PPF, like the AfDB's NEPAD Infrastructure Project Preparation Facility (IPPF), into an enhanced facility to prepare regional projects. But the ICA evaluation preempted its own recommendation by raising fundamental questions about the NEPAD IPPF's performance. After a decade of operation, IPPF still seemed unable to meet the technical challenges inherent in managing the full spectrum of preparation work:

> The additional organisational/ institutional, technical and financing challenges created by PPPs and regional projects […] has raised requirements in term of such skills and competencies and the financial resources required to provide them […] many if not most of the PPFs, have underestimated these challenges, but in certain instances, particularly in the case of IPPF, the gap between PPF ambition and ability to deliver has been extremely difficult to bridge. (CEPA, 2012, Vol. 1, 40)

The message of the ICA evaluation seems to have resonated with AfDB management. In July 2013, AfDB established Africa50 as a multi-billion-dollar preparation and financing facility targeting large PIDA-like infrastructure projects in Africa. Its stated purpose was "… to unlock private financing sources […] and […] accelerate the speed of infrastructure delivery in Africa" (AfDB 2013a). AfDB's initial presentations on Africa50 to its Board of Directors anticipated that two "business lines" would be needed for the facility to achieve its goals.

The first business line was a revolving project preparation fund, "Project Development" (PD), which was expected to cut the project preparation time to financial close from what was said to be the current average of seven years to less than three years. This fund would recover its costs from governments or private developers (plus a premium to cover losses on unsuccessful projects) either by taking repayment at project financial close or via carried interest shares in closed projects. Such a fund would meet its objectives by making "… skilled legal, technical and financial experts available to projects from an early stage of development" (AfDB 2013a, 2). It would also build on what AfDB claimed were its "recent successes" in overcoming early-stage project development bottlenecks and make use of AfDB's convening power to mobilize political support for necessary legal-regulatory reforms.

The second Africa50 business line was a financing fund, "Project Finance" (PF), which would collect large amounts of capital and make project investments available via bridge equity, senior secured loans, credit enhancements, refinancing, secondary transactions, etc. As part of this strategy, AfDB planned to raise debt in the international capital markets to augment Africa50's ability to finance its project pipeline. Much of this debt was expected to come from African countries themselves. AfDB hoped to raise as much as $22 billion by issuing bonds that African countries would buy using their foreign exchange reserves. To back the bond issue, Africa50 would be set up as a commercial corporate entity, legally and financially separate from the AfDB, with a credit rating of at least single-A to signal strong creditworthiness and an intention to preserve its capital base.

All of this was intended to mobilize non-traditional sources of finance such as institutional investors and international investment banks, in keeping with the global financial market changes after the 2007 financial crisis. The separate legal status also would allow Africa50 to circumvent the prudential limits of the existing AfDB financing windows, presumably including tight restrictions on what constituted a "regional" infrastructure project. AfDB calculated that it needed an early equity investment in this fund of $10 billion to achieve its aim of leveraging over $100 billion in investment.

Africa50's 2020 annual report indicated that after five years of full-time operation, the two business lines were struggling with the basic calculus of infrastructure project preparation in poor countries. The combination of too few projects reaching financial close and the high costs of project preparation meant that preparation costs of all the targeted projects could not be fully recovered from those few projects reaching financial closure. Table 8.1 indicates the annual profits and losses of the two Africa50 business lines from 2017 to 2021. The cumulative operating loss over this period was over $22.5

Table 8.1 *Annual profits and loss of Africa50's business lines, 2017–21*

Year	Project development	Project finance
2017	−30,068	−3,500,336
2018	−4,122,857	−3,062,253
2019	−9,258,560	277,742
2020	−5,898,875	4,340,662
2021	−8,805,000	7,555,000
Total	*−28,115,360*	*5,610,815*

Note: Figures shown are in $US.
Source: Africa50 Annual Reports.

million (in 2022, for the first time, Africa50's audited financial statements were not included in the annual report).

In 2020, Project Development expenses totaled over $11 million, while its revenue totaled just over $5 million, representing the most annual revenue ever generated. But this increase was mainly due to an innovative accounting practice introduced in 2020 for the first time. Almost all of this revenue ($4.7 million) was derived from fees charged to the sister fund, Project Finance, for "preferential access" to Project Development's pipeline, which in 2020 included only three projects to which preparation funding had been committed. Details of exactly what this access entailed, or why the access fee was so large, were not included in the annual report. The second business line, Project Finance, generated a profit of $4.3 million in 2020, about $1.6 million short of covering the total losses of the organization, resulting in an Africa50 overall operating loss for the fourth year in succession.

As of early 2021, Africa50 was pursuing a "recalibrated strategy" that apparently included expanding the sectors allowed for investment, considering project investments smaller than the original target of $20–80 million per project and exploring more opportunities to take minority stakes in projects. In 2021, Project Finance profit surged, driven by a "revaluation" of existing investments, but Project Development losses also surged, despite a $2.4 million fee paid by its sister fund.

8.6.2 The Global Infrastructure Facility (GIF)

A principal G20 response to the challenges outlined in the MDB Infrastructure Action Plan and reports of the Development Working Group was the official endorsement in 2014 of the Global Infrastructure Facility (GIF), a new multi-donor trust fund hosted and managed by the World Bank. The World Bank had proposed for some time that it should manage the preparation of transformational PPP projects using large amounts of IDA funding (World Bank 2011a; IDA 2013). GIF was also consistent with the recommendation of the ICA study (CEPA 2012) that a new "super PPF" should be created if it was found that scaling up existing PPFs, like the AfDB's NEPAD IPPF, would not be productive. (By creating Africa50, AfDB had already acknowledged that the IPPF was not the appropriate vehicle for this.)

GIF was formally established in April 2015. Its initial five-year pilot phase was funded with a capitalization of $94 million, contributed by Australia, Canada, China, Japan, Singapore, and the World Bank. GIF's structure and operations were tailored specifically to meet the recommendations of the Development Working Group reports and MDB Infrastructure Action Plan. In a 2014 report to the G20, the World Bank confirmed the GIF was not being created as one more conventional PPF, like the ones reviewed in the

ICA study. Rather, it was designed using a "fund of funds" approach. Its mission was to "coordinate and integrate" the efforts of the existing network of entities involved in the preparation and financing of "complex" infrastructure projects—MDBs, DFIs, donors, private investors, and governments. "Complex projects" were defined as those that required multiple parties to work together to structure, arrange, and provide financial support, as well as projects that required a blend of financial or risk mitigation instruments to attract long-term commercial finance. The definition emphasized projects that "... provide services to multiple countries or have a regional impact" (GIF 2015b, 3).

In other words, GIF activities would not be developed directly by GIF, but by "Technical Partners," to whom GIF funds would be transferred. The original Technical Partners were six MDBs: AfDB; AsDB; EBRD; EIB; IDB; and the World Bank Group. Eventually, several other MDBs became Technical Partners: AIIB, IsDB, and MIGA. "Advisory Partners," mostly from the private sector, included institutional investors, commercial banks, DFIs, and other organizations. GIF coordination of these actors was required to ensure "... collaboration and collective action on complex projects that no single institution could realize alone" (GIF 2014, 1). GIF would provide "end-to-end support," from upstream preparation through downstream structuring and transaction advice.

GIF's focus on projects with commercial potential and the ability to attract long-term private capital was expected to facilitate the recovery of GIF costs: "The bulk of the GIF's disbursements for project preparation and structuring are expected to be recovered through eventual reimbursement or fees upon successful project close" (3). Poverty reduction and sustainable growth were among GIF's targeted impacts, but GIF's operating guidelines required that only 20 percent of its activities be in LICs (GIF 2015a, 3). The GIF Results Framework admitted that "The GIF is not structured to monitor long term impact—that is, to what extent GIF-supported projects contribute to its ultimate development goals of poverty reduction and inclusive and sustainable growth in EMDEs [Emerging Markets and Developing Economies]" (GIF 2015b, 12).

By October 2018 it had become clear that GIF's funding would be depleted well before the pilot program end-date (June 30, 2020), and GIF launched a capital replenishment campaign (Danida 2019). By the end of the five-year pilot period in June 2020, GIF had approved a total of 93 project activities across 47 countries, in collaboration with five Technical Partners. The GIF's 2021 report to its donors claimed that it had "... successfully demonstrated its business model" by developing a robust pipeline and achieving its key targets (GIF 2021a). This judgment was reportedly based on a 2018 mid-term review conducted by independent consultants.

But GIF numbers present a different picture. By June 30, 2021, GIF had allocated $107.4 million of the funding it had received from donors. About 28 percent of this funding was used for administrative costs or fees paid to MDB Technical Partners, leaving 72 percent for projects. Only $1.2 million had been recovered by GIF via reflows from Technical Partners. Of the funding for projects, 8.8 percent went to LICs, well below the original 20 percent target. In terms of support for Technical Partners, 84 percent of GIF funding was used by the World Bank Group, raising questions about the extent to which actual coordination of multiple MDB-based PPFs was being achieved. Only two projects had reached financial closure over the five-year pilot period (GIF 2021a). In financial year 2021, GIF reported that four additional projects had reached financial closure.

The GIF projects reaching financial closure in 2021 included a street-lighting program in Brazil; port concessions in Ukraine; an airport in Bulgaria; and a telecommunications concession in Ethiopia (GIF 2021a, 11). Each of these projects was "complex" in the sense that more than one Technical Partner was involved. But exactly how these projects met other GIF eligibility requirements, and what GIF did to play a meaningful role in these projects (other than make grant funding available to Technical Partners) is not clear from published reports.

Faced with the need to seek funding replenishment for a marginally successful donor-funded program, GIF's 2021 reports to stakeholders requested massive new funding amounts well beyond what would be needed for simple replenishment. This increase was said to be required for the purposes of "Amplifying GIF's existing, validated business model" (GIF 2021b, 22). But presumably the funding increase would also help address GIF's overall weak project performance. GIF argued that funding scale-up was needed because, even though GIF was originally designed to provide "end-to-end support" both upstream and downstream, its performance had been limited by its lack of funding at both ends of the spectrum.

GIF reports offered no analysis or even anecdotal evidence to substantiate these funding requests. In lieu of that, the reports did include effusive testimonials from representatives of Technical and Advisory Partners who opined regarding the important role that GIF would play if its resources were increased. According to the GIF Advisory Council Co-chair: "[The GIF] should go from being 'pilot' to 'permanent' and, moreover, the GIF should be scaled-up massively, commensurate with the massive challenges of providing adequate infrastructure to people in the developing world" (GIF 2021b, 34).

In financial year 2022, GIF took steps to fully implement a "new strategic model" by intensifying upstream enabling environment support through a "scaled-up GIF approach," the introduction of a "Go-Deep product" involving comprehensive scans of emerging sustainable infrastructure project opportunities, as well as efforts to begin conceptualizing an "… upstream-to-downstream link through a concrete project pipeline and financing opportunities" (GIF 2022, 15). During 2022, GIF spent another $19 million on projects and claimed credit for three more financial closures.

8.7 THE MYTH OF THE PREPARATION GAP

The G20 infrastructure strategy developed by its working groups and MDBs was based on assumptions rather than evaluation and analysis but nevertheless became another powerful tool in support of PPP advocacy. The strategy was presented with little evidence to make a compelling case for the existence, much less importance, of a "project preparation gap," as opposed to the more traditional concept of an "investment gap":

- G20 reports had no basis on which to claim that the PPP track record suggested that a much larger future role in infrastructure investment could be played by PPPs. The G20 reports claimed that PPPs were already contributing as much as 30 percent of existing infrastructure investment (G20 2014). But it was clear from the PPI Database and various PPIAF studies that the figure was much lower, particularly in LICs. In 2019, a first comprehensive effort by the World Bank to research this question found that the private investment share in Africa, a G20 regional priority, was 5 percent (World Bank 2019c, 4).
- The claim that careful, well-funded project preparation, including upstream reforms to laws, regulations, and procedures, was needed to "enable" successful PPPs had been made about such projects since the World Bank's 2002 Private Sector Development Strategy (see Chapter 3). However, none of the G20 reports on PPFs or project preparation in general offered any compelling evidence or analysis confirming that under-funded project preparation was a more important reason for the lack of PPPs in poor countries than the fundamental reality of PPPs, that the resource expenditure needed for projects to reach sustainable levels of operation is almost impossible to justify on a value-for-money basis.
- Even if poor preparation could be shown to be a reason why PPPs have not been more widely successful, precisely how best to prepare successful projects, and how to do it cost-effectively, have never been clearly explained. Chapter 3 describes how the World Bank struggled in the early 2000s to arrive at best-practice recommendations for PPP-friendly legal-regulatory frameworks. That struggle has never ended. The World Bank's 2020 rankings of PPP legal and regulatory frameworks in 140 countries draws no clear correlation between "best-practice" framework

elements and PPP success, and therefore makes no recommendations regarding which of the many alternative framework elements surveyed are most important in facilitating PPPs (World Bank 2020).

- No rigorous analysis was presented by the G20 working groups confirming that the private sector was "misperceiving" the risks of PPPs in LICs. The Asian financial crisis beginning in 1997 had sharpened the private sector's appreciation of PPP risks in developing countries and contributed to a precipitous decline in such projects—it took 12 years for PPP investment in developing countries to recover in real terms (Leigland 2018). Ongoing cases of project collapses and renegotiations helped reinforce private sector risk perceptions. The 2012 paper commissioned by the G20 offered a dramatic argument claiming that risks to private investment were being systematically over-estimated in LICs (Roland Berger 2012). But the far more rigorous follow-up study by the OECD and World Bank (2015b) found no evidence of this.
- There was also no evidence presented that regional or cross-border infrastructure projects could be widely successful with more or better preparation. In fact, the evidence suggested that such projects would not be routinely successful regardless of how much was spent on preparation. The PPI Database confirmed that no developing country region had hosted significant numbers of multi-country PPP projects. It was well known that programs like IFC PPP Advisory and PIDG, not to mention private sponsors and investors, avoided such projects in LICs, opting instead for much smaller, less complicated, and less risky projects. Even with that reduced focus, these PPFs had limited success developing PPPs.
- Recovery of project preparation costs has proved to be almost impossible in LICs, as the experience of IFC PPP Advisory and PIDG has confirmed. Preparation costs in such countries are too high to be routinely covered by combinations of success fees and affordable retainers paid by governments. Plus, not enough projects reach financial closure for "claw-backs" from successful projects to cover the costs of unsuccessful ones. PIDG and IFC PPP Advisory required substantial amounts of donor grant funding to subsidize on-going project preparation in LICs; Africa50 and GIF have had no more success, despite more determined commitments to recover costs.
- Finally, as one World Bank researcher has put it, "… encouraging institutional investors to invest in private-sector infrastructure projects has been the holy grail of infrastructure financing for more than two decades" (PPIAF 2018). As a result, a significant amount of research has been undertaken to understand why institutional investors have been so reluctant to invest in infrastructure, particularly in poor countries. The risk-averse nature of institutional investors is motivated by a unique mix

of operating cost tolerances, financial regulations, return expectations, risk appetites, and portfolio-diversification targets. Better preparation of infrastructure projects is simply not enough to attract these investors to PPPs with high project and political risks and relatively low returns. PPIAF's 2018 study of institutional investor support for PPPs found no evidence to suggest that better project preparation or defining infrastructure as an investment asset class would successfully attract such investors to projects in developing countries (PPIAF 2018).[8]

8.8 CONCLUSIONS

By transforming the infrastructure finance problem into a project preparation one, this new strategic approach adopted by the G20 and its MDBs became a convenient distraction from the reality of PPPs in poor countries, which was already coming into focus through the work of practitioners in the mid-2000s: PPPs of any kind are so difficult and expensive to do, and resulting contracts are so fragile, that PPPs rarely are able to generate enough sustained revenues to outweigh the costs of preparation, financing, and operation. All of this was particularly true in LICs and with large, complicated projects, like regional, multi-country PPPs.

The distraction was convenient in several ways. First, it offered a plausible explanation for why the private sector was not solving infrastructure investment problems, as it was expected to do beginning with the rise in neoclassical economic thinking that underpinned structural adjustment lending programs in the 1980s. If project preparation was the problem holding back PPPs, then there was no need to question the confident belief that subjecting government-owned and managed infrastructure service systems to market forces and competitive pressures through some form of private participation would solve problems with financing and management.

Second, the distraction was also convenient for the international development community, donors and MDBs, because it helped perpetuate the belief that the private sector could, and therefore should, play a much larger role in sharing the massive investment burden created by what economists like William Easterly (2009) called the "do everything" approach initiated

---

[8] Many attempts to define infrastructure as an asset class had already been frustrated by the time that the G20's new strategy for infrastructure investment was being developed. This failure is usually attributed to the fact that broad definitions of an infrastructure asset class inevitably overlap with other asset classes and are therefore of little value for the purposes of adjusting strategic asset allocation to achieve portfolio diversification (Idzorek and Armstrong 2009).

by the MDGs. By setting up larger and better-managed PPFs, focusing on transformational, regional projects, and targeting long-term private sector finance, donors and MDBs could distract from their responsibility for the slow international response to the massive infrastructure deficits that the AICD study suggested may have been drastically mismanaged by donors and MDBs, at least in terms of the sector allocation of official development assistance (ODA) resources.[9]

[9] The G20's strategic shift to a focus on project preparation did not go unnoticed by the civil society critics of private participation in infrastructure. However, they tended to see the shift as less of a distraction and more of a brazen effort to satisfy "... private investors looking for high return" (Rohde 2015, 6).

PART IV

What have we learned about PPPs?

9. The costs and benefits of the transaction-only approach

9.1 INTRODUCTION

What have three decades of PPP advocacy taught us about public–private partnerships in developing countries? This chapter explores what we now know about the "transaction-only approach." Starting in the early 2000s, this approach is exemplified in the work of project preparation facilities (PPFs) like IFC's PPP Advisory and the Private Infrastructure Development Group (PIDG). It is now the preferred operating strategy used by hundreds of PPFs operating in multiple infrastructure sectors across the developing world, including the latest generation of PPFs like Africa50 and the Global Infrastructure Facility (GIF).

The transaction-only approach is based on several assumptions: First, with enough money and specialized expertise, sustainable infrastructure PPPs can be prepared and structured in the poorest developing countries. "Upstream" reforms, needed to create the ideal conditions for PPPs and ensure that PPP implementation results in expected benefits, can be implemented in parallel with project structuring, or even after projects are structured and the need for necessary reforms better understood. PPFs adopting this approach assume that upstream work is better left to development partners with the resources and long-term performance perspectives needed to facilitate legal and regulatory reforms, policy upgrades, capacity building, etc. In the meantime, project structuring by PPFs can and should carry on.

The second major assumption of the transaction-only approach is based on an acknowledgement that PPF project work can never by itself significantly close the infrastructure investment gap in the developing world. The gap, first documented by the *African Infrastructure Country Diagnostic* (AICD) study, is simply too large and the project "hit rates" of PPFs, even all of the largest PPFs combined, are far too low to even keep pace with, much less close, the ever-widening investment gap. But the PPF approach assumes that its value is in the demonstration effects generated by successful PPPs. The contention is that by completing even relatively small numbers of PPP projects, PPFs can successfully demonstrate the commercial or near-commercial viability of PPPs in a way that will incentivize more PPPs and broader market creation in developing countries. This is expected to happen as more and more prospective public and private partners observe the results of successful project structuring and are consequently encouraged to emulate the PPP approach.

But this transaction-only approach has not worked as expected, especially in the poorest countries. Some PPPs have reached financial closure in these countries and the numbers of projects and investment levels since the 1990s continue to fluctuate erratically. By 2012, total PPP investment in real terms had grown to a level that was approximately 80 percent higher than the previous peak in 1997. However, by 2020 the total had dropped again to roughly half the 1997 total. Since 2010, a variety of published assessments of regional and global spending on infrastructure in developing countries have estimated the private share of investment in most developing country regions to be in the range of about 5–20 percent (with a higher total for Latin America).

These assessments suggest that the private financing revolution expected in the mid-1990s never took place, despite the work of the global population of PPFs and their funding partners. But PPP advocates are encouraged by the fact that there seems to be no evidence that such a revolution cannot yet happen if PPFs and PPP units work harder to help PPPs gain traction in the developing world. This is the message delivered by advocates to bilateral donors and other development partners who fund most of the PPFs reviewed in this book. And PPP advocates have been extraordinarily successful in conveying this message.

This chapter examines these two basic assumptions underlying this transaction-only approach:

- What do we know now about "successful" PPP projects? Because success ultimately depends on the ability to attract private investment, what kinds of projects, in which infrastructure sectors, are preferred by the private sector? What kinds of projects do private investors avoid?
- Under what conditions are third parties (public and private) incentivized to replicate types of PPP projects in other settings or in other countries? In other words, to what extent and how do "successful" PPP projects generate demonstration effects that encourage replication?

9.2 WHAT DOES MARKET BEHAVIOR TELL US ABOUT "SUCCESSFUL" PPP PROJECTS?

9.2.1 The Dimensions of PPP Market Growth

After the Asian financial crisis, interest in PPPs in the developing world dropped sharply and remained low for seven years. The global PPP market started to rebound in 2004 and for the next eight years experienced a period of investment growth before starting another gradual decline that was exacerbated by the COVID-19 pandemic starting in 2020. In real terms, PPP investment matched the 1997 peak only after 15 years, and PPPs have exceeded that annual total in real terms only four times in the succeeding 25 years (2010, 2011, 2012, and 2015). The PPP recovery beginning in 2004 and peaking in 2012 was characterized by several key features:

- Market growth was overwhelmingly driven by major investments in *middle-income countries* (MICs), rather than in low-income countries (LICs) and least-developed countries (LDCs), the priority targets of most of the donor-funded PPFs. PPPs in LICs and LDCs have demonstrated no progress since the 1990s—attracting less than 1.4 percent of total PPP investment since 1995 (see Figure 1.2).
- Individual MICs like *India and Brazil* accounted for a large percentage of new PPP investments during this period of market growth. India introduced viability gap funding (VGF) subsidies for PPP projects in 2004, and from 2005 through 2012, over 600 PPP projects were completed, making the domestic Indian PPP market arguably the largest in the world (Government of India 2017, 92). In 2012, the independent power producer (IPP) program in Brazil accounted for over 80 percent of all greenfield power investment in the Latin America and the Caribbean (LAC) region (the LAC total was more than twice the total of any other developing country region that year).
- The PPP surge beginning in 2004 was driven almost exclusively by investments in *power and transport*—these sectors accounted for over 93 percent of all PPP-related investments. Power dominated in terms of total investment and numbers of projects. Three-quarters of all power projects exclusively involved power generation, almost all of them structured as independent power producer (IPP) projects.
- *Transport* ranked second to power in terms of total PPP investment and number of projects, with about half of all PPPs in the sector done as greenfield projects and half as brownfield projects. Road projects, mostly brownfield toll roads, constituted most of the subsector projects with over 47 percent of total global investment. Toll roads proved to be viable mostly in MICs—the usefulness of toll roads in LICs or LDCs is severely limited by a lack of vehicular traffic, combined with the inability of these governments to pay via shadow tolls or other unitary payment mechanisms that substitute for retail payments by drivers.
- Contrary to popular perceptions, projects involving investment in *information and communications technology* (ICT) have never played a significant role in global PPP market activity, and played no role in the PPP market recovery after 2004. Private investment in ICT has of course been massive, but nearly all of it has been mobilized through non-PPP mechanisms like

divestitures of state-owned telecoms, merchant projects, or purely private commercial investments. Projects in which the government role is limited only to licensing, rather than being involved in some way as a contracting authority, are generally not classified as PPPs.

- Defying conventional textbook wisdom, *greenfield PPPs*, involving the financing, construction and operation of new assets or facilities, were far more popular in developing countries after the Asian crisis than brownfield projects (involving existing facilities) and drove the recovery beginning in 2004. IPP projects, done on a greenfield basis and backed by government-guaranteed long-term take-or-pay off-take agreements, usually denominated in hard currency, emerged as the most desirable form of PPP in developing countries from the private sector's point of view.
- Since the global financial crisis in 2007–08, middle-income countries and their development partners have increasingly used a *blended finance* approach to make PPPs successful, by replacing much of the commercial finance with public money from government budgets or debt from donors, development finance institutions (DFIs), and MDBs. This is especially true for brownfield concessions. In 2015 (the first time that the World Bank differentiated public and private sources of PPP finance), private finance played a dominant role in energy sector projects, 96 percent of which were greenfield IPP projects (Table 9.1). That same year, transport projects, about half of which are brownfield projects, received more than half of their funding from governments and DFIs.

Table 9.1 *PPPs in energy and transport, sources of finance*

Source of investment	Energy sector	Transport sector
Private investment	65%	49%
Public investment	16%	41%
Development partners	19%	10%
Total investment	$31.7 billion	$20.7 billion
Percent brownfield	4%	48%

Note: All developing countries, 2015.
Source: Chao and Saha (2016).

9.2.2 The Dominance of Greenfield PPPs

The dominance of greenfield projects in the global PPP market growth achieved since the 1990s was not an intended consequence of efforts to use PPPs as structural adjustment tools in the 1980s and 1990s. Under structural adjustment, the objective was to find private sector solutions to problems with existing, or "brownfield," infrastructure service systems. These solutions were intended to make service systems better managed and less dependent on financial support from parent governments that had contributed to so much sovereign-backed over-borrowing.

Greenfield project solutions, involving private finance, construction, ownership, and management of new assets or systems, were already playing a role in private participation in infrastructure in the 1990s, but were not a structural adjustment priority largely because they were not viewed as having a direct, positive impact on the reform of existing SOEs. Greenfield projects did not represent the kind of PPP recommended by World Bank experts during the 1990s as the best way to "privatize" infrastructure service delivery (Guislain and Kerf 1995). Greenfield solutions included build–own–operate (BOO) and build–operate–transfer (BOT) projects.[1]

By the early 2000s, governments and the private sector were beginning to realize that although brownfield concessions seemed to work reasonably well in industrialized economies, they were much more problematic in the developing world, especially in the poorest countries. After reaching an investment peak in 1997, the Asian financial crisis exacted a severe toll on both brownfield and greenfield PPPs. But brownfield types took much longer to recover—15 years to match their 1997 investment total again in real terms. In 2012, middle-income countries like China and Brazil used high levels of government financial support to substitute for private investment and briefly propelled brownfield concessions back to their record 1997 investment level. Over the two decades since the onset of the Asian crisis, greenfield projects have dominated the world of PPPs in developing countries (Figure 9.1).

The ascendancy of greenfield concessions in the poorest countries has been especially dramatic. Figure 9.2 compares greenfield and brownfield PPP investment in MICs with those in LDCs and LICs. It shows that from 1996 to 2020, 83 percent of PPP investment in the poorest countries was via greenfield projects, and only 17 percent came via brownfield concessions. Over the same period, in MICs, 69 percent of PPP investments came via greenfield projects and about 31 percent from brownfield projects.

---

[1] Another widely used form of greenfield infrastructure project, which is not usually classified as a PPP, is the merchant project, involving the ownership, construction, and operation of assets by a private company at its own risk without government risk-sharing in the form of commitment to buy the services. In telecommunication or energy sectors, merchant projects normally operate in liberalized markets where the sale of services is unrestricted by a PPP contract with government—in other words, the private entity is free to sell the services to anyone who can pay.

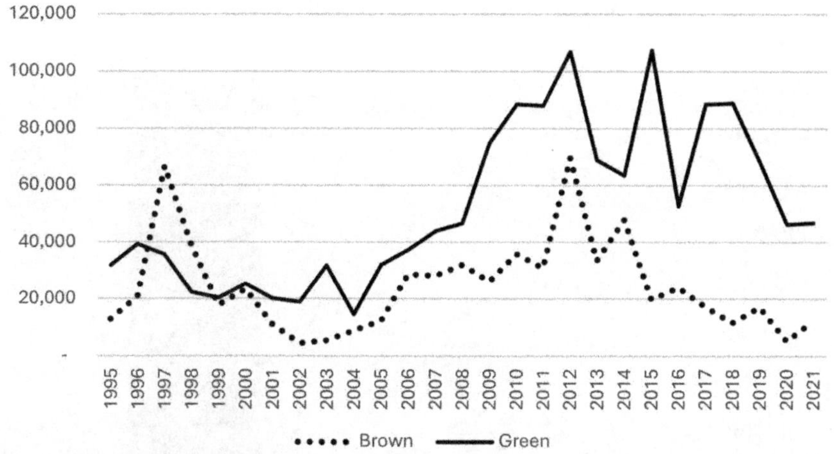

Note: US$ millions—2021 dollars.
Source: World Bank (2022).

Figure 9.1 Greenfield vs. brownfield PPPs, all developing countries, 1995–2021

In Africa, as of 2020, greenfield investment via BOTs and BOOs accounted for 78 percent of all PPP related investment since 1996 (Table 9.2). Greenfield power projects, most of which were IPP projects, made up 75 percent of greenfield investment and 60 percent of total PPP investment over that 26-year period.

9.2.3 Lessons Learned Regarding PPP Project Risks

To the extent that there was some PPP market recovery beginning in 2004, it was largely a function of investors learning how to understand and mitigate project risks, mostly by shifting risks to public partners, or simply avoiding projects in the riskiest sectors and countries, including the projects with the most pro-poor benefits (Leigland 2018).

The emerging dominance of greenfield PPPs in developing countries illustrates some of the lessons learned regarding PPP project risks. Conventional project finance wisdom argues that greenfield PPPs are inherently riskier than brownfield ones and that unless risk-weighted returns are pegged much higher to compensate for these risks, greenfield projects are less attractive to private investors. The principal risk is supposed to derive from the fact that greenfield projects typically are start-up projects that initially involve a significant investment of capital before they can start generating revenue. In contrast, brown-

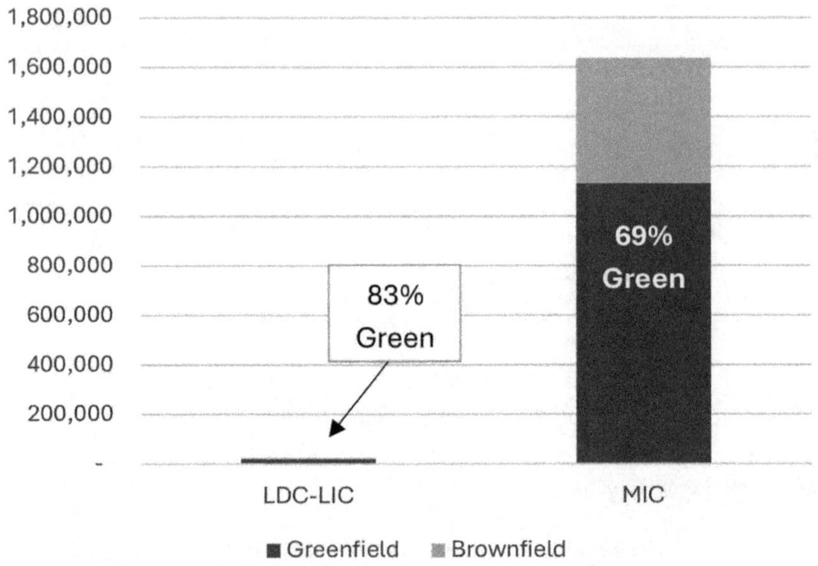

Note: US$ millions—nominal values.
Source: World Bank (2022).

Figure 9.2 *Greenfield PPPs as a percentage of all PPPs, by income status, 1995–2021*

Table 9.2 *PPP investment in SSA, 1995–2021*

Public–private partnerships								
Sectors	Brownfield Concessions		Greenfield BOTs/BOOs		Mgmt/Lease Contracts		Totals	
	US$ millions	No.	US$ millions	No.	US$ millions	No.	US$ millions	No.
Power	2,513	21	49,746	242	585	13	2,844	276
Transport	11,816	72	14,518	30	1,486	17	7,819	119
ICT	–	–	1,578	21	–	4	578	25
Water[a]	370	3	853	16	90	21	1,314	40
Totals	14,699	96	66,695	309	2,161	55	83,555	460

Notes: US$ millions—nominal values. [a] Includes sewerage and municipal solid waste.
Source: World Bank (2022).

field projects are thought to focus more on systems that are already functioning and generating at least some revenue.

The two specific types of risk that are said to be greater for greenfield PPPs than for brownfield PPPs are defined in the following ways:

- *Completion Risk.* Greenfield projects are assumed to face more "completion risk" associated with asset construction for a completely new service system because the scale of that work is much larger than construction normally would be to rehabilitate or extend a functioning service system. The larger the construction project the bigger are the challenges associated with design, construction, and choice of technology, the more likely are cost overruns, completion delays, permitting problems, flawed technology, and design mistakes. Large-size construction activity increases the challenges associated with the control and coordination of the multiple activities involved in developing and implementing the project—design, architecture, construction, finance, and operations.
- *Demand Risk.* Greenfield PPPs are also assumed to face higher levels of "demand risk" than brownfield projects because it is more difficult to estimate customer demand for new services than it would be for service systems already in operation. The developer of a greenfield PPP will not know with certainty whether demand—and resulting revenue generation—has been correctly estimated until the project commences operations and demand actually ramps up. This time-honored view holds that because brownfield concessions involve existing infrastructure assets, demand for services can be determined with a high degree of reliability from the operating track record.

These characterizations of completion and demand risks generally hold for greenfield and brownfield PPPs in industrialized countries, but much less so in developing countries. The difference can be summed up by saying that in developing countries many brownfield assets typically are in extremely poor condition. In these countries, the need for rehabilitation often reflects a situation that is different from the normal process of restoration or replacement of aging assets that is routine in industrialized countries. Rehabilitation in developing countries is often a response to years of substandard maintenance combined with inadequate performance monitoring. Not only are the assets dilapidated and neglected, but management information and basic record-keeping are frequently non-existent. Historical performance data is either inaccurate or unavailable. The precise condition, even the location, of underground assets like water pipes is often unknown. Customer records are often incomplete or missing—and it is not unusual to find that there is no way to tell how many end-users are even connected to existing service systems, much less paying their bills.

In these situations, the need for rehabilitation is often signaled not by risk-based modeling and analysis that predicts system failure, but by system breakdowns that have already occurred, requiring asset replacement rather than renewal or overhaul. These brownfield assets therefore are not classifiable as "mature operating assets" in the same way that brownfield service systems are often referred to in developed countries. In the early days of brownfield PPPs during the 1990s, poor project preparation meant that private operators were often surprised by the amount of asset investment, repair, and replacement needed to restore utility systems to full operation.

This means that completion risk is typically high for many brownfield PPPs in developing countries, because substantial new asset construction is often needed and required rehabilitation work or network extensions are larger and more costly than expected because of poor project preparation and incomplete information about operations. The poor quality of operating information also means that demand risk is high—it is often difficult to estimate customer demand and likely revenue generation for services that in terms of cost and quality are substantially different from services supplied previously.

9.2.4 New Strategies for Risk Mitigation

In practice, private sponsors of greenfield PPPs in developing countries quickly learned how to substantially mitigate completion and demand risks, especially after the project collapses during the Asian financial crisis. Completion risks were reduced by narrowly restricting the focus of greenfield projects to the construction of completely new assets and limiting as much as possible the kinds of projects taken on to well understood, standardized types and approaches. For example, private developers could repeatedly implement a succession of IPP projects in different countries using familiar BOT or BOO contracting models and power purchase agreements (PPAs), largely standardized technologies, with a suite of non-negotiable guarantees, risk mitigation instruments, and profit requirements. The outcomes of this work, in terms of cost and quality, eventually could be estimated with a high degree of certainty because the design of the work did not depend on responding to operating problems that were often unique to very different existing service systems. The need for unexpected follow-up repairs and rehabilitation to complete the work in such situations was minimal.

More importantly, demand risk for greenfield IPP projects could be handled contractually, with long-term PPAs denominated in hard currency and backed by sovereign guarantees and third-party enhancements like political risk insurance. Such contractual provisions effectively shifted demand risk to government owners of these projects. If demand or willingness to pay did not reach expected levels, governments would nevertheless be required by long-term PPAs to remunerate IPPs at originally agreed levels. Estimating demand for greenfield IPP projects became the sole responsibility of government owners, rather than private partners. The need for contract renegotiation to solve the cash flow problems of private partners was dramatically reduced.

Governments and private investors discovered early on that these characteristics of greenfield and brownfield PPPs in developing countries meant that existing project finance rules of thumb regarding the comparative risk profiles of these two kinds of projects did not apply strongly in these environments. World Bank data show that as brownfield concessions began to proliferate during the 1990s, they were significantly more likely to experience contractual distress or premature contract cancellation than greenfield concessions (World Bank 2022).

Over the two decades since the onset of the Asian crisis, greenfield projects account for most of the PPPs in developing countries. In contrast to the early 1990s, when recommendations and funding support from donors and MDBs gave investors comfort regarding brownfield concessions, these projects are now viewed as highly risky. Projects with the following risk mitigation characteristics have become by far the most popular with private investors and sponsors:

1. The financing, construction, and management of mostly new infrastructure assets; minimized investment in the rehabilitation of government assets (meaning that governments or government-owned utilities retain responsibility for dealing with existing assets that may have been poorly designed, built, or maintained).
2. The provision of wholesale as opposed to retail services, with payments for privately provided services made by a single government entity rather than thousands of retail end-users (meaning that all aspects of retail distribution—customer care, quality of service delivery, collection of end-user tariff payments, credit control, etc.—and all other aspects of sector and utility management remain the exclusive responsibility of governments or government-owned utilities).
3. Dollar-denominated payments made annually or biannually pursuant to long-term contracts regardless of the currency in which project revenues are generated (meaning that governments or government-owned utilities retain all risk associated with changes in exchange rates in cases where project revenues are in local currency).
4. Contract payments made on a "take-or-pay basis," requiring that payments be made if the service is available, whether or not the service is actually used (meaning that all demand risk associated with end-user unwilling-

ness or inability to pay for the service is retained by the government or government-owned utility).
5. Payments backed by sovereign guarantees as well as third-party guarantees like political risk guarantees (PRGs) or Multilateral Investment Guarantee Association (MIGA) guarantees (meaning that national governments make their strongest possible promise to pay and agree to the intervention of an international organization like the World Bank if payments are not made).

The importance for private investors and sponsors of the risk mitigation characteristics listed above explains why IPP projects, done on a greenfield (BOT or BOO) basis, often backed by take-or-pay, dollar-denominated PPAs, sovereign guarantees, and PRG or MIGA enhancements, represent by far the most widely used form of PPP in developing countries and the type of project most widely promoted by PPFs, like IFC PPP Advisory, PIDG, and others.

9.3 WHAT DO WE KNOW ABOUT DEMONSTRATION EFFECTS?

9.3.1 Case Study: Kigali Bulk Water PPP

The experience of PPP advocacy over the last 30 years has demonstrated that with enough money and specialized expertise, greenfield BOT or BOO projects can be done in many of the poorest countries, especially if the projects involve power generation (IPPs) or toll roads. These kinds of projects can often reach financial close without the need for "upstream" reforms because the various risk mitigation characteristics mentioned earlier are designed to protect private partners against various shortcomings in the upstream legal and policy environments in which these projects must operate.

No matter how much PPFs like the PIDG companies focused their work on greenfield IPP projects, their project work could never by itself significantly close the infrastructure investment gap in the developing world. But most of these facilities and programs operate under the assumption that the demonstration effects of even a few successful commercial or near-commercial projects will lead to project replication and market development.

Demonstration effects represent a phenomenon that is repeatedly referred to in the strategies of donors, DFIs, and MDBs. PIDG's five-year strategy emphasized the group's focus on "demonstration effects," "pioneering projects," and "catalytic effects" (e.g., PIDG 2019a). The World Bank Group's (WBG's) Independent Evaluation Group has identified demonstration effects generated by "pioneering investments" often involving "early movers" as among the most important "channels" through which group members like the

IFC and MIGA have tried to achieve long-standing WBG objectives of replication and market development (IEG 2019, 23). In its evaluation of the WBG's work on PPPs, IEG noted the potentially powerful impacts of demonstration effects even on upstream reforms: "Bank Group-supported transactions often created a market for PPPs through their demonstration effects and, at times, helped shape the regulatory environment. Demonstration and replication effects of individual PPPs may be as important as the actual transaction" (IEG 2015, 143).

Greenfield BOT projects now dominate the global PPP market in developing countries, so the many PPFs that continue to focus on these kinds of projects are rarely demonstrating anything new. But finding ways of using greenfield BOT models in a sector like water and sanitation, where the private sector has struggled to find a foothold, could be a significant test of the market development impacts of demonstration effects.

A greenfield BOT water project of that kind reached financial close in Rwanda in 2017 and began operations in 2021. The US$60.8 million project is known as the Kigali Bulk Water PPP. It supplies 40 million cubic meters of potable water per day to the government-owned and operated water distribution utility, known as the Water and Sanitation Corporation (WASAC). WASAC is responsible for retail water sales to end-users like households and businesses.

The project has been hailed in various local and international publications as "Africa's first water PPP" (e.g., Rwahigi 2015; Thomson Reuters 2018). It has won a host of "project of the year awards" (e.g., Africa Investor Awards 2018; *Infrastructure Journal* Global Awards 2018; Global Water Awards 2018; Principles for Responsible Investment Awards 2019). The project has also been celebrated as the only way to sufficiently scale-up private investment in the water sectors of developing countries to meet development objectives like the SDGs (Cattaneo 2018).

A number of leading development organizations collaborated to make this project possible—including IFC PPP Advisory, PIDG's Emerging Africa Infrastructure Fund (EAIF), the Multilateral Investment Guarantee Agency (MIGA), and the African Development Bank (AfDB). These actors have claimed that this project represents more than improved water supply services in Rwanda. Their claim is that the "demonstration effects" of this project are likely to motivate replication and thereby result in the scaling up of water sector investments in developing countries.

MIGA (who provided a political risk guarantee for the project) noted that "... it will have an important demonstration effect" (MIGA 2018). A case study, co-authored by EAIF and posted on the EAIF website, noted that "Dedicated funds, like EAIF, play a trailblazing, risk-reducing role in the sector, demonstrating what is possible and encouraging the private sector to invest in similar schemes with the public sector. The Kigali Bulk Water Supply project will serve as a model for other large-scale water projects in Africa" (Convergence et al. 2019). Rami Ghandour, managing director of Metito (the private concessionaire), called the project structure "... a model project for Africa, in terms of the business model and getting the private sector involved in the water sector" (*African Business* 2023).

In early 2023, the project became the first asset owned by a new company, Africa Water Infrastructure Development (AWID). The company is a partnership between Metito and British International Investment (BII), the U.K.'s development finance institution and impact investor. AWID will "... develop climate-smart water projects at scale," using Metito's "... viable commercial model for water infrastructure and provision in Africa" (Metito 2023). In other words, Metito and BII concluded that enough public and private partners across Africa will be motivated to replicate the Kigali model to warrant the creation of a new company to develop such projects "at scale" on a mostly commercial basis.

Because the Kigali Bulk Water PPP has now had several years of what the sponsor and financiers deem to have been successful operation, apparently meeting all of it contractual commitments, it seems possible now to begin assessing the nature of demonstration effects that the project might be generating. After the next section covering the project background, several key project characteristics are explored for their likely demonstration potential.

9.3.2 Kigali PPP Project Background

If successful and sustainable, the Kigali Bulk Water PPP will conclude a long history of attempts by development partners like the World Bank and IFC to assist the Rwandan government in reforming its water sector.[2] However, over most of that history, efforts to improve the efficiency of water distribution services in Rwanda took precedence over the search for new sources of water supply. Beginning in the 1980s reform recommendations focused on using brownfield PPP solutions to strengthen the management of the government's national water utility with lease contracts, management contracts, as well as long-term concessions.

In a comprehensive review of Rwanda's water sector performance published in 2005 by the World Bank and PPIAF, the priority concern remained the performance of the national utility, then a combined water and power utility known as Electrogaz. The report summed up the utility's problems in the following terms: low skill levels, over-staffing, high operational costs,

---

[2] For an overview of this history, see Leigland (2020b).

poor billing and collection performance, inadequate accounting and customer management, unsustainable debt burden, corruption, and high levels of non-revenue water (NRW) of over 40 percent. The report recommended a reform sequence, beginning with a management contract to focus on NRW reduction, followed by a long-term concession (involving private management of the utility and its commercial operation), followed eventually by consideration of full privatization. The need for additional water for Kigali was noted as a future concern that could eventually be addressed by the utility's private managers. By 2006, a management contract had been signed but collapsed before becoming fully operational. By 2010, another attempt to separate out and corporatize Electrogaz's water sector functions had failed, but the utility was renamed the Energy, Water, and Sanitation Authority (EWASA).

In 2010, the government engaged IFC PPP Advisory to structure a public–private partnership arrangement to finance, build, and operate a new water source for Kigali and nearby areas—this became the Kigali Bulk Water PPP. The IFC sourced technical assistance funding from PPIAF to successfully complete the process of creating a corporatized national water utility (now known as WASAC), but the transaction structure recommended by IFC marked the end of the long-term effort to use brownfield PPPs to strengthen water supply management. The structure proposed by IFC PPP Advisory was a 27-year greenfield BOT water supply project, meaning that the private partner's responsibilities were limited to the extraction, treatment, storage, and transmission of bulk water to WASAC. WASAC would continue to manage its own affairs, including all aspects of retail water provision, without private involvement. The project was awarded in 2015 to Kigali Water Limited (KWL), a wholly owned subsidiary of the Dubai-based Metito Group, and reached financial close in 2017 with loans from AfDB and EAIF.[3]

As the project structure was being finalized shortly before the scheduled financial closure in 2017, the government altered the structure of the PPP. The Rwanda Utilities Regulatory Authority (RURA) announced that the project was too expensive given existing end-user tariff levels. RURA demanded a 30 percent reduction in the bulk water price to be paid by WASAC for the wholesale water made available by the project. After a short negotiation, the price of water was reduced as RURA demanded, but in exchange the parties agreed to move the responsibility for financing, building, and operating the project's "forwarding infrastructure" (pumping station, transmission pipes, and storage

[3] In 2015, the World Bank once again proposed management contracts for the government's infrastructure utilities. The Bank's project appraisal document noted that the option was "… discussed and rejected by the GoR in view of the past experience" (World Bank 2015b, 9).

reservoirs) from the private partner as part of the BOT project to WASAC, who would handle this element as a public investment project. AfDB agreed to a $14 million concessional loan to the government for this part of the project. Total project cost dropped from $75 million to $61 million and the price of bulk water dropped accordingly (UNCDF 2018).

9.3.3 Demonstration Effects of the Kigali Bulk Water PPP

Research on PPP demonstration effects, undertaken since the early 2000s, remains remarkably limited, and provides little guidance about how demonstration effects work and which are most important. Most of this research involves case studies, limited surveys, and anecdotal information, often produced or sponsored by DFIs and MDBs directly involved in these projects (Castalia Strategic Advisors 2011b; Lion's Head 2018; IEG 2019). One systematic review offers insights about the demonstration effects of projects developed by DFIs and MDBs (Spratt and Collins 2012). One rigorous quantitative study seems to have produced only general insights on demonstration effects generated by a very narrow set of PPP project characteristics, such as the ways in which PPP project cancellations can demonstrate the need for governmental PPP programs to change their rules or procedures (Marcelo et al. 2017).

For the purposes of this chapter, six characteristics of the Kigali Bulk Water PPP were chosen based on the importance of each for both prospective public and private partners, the noteworthy nature of these characteristics, as well as their visibility—the fact that information on each of these characteristics has been publicly available without the need for extensive research. To what extent will these characteristics likely motivate others to replicate this project in other countries?

9.3.3.1 Preparation costs

Public and private stakeholders interested in similar kinds of projects in other countries will likely take note of the preparation process involved in this project, paying attention to who carried out preparation, how was it done, what did it accomplish, how much did it cost, and how was it paid for. The precise costs of this process have never been made public, but astute observers will try to understand at least the general outlines of the process to assess whether or not the successful results of preparation can be duplicated. Governments need to be sure they have enough money to finish the process—if not finished, whatever money has already been spent will likely be lost. Potential private sponsors need to have confidence that the process will reach completion as they begin their own preparation for bidding, which can often be quite expensive.

Preparation of the Kigali Bulk Water PPP, was carried out on behalf of the Rwandan government by IFC PPP Advisory, pursuant to an advisory agreement that became effective in 2010. IFC worked on the project until 2015, when commercial closure was marked by the signing key commercial documents by the preferred bidder. Full financial closure, involving lending commitments by AfDB and EAIF, took another two years of negotiation, during which the government received assistance from other advisers. IFC's costs were covered in a variety of ways: the government paid fees to IFC as required by the 2010 advisory agreement (an upfront one-time fee plus a monthly retainer fee); a success fee paid to IFC by the preferred bidder; grant funding made available by IFC-managed trust funds capitalized by donors; grants made available from a special "DevCo" trust fund capitalized by donors exclusively for IFC use and managed by PIDG; and possibly some contributions from IFC's corporate budget.

IFC was also able to access grant funding from the World Bank's Public–Private Infrastructure Advisory Facility (PPIAF), to carry out a reorganization and corporatization of the water and power utility, which resulted in a separate corporatized water utility, WASAC, to act as off-taker for the bulk water supply. In all, PPIAF claimed to have provided four years of technical assistance to WASAC beginning in 2011 (PPIAF 2015).

The total cost of project preparation in regions like Africa, for first-time projects in new sectors not counting lender costs or bidder costs, have been estimated at anywhere from 10 to 15 percent of total project cost (AfDB 2013a). Calculated on the basis of the original estimated project funding cost of US$75 million (see the breakdown in the next section), 10 percent would put preparation costs for this project at approximately US$7 million. Preparation costs for subsequent projects in other countries could be less, especially if there was no need to reorganize the government off-taker utility. But costs could also be higher in cases where government legal-regulatory frameworks require complicated and expensive analysis to justify PPPs. The Rwandan government did not pass a law covering PPPs until 2016 and did not detail project requirements regarding PPP preparation until 2018. The legal framework now in force requires preparation and government review of an extensive collection of elaborate analyses to justify projects of this kind, which likely would have significantly increased the preparation costs of the Kigali Bulk Water PPP as well as the time needed to prepare the project and obtain governmental approvals.[4]

---

[4] As of 2018, PPP justifications in Rwanda require, among other things, needs analysis; value-for-money assessment (including preparation of a public sector comparator); technical solutions options analysis; engineering due diligence; envi-

This generally available information on the preparation of the Kigali Bulk Water PPP suggests that it was an expensive and time consuming process, even for a country like Rwanda, which at the time of project financial closure was ranked second in sub-Saharan Africa in the World Bank's "Ease of Doing Business" survey (World Bank 2017). By 2019, Rwanda was ranked higher than all other African countries as well as developed countries like Spain, France, Switzerland, and Japan (World Bank 2019a). Nevertheless, without massive levels of concessional funding from donors, DFIs, and MDBs, it is unlikely that preparation of this project would have been possible.

9.3.3.2 Private investment

A second project characteristic of interest to public and private stakeholders in other countries is the amount of private investment attracted to a project like this. Private investment, particularly private equity, is of course the purpose of this kind of PPP and is a measure of the private partner's confidence in the profitability and sustainability of the project. Debt sourced from private commercial lenders also signals private sector confidence in the project—debt from DFIs can of course be important but also raises questions about whether or not the government could have accessed near-concessional funding from development partners to finance the entire project without private participation.

The general funding details of the Kigali Bulk Water Project have been disclosed in various publications (e.g., UNCDF 2018). The total original project cost was approximately US$75 million, with the various cost elements indicated in Table 9.3, which also includes an additional estimated cost of US$7 million for project preparation. EAIF, the lead arranger of the financing, combined with AfDB to finance US$41 million of the capital cost of the project. Of this total, US$38 million came in the form of senior debt and US$3 million as junior debt, all with loan tenures of 18 years.

It would be apparent to most interested observers that, other than Metito's equity and shareholder loan, there was no other private financial contribution to this project. Assuming US$7 million for project preparation and including the US$14 million for the forwarding infrastructure in the total project cost, US$82 million, the pure private sector investment in the project amounted to only about 13.3 percent of the total cost of the project. Pure private equity alone was only 2.4 percent of the total. The government's share of overall funding costs would include the tax refund (US$3 million), the AfDB loan to pay for the forwarding infrastructure (US$14 million), and a share of project

ronmental impact analysis; economic and social cost benefit analysis; financial analysis and modeling; risk assessment and allocation analysis; project structure assessment; procurement options analysis (Republic of Rwanda 2018).

Table 9.3 Kigali bulk water PPP, project funding, 2017

Type	Source	Amount in US$ millions
Loans to Metito	AfDB and EAIF	41
Loan to WASAC[a]	AfDB	14
Capital grant	Donors	6
Tax refund	Government	3
Shareholder loan	Metito	9
Sponsor equity	Metito	2
Project preparation	IFC, donors, Govt.	7
	Total	82

Note: [a] For the "forwarding" assets originally part of the project.
Source: Author's compilation from published reports.

preparation costs (conservatively estimated here to be about US$2 million). That puts the government's share of total project costs at about US$19 million or about 23 percent of the total indicated in Table 9.3.

Recent research has estimated that blended finance leverage ratios in low-income countries are indeed low—on average, MDBs, DFIs, and donors contribute about 73 percent of the total blended financed investment in low-income countries, to leverage about 27 percent from private partners (Attridge and Engen 2019). This means that in the case of the Kigali Bulk Water PPP the private partner contributed to the project's blended financial total slightly less than half the average private amount in low-income country projects.

9.3.3.3 Affordability

Public and private stakeholders interested in similar kinds of projects in other countries will of course pay attention to the affordability of such a project—will the public partner be able to meet financial commitments incurred under the agreement, ideally from its own revenue? If the utility must depend on intergovernmental transfers to pay its bills, this inevitably raises questions about the project from politicians and the general public and increases the possibility that such payments might be delayed or withheld, or newly elected politicians might insist on contract renegotiation to achieve a more affordable arrangement. A World Bank survey of 140 countries published in 2020 found that over 80 percent of these countries required an assessment of fiscal affordability as a key part of the official government process of justifying infrastructure PPPs (World Bank 2020).

Despite the relatively small amount of commercial investment in the Kigali Bulk Water PPP, the bulk water price was expensive. It illustrated the high costs of private participation via PPPs and this fact was immediately highlighted by the government's Office of the Auditor General (Republic of Rwanda 2022). In its 2021 annual audit report published after four months of the PPP's operation, the OAG noted that the cost to WASAC of the water produced by the new water treatment plant was three times the current average cost of production at WASAC's 25 other water treatment plants. The monthly invoice from the concessionaire's plant consumed 44 percent of WASAC's average total monthly sales revenue from all 25 of its plants. The OAG noted that not only could WASAC not fully settle its monthly water bills for the project, but that the situation was likely to get worse because the "take-or-pay" provisions of the PPP contract obligated WASAC to purchase the full capacity of the plant at a non-negotiable price regardless of how much water WASAC used. And pursuant to the contract, the price would increase annually to account for inflation.

As documented in the 2022 audit report, the price per cubic meter of water had indeed increased and was now substantially above the utility's most expensive selling price of water. Adding to WASAC's affordability problem was the fact that planning errors and delays in building the forwarding infrastructure, which WASAC had become responsible for, meant that since the beginning of the PPP's commercial operation the utility had paid for over seven million cubic meters of water that could not be sold to customers. The OAG labeled this a wasteful expenditure of over US$4.5 million. In its emphasis of the magnitude of these affordability problems, the OAG pointed out that WASAC's desperation to maximize its use of the water produced by the PPP, for which it was required to pay whether needed or used, left the utility with no choice but to significantly reduce water production at two other plants that were producing water far less expensively (Republic of Rwanda 2023).

Finally, and most importantly, WASAC's level of non-revenue water, water produced but not billed for, was still steadily increasing, further weakening WASAC's ability to cover the costs of the PPP's water from its own revenue. NRW had been at 41 percent in 2020, but had increased to 45 percent by the end of June 2022, amounting to about US$9 million in lost revenue in 2022 alone. As the 2022 audit report noted, "… the financial sustainability of WASAC Ltd is at stake if this trend is not addressed" (Republic of Rwanda 2023, 38). A clear, powerful demonstration effect of this project is reflected in the OAG reports: the project is not affordable for WASAC.

9.3.3.4 Risk transfer

Another project characteristic that both public and private stakeholders in other countries would take note of concerns the nature of public–private risk-sharing involved in the project. An understanding of risk allocation is essential in valuing the size of project returns and other benefits—both public and private partners seek appropriate levels of return for the project risks they assume. The 2020 World Bank survey of 140 countries cited earlier found that 74 percent of these countries required an assessment of project risks and risk sharing as part of the process of justifying infrastructure PPPs (World Bank 2020). The Rwandan government's PPP guidelines published in 2018 (after the Kigali Bulk Water PPP reached financial closure) stated that a "fair" allocation of risks depends on risks being commensurate with the project returns or gains allocated to the public and private partners in the project (Republic of Rwanda 2018, 9).

The structure of the Kigali Bulk Water PPP contract signed in 2017 reflected a sharp divergence from the kind of water sector public–private risk allocation recommended by Rwanda's development partners over the previous 25 years. Those earlier PPP recommendations routinely targeted more efficient use of existing (or "brownfield") assets via leases, management contracts, and concessions rather than an exclusive focus on adding new assets to the water system (via "greenfield" BOT projects). A brownfield concession, like the one recommended by the World Bank in 2005, would require a private partner to finance, repair, extend, rehabilitate, operate, and maintain existing assets. The private partner would be responsible for retail service management, billing and collections, customer care, tariff recommendations, etc. The private partner would be incentivized to solve operational problems like NRW, because such problems would reduce system revenues and, consequently, private profits. Some new assets (e.g., for a new water source and associated treatment) could be added to the system as part of such an arrangement but would be done in parallel with other activities and only after problems like NRW were addressed.

But the Kigali project reflects the private sector risk management strategy highlighted earlier. Because this is a BOT project involving new (greenfield) infrastructure assets, there is minimal risk of unanticipated, latent defects in assets that have a history of poor government construction or maintenance. The project involves wholesale as opposed to retail services, with payments for services made by a single government off-taker (vs. thousands of retail end-users), so the private partner faces minimal retail management risks (customer care issues, tariff issues, distribution problems like NRW, etc.). The private partner also faces minimal end-user demand risk because a long-term purchase agreement is structured on a take-or-pay payment basis, meaning that payment must be made whether or not the project's water is used or needed. Dollar-denominated payments by the government off-taker pursuant to a long-term contract eliminate currency mismatches for the private partner.

A sovereign guarantee is provided by the national government, as well as a third-party guarantee from MIGA.

The Rwandan government agreed to this allocation of risks by signing the BOT contract structured by the IFC. But the OAG audit reports have documented the inability of the government and WASAC to adequately mitigate many of the risks for which they have accepted full responsibility.

9.3.3.5 Additionality

Ways in which a PPP project demonstrates additionality are of strong interest to governments considering the replication of a particular model. "Additionality" refers to the achievement by a PPP project of total net benefit (in terms of a combination of cost, price, quality, quantity, risk transfer, etc.) that is more than would otherwise be achieved if the project were not implemented or was implemented in a substantially different way, for example as a public investment project or some other form of PPP. The 2020 World Bank survey of 140 countries cited earlier found that 76 percent of these countries required a comparative assessment of project value as part of the process of justifying infrastructure PPPs (World Bank 2020). Additionality is also something that donor-funded project preparation programs and facilities routinely claim to be targeting in their preparation of projects—the term appeared in the PIDG Five-Year Strategy over a dozen times (PIDG 2019a).

Governmental PPP legal-regulatory frameworks often require quantitative comparisons of PPP project value with "public sector comparator" (PSC) projects designed to provide the same service (see Chapter 6 for a discussion of PSC use by government PPP units). As of 2018, the Rwandan government has required the preparation of PSCs to make possible a value-for-money analysis confirming the expected additionality of PPP projects in the country. But this requirement did not apply to the Kigali Bulk Water PPP, which reached closure a year earlier. However, in the case of the Kigali project it does not take a value-for-money analysis to raise serious questions about the project's additionality in the minds of even casual observers.

First, it seems likely that the amount and nature of private investment in the Kigali Bulk Water PPP would raise questions in the minds of observers about the possibility that the government (or WASAC) might have sourced the full amount of financing for the project from concessional or near concessional sources without the need to incur the costs and complexities associated with a PPP arrangement. AfDB readily agreed to the US$14 million concessional loan to the government for the project's forwarding infrastructure, an essential part of the project. Given Rwanda's rapidly improving standing in rankings like the World Bank's *Doing Business* surveys, a public finance approach to the project seems to have been possible, especially considering how expensive the project's bulk water supply has been for WASAC.

Second, the OAG reports have raised questions about whether or not the PPP structure used in this case provided optimal benefits to WASAC. The need for private participation to facilitate capital investment may be somewhat unclear, but the need for private sector expertise in the operations, maintenance, rehabilitation, and extension of WASAC assets seems beyond doubt, particularly in light of the OAG reports. The 2023 audit report notes that 11 of WASAC's 25 water treatment plants were operating at less than 75 percent capacity because of delays in upgrading assets. The utility was delaying connections for thousands of new customers, and over 124,000 existing customers were being billed flat rates because of missing or inoperative water meters. NRW was reaching dramatic levels and threatening WASAC's financial sustainability. The risks associated with WASAC's acceptance of responsibility for the project's forwarding infrastructure, proved to be a serious mistake when the assets were not completed on time but payment for available bulk water was still required. This situation suggests that if some form of private participation was needed in the case of Rwanda's water sector, the form of it mostly likely to benefit WASAC would have been some type of brownfield PPP (concession, lease, management contract), rather than a BOT that focused exclusively on new water supply assets.

9.3.3.6 Sector applicability

Finally, and perhaps most importantly, for a project like Kigali Bulk Water PPP to encourage replication in the water sectors of other countries it needs to demonstrate that it effectively addresses an important, widespread problem that exists in those sectors. For example, greenfield BOT and BOO structures have repeatedly demonstrated their applicability in the power sectors of developing countries, resulting in the rapid spread of the IPP project model in multiple countries because of its ability to facilitate private investment in large, capital-intensive electricity generation projects. This success has much to do with the basic characteristics of the electricity sector. The principal investment need in the sector is generation—electricity is relatively inexpensive to transport, but expensive to generate and store, so power must be generated constantly and safely using large, complicated facilities. Because multiple generation facilities can use the same basic transmission assets with relatively inexpensive enhancements, the sector can accommodate multiple, competing generators of electricity, public or private.

The water sector has much stronger natural monopoly characteristics than electricity, because water supply is primarily a transport challenge. Water is relatively expensive to transport, especially given health and safety considerations, but relatively inexpensive to source, treat, and store. This complicates the creation of competitive markets for water in two ways: First, it means that for a given water service area, it is usually impractical to have more than one service provider—different water sources in different locations usually cannot share transmission assets, and it is usually too expensive to build new transmission assets for each new source of water.

Second, in jurisdictions like the urban areas of Africa, the principal local sources of available water are already being exploited and some form of basic water transport infrastructure already exists, usually in the form of underground pipe networks. Because of this, the essential capital investment needs in the sector typically involve rehabilitation of existing assets and extension of existing distribution systems, rather than developing new sources of water. This usually makes the investment needs in the water sector much less than in a sector like electricity. The World Bank's first comprehensive effort to estimate the infrastructure investment needs in African countries, the *African Infrastructure Country Diagnostic* (AICD), demonstrated that water investment accounted for about 30 percent of the total infrastructure financing gap in Africa, compared with 60 percent for electricity (Foster and Briceño-Garmendia 2010).

Of course, the water sectors of most developing countries often need new assets, such as water treatment and water storage facilities, etc. And sometimes these assets can be complicated and expensive, for example in the case of water re-use or desalination. But most of the time new sector assets do not require investments large enough to justify the cost and complexity of project finance and private participation, as is more often the case with larger and more expensive electricity generation assets.

The PPP investment track record in sub-Saharan Africa (SSA) dramatically underscores the power sector's use of greenfield projects (mostly IPP projects) to attract over 40 times more capital investment than the water sector (Figure 9.3).

The water sector's primary investment need for asset rehabilitation and system extension, rather than major investment in large new capital assets for sourcing and treating water, puts into perspective the 30 years of recommendations made by development partners to the Rwandan government regarding the need for brownfield PPPs in the country's water sector. The need for additional sources of water for Kigali had been growing since the time of the country's devastating civil war in the early 1990s. But investing in new water sources for the city was not cost-effective without reductions in NRW that could only result from asset rehabilitation and more effective system management. As the World Bank argued in 2005, this indicated the need for a brownfield PPP approach that included new asset construction as a necessary but not sufficient element. Rwanda's water sector investment needs reflected common, widespread problems in the sector, but not problems that could be adequately addressed with greenfield solutions alone. The Kigali Bulk Water PPP demonstrated for government officials in other developing countries the use of a project structure that did not support their primary investment needs in most cases.

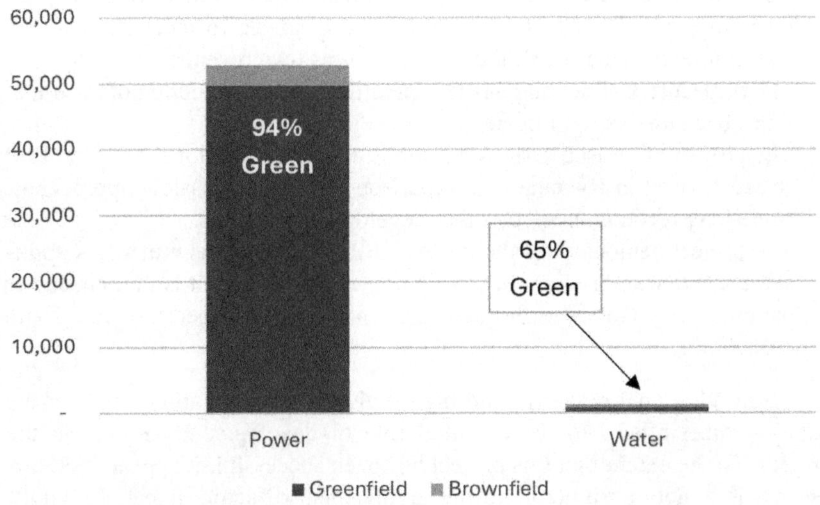

Note: US$ millions—nominal values.
Source: World Bank (2022).

Figure 9.3 PPP investment in SSA, power vs. water, 1995–2021

9.4 CONCLUSIONS

This assessment of demonstration effects generated by the Kigali Bulk Water PPP suggests several conclusions:

First, although the public and private partners involved in this project have all claimed that it would generate significant positive demonstration effects likely to facilitate replication, specific effects have not been identified by any of these partners.

Second, a review of six noteworthy and highly visible project characteristics that are likely to be of interest to public and private actors in other countries, and therefore likely to generate demonstration effects, suggests that most of these characteristics will not encourage replication:

- The project preparation process was expensive and time consuming. It would have been impossible for the government to pay for such a process without considerable amounts of grant funding from development partners.
- The project attracted relatively little private investment, especially considering the costs and complications of preparing and tendering the PPP transaction.

- The wholesale water sold to the government's water utility, WASAC, has been so expensive that the utility has been unable to meet its financial commitments under the PPP contract from its own revenue.
- The project risk allocation has left the utility with a collection of risks that it has been unable to mitigate.
- The project has raised serious questions about the additionality of the PPP structure used in Rwanda in comparison with other possible approaches, some long recommended by other development partners.
- The project demonstrates the use of a PPP model that is much less applicable in the water sectors of developing countries than it is in their power or transport sectors—where the model has clearly helped motivate some replication.

Third, an additional powerful and highly visible demonstration effect of the Kigali project relates to the essential role of development partners in the project. To the extent that this project has been successful, it appears that this success is largely attributable to the involvement of actors like IFC, AfDB, PIDG, and MIGA. Because of the extensive public relations efforts of these development partners, their contributions in making the project succeed have been well publicized and amount to what is probably the single most visible demonstration effect of the project. The effect is positive in the sense that this kind of a project is clearly a priority for these development partners, who may be willing to help with similar projects (although their capacity to repeat this heavily subsidized approach to preparation and finance is probably limited). At the same time, the demonstration effect of this involvement is likely negative in the sense that, as at least one study has pointed out, the benefits made possible by the involvement of development partners in such a project are almost impossible for private participation to replicate and therefore would never be attempted:

> In many cases it is precisely these features that make a project possible, and they are a direct result of DFIs' rather unique position. It is thus not always possible for private actors to follow DFIs example and make the same investments, as they do not enjoy the advantages that made these investments possible in the first place. (Spratt and Collins 2012, 4)

10. South Africa's renewable energy IPP program: the rediscovery of upstream project preparation

10.1 INTRODUCTION

The ultimate objective of the public–private partnership (PPP) advocates, especially project preparation facilities (PPFs) like the Private Infrastructure Development Group (PIDG) and IFC PPP Advisory, is to encourage replication of PPPs as a principal solution to the problem of financing more and better quality infrastructure in developing countries. Subsidized funding and expertise, if supplied in enough quantities, can help individual PPPs reach financial closure in almost any country, but the numbers of projects done that way and the associated benefits are far too small relative to the overall infrastructure investment problem for such isolated projects to be considered part of a meaningful solution. The ideal form of PPP scale-up would be the development of markets for projects involving private participation, in the sense of governments offering multiple projects to multiple private companies who are willing and able to compete for project opportunities that need minimal subsidy support.

The transaction-only approach favored by most of the PPFs that have proliferated since the early 2000s has not generated this kind of scale-up. The World Bank's PPI Database confirms that the creation of PPP markets in this sense has been extremely rare in developing countries, but particularly so in low-income countries. In the few cases where PPP markets have achieved some limited form of sustained competitive activity, the reasons have had much less to do with the demonstration effects generated by isolated, heavily subsidized projects than with improvements and reforms in the upstream project environment—in other words, actions necessary to lay the groundwork necessary to enable downstream transactions. Donor-financed PPFs pursuing the transaction-only approach to project development typically circumvent, rather than directly address, the important upstream obstacles to PPP market development, like lack of political support, inadequate regulations and policies, and weak PPP program management. These facilities complete isolated projects, then move on usually without ever calling attention to, much less addressing, the problems that effectively limit PPP project scale-up.

A recent example in the developing world of the importance of upstream preparation for the achievement of market-like PPP behavior was the remarkable, if short-lived, success of South Africa's Renewable Energy Independent Power Producer Procurement Programme (REIPPPP). Between 2012 and 2015, the program attracted $19 billion in private investment in 92 independent power producer (IPP) projects, totaling 6,327 MW, with wind and solar photo voltaic (PV) prices among the lowest in the world. The generating capacity added to the South African grid by the program in four years was more than the total existing installed capacity of every other sub-Saharan Africa (SSA) country. Over this period, South Africa ranked among the top ten countries globally in renewable energy IPP investment, ahead of Canada, Brazil, Spain, and France. One large equity investor noted that REIPPPP was the most successful public effort to attract private investment in infrastructure in Africa (Eberhard et al. 2014).

South Africa's program incorporated upstream preparation in a fashion similar to that recommended as part of the World Bank's more deliberative approach to PPPs, adopted after the end of policy-based lending in the 1990s. The approach was articulated in the 2000–2001 World Development Report (World Bank 2000, 87) and the Bank's 2002 private sector development strategy (World Bank 2002b). South Africa's REIPPPP is noteworthy also because it was domestically designed, managed, and financed. The individual IPP projects were not prepared or financed with subsidies from donors or development banks, although the International Finance Corporation (IFC) provided financing for some of the projects and closely monitored program results. The market-building success of South Africa's program led directly to an IFC program intended to duplicate REIPPPP success ("Scaling Solar"), and influenced IFC's transformational adoption of its new "upstream" project development strategy in 2020 ("IFC 3.0"). This chapter summarizes the REIPPPP approach and how its short-lived success influenced the IFC and others.

10.2 REIPPPP'S UPSTREAM SUCCESS FACTORS

10.2.1 High-level Political Support

A large measure of REIPPPP success is attributable to a number of upstream policies and program characteristics that resulted from careful planning and timely action by politicians and government managers. For as long as it lasted, chief among these factors was the high-level political support for the program. Political leadership has long been recognized as critical to the success of PPP programs in Africa, beginning with the evaluations done of the African privatization programs in the 1980s and 1990s (Jones et al. 2002). The successful completion of one of Africa's first, high-profile PPP successes, the 1997 Maputo toll road concession, largely resulted from the enthusiastic, coordinated, high-level support provided personally by the presidents of Mozambique and South Africa, Joaquim Chissano and Nelson Mandela. The two presidents appeared at an investor conference in 1996 to encourage private investment in the concession and over 180 other commercial projects along the transport corridor from Johannesburg to Maputo (Mandela 1996).

IFC PPP Advisory attempts to lock in political commitment to PPP projects with which it assists by identifying key government commitments in the financial advisory service agreements (FASAs) that each government must sign before IFC assistance can proceed. The FASAs normally require governments to pay an upfront fee as well as monthly retainer fees to IFC for the advisory work, guaranteeing that governments have an investment in making sure the project development process is successful. More importantly, FASAs also usually detail the proposed PPP project structure that government clients commit to supporting by signing the agreement.

When REIPPPP began designing its tender program in 2011, it benefitted from a relatively long history of policy statements supporting the use of renewable energy for climate change mitigation and economic development, especially job creation. This was not too different from other African countries. However, the degree of high-level political support that was signaled by South African President Jacob Zuma's commitments to green energy during the COP15 and COP17 meetings was very different indeed. This support from the president was a surprise—South Africa voluntarily committed to reduce carbon emissions although it faced no binding obligations under the United Nations Framework Convention on Climate Change or the Kyoto protocol. For a country so dependent on coal for its energy, and facing extraordinary poverty and development challenges, this was a striking break from the past.

Another form of political support came in the form of high-level government decisions to shift responsibility for developing IPP projects from the country's powerful state-owned, vertically integrated power utility, Eskom, to the Department of Energy (DOE). By the late 2000s, the country clearly needed new generating capacity and the government had unmet renewable energy targets dating from 2003. Eskom had been tasked with procuring renewable energy IPP projects but failed to complete any projects. The failure was likely due to Eskom's reluctance to open the sector to competition that could cast the efficiency of its own operations in an unfavorable light (Eberhard et al. 2014).

Because of Eskom's unwillingness or inability to make progress with IPP projects, DOE took direct control of the program, which became REIPPPP. DOE also sought the assistance of the National Treasury's Public–Private Partnership Unit to manage the process. A small team of mostly mid-level technical staff from DOE and the PPP Unit established a project office that functioned effectively outside of the formal departmental structure of national government to act as manager of the REIPPPP process.

The DOE IPP project unit managing REIPPPP did a remarkable job of maintaining political support for as long as it did. Some of the ways in which this happened included the following:

- *A compelling case for renewable energy*. The DOE IPP unit repeatedly made the case for the program at every opportunity, in informal government meetings, conferences, cabinet meetings, and presentations before Parliament—no one was allowed to forget that the program had strong justifications and had been personally sanctioned by the president.
- *Off-budget program funding*. The transaction costs for the REIPPPP program were high, but after using some small donor grants to initiate operations the DOE unit established a mechanism to successfully capture fees from closed projects. This self-sustaining feature kept the program off budget and helped pre-empt criticism from Eskom and others that it was too expensive.
- *Accelerated roll-out of generating capacity*. Despite the high initial costs of renewable energy, at least when the program started, REIPPPP offered something that most South Africans thought they urgently needed in 2011 in the wake of widespread power cuts—a relatively fast roll out of new power-generating capacity.
- *Sharp cost reductions*. The use of competitive bidding and multiple tender rounds helped tariffs drop precipitously after the first round of bidding, and this reduction was a major factor in the government's willingness to continue its support for REIPPPP as a "successful" program.
- *Non-negotiable contracts*. The REIPPPP team used well designed, non-negotiable contract documentation to control bidder gamesmanship and restrict time-consuming negotiations. The approach resonated with government officials who wanted assurances that the program was managed by and for the government, rather than private businesses.

10.2.2 Socio-economic Benefit Requirements

Another important feature of this program that helped to generate support from politicians and the general public was its emphasis on socio-economic benefits (Leigland and Eberhard 2018). These non-price factors in bid evaluation were somewhat confusing and expensive for bidders to respond to but nevertheless helped cement high-level stakeholder support. Organized in bid documents under the heading of "economic development requirements," these factors were designed to incentivize bidders to promote job growth, domestic industrialization, community development, and black economic empowerment.

The focus of REIPPPP on local content requirements was also significantly different from that required under existing South African frameworks like the government's Preferential Procurement Policy Framework Act (PPPFA), promulgated in 2000, or the Broad-Based Black Economic Empowerment (BBBEE) Act of 2003 with its Code of Good Practice published in 2007. An exemption was granted from the PPPFA's requirement that 90 percent of the bid score be allocated to price with the remaining 10 percent allocated to compliance with preference categories (or an 80/20 split for smaller contracts). Instead, REIPPPP divided bid scoring on a 70/30 basis, with the former allocated to price and the latter to non-price "economic development" criteria.

These departures from existing requirements encouraged government officials to view REIPPPP as a program that, in the words of the first request for proposal (RFP), "... is inherently excellent for achieving positive socio-economic outcomes" (Republic of South Africa 2011, 11). Government officials clearly saw a potential to boost local manufacturing in a sector that was nearly non-existent. Because of the distributed nature of renewable energy generation, project sites offered an unusually intense business focus on rural areas that otherwise would have little potential to attract investment. The effort to capture socio-economic benefits as part of the program garnered political and public support and helped the program turn into something more than a one-off project exercise.

10.2.3 Sector Policies and Plans

REIPPPP took on market-like characteristics largely because it offered the prospect of multiple bid rounds involving a relatively stable pipeline of potentially profitable private sector investment opportunities. Private sector actors became convinced that the process would continue as promised and that it was prudent to invest in pre-project preparation and due diligence so that they could compete in multiple bid rounds if necessary to win a desired number of project opportunities. This gradually expanded the number of bidders and made the bid rounds increasingly competitive.

All of this was possible because at the time the South African government used a well-developed, transparent sector planning process that gave the private sector comfort that sector officials were following established planning rules and would not suddenly shift course in terms of seeking and sustaining private investment. The post-apartheid South African Government originally strengthened this process by taking power planning authority away from Eskom to ensure that planning was not done exclusively in the utility's interests. The new formal planning system mandated the DOE to produce an electricity plan, known as the Integrated Resource Plan (IRP). Based on this plan, the Minister of Energy issued periodic determinations regarding how much new power generation was needed, and from which sources. The sector electricity regulator, the National Energy Regulator of South Africa (NERSA), could only license new capacity within the bounds set by these ministerial determinations.

The post-apartheid government also quickly recognized that IPPs should be allowed to enter the market to enhance the country's power generating capacity. Following the publication of the Energy Policy White Paper in 1998, the South African Cabinet proposed a 70:30 share of power-generating responsibility between Eskom and the private sector, and work commenced on the design of a competitive wholesale power exchange. However, with looming Eskom power shortages, the prospective wholesale market was abandoned in 2004 in favor of the existing single-buyer model with Eskom serving as the off-taker. IPPs were still expected to play a significant role in power generation, but the policy and regulatory framework for IPP projects was not immediately put in place and as noted earlier, Eskom was unable or unwilling to procure cogeneration and baseload IPP projects. No IPP contracts were signed except for a handful of short-term power purchase agreements with industrial generators, which amounted to less than 400 MW.

After the 2009 COP15 meeting in Copenhagen, South Africa also began to transform the content of its energy plans, requiring that renewable energy play a significant role in the nation's power generation mix. For the first time, the IRP 2010–30 incorporated a carbon emissions cap and included renewable energy objectives, with 17.8 GW of solar and wind energy capacity planned by 2030. More than most countries, South Africa relies heavily on coal and compared with the rest of Africa has a highly energy-intensive economy. These factors resulted in South Africa's carbon emissions (on a per capita and GDP basis) being disproportionately high (although, in total, they amount to little over one percent of global emissions). South African policymakers were mindful of risks that these emission levels might pose to the economy's future international competitiveness. They were also aware that the country had considerable potential for some types of renewable energy generation. All these considerations influenced President Zuma's commitments to renewable energy, which helped launch and sustain REIPPPP.

10.2.4 Program Design: Size and Sector Focus

The narrow focus of REIPPPP on renewable energy IPPs played a strong role in the ability of the program to attract multiple investors as well as maintain domestic and international political support. This was not a broad PPP program focusing on a wide variety of project types, some of which might not generate many private sector opportunities. The South African government had attempted such an approach years earlier with a state-of-the-art PPP legal-regulatory framework and a national PPP unit. But that approach was unsuccessful in stimulating ongoing market-like PPP activity, as it was in many other developing countries. REIPPPP was focused on a single kind of PPP, involving greenfield power generation, which had already become the most widely used type of private participation in infrastructure in the form of IPP projects.

Climate change concerns provided part of the motivation for the REIPPPP project focus. Such concerns were being heavily promoted by development partners and were increasingly being taken up by African actors like Regional Economic Communities (RECs) and other regional bodies. Rising fossil fuel prices also began to incentivize more serious government consideration of the use of renewable energy, along with the emergence of more reliable, less expensive, renewable energy technology.

REIPPPP also tapped into South Africa's need to quickly roll out more electricity generation. In the 1970s, overestimations of power demand growth led to Eskom investments that created an oversupply of power. By the end of the 1990s, South African's had become comfortable with electricity prices that were among the lowest in the world. But by 2004, after years of little or no investment, the over-supply of power was quickly disappearing and power cuts—once unthinkable in South Africa—were becoming a distinct possibility. Electricity prices began to sharply increase, alarming Eskom's customers, and prompting urgent calls for a rapid scale-up in generation.

Eskom resisted IPPs because private participation would threaten the utility's sector dominance. But by the mid-2000s, it was clear that Eskom mismanagement was failing to implement its own large-scale generation projects quickly enough to close the supply–demand gap. Renewable energy IPP projects tended to be small- to medium-sized (often less than 100 MW), but multiple projects of this kind could make large contributions to national power generating capacity. As REIPPPP eventually demonstrated, with construction periods of around 12 months, IPP projects could quickly add relatively large amounts of solar- or wind-generating capacity to the national grid, far faster than the time needed to construct hydro or coal-fired generation facilities.

In terms of important market factors impacting the program, the global slow-down in renewable energy markets in industrialized economies at the time meant a program the size of REIPPPP attracted considerable attention from the international private sector. The overcapacity in the global market combined with technological improvements and manufacturing advances, along with REIPPPP's well designed and transparent tendering program, to result in over 90 IPP projects demonstrating remarkably low energy prices.

10.2.5 Legal and Regulatory Adjustments

One of the most important factors in REIPPPP's ability to "scale-up" the use of PPPs by successfully completing multiple IPP projects involved a decision to exempt the program's projects from South Africa's legal and regulatory rules governing the development and approval of PPP projects. These rules, discussed earlier in Chapter 6, were originally established as essential elements of a best-practice PPP policy framework in South Africa. The key requirement was that analytical methodologies like value-for-money (VfM) assessments were necessary to demonstrate that a PPP structure was warranted for infrastructure projects rather than some form of traditional public investment. The analytical approach was rigorous, but in requiring such methodologies, governments are rarely able to balance the need for consistent, compelling analysis with the capabilities of government staff to implement or at least understand the analytical results if produced by consultants or development partners.

This problem reflects a difficult balancing act facing developing country governments like South Africa's. On the one hand, simply requiring the use of different kinds of analysis to justify a PPP project does not go far enough unless detailed analytical methodologies are also specified so that analyses can be done consistently, and the expected value of projects can be assessed on a comparable basis. On the other hand, sophisticated methodologies may be too complicated, time-consuming, or expensive for government officials to use effectively and consistently. An example is the widespread requirement to use "public sector comparators" (PSCs) in VfM analysis, which was a key element of the South African legal-regulatory framework for PPPs (see the discussion of PSCs in Chapter 6).

Had REIPPPP been defined as a PPP program, with its projects subject to the government's rules regarding the justification of projects, REIPPPP's use of multiple bid rounds to procure over 90 IPP projects would have been impossible. The REIPPPP manager had considerable prior experience as a senior official in National Treasury's PPP Unit and well understood the problems created if REIPPPP's projects were classified as "PPPs." Each project would have been required to laboriously follow two dozen preparation steps and wait for four separate government signoffs before project development could finish.

A regulatory review arranged by the REIPPPP program manager determined that REIPPPP was not required to follow National Treasury Regulation rules for evaluating and approving public–private partnerships (PPPs). The review found that the PSC process was not applicable to REIPPPP projects because Eskom, which signed the power purchase agreements with private sponsors, was a state-owned enterprise rather than a government agency, and therefore its purchase of power was not subject to National Treasury's PPP regulations for governmental entities. REIPPPP was classified as a non-governmental program even though the procurement process was formally the responsibility of DOE, and IPP contracts were backed by sovereign guarantees. Although the program was exempted from PPP requirements, it eventually went through the motions of demonstrating VfM, presumably to fulfill at least the spirit of the government's PPP regulations, by requesting bidders to voluntarily submit their own VfM justifications.

10.2.6 Program Management

South Africa's REIPPPP also benefitted from a program characteristic that is extremely rare in developing countries, but essential in attracting and maintaining the kind of strong private sector interest required to turn several one-off projects into an ongoing PPP market: capable, private sector-friendly program management.

The South African president and other senior officials supported the program, at least initially, but the program unit was also effectively led by a senior manager from the National Treasury PPP Unit who had worked there since its creation in 2000. She had helped establish Treasury's rigorous PPP project appraisal framework and had been involved with DOE's efforts to promote IPP projects as early as 2007. She was able to interact convincingly with senior government officials, effectively explain and defend the program in meetings with stakeholders, deal with development partners, select and manage consultants, communicate with the private sector, and manage a complicated procurement and contracting process.

The program manager also surrounded herself with a team that was familiar with private sector infrastructure projects, as well as most of the bankers, lawyers, and consultants involved in such projects in South Africa. Because of this, the unit did not start out with the level of mistrust of private business that has sometimes characterized other government agencies in South Africa. Dialogue with private sector counterparts on key REIPPPP design and implementation issues began almost immediately and continued throughout the process. The program was managed from the outset in a fashion that was tailored toward generating enthusiastic participation by private sector players without compromising the government's interests or objectives.

The program made extensive use of private domestic and international advisers to design and help manage the program, review bids, and incorporate lessons learned into the program as it progressed through the bid rounds. By maintaining the high quality of transaction advice, the program unit avoided criticism from the private sector and independent industry experts. The program was able to stay off the government budget while also covering the considerable costs of these consultants, as well as the costs of offices, a website, various databases, and an extensive communications program using revenues from bidder registration fees and fees paid by successful IPP project companies. This self-financing character also allowed the program to maintain a largely ad hoc institutional status. The IPP project unit was officially a part of the Department of Energy but acted at arm's length from the department as a kind of semi-independent project office. This allowed and, to some extent, encouraged an operating approach that emphasized entrepreneurial problem solving to make the program successful, rather than an approach focused on the enforcement of bureaucratic rules and procedures.

10.2.7 Competitive Tendering

An aspect of program management that was particularly important in REIPPPP's success was the use of competitive tendering. Tendering of PPPs has now been widely acknowledged world-wide as the best-practice approach to the selection of private partners. Of the 140 countries surveyed by the World Bank in 2020, 96 percent have rules requiring competitive bidding of PPPs based on published selection criteria (World Bank 2020). About 70 percent of the economies surveyed allowed direct negotiations of PPP projects under certain conditions, with most specifying the circumstances in which this method can be used.

But this remains a challenging area with constant pressure to circumvent competitive processes. Donor-funded transaction advisers and investors like the PIDG companies avoid tendering because it slows down their constant effort to complete projects and meet their principal performance targets. IFC PPP Advisory requires client governments to use tendering to select private partners, but refuses to compete for transaction advisory work, requiring most clients to circumvent their own rules for competitively selecting PPP advisers.

The key advantages of tendering are transparency and the value-for-money likely to result from competition. The frequent use of non-competitive sole source awards can give the private sector the impression that the procurement process is non-transparent with unclear procedures that sometimes may allow weak bidders to unfairly capture tenders. This may deter capable and qualified private-sector bidders from competing for PPPs when tendering is used.

REIPPPP's procurement process was efficient, professional, and competitive. It issued timely RFPs, employed clear qualification and evaluation criteria, used bankable contract documents, as well as appropriate credit enhancements, like sovereign guarantees. The use of non-negotiable contract documents drew strong support from government officials, but the private sector also generally approved of the process because the quality of the documentation was high and relieved preferred bidders from long and costly negotiations to finalize contracts. The processes of tendering and related document storage were also highly secure, managed from a facility at a confidential location with highly restricted access, 24-hour guards, and 24-hour recorded electronic surveillance. This gave private-sector bidders comfort in the integrity of the bidding process.

10.3 REIPPPP'S RAPID RISE AND FALL

10.3.1 The Value of a Facilitative Investment Climate

Upstream strategies and policies contributed strongly to REIPPPP's success but some of the most critical upstream success factors are beyond the ability of policymakers in most developing countries to achieve in the short to medium term, much less sustain over the long term. Probably the most important of these factors in 2011 was South Africa's investment climate. "Investment climate" refers to a list of desirable socio-economic country characteristics that facilitate private investment in infrastructure. The list includes things like macro-economic stability, an active capital market, an efficient banking system, a history of upholding contracts, readily available access to arbitration, the relative absence of corruption, the availability of a well-educated and productive workforce, and a growing economy with a government focus on expanding the private sector's role in it via multiple investment opportunities. Much of REIPPPP's attraction for investors can be summed up by the fact that in 2011, South Africa ranked at or near the top of all African countries in terms of these characteristics.

A weak investment climate does not necessarily rule out sustainable PPPs, even in the poorest countries. This fact has buoyed the efforts of transaction-only PPFs who have used subsidized preparation and investment, and private sector risk mitigation, to conclude IPP projects in some of Africa's most challenging investment environments. But the attractiveness of the investment climate does contribute to the competitiveness of project bids and, as a direct result, can help lower the cost of projects. In the past, the more robust investment climates in Africa's middle-income countries, reflected in more investment-grade credit ratings, facilitated more and larger project-financed PPPs on more favorable terms than in Africa's primarily low-income countries (Gratwick and Eberhard 2008).

Credit ratings are probably the most widely referred to short-hand measures of a country's investment climate strength. They gauge the likelihood that an entity (sovereign government, commercial bank, or corporate enterprise) will be willing and able to repay its debts on time. Historically, several African middle-income countries (South Africa, Mauritius, Botswana, Namibia, etc.) have achieved "investment grade ratings" (BBB− or higher). None of the low-income countries in Africa have achieved investment grade ratings, and their debts are perennially categorized as "speculative" from an investment point of view. South Africa's 2011 investment grade rating matched the rating of Eskom, who was responsible for purchasing the energy produced by the new IPP projects. This meant that banks and investors would accept sovereign guarantees without requiring an additional layer of political risk insurance, as would have been the case for large PPPs in almost every other African country.

Credit ratings are usually just the starting point for private investors as they try to assess the nature of the investment climate in countries where they may invest. A large and ever-growing population of data sources was already available for investors when REIPPPP was initiated, providing pre-packaged evaluations of the prospects for investment success in most developing countries (e.g., Rand Merchant Bank 2011). In 2011, all of these sources routinely ranked South Africa as by far the strongest economy on the continent and the most desirable investment location. The country's banking sector was the largest, deepest, and most sophisticated in Africa. While perceived to be conservative and expensive, South African banks were essential in helping REIPPPP achieve so many closed transactions in a relatively short period of time. South Africa also had a wide array of other kinds of sophisticated advisory services needed for REIPPPP projects, including legal firms and technical consultants to help with the design of competitive bids and project implementation.

10.3.2 The Failure to Extend and Sustain Upstream Reforms

REIPPPP ultimately came to a premature end in 2015 because of a failure to sustain its high-level political support, the inability to go further with needed sector reforms, and the sharply diminishing strength of the country's investment climate. The program's high level political support evaporated when the national, state-owned power utility, Eskom, began to take action to slow and disrupt REIPPPP implementation. As the economy's largest state-owned enterprise, Eskom had considerable political influence. And to make a program like REIPPPP successful over the long term, politicians must be willing to tolerate reductions in (or elimination of) sector domination by large, state-owned utilities of this kind. This means forgoing many of the traditional political benefits that these SOEs often provide in the developing world, including highly paid patronage jobs, extra employment and social safety net benefits for lower-income constituents, as well as opportunities to isolate debts and revenue shortfalls from general budgets.

By 2014, some South African politicians and government officials had become interested in preserving Eskom's sector domination. It was becoming clear that President Zuma had decided to pursue a massive nuclear power development program with the help of Russia's Rosatom State Nuclear Energy Corporation. Apparently the president decided that Eskom should own and manage the large new fleet of nuclear generation facilities and that such a program would mean that renewable energy projects would no longer be priorities. Various South African energy experts were unable to convince government policymakers that REIPPPP's success in rapidly adding new generation capacity meant that the expensive nuclear program would not represent value for money (BUSINESSTECH 2016).[1]

As REIPPPP began to successfully produce projects, Eskom and its political allies began to publically criticize the program, arguing among other things that the IPP projects were too expensive. Eventually, Eskom began to slow its transmission planning in order to delay IPP project grid connections. Eskom declared in mid-2016 that it would not sign additional power purchase agreements (PPAs) for renewable projects because of what it said were the high costs of these long-term commitments. This left a large number of procured projects in limbo, along with the entire sequence of new bid rounds. The local industrial development component of REIPPPP also came to a halt. This component had begun to stimulate local business development by requiring that some system components be sourced locally. After Eskom stopped signing PPAs, many of these local business start-ups eventually closed.

The country's political leadership at the time did little to protect REIPPPP. The highly effective REIPPPP program manager was summarily replaced without explanation. The status of the REIPPPP program office was formalized and it was forced to become less entrepreneurial and made to focus more on enforcement of bureaucratic rules and procedures than on problem solving. Some efforts have been made to restart REIPPPP bid rounds, but the program had suffered serious long-term reputational damage and never again generated projects as it did in the 2012–15 period. South Africa's nascent "market" for power generation PPPs had been effectively closed after only a few years of successful operation.

The demise of REIPPPP signaled a victory for Eskom and its political patrons in protecting its sector dominance from the threat posed by IPPs. But the utility's over-staffing, mismanagement, and unprecedented levels of internal looting were also becoming evident as the country began to experience longer and more frequent power cuts. By the end of 2017, Eskom had lost all three of its investment-grade credit ratings. Mismanagement in Eskom and South Africa's other state-owned enterprises was also instrumental in undermining the strength of the country's investment climate. Marginal downgrades in the country's sovereign ratings had already begun in mid-2012. In April

1 The nuclear program never started as planned, but has never left the list of government energy sector priorities.

2017, both S&P and Fitch downgraded the country's foreign currency rating to junk status, ending years of investment-grade ratings.

By 2018, Eskom's outstanding debt totaled R387 billion, almost 60 percent of which had been sovereign guaranteed—almost three-quarters of all sovereign-guaranteed borrowing by the country's state-owned enterprises (Hofstatter 2018). Declining power sales, increasing costs, corruption scandals, painful power outages, and repeated unsuccessful requests for the regulator to allow double-digit tariff increases eventually led to frantic large-scale government efforts to reform the country's power sector. Those efforts continued without resolution or even clear signs of progress in 2024. The country's sovereign credit rating further declined.

The successes of REIPPPP underscored the importance of the upstream legal, regulatory, and policy environment in achieving market-like scale-up of PPPs. But REIPPPP's ultimate demise illustrates how fragile this kind of market behavior can be and how fully institutionalized and comprehensive such reforms must be to sustain change. This supports the point made in Chapter 9 that by themselves one-off greenfield IPP projects do little or nothing to solve sector problems caused by mismanaged and corrupt state-owned enterprises that often dominate these infrastructure sectors in developing countries.

10.4 REIPPPP'S INFLUENCE: IFC'S SCALING SOLAR PROGRAM

10.4.1 A One-stop Shop for IPPs

REIPPPP's success, however brief, had considerable influence on some of the development partners who recognized that the South African program had come close to establishing a functioning, competitive market for PPPs. Because of its success in South Africa, extensive upstream preparation clearly seemed to have more potential than transaction-only approaches. This realization had a particular impact on IFC. Power sector investment had long been a priority for IFC, but IFC PPP Advisory had struggled with renewable energy IPP projects. An IFC survey of potential solar markets (completed well before the full impacts of REIPPPP had been documented) noted the unique accomplishments of the South African program: "... very little investment is taking place, except in South Africa where the hugely successful renewable energy procurement program has attracted more than US$3 billion of investments and made it, quite literally, the shining beacon of the region. Elsewhere? Nothing. Literally nothing" (Fergusson et al. 2015, 114).

Earlier efforts to develop solar IPP projects in other African countries had focused on the use of feed-in tariffs (FiTs), promoted by donors, DFIs, and

MDBs. FiTs had long been the default option recommended by development partners because of the widespread use of FiTs in industrialized economies. A FiT is a guaranteed minimum price per unit of power, over a stated fixed-term period. The philosophy behind FiTs is that because existing electricity tariffs are thought to be too low to fully compensate investors who design, build, and operate renewable energy facilities, governments should agree to higher than normal tariffs for these producers as a way to accelerate these investments.

In South Africa, as in some other developing countries, FiTs had not incentivized the right amount of solar power in the right locations, or at the best prices for governments because competitive service pricing was not involved. These were directly negotiated contracts, proposed by interested sponsors on a self-selected basis. The contracts were slow and expensive to conclude because they entailed high transaction costs, were hampered by limited government capacity to negotiate transactions, and plagued by high perceived risk. In other words, in many developing countries, this approach did not result in project replication or market development.

IFC PPP Advisory realized that, as with REIPPPP, governments needed to actively manage the process of selecting private sponsors to get multiple transactions of the kind that would be most beneficial: "Reflecting back on what made South Africa and other programs a success, we identified the key ingredients of scale, transparent competition, a bankable contractual framework, repetition" (Fergusson et al. 2015, 115). Active management meant a host of upstream preparation activities to lay the groundwork for multiple downstream transactions. These activities included the following:

1. The pre-tender preparation of bankable, non-negotiable template documents and arrangements for "stapled" financing from IFC Investment (automatically available to winning bidders). These upstream activities would accelerate low-cost tender preparations and help avoid drawn-out contract negotiations. This could help maximize project delivery speed and efficiency.
2. The pre-selection of project sites would minimize uncertainty, ensuring each project was optimized for the grid. The addition of pre-structured stapled political risk insurance and off-taker credit enhancement would strengthen private supplier risk mitigation and encourage tender participation.
3. Working with government planners to prepare an offering of multiple projects and multiple auction rounds would also encourage bidder interest (as with REIPPPP, losing bidders in one tender round would still have opportunities to be successful in subsequent rounds). IFC hoped to eventually set up "Scaling Solar" programs in multiple African countries

to create a regional market in solar IPP projects to maintain replication and market momentum.

The key to Scaling Solar was the creation of what the IFC called a "one-stop shop" for IPPs—a massive amount of upstream preparation to provide everything needed ahead of tenders, help in designing and managing the actual tender processes, plus the availability of financing products that preferred bidders could access as soon as tenders were completed. All of this was designed to help transactions reach financial closure as quickly as possible. The process required a considerable amount of financial assistance and technical expertise because of the need to implement such a wide range of upstream activities: project identification, site location, legal and technical feasibility assessment, document preparation, tender design, coordination of World Bank Group (WBG) credit enhancements and stapled financing options. The difficulty of doing all of this was exacerbated by the IFC pledge that the process, from initial feasibility assessments to financial close, would be completed in 12 months (Fergusson et al. 2015).

In 2015, IFC Advisory proposed the first Scaling Solar program to the Zambian government. The program represented millions of dollars in assistance and very low risks to the government because every important aspect of the program would be managed or overseen by IFC. The government agreed and in July 2015 a request for pre-qualification was issued for two projects. Forty-eight solar developers responded and 11 were prequalified, all well known in the international marketplace. In February 2016, a request for proposals was issued to the prequalified firms, and after proposals were submitted and evaluated, the winning bids were announced in June 2016. The tenders resulted in winning bids of 6c kWh for a 52 MW project and 7.8c kWh for a 34 MW project.

The Zambian bids attracted considerable attention in SSA. The bids were not only lower than the best prices achieved by the South African REIPPPP Program, but also comparable to prices achieved in the most advanced frontier solar markets. The achievement of the Zambian program was not lost on countries like Uganda and Nigeria, where government officials began to insist on prices of no more than USc 7–8 kWh for new projects, or in some cases, even for projects for which PPAs had already been signed. A second round of Scaling Solar tendering was eventually implemented in Zambia, targeting 500 MW. Subsequent Scaling Solar programs were later announced in Senegal, Madagascar, Ethiopia, and Uzbekistan.

10.4.2 Questions about the Success of Scaling Solar

The market-building impacts of the Scaling Solar programs were not as strong and sustainable as IFC hoped. Scaling Solar did indeed involve a "one-stop shop solution" as IFC claimed, but almost every important aspect of the program was handled by IFC PPP Advisory. A variety of donors provided the large amounts of funding necessary for the upstream preparation, but only on condition that IFC manage the process. IFC Investment agreed to offer stapled financing automatically to the preferred bidder as long as IFC PPP Advisory managed the tender process and all bid document preparation.

IFC argued that the Scaling Solar program would build counterpart government capacity because the host country agencies and personnel would be involved in preparing the projects and managing the procurement process. But the very limited exposure of government counterparts to a single tender exercise, implemented in world-record time and almost completely designed and managed by IFC meant that very little sustainable capacity development took place. As a DFID case study of the program later pointed out, Scaling Solar involved almost no focus on the long-term sustainability of the program itself (DFID 2017).

If a program like Scaling Solar was going to be more than a one-off tender exercise, it needed to incorporate a more extensive collection of upstream reforms: enhanced capacity of government staff, sector reforms involving market structure (e.g., grid code amendments), legislation, regulation (e.g., IPP project licensing), master planning, and customer pricing, etc. These kinds of reforms arguably were needed *before* a program like Scaling Solar was implemented. As with most power sectors in Africa, Zambia's sector was plagued by weak planning, faulty regulation and customer pricing, and dominated by a poorly managed, vertically integrated, state-owned utility. Needed "upstream" legal and regulatory reforms, as well as meaningful capacity building, were conspicuously ignored by the Scaling Solar program.

In the aftermath of the first Scaling Solar program in Zambia, several independent evaluations have suggested that the desperate IFC effort to meet the 12-month deadline for financial closure may have compromised some of the program's claims of success. In contrast to REIPPPP's effort to achieve a fair balance of project risks between public and private partners, Scaling Solar shifted most of the significant project risks and project development costs away from private developers to the IFC, donors, or the government. In the words of the DFID case study mentioned above, the program "... effectively removes material risk from the project ..." (DFID 2017). IFC not only prepared the projects, they also offered most of the financing. And a significant share of the financing was offered on concessional grounds—something that may have been unnecessary given the interest of commercial banks in these projects (Kruger and Eberhard 2018). DFID's case study noted that all this de-risking left only a few areas for differentiation among bidders in a competitive tender, such as the size of equity returns, pricing of engineering, procurement, construction (EPC) contracts, and owner's overheads (DFID 2017). The ability to compete based on these factors could mostly be reduced to the amount of technical and financial resources available to competing bidders, so small developers were effectively excluded from the competition.

More recent evaluations have raised additional questions about the accuracy of information released by the IFC regarding the "success" of the Zambia program. A U.S. Agency for International Development (USAID) evaluation in 2018 found that the publicly announced tariffs were inconsistent with the published tender requirements, because they included extra and unquantified post-award tax breaks for the winning bidders and lower than required equity requirements (USAID 2018). The USAID study concluded that the key stated objective of the project, the mobilization of private sector finance, had clearly not been met. For the first round of the Zambia program, 80 percent of the nominal financing was provided by IFC and other concessional financing sources.

A 2021 study by published by the Energy for Growth Hub confirmed that despite official claims that implicit and explicit subsidies played minimal roles in the Zambian IPPs, the level of both kinds of subsidy was substantial. The study identified concessional finance plus free land, tax breaks, project preparation funding, a guarantee provided by the World Bank, plus the implicit guarantee related to any kind of DFI finance in projects of this kind (Emery 2023).

The impetus for Scaling Solar's approach to market development, and perhaps some of its shortcomings, may have resulted in part from a sense of urgency around the need to promote IFC's strategic investment interests. Scaling Solar was designed at a time when IFC Investment was aggressively expanding its lending for renewable energy power generation projects. From 2005 to 2008, IFC's lending to IPPs (for both renewable energy and thermal plants) surged into a dominant position in the organization's infrastructure lending portfolio, expanding the IPP share of all commitments from 29 percent in 2001–04, to just over 40 percent. But from 2009 to 2012, lending to thermal projects fell off by 32 percent and lending to renewable energy IPP projects (including hydropower projects) remained flat. To maintain power generation's share of the portfolio in the face of sharply increasing lending for transportation projects, IFC ramped up lending for renewable projects by 32 percent over the 2013–16 period (Kenny et al. 2018). Scaling Solar issued its first request-for-prequalification (RFPQ) in July 2015.

If the Zambian program and other "Scaling Solar" programs planned for other countries had completed as many IPP projects as hoped, their use of

IFC Investment's stapled financing options could have generated substantial benefits for IFC's lending portfolio. But these programs could not be replicated without IFC PPP Advisory's almost total control of preparation and the donor funding that IFC's involvement attracted. In addition, preferred bidders selected by these tenders were not obligated to take advantage of the stapled financing options. Other DFIs interested in financing renewable energy IPP projects were sometimes willing to offer concessional funding for well-prepared projects, at prices that IFC could not match. As of May 2023, the Scaling programs had delivered similarly subsidized projects in only two additional countries (Senegal and Uzbekistan), leading one expert observer to conclude that "… the initiative did not fulfill its grand vision of providing a demonstration model that could be replicated widely" (Kenny 2023).

10.5 "IFC 3.0": MAINSTREAMING UPSTREAM PREPARATION

10.5.1 Lessons Learned

The Scaling Solar experience suggested several realities regarding IFC PPP Advisory transaction work:

- With enough subsidized upstream preparation and private sector risk mitigation, one-off PPPs (offering highly affordable services) could reach financial closure in low-income countries in a relatively short period of time.
- The process, without the direct management by IFC PPP Advisory and coordination with IFC Investment, was unlikely to be repeated in other settings; the chances for significant scale-up and market-like behavior in countries where IFC was not leading a process like this seemed remote unless engagements could be longer in duration (starting further upstream) and supported with more resources.

These lessons had significance for IFC at a time when the organization was trying to maintain its investment numbers in the face of competition from DFIs such as FMO, PROPARCO, and DEG, who also specialized in lending at near-commercial terms to private companies and financial institutions. Questions about IFC's ability to achieve—and ultimately take advantage of—PPP scale-up and market-like behavior were also being asked by others in the WBG at this time.

IEG issued a 2013 assessment of the monitoring and evaluations systems of the IFC. The assessment found that IFC PPP Advisory was effectively capturing the outputs of its work, meaning the number of projects tendered, projects closed, etc. But the program was not effectively capturing data on project outcomes, meaning the broader changes resulting from those outputs, which would include longer-term results like project replication or market development. For PPP advisory, there was no formal, systematic follow-up after an activity was deemed to be completed. Follow-up evaluation was handled through "… ad hoc or selective post completion initiatives or external evaluations …" (IEG 2013, 42). In other words, IFC PPP Advisory did not have an effective method for understanding what kinds of market-building outcomes its work might be having. This also meant that they had no ex ante way of selecting PPP projects with the highest potential for replication and market development.

A few years later, IEG spelled out the consequences of IFC's failure to focus on outcomes as well as outputs. IEG's annual performance review of the entire WBG from 2014 to 2016 evaluated samples of projects and found that development outcome ratings for both IFC Investment and IFC Advisory were in sharp decline (IEG 2017). Outcome ratings for IFC Investment projects dropped to 50 percent, well below IFC's corporate target of 65 percent. Development effectiveness for IFC Advisory Services dropped from 63 percent in financial year 2011–13 to 49 percent in financial year 2014–16, the lowest rating since IEG started such reviews in 2008. IFC activities were achieving outputs, but not outcomes: "Simply put, while a large share of advisory projects were rated satisfactory or better for delivering the intended outputs (for example, report, training, products, and so on), expected outcomes or the short- or medium-term changes resulting from the project were not achieved" (47).

10.5.2 IFC's New Upstream Strategy

IEG's 2017 findings regarding IFC performance attracted a considerable amount of attention inside as well as outside IFC. Later that year, the WBG issued a document outlining a new group-wide strategy for infrastructure finance that became known as the "cascade approach." This approach called for a dramatic shift from traditional default models in which governments played primary roles in financing and implementing infrastructure projects to a model in which private sector involvement was prioritized whenever feasible, with governments involved only as a last resort (WBG 2017b). So, instead of starting with public finance as the default option and bringing in the private sector only when necessary, the new WBG approach reversed the process, calling for initial consideration of direct private finance, moving to PPPs if necessary, and considering public finance only if no private options were feasible.

Among other things, the WBG promotion of the cascade approach prioritized the need for IFC to immediately address the IEG performance findings and find a way to better guard its market share against the growing number of DFI competitors. The solution was a much bigger and better version of the Scaling Solar strategy: using more resources to move further upstream, and coordinate the work of IFC Advisory and IFC Investment to play a direct, combined role in the preparation of downstream projects in which IFC would be positioned to invest. The traditional conflict-of-interest prohibition against IFC Advisory and IFC Investment working together on the same projects had been overlooked for the purposes of Scaling Solar. For the new strategy, that prohibition was officially ended in the interest of finding desperately needed new investment opportunities.

The ambitious new long-term IFC strategy started development in 2017, was discussed with the IFC board in 2018, and reached a more thorough articulation in *IFC 3.0: Creating Markets and Mobilizing Private Capital* (IFC 2020a). The strategy called for IFC to reach $48 billion in total long-term finance commitments by 2030, with 40 percent in IDA and fragile or conflict affected countries—a four-fold increase over 2021 commitments in those countries.

To meet these new targets, IFC acknowledged the "... critical need to address the shortage of bankable transactions" (IFC 2020a, 11). It was already clear that the existing business models used by both IFC Investment and IFC PPP Advisory would not allow them to meet the ambitious "IFC 3.0" performance targets. Both approaches were reactive and opportunistic rather than proactive and strategic. IFC Investment had traditionally focused on private firms that initiated financing requests and relied on repeat clients for more than half of its business (Kenny 2021). IFC PPP Advisory had pursued its transaction-only approach, working with public sector clients, and selecting projects opportunistically in the sense that deals were prioritized if they could reach commercial closure relatively quickly without requiring lengthy and expensive upstream reforms.

This downstream transaction focus had worked for IFC PPP Advisory in achieving modest numbers of commercial closures in middle-income countries. But the approach did not work well in low-income countries where more time and effort were needed on upstream legal, regulatory, and capacity building activities in order to prepare the groundwork for the structuring and tendering of PPP transactions. Quadrupling the number of project closures in IDA countries would not be possible without early-stage work to generate realistic pipelines of potential PPPs.

To find the bankable transactions it needed, the organization created a new department, "IFC Upstream." Its purpose was "... to support the creation and realization of specific projects for which IFC is a likely financing partner ..."

(IFC 2020a, 22). By 2020 IFC began the process of hiring hundreds of new staff to focus on upstream operations, organized in four Global Upstream Units, 15 Regional Upstream Units, and a Global Upstream Department. The majority of IFC PPP Advisory resources were to be shifted to Upstream (23). By the beginning of 2022, InfraVentures had already been absorbed into the Upstream program.

Several principles were also established to guide this upstream work:

- "Upstream activity is broadly defined as all activity that lays the groundwork for development of a particular sector or project, enabling it to attract private sector investment" (IFC 2020a, 8).
- It will focus on "... creating new and stronger markets, particularly in countries that have benefited least from private investment" (3).
- The work will require "... a shift in IFC's approach from separate investment and advisory engagements to one that systematically coordinates advisory with investment and policy advice to create the upstream conditions for market creation while also building a near-term investment pipeline ..." (9).
- IFC is "... mainstreaming its approach to upstream ..." meaning that this represents organization-wide change, with both Investment Services and Advisory Services restructured to accommodate the new approach (5).
- "Upstream" work would begin considerably earlier than preparation work for Scaling Solar. PPP Advisory staff were asked to "... have a clear line of sight to a potential IFC Investment within 5 years" (IFC 2020b, 3).

10.5.3 A Framework for Anticipating and Measuring IFC's Outcomes

To commit so much funding and personnel to upstream work in the hopes that it would result not only in downstream projects, but also market-building outcomes, IFC needed a new project analytical framework that could resolve the monitoring and evaluation shortcomings identified by IEG in 2013. Ideally, this would be framework that could accurately anticipate the likelihood of output achievement (measured by output indicators like numbers of tendered projects or commercially closed transactions). The framework would also need to anticipate the likely longer-term outcomes of closed projects—whether or not a project output would also create an outcome like project replication or market development. Such a system would inform ex ante project selection and design, and help ensure that resources used for upstream work were not wasted on one-off projects incapable of leading to further development change. The system could also be used for ex post monitoring and evaluation.

IFC started piloting its Anticipated Impact Measurement and Monitoring (AIMM) system in July 2017 (IFC 2019). AIMM was an elaborate suite of analytical tools incorporating hundreds of assumptions about the relationships between project outputs and outcomes and the nature of "markets" and market development.[2] The two key analytical concepts used in evaluating projects are:

- *Market outcomes*—these are the attributes of markets that IFC projects might help develop:
  - Competitiveness
  - Resilience
  - Integration
  - Inclusiveness and
  - Sustainability.
- *Market creation channels*—these are the ways in which projects help achieve each of the market outcomes:
  - Demonstration and replication effects
  - Actions that contribute to promoting competition
  - Putting in place enabling frameworks and
  - Building skills and capacity that open the market to new opportunities.

To determine an overall rating of a project's potential to produce intended outcomes, projects needed to be assessed in terms of the development "gap" addressed by the project (the size of the development challenge relative to the size in similar client countries). The rating also needed to incorporate an estimation of the intensity of the project's impact, which depends on the project's design, size, duration, etc. IFC staff were also warned to consider the need for counterfactual, "no project" assessments of outcomes, the possibility that projects can have negative outcome effects, the fact that outcomes will likely happen long after projects have started operations, the risk of double counting outcomes, etc.

The IFC 3.0 strategy was an acknowledgment that the downstream transaction-only PPP strategy that had dominated PPF work for the previous 25 years had not been successful in leading to project replication and market development in the poorest countries. AIMM underscored this by cautioning that individual transactions cannot be expected to make significant and immediate systemic market changes. AIMM noted that such projects typically have only an incremental impact on market development.

---

2 Publicly available AIMM documents note that the framework was developed based on research and IFC experience, but no supporting documents or references are identified.

Demonstration effects that motivate market entry and project replication are rare, especially if the effects are generated by isolated, one-off projects. Such effects can also be negative or misleading and can discourage market entry. Other "channels" of market creation, like better enabling frameworks, skill development, or innovations that promote competition, are often equally if not more important. More than one type of intervention is usually necessary to move a market to the next stage of development. AIMM pointed out that programmatic approaches involving "… concerted and cumulative World Bank Group efforts over time" are often needed to generate tangible market outcomes and sustainable changes (IFC 2019, 6).

10.6 CONCLUSIONS

Although short-lived, the remarkable success of South Africa's REIPPPP program prompted IFC appreciation, after nearly two decades, of the wisdom of the recommendations about PPPs reached in the World Bank's 2002 Private Sector Strategy—that focusing on transaction assistance would not be enough to facilitate PPP replication in developing countries. Extensive upstream work on factors "extraneous" to transactions was needed to prepare the groundwork for sustainable projects.

But IFC's ultimate intentions with this upstream work are not completely clear. The work undertaken by IFC Upstream may be mostly a matter of identifying and facilitating legal and regulatory reforms, carrying out capacity building, and clearly conceptualizing possible projects. This might reflect a genuine intention to trigger project replication and market behavior involving projects that eventually would be done by public and private actors, without the involvement of donors and DFIs like IFC or subsidized preparation and investment offered by donors. But IFC policymakers undoubtedly know that this kind of outcome is unlikely. As noted in Chapter 9, DFI project successes are often more than anything else the result of DFI involvement, something that private sector actors cannot replicate.

IFC's market development strategy may be aiming at something else. The 2015 IEG review of the WBG's PPP work identified the main upstream problem limiting project replication as one of "client commitment," and suggested that "For projects that involve commitments from multiple stakeholders, IFC should engage in a pre-mandate assignment to identify and map stakeholders and engage in discussions with them to determine their support for the projects" (IEG 2015, xxiii).

"Client commitment" is often another way of saying that clients are unconvinced to proceed with a PPP, the only solution offered in the past by IFC PPP Advisory. Will IFC's new emphasis on upstream work be more about objective technical advice or PPP advocacy? Will comparative VfM assessments be done to show clients how and why PPPs are better solutions to infrastructure problems than alternatives like enhanced forms of traditional public investment? Is this an effort to scale-up the use of PPPs in the sense of establishing sustainable markets in such projects in developing countries, or just a more comprehensive, longer-term effort to help IFC meet its own investment targets?

PART V

Conclusions

11. Conclusions to *The Rise and Fall of Public–Private Partnerships*

11.1 THE FUTURE OF PPPS

The private sector has already passed judgment on the future of public–private partnerships (PPPs). Some isolated, heavily subsidized projects will continue to reach closure, mostly in middle-income countries. But projects will only do so if the ratio of private returns to private risks is acceptable to private partners. Private investors and sponsors are now familiar enough with these projects to understand that there are only a very limited set of contracting arrangements that are likely to achieve what from their perspective are acceptable ratios of that kind. Consequently, most private investment in infrastructure will increasingly focus on projects involving highly secure revenue streams and strong forms of private sector risk mitigation. The vast majority of these projects will be greenfield, wholesale, build–operate–transfer (BOT) and build–own–operate (BOO) projects, supported with subsidies for preparation and investment, involving long-term service purchase agreements and unitary payments in hard currency backed by various kinds of guarantees. Brownfield PPPs involving private rehabilitation and operation of assets long owned and maintained by government entities, and projects depending on retail service revenues for commercial viability (with tariffs set by government regulators), already seem well on their way to extinction.

Efforts to enable project replication and market-like behavior will likely continue to show little success. Demonstration effects of one-off projects have never incentivized this kind of behavior, despite a quarter century of effort. The sort of upstream project environments necessary to facilitate PPP market behavior, like the one that benefitted South Africa's renewable energy independent power producer program for several years, can rarely be developed in the near- to medium-term, unless countries already have strong investment climates. The enormous effort by the International Finance Corporation (IFC) to marshal resources for upstream preparation of PPPs, pursuant to the organization's "IFC 2.0" strategy, may generate more projects financed by the IFC, but is unlikely to achieve outcomes involving projects reaching closure without the involvement of development finance institutions (DFIs).

The principal unanswered question about the future of PPPs is how soon will donors and multilateral development banks (MDBs) who support what this book refers to as PPP advocacy manage to free themselves of misconceptions regarding what PPPs are and what they can achieve. Development partners should consider moving on to a more balanced form of support that includes stronger efforts to expand and improve various types of mostly conventional public investment and management of infrastructure. In light of all the available evidence, there appear to be no compelling reasons for donors to continue funding project preparation facilities (PPFs) that exclusively focus on developing individual PPP projects without rigorously assessing alternatives to PPP approaches.

But changes in the prevailing approach will not be easy. PPP advocacy has been extraordinarily successful in convincing the development community to support the idea that PPPs can be significantly scaled up to solve infrastructure problems in developing countries. That support has included enormous amounts of funding provided by donors and MDBs to PPFs to promote the use of PPPs and prepare projects on behalf of developing country counterparts. That level of support has remained very strong for a long period of time despite poor performance because PPP advocates have managed to avoid rigorous evaluations of their activities.

Lant Pritchett's attempt to explain why evaluation is so poorly done in foreign aid programs offers a political economy explanation for this avoidance. Pritchett describes advocates, the most entrepreneurial of whom he calls "true believers," as those who initiate, administer, and promote budget expansion of single-problem, single-solution facilities, like the PPP advocacy programs and PPFs discussed here. But these advocates rarely support rigorous program evaluation because of the risks that evaluations may cost them essential support from donors and other "core supporters" who are needed for program sustainability. Instead, advocates must persuade core supporters to continue funding their work by relying on anecdotal evidence in the form of success stories and testimonials to confirm the efficacy of their programs. Pritchett uses the admittedly awkward term, "persuadability," to describe how amenable core supporters are to promotional or persuasive activities by true believers who staff the many PPFs that survive on donor money.

11.2 THE LAST PPP ADVOCACY ARGUMENT

Despite the accumulating evidence of poor PPP performance, many "core supporters" are still convinced by the last and in many ways the most enduring argument in favor of PPPs: that there is no other alternative but to turn to the private sector for help with infrastructure investment. Among other things, this argument makes it easier to accept that significant up-front project appraisal work is not necessary to confirm project additionality. This "no alternative" argument supports the claims made by governments in many developing countries that they have little room to expand their budgetary expenditure on infrastructure because of their inability to increase own-source revenue from taxes and user-fees, and limited capacity to borrow to finance infrastructure investment.

However, in many cases these claims are simply not supported by evidence—governments often can do much more to generate own-source revenue by setting tariffs to target end-users who can pay for services, cross-subsidizing services to ensure benefits for poor customers, improving the collection rates for taxes and user fees, optimizing systems of intergovernmental grants and loans, etc. More effective revenue generation also increases the likelihood that government utilities can borrow on their own account from bond markets or commercial banks to finance infrastructure investments. This kind of borrowing requires utilities to plan capital investment activities that are bankable and commercially viable and meet the compliance and due diligence requirements of regulators and investors. Municipal bond markets are already developing on this basis in middle-income countries like India, China, Brazil, Columbia, and Mexico.

Major improvements in all of these areas are often possible, but are time-consuming and nearly always risk antagonizing powerful entrenched interests that benefit in some way from the status quo. Governments and their development partners prefer to find ways of circumventing such problems rather than trying to solve them directly, and this is of course a major part of the motivation for attempting to use private finance to pay for things like infrastructure investment.

But even in cases where budgetary envelopes cannot be significantly expanded, this still does not necessarily mean that governments have no real choice other than to explore private participation as the only way to significantly improve the quality and quantity of infrastructure services in these countries. Private participation in the form of PPPs has never exceeded 10–15 percent of total infrastructure investment in developing countries, with much lower percentages in low-income countries. It is also clear that, across the developing world, most of the financing for private participation comes from non-private sources like DFIs, donors, public banks, and public equity (World Bank 2019c). The public sector, including general-purpose public entities like treasury departments and ministries, as well as special-purpose entities like state-owned enterprises (SOEs), remains the dominant source of finance for water, energy, and transport in the developing world. Even in upper middle-income countries, PPPs are mostly additional forms of infrastructure investment, not replacements for public projects.

If government departments and SOEs account for 95 percent of infrastructure investment in a region like sub-Saharan Africa (SSA), then finding ways of increasing the efficiency of the ways in which government entities select, prepare, and manage their public investments could have substantial beneficial impacts on the quality and quantity of infrastructure service provision. Making even marginal improvements in the efficiency of that kind of investment, or facilitating reductions in investment needs through operational improvements, would have a far larger impact on the quality of infrastructure services provided in developing countries than spending huge amounts of time and money preparing a handful of opportunistically selected, highly subsidized PPPs that can only be replicated with end-to-end support from development partners.

11.3 ALTERNATIVES TO PPPS

Since the mid-2010s, understanding and improving public investment has become a much more active field of innovative research, with a practical emphasis on best-practice recommendations. In several ways, these developments have significantly undermined the "no alternative" arguments made by PPP advocates, as follows.

11.3.1 Reform of State-owned Enterprises

A decade after the end of structural adjustment lending programs, the Africa Infrastructure Country Diagnostic (AICD) noted that SOEs were "here to stay" (Foster and Briceño-Garmendia 2010). More recent efforts to assess the extent of SOE privatization in regions like SSA have confirmed that little progress has been made (Estrin and Pelletier 2018). Africa remains the developing country region with the largest percentage of infrastructure utilities under state ownership. However, even in Organisation for Economic Co-operation and Development (OECD) countries the role of SOEs in infrastructure investment is increasing (IMF 2020). The realization that SOEs are "here to stay" has led to the view that SOEs need to be reformed rather than removed via privatization as a way to significantly improve infrastructure investment and management. The acceptance of this view has reached the point where serious research endorses decisions by some OECD countries to deploy enhanced SOE models as alternatives to privatized SOEs or PPPs. In Denmark, for example, the government has rejected PPP models for large transport projects in favor of an SOE model that combines professional boards of directors and management with financing via state guaranteed-loans and user-charges (Christensen and Greve 2018).

11.3.2 Municipal Bond Market Development

The benefits of municipal bond issuance have long been well known to officials in developing countries, if only because of the powerful example of the U.S. municipal market. Countries like India, Indonesia, and the Philippines started trying to emulate elements of the U.S. municipal bond market in the 1990s (Leigland 1997). They continue to work on the legal, regulatory, and policy reforms needed to enable municipal bond market activity. But other kinds of work are needed as well and are being addressed in some countries. India sold its first municipal bond issue without a state guarantee in 1998. Arguably its legal-regulatory framework for municipal bond issuance has been in place since then. But the issuance track record since 1998 has shown little signs of growth, with only about two dozen issuers selling bonds since the first issue. The problem now being addressed in India is the need for "upstream" municipal bond preparation that takes place 12–18 months prior to the actual sale of bonds. This preparation is essential in India because although over 160 potential municipal bond issuers are considered creditworthy (with credit ratings of at least "BBB"), bond issues in India need to be rated "AA" or above to meet prudential investment requirements that permit the market's largest investors—pension funds, insurance companies, and mutual funds—to purchase these securities (Srikumar and Venkataraman 2023). So, in its simplest form this upstream preparation consists of work to help already creditworthy municipal governments achieve the "AA" rating necessary for a successful bond sale in India. Such preparation typically focuses on fully meeting the compliance and due diligence requirements specified by regulators and credit rating agencies, and emphasizing improvements to accounting procedures and financial reporting. In India, various levels of government are currently identifying ways of financing this kind of upstream preparation.

11.3.3 Public Investment Management (PIM)

The challenge of identifying the institutions and procedures required to efficiently oversee and manage public investments has become the focus of an emerging body of literature on PIM. Economists and public management experts are attempting to develop tools to help poor countries improve the quality and cost-effectiveness of their investment expenditures (Fainboim et al. 2013; IMF 2015; ODI 2015, 2016). The emphasis in this literature has been on near-term results in low-capacity environments. In other words, the sophisticated project planning, budgeting, and management systems in developed countries have been largely bypassed because of their inability to provide practical results in most developing country environments. Instead, experts have begun to identify essential features of PIM systems that reduce key risks but which can be implemented by public officials in these countries.

11.3.4 Hybrid Infrastructure Project Structures

Given the increasingly apparent limitations of PPPs, combined with the growing sophistication of PIM approaches, it is no surprise that some governments have experimented with alternative project structures that technically may not be PPPs as conventionally defined because of a limited risk-sharing. Some of these hybrid structures offer ways of taking more advantage of private sector efficiencies, and in some cases access to finance, than would be the case with traditional public investment. And because these are hybrids, this access to private participation benefits can sometimes be achieved without enduring the high costs, delays, and political controversy often associated with PPPs. Here, India's experimentation with enhanced engineering, procurement, construction (EPC) contracts and so-called "hybrid annuity model" (HAM) contracts is illustrative (Leigland 2020a). Compared with PPP models widely used in India until 2013, these project structures involve less risk for private partners, but also less profit and more government control. A preliminary analysis published by the Asian Development Bank (AsDB) found that the value-for-money (VfM) generated by both HAMs and EPCs was higher than for conventional contracts used by the Indian government for most public investment projects (Peri et al. 2019). IFC PPP Advisory helped pioneer the use of HAM contracts in India but does not seem to have promoted the approach in other countries, perhaps because these are not usually classified as PPPs.

11.4 WHAT SUSTAINS PPP ADVOCACY?

If the "no alternative" argument is so easily discredited, what has delayed actions by donors needed to control the excesses of PPP advocacy? What has postponed the decline in donor funding that should have steadily accelerated as PPFs consistently fail to meet ever more ambitious PPP performance promises? From time to time, individual donors have become disenchanted with PPFs like GPOBA, PPIAF, and PIDG, and have withdrawn funding as a result. But this has never turned into a trend involving most of the donors who fund these facilities. At higher levels of the development community, the general enthusiasm for PPPs seems largely undiminished despite three decades of under-performance. In tracing the evolution of PPP advocacy since the mid-1990s several key reasons for this sustained enthusiasm stand out, as follows.

11.4.1 Ideology

The first and most important reason is that PPP advocacy is a by-product of the powerful ideological faith in private sector-oriented market-based solutions to economic problems. This is the same faith that fueled what World Bank officials later admitted was a "euphoria over privatization" under structural adjustment—the faith has manifested itself in many other areas of public policy since the 1980s. Privatization and PPPs were not two different approaches as has been argued by PPP advocates since the early 2000s. Nor did the faith in market-based solutions die with the reluctant abandonment of structural adjustment's privatization imperatives. The power of this faith and its widespread impacts on social and economic policy in OECD countries have until relatively recently been ignored or underestimated except by critics deemed to be too ideological to be taken seriously by mainstream politicians and policy makers. After the global financial crisis, academic researchers began to treat the unshakable faith in the power of the market as a subject of study. More recently, popular historical accounts by journalists and academicians have begun to explore the social and economic implications of this widespread market-based ideology (Slobodian 2018; Appelbaum 2019; Gerstle 2022; Oreskes and Conway 2023). The point is, this is a powerful, pervasive, and enduring world view that continues to buoy PPP advocacy despite the absence of rigorous evaluations demonstrating compelling benefits.

11.4.2 Crises

A second reason for the ability of PPP advocacy to continue to attract strong donor support has been the succession of major infrastructure-related crises that seem to be beyond solution by the existing global aid system. The Millennium Development Goals (MDGs) were followed by the even more ambitious and less achievable Sustainable Development Goals (SDGs). Climate change began to emerge as a massive, dangerous, and seemingly intractable infrastructure problem. The COVID-19 pandemic took infrastructure investment challenges to a new level, especially in low-income countries (LICs). Unlike the Asian financial crisis in 1997 or the global financial crisis a decade later, the pandemic impacted LICs with simultaneous external and domestic shocks—collapsing demand for exports, falling commodity prices, weakening foreign direct investment combined with diminished domestic economic activity, dramatic decreases in tourism revenues, a fall in remittances, declining tax revenues, increasing food insecurity, and growing demands on governments to mitigate the spread of the virus. Repeated infrastructure challenges generated by these kinds of crises, make the need for finding large new sources of investment seem particularly urgent, and suggest that more effort should be applied in attracting private investors to participate in projects.

11.4.3 Self-defense

A third reason for the undiminished strength of PPP advocacy became apparent with the development community's reactions to the emergence of evidence regarding the immense size of the infrastructure investment gap in the developing world, first documented reliably in studies like AICD in 2010. The reaction was surprise and a measure of embarrassment. Established development institutions were sharply criticized by the likes of the G24, and G20 officials threatened to modify the mandates of national and international development banks to force them into more infrastructure investment in poor countries. Donors and MDBs claimed that they were already doing all they could in these countries, well aware that sourcing additional funding from member countries would be difficult so soon after the global financial crisis. The development establishment shifted blame to the private sector, and its trillions of dollars in resources, for the lack of infrastructure investment. Because the private sector had more than enough money for needed investment, the G20 and the leading MDBs reframed the problem as a "preparation gap." The real challenge was not in closing an investment gap, requiring more money to be channeled through donors and MDBs, but in finding more effective ways of attracting private sector investment into infrastructure projects. Already established PPFs, like PIDG and IFC PPP Advisory, focused on preparing projects for private investment, although had not achieved the widespread replication of projects that was needed. But these PPFs were excused as having insufficient resources to effectively do so. The problem was dismissed as the result of insufficient funding for preparation and lack of coordination among PPFs, rather than shortcomings in the basic PPP mechanism—a far more daunting prospect. The G20 concluded that new, larger, and better-funded PPFs like the Global Infrastructure Facility (GIF) and Africa50 were needed to address the problem. Meanwhile, existing PPFs like PIDG, PPIAF, and IFC PPP Advisory now also had more compelling arguments for additional funding. But the disappointing performance of PPFs of any kind continues to raise questions about the wisdom of focusing on PPP project preparation rather than the search for more effective ways of addressing traditional public investment management approaches to infrastructure financing and management.

11.4.4 Strategic Self-interest

A fourth reason for the endurance of PPP advocacy has to do with the sheer size and geographical spread of the global community of PPP true believers and core supporters, now involving thousands of facilities, funds, programs, associations, government PPP units, private sector sponsors, operators, investors, conference organizers, consulting firms, training providers, etc. This community acts as a world-wide lobbying coalition whose members sometimes appear to be advocating the use of PPPs primarily as a way to protect their own jobs and influence rather than to improve infrastructure service delivery. Operating mostly as single-purpose actors, employed solely for the purpose of facilitating PPPs, these organizations and individuals have spent billions of dollars over the last 25 years to promote the use of PPPs usually without consistently or rigorously analyzing the costs and benefits of individual PPPs, or the comparative value of alternative approaches involving traditional public investment.

11.5 CONCLUSIONS

These reasons help explain the continued existence of the PPP paradox described in the introduction to this book. Although a mounting body of reliable evidence exists regarding the lack of PPP success in developing countries, such projects are tremendously over-sold by advocates. PPPs attract far more attention and resources than they should compared to alternative approaches to infrastructure development which have the potential for much larger and more sustainable benefits. This situation will continue until bilateral donors, who act as the core supporters of PPP advocacy, examine their own incentives for a lack of attention to more important and cost-effective infrastructure service delivery solutions.

12. Postscript: revisiting the seven deadly sins of donors

12.1 INTRODUCTION

Underpinning the endurance of public–private partnership (PPP) advocacy is the willingness of donors to continue providing financial support to project preparation facilities (PPFs) and other advocacy programs profiled in this book. This willingness reflects what Lant Pritchett called the "persuadability" of "core supporters" (Pritchett 2008). A helpful short-hand guide in understanding the various dimensions of this persuadability is the well-known paper by Nancy Birdsall, "Seven Deadly Sins: Reflections on Donor Failings" (Birdsall 2005). Originally prepared for a development conference in Bangladesh, and republished many times thereafter, the paper deals with the shortcomings of "donors"—broadly defined to include multilateral development banks (MDBs), development finance institutions (DFIs), bilateral donors, and others—as providers of development assistance. Birdsall's paper focused mostly on the quality of aid rather than the quantity, reflecting her conviction that problems with aid quality were important because "… they reduce considerably the effective value of the aid that is transferred, and in the most aid-dependent countries may well mean that the way the 'business of aid' is conducted actually undermines those countries' long-term development prospects" (3).

Now nearly two decades old, the paper captures donor shortcomings at a time when support for PPPs was ramping up to counteract the sharp drop in enthusiasm for such projects after the Asian financial crisis. Birdsall's paper did not focus specifically on PPP-related assistance, but her discussion of the "seven deadly donor sins" helps explain donor willingness to accept the non-rigorous claims disseminated by PPP advocates regarding the efficacy of their programs. That Birdsall's discussion is still so relevant today, particularly for PPP advocacy, reflects the persuasive power of this advocacy and suggests that donor support for it will be difficult to change.

12.2 THE SEVEN DEADLY DONOR SINS OF PPP ADVOCACY

12.2.1 Impatience (With Institution-Building)

Birdsall pointed out that the most fundamental development challenge involved the need to create and sustain the economic and political institutions required to support equitable and sustainable growth—economies without the right institutions were clearly failing to develop. But a significant segment of the development community did not have the patience (or the ability to commit long-term funding) necessary to build such institutions. These donors opted instead for programs and projects in which short-term inputs could generate visible near-term outputs. In their impatience to achieve such outputs, MDBs and donors often relied on specially created government agencies like project implementation units and privatization agencies to implement these programs and projects in a manner that circumvented what were perceived to be the bureaucratic constraints of recipient governments. But Birdsall noted that such efforts were being driven by a kind of "willful naiveté" regarding political realities in these countries and often undermined efforts by counterparts to effect their own meaningful reforms of the existing institutional framework (6).

This kind of donor impatience and naiveté has been precisely reflected in donor funding of PPFs, as well as the creation of specialized government PPP units. These efforts are designed to take PPP project preparation out of the hands of counterpart officials normally tasked with decisions about infrastructure investment, in order to avoid bureaucratic hurdles and accelerate project development. This donor involvement emphasizes short-term inputs of technical assistance and expertise provided by foreign experts to generate near-term outputs, measured by the financial closure of handfuls of opportunistically selected PPP transactions. In the transaction-only PPF approach, institutional reforms or staff capacity building are typically ignored completely, as are any kind of long-term monitoring and evaluation of impacts. Underlying problems with infrastructure finance, service delivery, tariff setting, etc., are left to client governments to deal with. The increasing focus on greenfield PPPs like IPP projects means that governments and their utilities need to solve long-standing problems with retail service delivery, including end-user willingness and ability to pay, in order to make the PPP projects affordable. But this has rarely happened. Efforts by other donors to persuade clients to institute PPP-friendly legal and regulatory reforms, or create new PPP units to manage project development, also distract from the more fundamental political, economic, and institutional problems limiting investment. Most donors have no patience to address such problems.

12.2.2 Envy (Collusion and Coordination Failure)

Birdsall noted the rapid proliferation of donors working in developing countries and the fragmentation of aid and increasing transaction costs associated with this. She noted that donors tend to avoid competition with each other as well as meaningful collaboration. Instead, they collude, like suppliers in the absence of a competitive market. She referred to William Easterly's description of this as a "cartel of good intentions"—client countries have little opportunity to complain or to request alternative solutions to problems that donors think that only they fully understand (Easterly 2009). Although they are "customers," client governments are unable to reward successful aid agencies and discipline unsuccessful ones. The duplication of effort resulting from collusion permits the diffusion of blame when expected long-term impacts in recipient countries do not materialize as expected.

At the time that Birdsall's essay was first published, the Public Private Infrastructure Facility (PPIAF) already had 15 donors and the Private Infrastructure Development Group (PIDG) had nine. Because these and many other PPP advocacy programs are multilateral in nature, involving common pools of funds, the transaction costs of dealing with so many donors are minimized. But the negative effects of collusion are intensified—PPIAF, PIDG, and most other PPFs are single-problem, single-solution "true believer" facilities in the sense that to receive this support, client governments must agree to PPP solutions to infrastructure investment problems and effectively forego consideration of alternative public investment options. There is no healthy competition among PPIAF or PIDG donors that leads to the identification and support for alternative solutions. Donors delegate to program managers or secretariats the job of picking specific countries and projects and monitoring and evaluating outcomes. This continues to facilitate the collusion and diffusion of blame that Birdsall and Easterly identified two decades ago.

As long as these donor-funded programs continue to achieve a few visible successes each year, all of the participating donor members can take some credit for success. Individual donor contributions are relatively small compared to the size of the total preparation costs so individual contributions seem to be leveraging much larger investment. No one has an interest in assessing the value for money of all the donor contributions relative to total investment mobilized, and benefits like demonstration effects and positive market development impacts are routinely claimed but not confirmed via evidence-based evaluations. By spreading PPP advice and transaction assistance so thinly across so many developing countries, involving so many donors, the persistent inability to kick-start PPP market activity in any of these beneficiary countries or even replicate PPPs developed with donor assistance can be dismissed as premature issues of concern: more work is needed.

12.2.3 Ignorance (Failure to Evaluate)

Birdsall recognized that rigorous evaluations of donor-funded aid programs and projects were extremely rare:

> Official and private agencies that develop and manage development assistance programs hesitate, with some justification, to advertise the limits of their craft. In the donor countries that finance assistance, suspicion that much such assistance is wasted runs high, and exposure of a program's current shortcomings could reduce its future funding. (11)

She cited Pritchett's political economy explanations regarding why such evaluations are not in the interests of true believers—little new knowledge is expected to result from such evaluations, evaluations can be costly and distracting, rigorous evaluations can be difficult to do well (particularly if they involve things like counterfactual analysis), attribution of results can be difficult, and above all the results of evaluations are difficult to anticipate (Pritchett 2008). Even positive evaluations can be problematic if results fail to fully live up to the non-rigorous claims of program efficacy made frequently by donor-funded facilities or programs as part of their public relations efforts. Pritchett's political economy explanation of this topic concluded that "If a program can already generate sufficient support to be adequately funded, then knowledge is a danger" (142).

The donor-funded PPP advocacy programs and facilities reviewed in this book consistently demonstrate this effort to avoid rigorous evaluation. Backed by the strong beliefs of core supporters regarding the efficacy of market-based, private participation as a solution for public infrastructure investment and management problems, facilities and programs like PPIAF, PIDG, IFC PPP Advisory, and GIF have found that rigorous, fully independent program evaluations have not been necessary to mobilize adequate levels of operational funding. Donors of course normally require some form of evaluation but typically allow most of these PPP advocacy facilities to manage their own evaluations and report on the results. The evaluations are typically carried out by carefully selected consultants (most of whom are also PPP true believers) with track records of non-critical assessments, and a willingness to negotiate evaluation findings with their clients.

The staff of bilateral donor organizations often lack the technical expertise to critique such evaluations. But in any case, the longer that financial support is provided to a PPF, the less likely are donors to be receptive to a critical evaluation recommending radical course changes. Such recommendations cast doubt on the wisdom of past support for such programs. Birdsall's general comment on this "sin of ignorance" is particularly relevant for donor-funded

PPP advocacy: "The lack of emphasis on good evaluation has been immensely costly. In the absence of timely, credible, and independent evaluation, many aid dollars have been misdirected" (12).

12.2.4 Pride (Failure to Exit)

Birdsall noted that although donors are typically impatient for results, they also tend to be reluctant to exit from programs and countries where their aid is not helping as expected. She explained that impatience and inability to exit are not inconsistent. Once committed to a program, donors tend to be motivated by what Birdsall called "misguided optimism," combined with an enlightened commitment to "do something" for reform-minded government clients. Pritchett's comments on the reluctance of advocates to carry out rigorous evaluations are relevant here as well. Once donors have invested in a program, evaluations with the potential to expose poor performance, much less question a program's reason for being, are rarely encouraged. "Strategic ignorance" is preferred to any kind of analysis that might justify abrupt program termination.

As an example of this reluctance to exit, Birdsall cited the phenomenon of repeated rounds of unsuccessful structural adjustment loans provided to the same countries by the International Monetary Fund (IMF) and World Bank. Easterly's well-known research (2002) found that the faith in the adjustment approach was so strong that instead of raising serious questions about this repetition, the unsuccessful results of earlier adjustment loans were used to justify the need for new loans. The same kind of logic is reflected in PPP advocacy. The minimal progress in jump-starting widespread use of PPPs in poor countries has been used by true believers to justify using even more resources "to finish the job" rather than consider alternative approaches. In other words, as with adjustment loans, PPP failure is automatically seen as a reason to provide more support for these projects rather than a reason to change or discontinue support. The disappointing first-phase results of GIF were interpreted to mean that the facility needed a scale-up of donor resources and a dramatically expanded menu of PPP support instruments.

The development community often pays lip service to the need to include "exit strategies" in the design of aid programs. Usually this means identifying performance criteria in program design which signal the point at which a funding cut-off is sensible, either because the program has successfully reached its objectives or because the objectives clearly will not be reached. But such strategies are strongly resisted by the management and staff of PPFs, who find hard decision rules of this kind threatening. They typically delay consideration of program closure as long as possible, arguing that "success is just around the corner."

The 2008 independent review of DFID's rapidly expanding private sector infrastructure (PSI) portfolio registered DFID's commitment to formalize exit strategies for its PSI facilities (WSP 2008). But such strategies were never prepared for DFID-funded facilities like PIDG, DevCo, PPIAF, and GPOBA. By the late 2000s, many of PIDG's donors had become concerned about the program's lack of exit strategies and the prospect that PIDG facilities would never become self-sustaining as originally promised. But in a special meeting of PIDG donor members in Bern, Switzerland, in May of 2010, PIDG management assured them that "the job is not yet done," and the consideration of exit conditions was premature. In 2018, the donors allowed PIDG and its core subsidiary facilities to be transformed into limited liability companies, implying a PIDG willingness to finally accept more commercially oriented performance assessments. But PIDG has never become self-sustaining and continues to operate mostly on the basis of donor contributions. None of the core PIDG facilities has ever developed exit strategies.

12.2.5 Sloth (Pretending Participation is Sufficient for Ownership)

Birdsall noted the long-standing tendency of donors to eagerly misinterpret client government willingness to accept "bribe-like transfers" and participate in development project implementation as signals that clients have taken "ownership" of a reform agenda. This was of course one of the fallacies associated with structural adjustment lending, the mistaken assumption by the World Bank that client government agreement to loan conditions indicated agreement with and ownership of the resulting adjustments. Birdsall's essay explored this phenomenon in other areas of aid policy, like the tendency to assume that donor requirements for civil society consultations regarding the design of proposed donor-funded development programs somehow guaranteed significant levels of popular "ownership" of such programs.

This kind of misunderstanding regarding the ways in which governments or their citizens take ownership of reform agendas is also apparent in PPP advocacy, particularly in the conviction by PPP advocates that governments in developing countries are gradually being convinced of the value of PPP projects. Because governments are willing to accept transaction assistance for the handful of PPPs in these countries which have the potential to be sustainable projects does not necessarily mean that governments have become true believers in the value of PPP projects. These governments typically have neither the technical capacity, the financial resources, nor the interest required to replicate the heavily subsidized support that donor-funded PPFs can bring to bear for such projects. Government willingness to acquiesce while a PPF develops such a project or donor funding helps to set up and staff a PPP unit, but has little to do with ownership of a reform agenda. Similarly, the idea that the demonstration effects generated by a heavily subsidized PPP reaching financial closure will motivate replication by governments, seriously ignores the fact that demonstration effects are often negative, and by themselves are rarely the single most important factor motivating policy ownership.

12.2.6 Greed (Unreliable as Well as Stingy Transfers)

Birdsall criticized what she considered to be small amounts of development funding provided by donors, as well as the volatile and unpredictable quantities of such funding. The unreliability of donor flows has always been a problem because without assurance of continuing flows for particular kinds of activities or investments, counterpart governments are limited in what they can do with the donor money. A simple example is the reluctance to use donor money for new investment in infrastructure without any certainty that funding will be available to help with recurrent costs of asset maintenance. In other situations, the benefits of donor-funded investments or activities might be optimized if follow-on changes were made to government policies or procedures, staffing, budgets, etc. But without any assurance that funding would continue, or become available from other sources, it might not be cost-effective to introduce those kinds of changes, so they are delayed or not made.

Birdsall's claims regarding the insufficiency and unreliability of donor funding applies to PPP advocacy in several ways. First, donor funding for PPP advocacy is highly fragmented—it is provided in relatively small amounts by multiple donors, is randomly spread across the developing world, and is applied opportunistically in dozens of different countries to prepare projects or set up PPP units. This kind of support provides governments with none of the assurances they need to justify long-term changes to policies, procedures, institutions, staffing, or budgets to create more of a user-friendly enabling environment for PPPs. Even if evidence existed demonstrating that infrastructure PPPs could provide significant value for developing economies, this fragmented style of donor support would militate against the full, sustainable institutionalization of PPP programs.

Second, arguably too much donor funding is made available for the global effort to promote PPPs. The opportunity costs of this total volume of support are high because alternative solutions to infrastructure investment problems are deprived of badly needed support. Arguably, far too little funding support is made available to explore and institutionalize infrastructure investment solutions that have much higher potential value for developing countries, such as the various dimensions of public investment management.

12.2.7 Foolishness (Underfunding of Global and Regional Public Goods)

Birdsall concluded her account of donor "sins" with criticism of donor unwillingness or inability to focus on global or even regional public goods. She argued that "Multi-country physical infrastructure projects should be a priority, despite the fact they may take longer to design and organize and may not seem to have the immediate ownership or easily measurable effects in relation to the Millennium Development Goals" (Birdsall 2005, 21).

Large regional infrastructure projects continue to desperately require attention in regions like Africa, where the small size of many countries means that if they have substantial water or power resources, they usually cannot justify the full exploitation of such resources based on their own national service delivery requirements. The *Africa Infrastructure Country Diagnostic* (AICD) study identified such projects as one of the few ways of adequately scaling up power supply in Africa (Foster and Briceño-Garmendia 2010). Inga III, discussed in Chapter 7, is perhaps the best-known example of this kind of project.

As indicated in earlier chapters, the importance of regional infrastructure projects in Africa has long been strongly championed by groups like the African Union, NEPAD, and later by the G20. Bilateral donors like the U.K.'s Department for International Development (DFID) helped finance the original *Programme for Infrastructure Development in Africa* (PIDA) study of Africa's regional infrastructure investment needs issued in 2012. The German development agency GIZ has provided support for the PIDA program as it developed its revised Priority Action Plan, beginning in 2019. But overall, donor support for regional infrastructure in Africa has seemed half-hearted, with much less support provided, for shorter periods, than the support provided to PPP advocacy programs and facilities. DFID involvement was conspicuously absent in the process of revising the PIDA study.

PPPs are clearly not a solution to the problem of too few regional infrastructure projects, despite the ambitions of the African Union's PIDA program. Some measure of private financing is often essential simply because large regional projects are too big for MDBs and bilateral donors to handle without additional financial support. But as the evidence confirms, any kind of infrastructure investment project in a poor country, which involves private participation, faces difficult challenges associated with cost and complexity. Regional projects with multiple country "owners" accentuate these challenges. It is no secret that PPFs like PIDG and IFC PPP Advisory seek to avoid large regional projects whenever possible, while PPFs established to focus directly on regional infrastructure projects, like the NEPAD Infrastructure Project Preparation Facility hosted by the African Development Bank, have been notably unsuccessful.

But finding a viable project structure within which to blend public and private resources for the development and financing of infrastructure is not the most important problem limiting the development of regional or cross-border infrastructure. Birdsall recognized that issues regarding the ownership of and responsibility for regional projects had already long confused donors and MDBs and slowed the pace of regional project implementation. Twenty years after Birdsall's essay, development partners have still not fully resolved these issues. Because virtually every large infrastructure project in Africa requires support from multilateral development banks, MDB definitions of regional projects are extremely important. Like the private sector, which prefers to deal with sovereign governments rather than supranational entities, MDBs favor relationships with sovereign governments. MDBs typically define regional projects in ways that emphasize leading roles for one of the individual sovereign governments involved. All of this makes it extremely difficult for MDBs to support projects with multi-country owners.

12.3 ARE THERE "DONOR FIXES" FOR THE EXCESSES OF PPP ADVOCACY?

Birdsall concluded each of the seven discussions of donor "deadly sins" with sections recommending "Donor Fixes," which summarized some of the actions donors could take to mitigate the effects of these "sins" in the interests of improving "the effective value of aid." Many of these "fixes" are still relevant today, particularly for PPP advocacy:

1. *Impatience (with institution building).* Birdsall noted that the "real fix" for this kind of impatience is possible only after donors acknowledge how fundamental for development are well-functioning government institutions. Donors need to focus more on the long-term strengthening of government institutions than on using short-term inputs to circumvent existing institutions and pursue visible near-term outputs (7). With regard to PPP advocacy, there is still a need for a much stronger focus on the institutions responsible for infrastructure investment planning and management and less of an effort to bypass these institutions by using short-term funding of PPFs and PPP units to pursue small numbers of opportunistically selected PPP transactions.
2. *Envy (collusion and coordination failures).* Birdsall argued that donors could make themselves more accountable by giving recipient governments access to independent evaluation funds that use pooled donor resources to carry our periodic assessments of each donor's cooperative behavior in their countries (10). With regard to PPP advocacy, donors need to reconsider joining multi-member trust funds promoting PPP-only

solutions, especially in light of accumulating evidence regarding the disappointing performance of infrastructure PPPs. Do client governments have adequate opportunity to express their views on the value of PPPs and explore alternative types of infrastructure investment and management solutions?

3. *Ignorance (failure to evaluate).* Birdsall argued that donors like the World Bank and other MDBs should finally accede to demands for independent evaluation of their effectiveness from "groups on the left, right and center" (13). One way to do this, described above, would be to finance an independent entity that would in turn finance and manage evaluations of selected donor programs. With regard to PPP advocacy, any kind of objective, independent evaluation of the performance of donor funded PPFs and PPP units would represent a major step forward, especially if such evaluations make an effort to assess the value-for-money of such activities compared with programs to improve the efficiency of conventional public investment management.
4. *Pride (failure to exit).* Birdsall noted that donors must rein in their "... enlightened but misguided optimism that success is always just around the corner" (14). Large donor-funded programs should as a rule build in exit conditions as the natural default, making continued funding support contingent on the achievement of performance targets rather than a foregone conclusion. There seems to be little debate about the fact that PPFs and other donor supported PPP advocacy programs should have exit strategies as well, but donors have never widely insisted that such strategies be prepared, perhaps reflecting their continuing belief that PPP success is "just around the corner."
5. *Sloth (pretending participation is sufficient for ownership).* Birdsall acknowledged that incentivizing government ownership of reform agendas is a complex challenge for which there is no single solution. But she cautioned donors that "Promises and 'participation' are not an adequate substitute for political ownership, and are no better than traditional conditionality as guarantees of change" (16). With regard to PPFs, donors should require, as a condition for funding renewal, a thorough investigation of claims that client governments are satisfied with the outcomes PPP projects and taking ownership of the agendas. Client government ownership of donor-funded PPP projects and programs should be confirmed not just assumed.
6. *Greed (unreliable as well as stingy transfers).* Birdsall recommended ways of increasing donor financial flows for development assistance, and making flows less unpredictable and volatile (19). With regard to PPP advocacy, a similar step forward now would be to more strategically and programmatically focus current levels of funding provided to PPFs

like PIDG, GIF, PPIAF, and IFC PPP Advisory on narrower, carefully selected collections of recipient countries and sectors. This could provide higher levels of sustained assistance, and better highlight the actual long-term performance of these advocacy programs.

7. *Foolishness (underfunding of global and regional public goods).* Birdsall's concern, still largely valid today, was that donors do not seem to fully recognize the importance of regional infrastructure. "Financing of global and regional public goods needs a big push. The case for regional programs in Africa is especially obvious …" (23). If anything, this challenge is even bigger now than it was 20 years ago. Donors still need to find ways of dealing with multiple government owners of projects as well as supranational bodies that act as influential regional stakeholders. Private investment will be needed for very large regional projects, along with public finance, but the evidence is also clear now that regional or cross-border PPPs will not solve problems with regional infrastructure investment. Donors will need to employ new modalities to make such projects work and should stop encouraging the unrealistic expectations of regional organizations like those in Africa regarding the likelihood that traditional forms of private participation will solve regional problems.

References

Abadie, R. 2008. "Infrastructure Finance—Surviving the Credit Crunch." London: PricewaterhouseCoopers.

AfDB [African Development Bank]. 2000. "Privatization of Public Enterprises in Zambia: An Evaluation of the Policies, Procedures and Experiences." AfDB Economic Research Paper No. 35, prepared by C.M. Fundanga and A. Mwaba, January 1. https://www .afdb .org/ fr/ documents/ document/ working -paper -35 -privatization -of -public -enterprises -in -zambia -an -evaluation -of -the -policies -procedures -and -experiences -8978.

AfDB [African Development Bank]. 2013a. "Africa50: Questions and Answers." Memorandum to the AfDB Board of Directors from Secretary General, C. Akintomide (July 16).

AfDB [African Development Bank]. 2013b. "INGA Site Development Electricity Access Support Project (PASEL)." Project Appraisal Report, October. Tunis, Tunisia: African Development Bank.

Africa50. 2018. *Annual Report and Financial Statements for the Year Ended 31 December 2018*. Casablanca, Morocco: Africa50.

African Business. 2023. "Should Private Companies Play a Role in Africa's Water Sector?" Tom Collins, *African Business Online Magazine*. January 20. https://african.business/2023/01/resources/should-private-companies-play-a-role-in-africas-water-sector.

African Energy. 2021. "Zesco's Debt Balloons to $3.5bn." *African Energy Newsletter*, October 24. https://www.africa-energy.com/article/zescos-debt-balloons-35bn.

African Union. 2020. *Elaboration of the 2021–2030 Priority Action Plan for the AU Program for Infrastructure Development in Africa (PIDA) – The Integrated Corridor Approach – "A Holistic Infrastructure Planning Framework to establish PIDA-PAP 2."* Addis Ababa, Ethiopia: The African Union, February 27.

Aguas Argentinas S.A. Concession Contract. 1993. *Concession Agreement entered into between the Argentine State and Aguas Argentinas S.A.* April 28.

Ahadzi, M., G. Bowles. 2004. "Public-Private Partnerships and Contract Negotiations: An Empirical Study." *Construction Management and Economics* 22(9): 967–978.

Alcazar, L., M.A. Abdala, M.M. Shirley. 2000. "The Buenos Aires Water Concession." Policy Research Working Paper No. 2311. Washington, D.C.: World Bank.

Alexander, N. 2013. "Responsible Investment in Infrastructure: Recommendations for the G20." Washington, D.C.: Heinrich Böll Foundation North America (October). https://us.boell.org/sites/default/files/responsible_investment_in_infrastructure.pdf.

Alexander, N. 2015. "The World Bank: In the Vanguard of an Infrastructure Boom." Washington, D.C.: Heinrich Böll Foundation North America (February). https://us .boell.org/en/2015/02/03/world-bank-vanguard-infrastructure-boom.

Andrés, L.A., J. Schwartz, L. Guasch. 2013. *Uncovering the Drivers of Utility Performance: Lessons from Latin America and the Caribbean on the Role of the Private Sector, Regulation, and Governance in the Power, Water, and Telecommunication Sectors*. Washington, D.C.: World Bank.

Ansar, A., B. Flyvbjerg, A. Budzier, D. Lunn. 2017. "Big is Fragile: An Attempt at Theorizing Scale." In B. Flyvbjerg (ed.), *The Oxford Handbook of Megaproject Management*, 60–95. London: Oxford University Press.

APEC [Asia-Pacific Economic Cooperation]. 2008. "Joint Ministerial Statement: 2008." 15th Finance Ministers' Meeting, November 5–6, Trujillo, Peru.

Appelbaum, B. 2019. *The Economists' Hour: False Prophets, Free Markets, and the Fracture of Society*. Boston, MA: Little, Brown & Company.

Arthur D. Little. 2020. "Successful Public-Private Partnerships: How Countries Should Set Up an Effective Ecosystem for Public-Private Partnerships." ADL Viewpoint by C. Stella and S. Menassa, October. https://www.adlittle.com/en/insights/viewpoints/successful-public-private-partnerships.

AsDB [Asian Development Bank]. 2017. *Meeting Asia's Infrastructure Needs*. Manila: Asian Development Bank.

ASI [Adam Smith International]. 2014. "Assessment of Project Preparation Facilities in Asia." Report prepared for the G20 Development Working Group.

Attridge, S., L. Engen. 2019. *Blended Finance in the Poorest Countries: The Need for a Better Approach*. London: Overseas Development Institute, April. https://www.odi.org/sites/odi.org.uk/files/resource-documents/12666.pdf.

AU [African Union], African Development Bank, NEPAD. 2009. "Programme for Infrastructure Development in Africa (PIDA) General Terms of Reference." Addis Ababa, Ethiopia: The African Union.

AUC [Africa Union Commission], African Development Bank (AfDB), UN Economic Commission for Africa (UNECA), NEPAD Planning and Coordinating Agency (NPCA). 2012. *Program for Infrastructure Development in Africa: Interconnecting, Integrating and Transforming a Continent*. Addis Ababa, Ethiopia: The African Union. https:// www .afdb .org/ en/ topics -and -sectors/ init iativespar tnerships/ programme-for-infrastructure-development-in-africa-pida/.

Augenblick, M., B.S. Custer. 1990. "The Build, Operate, and Transfer ("BOT") Approach to Infrastructure Projects in Developing Countries." Policy, Research, and External Affairs Working Paper WPS 498, August. Washington, D.C.: World Bank.

Bakovic, T., B. Tenenbaum, F. Woolf. 2003. "Regulation by Contract: A New Way to Privatize Electricity Distribution?" World Bank Working Paper 14. Washington, D.C.: World Bank.

Bayliss, K., B. Fine. 1998. "Beyond *Bureaucrats in Business*: A Critical Review of the World Bank Approach to Privatization and Public Sector Reform." *Journal of International Development* 10(7): 841–855.

Bayliss, K., E. Van Waeyenberge. 2017. "Unpacking the Public Private Partnership Revival." *The Journal of Development Studies* 54(2): 1–17.

Bel, G., P. Bel-Pinana, J. Rosell. 2017. "Myopic PPPs: Risk Allocation and Hidden Liabilities for Taxpayers and Users." *Utilities Policy* 48(4): 147–156.

Bhattacharya, A., M. Romani, N. Stern. 2012. "Infrastructure for Development: Meeting the Challenge." Policy paper sponsored by The Centre for Climate Change Economics and Policy, the Grantham Research Institute on Climate Change and the Environment, in collaboration with the Intergovernmental Group of Twenty-Four on International Monetary Affairs and Development (G-24) (June). http:// www .lse .ac .uk/GranthamInstitute/wp-content/uploads/2014/03/PPinfrastructure-for-development -meeting-the-challenge.pdf.

Birdsall, N. 2005. "Seven Deadly Sins: Reflections on Donor Failings." Working Paper No. 50. Center for Global Development, December. Washington, D.C.: Center for Global Development.

BNP Paribas. 2009. "Preliminary Financial Feasibility Study—Project Inga 3." Unpublished report prepared for the World Bank and the Public-Private Infrastructure Advisory Facility, December.
Boardman, A.E., M. Hellowell. 2016. "A Comparative Analysis and Evaluation of Specialist PPP Units' Methodologies for Conducting Value for Money Appraisals." *Journal of Comparative Policy Analysis: Research and Practice* 19(3): 191–206.
Boardman, A.E., A. Vining. 2012. "The Political Economy of Public-Private Partnerships and Analysis of their Social Value." *Annals of Public and Cooperative Economics* 83(2): 117–141.
Bosshard, P. 2012. "Infrastructure for Whom? A Critique of the Infrastructure Strategies of the Group of 20 and the World Bank." International Rivers (May). https://www.internationalrivers.org/sites/default/files/attached-files/infrastructure_for_whom_report.pdf.
Bourguignon, F. 2006. "Rethinking Infrastructure for Development." Closing Remarks, Annual Bank Conference on Development Economics, Tokyo, Japan, May 30.
Bradburd, R. 1992. "Privatization of Natural Monopoly Public Enterprises: The Regulation Issue." World Bank Working Paper WPS 864, April. Washington, D.C.: World Bank.
Bretton Woods Project. 2015. "Throwing Evidence to the Wind? The World Bank Continues Pushing PPPs." September 25. https://www.brettonwoodsproject.org/2015/09/throwing-evidence-to-the-wind-the-world-bank-continues-pushing-ppps/.
Brinkerhoff, D.W., J.M. Brinkerhoff. 2011. "Public-Private Partnerships: Perspectives on Purposes, Publicness, and Good Governance." *Public Administration and Development* 31(1): 2–14.
Brook, P. J., S.M. Smith. 2001. *Contracting for Public Services: Output-based Aid and its Applications*. Washington, D.C.: World Bank.
Buchs, T.D. 2003. "Privatization in sub-Saharan Africa: Some Lessons from Experiences to Date." Unpublished IFC Working Paper, December.
Burger, P., I. Hawkesworth. 2011. "How to Attain Value for Money: Comparing PPP and Traditional Infrastructure Public Procurement." *OECD Journal on Budgeting* 11(1): 1–56. https://www.oecd.org/gov/budgeting/49070709.pdf.
BUSINESSTECH. 2016. "Zuma: Nuclear Plan Will Roll Out at an Affordable Pace." BUSINESSTECH News24Wire, February 11.
Campbell-White, O., A. Bhatia. 1998. *Privatization in Africa.* World Bank Directions in Development. Washington, D.C.: World Bank.
Candoy-Sekse, R. 1988. "Techniques of Privatization of State-Owned Enterprises, Volume III." World Bank Technical Paper No. 90. Washington, D.C.: World Bank.
Castalia Strategic Advisors. 2005. "Experience with Private Participation in Sub-Saharan African Infrastructure: What are the Lessons for Future Policy?" Unpublished report prepared for the African Infrastructure Department of the World Bank.
Castalia Strategic Advisors. 2007. "Key Challenges to Public Private Partnerships in South Africa: Summary of Interview Findings." Report to the Support Programme for Accelerated Infrastructure Development (SPAID), jointly sponsored by the Presidency of the Republic of South Africa and the Business Trust, Pretoria, April.
Castalia Strategic Advisors. 2011a. "2010 Progress Review of InfraCo." Report to the Private Infrastructure Development Group, January.
Castalia Strategic Advisors. 2011b. "Evaluation of the Demonstration Effect of IFC's Involvement in Infrastructure in Africa, Final Report." Report commissioned and funded by the IFC and the Private Infrastructure Development Group through DevCo,

February. https://studylib.net/doc/18349592/evaluation-of-the-demonstration-effect-of-ifc-s-involveme.

Cattaneo, E. 2018. "Kigali Water: Lessons from One of sub-Saharan Africa's First water PPPs." World Bank Blog, March 22. https://blogs.worldbank.org/ppps/kigali-water-lessons-one-sub-saharan-africa-s-first-water-ppps.

CEE Bankwatch Network. 2008. "Never Mind the Balance Sheet: The Dangers Posed by Public-Private Partnerships in Central and Eastern Europe." CEE Bankwatch Network (November). http://bankwatch.org/documents/never_mind_the_balance_sheet.pdf.

CEPA [Cambridge Economic Policy Associates]. 2012. "Infrastructure Consortium for Africa (ICA) Assessment of Project Preparation Facilities for Africa." Report to the ICA Secretariat, in association with Nodalis Conseil, September. https://www.icafrica.org/fileadmin/documents/Knowledge/ICA_publications/ICA-PPF-Study%20Report-ENGLISH-VOL%20A.pdf.

Chan, A.P.C., P.T.I. Lam, D.W.M. Chan, E. Cheung, Y. Ke. 2010. "Critical Success Factors for PPPs in Infrastructure Developments: Chinese Perspective." *Journal of Construction Engineering and Management* 136(5): 484–494.

Chao, J., D. Saha. 2016. *Sources of Financing for PPP Investments 2015*. Washington, D.C.: World Bank. https://ppi.worldbank.org/content/dam/PPI/resources/ppi_resources/topic/2015-PPP-Investments-Sources.pdf.

Christensen, L.T., C. Greve. 2018. "Choosing State-Owned Enterprises Over Public Private Partnerships for Infrastructure Governance: Explaining Institutional Change with Evidence from Denmark's Transport Sector." *International Public Management Review* 18(2): 137–161.

Churchill, A. 1990. "Introduction." In J. Besant-Jones (ed.), *Private Sector Participation in Power through BOOT Schemes*, 1–4. Washington, D.C.: World Bank.

Commission for Africa. 2005. "Our Common Interest." Report of the Commission for Africa, London.

Convergence, Private Infrastructure Development Group (PIDG), Emerging Africa Infrastructure Fund (EAIF). 2018. "Case Study of the Emerging Africa Infrastructure Fund Ltd." December. https://www.eaif.com/wp-content/uploads/2019/01/Convergence-EAIF-Case-Study-2018.pdf.

CPCS. 2021. "Municipal PPP Framework and Guidelines Review, Volume I, Main Report." Report prepared for National Treasury, Republic of South Africa, March.

Craig, J. 2000. "Evaluating Privatisation in Zambia: A Tale of Two Processes." *Review of African Political Economy* 27: 357–366.

CRISIL. 2010. "Project Implementation Review of the NEPAD Infrastructure Short Term Action Plan (STAP)." Report prepared by CRISIL Infrastructure Advisory for the African Development Bank, Tunis.

Danida. 2019. "Concept Note: Contribution to Global Infrastructure Facility." Ministry of Foreign Affairs of Denmark, September.

De Fiore, F., H. Uhlig. 2005. "Bank versus Bond Finance: What Explains the Difference between US and Europe?" European Central Bank Working Paper Series No. 547, November.

De Lemos, T., M. Betts, D. Eaton, L. Tadeu De Almeida. 2000. "From Concessions to Project Finance and the Private Finance Initiative." *The Journal of Project Finance* 6(3): 19–37.

De Luca, L. 1998. *Labour and Social Dimensions of Privatization and Restructuring (Public Utilities: Water, Gas, Electricity)*. Geneva: International Labour Office.

de Villiers, S. 2021. "How SA's Municipalities became the Wild West of Mismanagement." *Financial Mail*, July 2. https://www.businesslive.co.za/fm/opinion/2021-07-02-shirley-de-villiers-how-sas-municipalities-became-the-wild-west-of-mismanagement/.

Della Croce, R., F. Stewart, J. Yermo. 2011. "Promoting Longer-Term Investment by Institutional Investors: Selected Issues and Policies." *OECD Journal: Financial Market Trends*, 2011(1): 1–20.

DFID [Department for International Development]. 1997. "Eliminating World Poverty: A Challenge for the 21st Century." White Paper No. 1. London: DFID.

DFID [Department for International Development]. 2000. "Eliminating World Poverty: Making Globalisation Work for the Poor." White Paper No. 2. London: DFID.

DFID [Department for International Development]. 2002. "Making Connections: Infrastructure for Poverty Reduction." London: DFID.

DFID [Department for International Development]. 2006. "Eliminating World Poverty: Making Governance Work for the Poor." White Paper No. 3. London: DFID.

DFID [Department for International Development]. 2017. "Case Study: IFC's Scaling Solar Programme, Zambia." Infrastructure and Cities for Economic Development (ICED) Evidence Library. http://icedfacility.org/wp-content/uploads/2017/12/ICED_Case_Zambia-Scaling-Solar.pdf.

Easterly, W. 2002. "What Did Structural Adjustment Adjust? The Association of Policies and Growth with Repeated IMF and World Bank Adjustment Loans." Center for Global Development Working Paper 11. Washington D.C.: Center for Global Development.

Easterly, W. 2007a. "The Ideology of Development." *Foreign Policy*, July/August. https://foreignpolicy.com/2009/10/13/the-ideology-of-development/.

Easterly, W. 2007b. "Are Aid Agencies Improving?" Global Economy and Development Working Paper No. 9, September. Washington, D.C.: The Brookings Institution.

Easterly, W. 2009. "The Cartel of Good Intentions." *Foreign Policy*, November. https://foreignpolicy.com/2009/11/11/the-cartel-of-good-intentions/.

Eberhard, A., K. Gratwick. 2010. "IPPs in Sub-Saharan Africa: Determinants of Success." Management Programme in Infrastructure Reform and Regulation. Cape Town: University of Cape Town, Graduate School of Business.

Eberhard, A., K. Gratwick, E. Morella, P. Antman. 2016. *Independent Power Projects in Sub-Saharan Africa: Lessons from Five Key Countries*. World Bank Directions in Development. Washington, D.C.: World Bank.

Eberhard, A., J. Kolker, J. Leigland. 2014. *South Africa's Renewable Energy IPP Program: Success Factors and Lessons*. Report sponsored by the World Bank Institute and the Public Private Infrastructure Advisory Facility (PPIAF). Washington, D.C.: World Bank.

EBRD [European Bank for Reconstruction and Development]. 2019. "MDB Infrastructure Cooperation Platform: Project Preparation Workstream Phase II: Reference Note on Project Preparation across the Full Project Cycle." London: EBRD.

EIU [Economist Intelligence Unit]. 2015. *Evaluating the Environment for Public-Private Partnerships in Africa: The 2015 Infrascope*. London: EIU.

Emery, T. 2023. "Solar Can't Scale in the Dark: Why Lessons about Subsidies and Transparency from IFC's Scaling Solar Zambia Can Reignite Progress toward Deploying Clean Energy." Energy for Growth Hub, May. https://www.energyforgrowth.org/wp-content/uploads/2023/05/2023-05-08_Emery_Scaling-Solar.pdf.

EPEC [European PPP Expertise Centre]. 2014. *Establishing and Reforming PPP Units: Analysis of EPEC Member PPP Units and Lessons Learnt*. Luxembourg: European Investment Bank.

Estache, A. 2005. "What Do We Know about Sub-Saharan Africa's Infrastructure and the Impact of Its 1990s Reforms?" Universite Libre de Bruxelles, Ecares Working Paper, May 25.

Estrin, S., A. Pelletier. 2018. "Privatization in Developing Countries: What Are the Lessons of Recent Experience?" *The World Bank Research Observer* 33: 65–102.

Eurodad. 2020. "Why Public-Private Partnerships Are Still Not Delivering." December. https:// www .eurodad .org/ why _public _private _partnerships _are _still _not_delivering.

European Commission. 2003. "Guidelines for Successful Public-Private Partnerships." European Commission, Brussels. http://ec.europa.eu/regional_policy/sources/docgener/guides/ppp_en.pdf.

Fainboim, I., D. Last, E. Tandberg. 2013. "Managing Public Investment." In M. Cangiano, T. Curristine, M. Lazare (eds.), *Public Financial Management and Its Emerging Architecture*, 311–337. Washington, D.C.: International Monetary Fund.

Farquharson, E., J. Encinas. 2010. "The UK Treasury Infrastructure Finance Unit: Supporting PPP Financing During the Global Liquidity Crisis" (March). Washington, D.C.: World Bank.

Fatokun, A., A. Akintoye, C. Liyanage. 2015. "Renegotiation of Public Private Partnership Road Contracts: Issues and Outcomes." In A.B. Raidén and E. Aboagye-Nimo (eds.), *Proceedings of the 31st Annual ARCOM Conference*, September 7–9, 1249–1258. Lincoln, U.K.: Association of Researchers in Construction Management.

Fay, M., L. Andres, C. Fox, U. Narloch, S. Straub, M. Slawson. 2017. *Rethinking Infrastructure in Latin America and the Caribbean: Spending Better to Achieve More*. Washington, D.C.: World Bank.

Fay, M., H.I. Lee, M. Mastruzzi, S. Han, M. Cho. 2019. "Hitting the Trillion Mark: A Look at How Much Countries Are Spending on Infrastructure." Policy Research Working Paper 8730. Sustainable Development Practice Group (February). Washington, D.C.: World Bank.

Fergusson, J., D. Croft, Y. Charafi. 2015. "Scaling Solar: Making the Sun Work for Africa." *2015 Africa Energy Yearbook*. London: EnergyNet Ltd.

Fioravanti, R., L. Carolina, A. Deep. 2019. "Filling the Infrastructure Investment Gap. The Role of Project Preparation Facilities: An Overview of MDBs and the Inter-American Development Bank approach." IDB Discussion Paper (IDB-DP-00603). Washington, D.C.: Inter-American Development Bank.

Fitch Ratings. 2009. "Large Projects, Giant Risks?" Report by Fitch Global Infrastructure & Project Finance. Fitch Ratings, New York, May 18.

Fitzgerald, P. 2004. "Review of Partnerships Victoria Provided Infrastructure." Final Report to the Treasurer, State Government of Victoria, Australia.

Flyvbjerg, B. 2014. "What You Should Know about Megaprojects and Why: An Overview." *Project Management Journal* 45(2): 6–19.

Foster, V., C.M. Briceño-Garmendia. 2010. *Africa's Infrastructure: A Time for Transformation*. AICD Flagship Report. Washington, D.C.: World Bank.

Fraser, A., J. Lungu. 2009. "Six Problems: Privatisation and the Zambian Copper Mines." *African Analyst* 4(1): 28–43.

G20. 2010. "Multi-Year Action Plan on Development." G20 Seoul Summit 2010, Annex II. https:// www .oecd .org/ g20/ summits/ seoul/ Annex2 -Multi -Year -Action -Plan-Development.pdf.

G20. 2011a. "High Level Panel on Infrastructure Recommendations to G20: Final Report." Submission to the G20, October 26.

G20. 2011b. "Infrastructure Action Plan: Submission to the G20 by the MDB Working Group on Infrastructure." Washington, D.C.: World Bank. http://documents.worldbank .org/curated/en/828751468331900533/pdf/655610BR0v10Se0Official0Use0Only090 .pdf.

G20. 2014. "Report on Infrastructure Agenda and Response to the Assessments of Project Preparation Facilities in Asia and Africa." Report to the G20 by the Development Working Group on Infrastructure.

Galetovic, A., E. Engel, R. Fischer. 2017. "Renegotiations in Public-Private Partnerships: Theory and Evidence." In *Public Private Partnerships for Transport Infrastructure: Renegotiation and Economic Outcomes*, International Transport Forum Roundtable Reports, No. 161, 37–56. Paris: OECD Publishing.

Geddes, R.R., E. Reeves. 2017. "The Favourability of U.S. PPP Enabling Legislation and Private Investment in Transportation Infrastructure." *Utilities Policy* 48(C): 157–165.

Gerstle, G. 2022. *The Rise and Fall of the Neoliberal Order: America and the World in the Free Market Era.* Oxford: Oxford University Press.

GIF [Global Infrastructure Facility]. 2014. "Global Infrastructure Facility: Update for G20—September 2014." http:// www .g20 .utoronto .ca/ 2014/ 11 %20Global %20Infrastructure%20Facility%20-%20Update%20for%20G20.pdf.

GIF [Global Infrastructure Facility]. 2015a. "Global Infrastructure Facility Operating Guidelines." April 20. https://www.globalinfrafacility.org/.

GIF [Global Infrastructure Facility]. 2015b. "Global Infrastructure Facility Results Framework." May 25. https://www.globalinfrafacility.org/.

GIF [Global Infrastructure Facility]. 2021a. "GIF Annual Highlights 2021: A G20 Initiative Promoting Sustainable and Quality Infrastructure Investments in Emerging Markets." Washington, D.C.: World Bank. https://www.globalinfrafacility.org/.

GIF [Global Infrastructure Facility]. 2021b. "The Global Sustainable Infrastructure Challenge and the GIF Response." https://www.globalinfrafacility.org/.

GIF [Global Infrastructure Facility]. 2022. *GIF Highlights Report 2022: Unlocking Private Capital for Sustainable, Quality Infrastructure*. Washington, D.C.: World Bank. https://www.globalinfrafacility.org/.

Gomez-Ibanez, J. 2007. "Alternatives to Infrastructure Privatization Revisited: Public Enterprise Reform from the 1960s to the 1980s." World Bank Policy Research Working Paper No. 4391. Washington, D.C.: World Bank.

Government of India. 2017. "India: Three Year Action Agenda, 2017–18 to 2019–20." Report of the National Institution for Transforming India (NITI Aayog). New Delhi: NITI Aayog.

Gratwick, K.N., A. Eberhard. 2008. "An Analysis of Independent Power Projects in Africa: Understanding Development and Investment Outcomes." *Development Policy Review*, 26(3): 309–338.

GRM International AB. 2010. "Review of the Swedish Contributions to Private Infrastructure Development Group Final Report." November.

GTAC [Government Technical Advisory Centre]. 2015. *Government Technical Advisory Centre and National Treasury Programme 8: Technical Support and*

Development Finance. Annual Report 2014/15. Pretoria: South African National Treasury. http://www.gtac.gov.za.

Guasch, J.L. 2004. *Granting and Renegotiating Infrastructure Concessions: Doing It Right*. Washington, D.C.: World Bank.

Guislain, P., M. Kerf. 1995. "Concessions—The Way to Privatize Infrastructure Sector Monopolies." Public Policy for the Private Sector No. 59 (October). Washington, D.C.: World Bank.

Hall, D. 2015. "Why Public-Private Partnerships Don't Work: The Many Advantages of the Public Alternative." Public Services International Research Unit (February). https://www.world-psi.org/sites/default/files/rapport_eng_56pages_a4_lr.pdf.

Hammami, M., J.-F. Ruhashyankiko, E. Yehoue. 2006. "Determinants of Public Private Partnerships in Infrastructure." IMF Working Paper No. 06/99. Washington, D.C.: International Monetary Fund.

Harris, C. 2003. "Private Participation in Infrastructure in Developing Countries: Trends, Impacts and Policy Lessons." Working Paper No. 5. Washington, D.C.: World Bank.

Hart, O. 2003. "Incomplete Contracts and Public Ownership: Remarks, and an Application to Public-Private Partnerships." *Economic Journal* 113(486): 69–76.

Hegstad, S.O., I. Newport. 1987. "Management Contracts: Main Features and Design Issues." World Bank Technical Paper No. 65. Washington, D.C.: World Bank.

Hellowell, M. 2010. "The UK's Private Finance Initiative: History, Evaluation, Prospects." In G. A. Hodge, C. Greve, A. E. Boardman (eds.), *International Handbook on Public–Private Partnerships*, 307–332. Cheltenham, U.K.: Edward Elgar Publishing.

Hellowell, M., V. Vecchi. 2012. "An Evaluation of the Projected Returns to Investors on 10 PFI Projects Commissioned by the National Health Service." *Financial Accountability and Management* 28(1): 77–100.

Hodge, G.A., C. Greve. 2007. "Public-Private Partnerships: An International Performance Review." *Public Administration Review* 67(3): 545–558.

Hodges, J. 2009. "Delivering the Goods: Multi-Donor Approaches to Project Development and Funding." IFC Smart Lessons (September). Washington, D.C.: International Finance Corporation.

Hofstatter, S. 2018. "Counting the Cost of State Capture." *Financial Mail*, September 6.

Husain, I., R. Faruqee (eds.). 1994. *Adjustment in Africa: Lessons from Country Case Studies*. Washington, D.C.: World Bank.

Hyun, S., D. Park, S. Tian. 2018. "Determinants of Public–Private Partnerships in Infrastructure in Asia: Implications for Capital Market Development." Asian Development Working Paper Series 552, Asian Development Bank, Manila.

ICA [Infrastructure Consortium for Africa]. 2006a. *Infrastructure Project Preparation Facilities: User Guide*. Infrastructure Consortium for Africa. Tunis: AfDB. https://www.icafrica.org/en/knowledge-hub/article/infrastructure-project-preparation-facilities-user-guide-africa-14/.

ICA [Infrastructure Consortium for Africa]. 2006b. "Strengthening Donors' Cooperation in Support of NEPAD Infrastructure Projects Preparation: The 'Tunnel of Funds' Concept." Unpublished PowerPoint presentation by AfDB NEPAD Unit, April 11.

IDA [International Development Association]. 2009. "A Review of the Use of Output-Based Aid Approaches" (November). IDA15 Mid-Term Review. Washington, D.C.: World Bank.

IDA [International Development Association]. 2013. "IDA Support to Transformational Projects with Regional Impact" (March). IDA Resource Mobilization Department, Concessional Finance and Global Partnerships. Washington, D.C.: World Bank.

Idzorek, T., C. Armstrong. 2009. "Infrastructure and Strategic Asset Allocation: Is Infrastructure an Asset Class?" Report prepared by Ibbotson Associates, sponsored by First American Funds/FAF Advisors, January.

IEA [International Energy Agency]. 2017. *Renewable Energy Auctions: Analysing 2016*. Paris: IEA. http://www.irena.org/publications/2017/Jun/Renewable-Energy-Auctions-Analysing-2016.

IEG [Independent Evaluation Group]. 2008. "Nigeria Country Assistance Evaluation: The World Bank in Nigeria, 1998–2007" (June 30). Report of the World Bank's Independent Evaluation Group. Washington, D.C.: World Bank.

IEG [Independent Evaluation Group]. 2010. "Cost-Benefit Analysis in World Bank Projects" (June). Report of the World Bank's Independent Evaluation Group. Washington, D.C.: World Bank.

IEG [Independent Evaluation Group]. 2011. "Trust Fund Support for Development: An Evaluation of the World Bank's Trust Fund Portfolio." Report of the World Bank's Independent Evaluation Group. Washington, D.C.: World Bank.

IEG [Independent Evaluation Group]. 2013. "Biennial Report on Operations Evaluation: Assessing the Monitoring and Evaluation systems of IFC and MIGA." Report of the World Bank's Independent Evaluation Group. Washington, D.C.: World Bank.

IEG [Independent Evaluation Group]. 2015. "World Bank Group Support to Public-Private Partnerships: Lessons from Experience in Client Countries, FY02–12." Report of the World Bank's Independent Evaluation Group. Washington, D.C.: World Bank. http://documents1.worldbank.org/curated/en/405891468334813110/pdf/93629-REVISED-Box394822B-PUBLIC.pdf.

IEG [Independent Evaluation Group]. 2017. "Results and Performance of the World Bank Group 2017." Report of the World Bank's Independent Evaluation Group. Washington, D.C.: World Bank.

IEG [Independent Evaluation Group]. 2019. "'Creating Markets' to Leverage the Private Sector for Sustainable Development and Growth: An Evaluation of the World Bank Group's Experience through 16 Case Studies" (April 26). Report of the World Bank's Independent Evaluation Group. Washington, D.C.: World Bank.

IFC [International Finance Corporation]. 2002. *IFC Annual Report 2002*. Washington, D.C.: International Finance Corporation. https://www.ifc.org/wps/wcm/connect/publications_ext_content/ifc_external_publication_site/publications/previous-annual-reports.

IFC [International Finance Corporation]. 2007. "Global Infrastructure Project Development Fund Board Paper (Annex 4), Project No. 25792" (September). Washington, D.C.: International Finance Corporation.

IFC [International Finance Corporation]. 2010. *IFC Annual Report 2010*. Washington, D.C.: International Finance Corporation. https://www.ifc.org/wps/wcm/connect/publications_ext_content/ifc_external_publication_site/publications/previous-annual-reports.

IFC [International Finance Corporation]. 2019. "IFC's Anticipated Impact Measurement and Monitoring (AIMM) System: Project Assessment and Scoring Guidance Note" (March). Washington, D.C.: International Finance Corporation.

IFC [International Finance Corporation]. 2020a. *Strategy and Business Outlook FY21–FY23: A Focus on Execution* (April 9). Washington, D.C.: International Finance Corporation. https://documents1.worldbank.org/curated/en/402581596012370986/pdf/IFC-Strategy-and-Business-Outlook-FY21-FY23-A-Focus-on-Execution.pdf.

IFC [International Finance Corporation]. 2020b. "CTA and Upstream." Unpublished PowerPoint Presentation, March.

IMF [International Monetary Fund]. 2015. *Making Public Investment More Efficient*. Washington, D.C.: International Monetary Fund.

IMF [International Monetary Fund]. 2020. *Government Support to State-Owned Enterprises: Options for Sub-Saharan Africa*. Washington, D.C.: International Monetary Fund.

IMF [International Monetary Fund]. 2021. "IMF Investment and Capital Stock Dataset (ICSD) 2021: Manual & FAQ – Estimating Public, Private, and PPP Capital Stocks." Washington, D.C.: International Monetary Fund.

Independent Online. 2010. "DRC in Power Play as It Scraps Inga 3 Venture." Independent Online, February 27. https://www.iol.co.za/business-report/economy/drc-in-power-play-as-it-scraps-inga-3-venture-696575.

InfraCo. 2007. "Business Plan for a Proposed Expansion of Operations." London: InfraCo Africa.

Iossa, E., D. Martimort. 2015. "The Simple Micro-Economics of Public Private Partnerships." *Journal of Public Economic Theory* 17(1): 4–48.

Irwin, T., M. Klein, G.E. Perry, M. Thobani. 1997. "Dealing with Public Risk in Private Infrastructure." World Bank Latin American and Caribbean Studies. Washington, D.C.: World Bank.

Irwin, T., S. Mazraani, S. Saxena. 2018. "How to Control the Costs of Public-Private Partnerships." Fiscal Affairs Department, International Monetary Fund. Washington, D.C.: International Monetary Fund.

Izaguirre, A.K. 2009. "Assessment of the Impact of the Crisis on New PPI Projects: Update 2." Private Participation in Infrastructure Database, World Bank, Washington, D.C.

Jones, L., U. Jammal, N. Gokgur. 2002. "Impact of Privatization in Cote D'Ivoire." Report Prepared by the Boston Institute for Developing Economies (BIDE) for Privatization Committee, Government of Côte d'Ivoire, Boston, July 15.

Kenny, C. 2020. "Development Finance Institutions Should Be Instruments of Public Policy, Not Private Gain." CGD Blog Post, March 18. https://www.cgdev.org/blog/development-finance-institutions-should-be-instruments-public-policy-not-private-gain.

Kenny, C. 2021. "IFC 3.1?" CGD Note, June. https://www.cgdev.org/sites/default/files/ifc-three-point-one.pdf.

Kenny, C. 2023. "The IFC and (De)Scaling Solar." CGD Blog Post, May 8. https://www.cgdev.org/blog/ifc-and-descaling-solar.

Kenny, C., J. Kalow, V. Ramachandran. 2018. "Inside the Portfolio of the International Finance Corporation: Does IFC Do Enough in Low-Income Countries?" Center for Global Development Policy Paper 115. Washington, D.C.: Center for Global Development. https://www.cgdev.org/publication/insideportfolio-international-finance-corporation-does-ifc-do-enough-low-income.

Kerf, M., R.D. Gray, T. Irwin, C. Levesque, R.R. Taylor. 1998. "Concessions for Infrastructure: A Guide to their Design and Award." World Bank Technical Paper No. 399. Washington, D.C.: World Bank.

Kikeri, S., J. Nellis, M. Shirley. 1992. *Privatization: The Lessons of Experience*. Washington, D.C.: World Bank.

Klein, M. 1998a. "Bidding for Concessions." World Bank Policy Research Working Paper No. 1957. Washington, D.C.: World Bank.

Klein, M. 1998b. "The Case for Periodic Rebidding of Concessions." Public Policy for the Private Sector, Viewpoint Note 161. Washington, D.C.: World Bank.

Klein, M. 1998c. "One Hundred Years after Bretton Woods: A Future History of the World Bank Group." *EIB Papers: International Financial Institutions in the 21st Century* 3(2): 30–59.

Klein, M. 1999. "The Impact of the Financial Crises on the Power Sector of Transition Countries." In *Energy After the Financial Crises: Energy and Development Report 1999*. Washington, D.C.: World Bank.

Klein, M. 2003. "Foreword" to "Private Participation in Infrastructure in Developing Countries: Trends, Impacts and Policy Lessons." Working Paper No. 5. Washington, D.C.: World Bank.

Klein, M. 2015. "Public-Private Partnerships: Promise and Hype." World Bank Policy Research Working Paper No. 7340. Washington, D.C.: World Bank.

Klein, M., B. Hadjimichael. 2003. *The Private Sector in Development: Entrepreneurship, Regulation, and Competitive Disciplines*. Washington, D.C.: World Bank.

Klijn, E.H., J. Koppenjan. 2016. "The Impact of Contract Characteristics on the Performance of Public-Private Partnerships." *Public Money and Management* 36(6): 455–462.

Kotze, R., A. Ferguson, J. Leigland. 2000. "Government Facilitation of Public-Private Infrastructure Projects: Lessons from South Africa." *Journal of Project Finance* 6(1): 61–70.

Kruger, W., A. Eberhard. 2018. "Renewable Energy Auctions in sub-Saharan Africa: Comparing the South African, Ugandan, and Zambian Programs." *Wiley Interdisciplinary Reviews: Energy and Environment* 7(4), July/August.

Kumar, G., I. Lieberman, Y. Mumssen. 2010. "Access to Finance in Output-Based Aid." GPOBA OBA Working Paper No. 11. Washington, D.C.: World Bank.

Lee, N. 2019. "Trillions for the SDGs? Time for a Rethink." *OECD Development Matters*. https://oecd-development-matters.org/2019/01/17/trillions-for-the-sdgs-time-for-a-rethink/.

Leigland, J. 1994. "Public Authorities and the Determinants of their Use by State and Local Governments." *Journal of Public Administration Research and Theory* 4(4): 521–544.

Leigland, J. 1997. "Accelerating Municipal Bond Market Development in Emerging Economies: An Assessment of Strategies and Progress." *Public Budgeting & Finance* 17(2): 57–79.

Leigland, J. 2018. "Changing Perceptions of PPP Risk and Return: The Case of Brownfield Concessions." *The Journal of Structured Finance* 23(4): 47–56.

Leigland, J. 2020a. "Hybrid Infrastructure PPPs in India: Costs, Benefits, and Emerging Risks." *Journal of Structured Finance* 26(1): 45–55.

Leigland, J. 2020b. *Public-Private Partnerships in Sub-Saharan Africa: The Evidence-based Critique*. Oxford: Oxford University Press.

Leigland, J., A. Eberhard. 2018. "Localisation Barriers to Trade: The Case of South Africa's Renewable Energy Independent Power Program." *Development Southern Africa* 35(4): 569–588.

Leigland, J., A. Roberts. 2007. "The African Project Preparation Gap: Africans Address a Critical Limiting Factor in Infrastructure Investment." Gridlines Series No. 18, Public Private Infrastructure Advisory Facility (PPIAF). Washington, D.C.: World Bank.

Leigland, J., H. Russell. 2009. "Another Lost Decade? Effects of the Financial Crisis on Project Finance for Infrastructure." PPIAF Gridlines Series No. 48, Public-Private Infrastructure Advisory Facility (PPIAF). Washington, D.C.: World Bank.
Lemma, A. 2013. "Literature Review: Evaluating the Costs and Benefits of Centralised PPP Units." Overseas Development Institute, Economic and Private Sector PEAKS, April. https://assets.publishing.service.gov.uk/media/57a08a49e5274a31e0000510/Evaluating_the_Costs_and_Benefits_of_Centralised_PPP_Units_24.pdf.
Levinsohn, D., D. Reardon. 2007. "Municipal PPP Projects in South Africa: Obstacles and Opportunities." IP3 Public-Private Partnership Information Series, Washington, D.C.
Lion's Head. 2018. "Demonstration Effects of EAIF and GuarantCo Transactions on Infrastructure Finance Markets." Final Report prepared for the Private Infrastructure Development Group (PIDG).
Mandela, N. 1996. Speech at the Maputo Development Corridor Investor Conference, May 6. South African History Online. http://www.sahistory.org.za.
Manibog, F., R. Dominguez, S. Wegner. 2003. *Power for Development: A Review of the World Bank Group's Experience with Private Participation in the Electricity Sector*. World Bank Operations Evaluation Department, IFC Operations Evaluation Group, MIGA Operations Evaluation Unit. Washington, D.C.: World Bank, International Finance Corporation, Multilateral Investment Guarantee Agency.
Marcelo, D., S. House, C. Mandri-Perrott, J. Schwartz. 2017. "Do Countries Learn from Experience in Infrastructure PPP? PPP Practice and Contract Cancellation" (May). Policy Research Working Paper 8054. Washington, D.C.: World Bank.
Marriott, A. 2014. "A Dangerous Diversion: Will the IFC's flagship health PPP bankrupt Lesotho's Ministry of Health?" Oxfam Briefing Note, Oxfam International (April). https://www.oxfam.org/sites/www.oxfam.org/files/bn-dangerous-diversion-lesotho-health-ppp-070414-en.pdf.
M'Bida, A., E. Maussion. 2020. "Dam Doubts: DRC's Giant Inga III Dam: Spanish Firm ACS Throws in the Towel." *The Africa Report*, January 24. https://www.theafricareport.com/22572/drcs-giant-inga-iii-dam-spanish-firm-acs-throws-in-the-towel/.
Metito. 2023. "Africa Receives Investment Boost to Develop Water Infrastructure." Metito press release, March 15. https://www.metito.com/news-detail/africa-receives-investment-boost-to-develop-water-infrastructure.
MIGA [Multilateral Investment Guarantee Agency]. 2018. "Kigali Bulk Water Supply Project: Project Brief." November 17. https://www.miga.org/project/kigali-bulk-water-supply-project.
Ministry of Foreign Affairs of the Netherlands. 2013. *Public-Private Partnerships in Developing Countries: A Systematic Literature Review*. Policy and Operations Department (IOB) Report No. 378. The Hague: The Netherlands: Ministry of Foreign Affairs of the Netherlands.
Mumssen, Y., L. Johannes, G. Kumar. 2010. *Output Based Aid: Lessons Learned and Best Practices*. Washington, D.C.: World Bank.
Nellis, J. 1989. "Contract Plans and Public Enterprise Performance." World Bank Discussion Paper No. 48 (February). Washington, D.C.: World Bank.
Nellis, J. 2005. "The Evolution of Enterprise Reform in Africa: From State-Owned Enterprises to Private Participation in Infrastructure—and Back?" World Bank ESMAP Technical Paper No. 084. Washington, D.C.: World Bank.
Nelspruit TLC [Transitional Local Council]. 1996. *Nelspruit Concession for Water Supply and Sanitation Services: Request for Proposals (RFP)*. December 9.

Nelspruit TLC [Transitional Local Council]. 1999. *Concession Agreement Entered into between Nelspruit TLC and the Greater Nelspruit Utility Company (Proprietary) Limited.* April 21.

NIAF [Nigeria Infrastructure Advisory Facility] Phase II. 2015. "Final Report of the Technical Review Panel to DFID." TRP Annual Review No. 7. September.

Nwangwu, G. 2016. *Public Private Partnerships in Nigeria: Managing Risks and Identifying Opportunities*. London: Palgrave Macmillan.

ODI [Overseas Development Institute]. 2015. *Bricks and Dollars: Improving Public Investment in Infrastructure*. ODI Report prepared by T. Hart, P. Krause, M. Miller. London: Overseas Development Institute.

ODI [Overseas Development Institute]. 2016. *Public Investment Management: A Public Financial Management Introductory Guide*. ODI Report prepared by M. Miller, S. Mustapha. London: Overseas Development Institute.

ODI [Oversees Development Institute]. 2018. *Clean Energy Project Preparation Facilities: Mapping the Global Landscape*. Research report prepared by D. Nassiry, S. Pickard, S. Whitley, A. Scott. London: Overseas Development Institute. https://odi.org/en/publications/clean-energy-project-preparation-facilities/.

OECD [Organisation for Economic Co-operation and Development]. 2010. *Dedicated Public Private Partnership Units: Survey of Institutional and Governance Structure*. Paris: OECD Publishing.

OECD [Organisation for Economic Co-operation and Development]. 2017. *Blended Finance: Mobilising Resources for Sustainable Development and Climate Action in Developing Countries*. OECD Policy Perspectives (October). file:///C:/Users/JL/Documents/Blended%20finance/Blended-finance-Policy-Perspectives.%20OECD.pdf.

OECD [Organisation for Economic Co-operation and Development]. 2018. *OECD Survey of Capital Budgeting, Infrastructure Governance and PPPs.* Paris, France: OECD Publishing.

OECD [Organisation for Economic Co-operation and Development], World Bank Group. 2015. "Risk and Return Characteristics of Infrastructure Investment in Low Income Countries" (September 3). Paris, France: OECD Publishing.

Oreskes, N., E.M. Conway. 2023. *The Big Myth: How American Business Taught Us to Loathe Government and Love the Free Market.* London: Bloomsbury Publishing.

Palmer, K. 2014. "Innovation in International Development Assistance: Ten Years of the Private Infrastructure Development Group (PIDG)." https://efdafrica.org/site/assets/files/1045/pidg_article-_final_pmu.pdf.

Peri, R., C. Chen, D. Dey. 2019. "Hybrid Annuity Contracts for Road Projects in India." ADB South Asia Working Paper Series No. 68, December. Manila: Asian Development Bank.

Peterson, G. 2003. "Banks or Bonds? Building a Municipal Credit Market." Washington, D.C.: The Urban Institute.

PIDG [Private Infrastructure Development Group]. 2003. "Consultation Document on a Proposal to Establish an Infrastructure Project Development Company (DEVCO)." Unpublished paper, March.

PIDG [Private Infrastructure Development Group]. 2008. "An Approach to Supporting Private Sector Participation in Infrastructure: Benefits, Challenges and Lessons Learnt from the PIDG." Unpublished paper, June.

PIDG [Private Infrastructure Development Group]. 2012. *Annual Report 2012.* London: Private Infrastructure Development Group. https://www.pidg.org/.

PIDG [Private Infrastructure Development Group]. 2013. *Annual Report 2013*. London: Private Infrastructure Development Group. https://www.pidg.org/.
PIDG [Private Infrastructure Development Group]. 2015. *Annual Report 2015*. London: Private Infrastructure Development Group. https://www.pidg.org/.
PIDG [Private Infrastructure Development Group]. 2019a. *Five-Year Strategic Plan, 2019–2023*. London: Private Infrastructure Development Group. https://www.pidg.org/wp-content/uploads/2020/09/PIDG-Five-Year-Strategic-Plan_2019-2023_published_pages.pdf.
PIDG [Private Infrastructure Development Group]. 2019b. "Results Monitoring Database." https://www.pidg.org/our-impact/results-monitoring-database/.
PIDG [Private Infrastructure Development Group]. 2020. *PIDG Annual Review 2020*. London: Private Infrastructure Development Group.
PIDG [Private Infrastructure Development Group]. 2021. *PIDG Annual Review 2021*. London: Private Infrastructure Development Group.
PPIAF [Public-Private Infrastructure Advisory Facility]. 2007. *Public-Private Partnership Units: Lessons for their Design and Use in Infrastructure*. Washington, D.C.: World Bank.
PPIAF [Public-Private Infrastructure Advisory Facility]. 2009. *Toolkit for Public-Private Partnerships in Roads and Highways*. Washington, D.C.: World Bank.
PPIAF [Public-Private Infrastructure Advisory Facility]. 2015. "PPIAF Helps the Government of Rwanda Manage Private Sector participation in the Water Sector." Washington, D.C.: World Bank.
PPIAF [Public-Private Infrastructure Advisory Facility]. 2018. *Contribution of Institutional Investors: Private Investment in Infrastructure 2011–H1 2017*. Washington, D.C.: World Bank.
Pritchett, L. 2008. "It Pays to Be Ignorant: A Simple Political Economy of Rigorous Program Evaluation." In W. Easterly (ed.), *Reinventing Foreign Aid*, 121–144. Cambridge, MA: The MIT Press.
Rand Merchant Bank [RMB]. 2011. *RMB FICC Research: Where to Invest in Africa*. https://www.rmb.co.za/files/pdf/landing/where-to-invest-in-africa/where-to-invest-in-africa-2011-edition.pdf.
Republic of Rwanda. 2018. "Public Private Partnership Guidelines." Official Gazette No. 29bis of July 16.
Republic of Rwanda. 2022. "Report of the Auditor General of State Finances for the Year Ended 30 June 2021." Kigali, Rwanda: Office of the Auditor General of State Finances.
Republic of Rwanda. 2023. "Report of the Auditor General of State Finances for the Year Ended 30 June 2022." Kigali, Rwanda: Office of the Auditor General of State Finances.
Republic of South Africa [RSA]. 2011. "REIPPPP Tender Notices and Briefing Notes." Department of Energy. http://www.ipp-renewables.co.za.
Republic of Zambia. 2017. "Report of the Committee on National Economy, Trade and Labour Matters on the Public-Private Partnership (Amendment) Bill for the Second Session of the Twelfth National Assembly." Report by the National Assembly. Lusaka: National Assembly of Zambia.
Reuters. 2020. "DRC's Giant Inga III Dam: Spanish Firm ACS Throws in the Towel." Reuters, February 11. https://www.theafricareport.com/22572/drcs-giant-inga-iii-dam-spanish-firm-acs-throws-in-the-towel/.

Rohde, N. 2015. "'Assembly Lines' for Project Development: The Role of Infrastructure Project Preparation Facilities (PPFs)." Report prepared for Heinrich Böll Stiftung, New York.

Roland Berger. 2012. "Misperception of Risk and Return in Low Income Countries." Report prepared for the G20 Development Working Group.

Ross, T.W., J. Yan. 2015. "Comparing Public-Private Partnerships and Traditional Public Procurement: Efficiency vs. Flexibility." *Journal of Comparative Policy Analysis* 17(5): 1–19.

Rwahigi, M. 2015. "Rwanda Signs Water Purchase Agreement with Metito to Increase Access to Clean Safe Water." *Hope Magazine*, April 1.

Sachs, J.D. 2006. *The End of Poverty: Economic Possibilities for Our Time*. New York: Penguin.

Saha, D., F.T. Ibrahima. 2020. "Who Finances Infrastructure, Really? Disentangling Public and Private Contributions." World Bank Blog, January 15. https://blogs.worldbank.org/en/ppps/who-finances-infrastructure-really-disentangling-public-and-private-contributions.

Saldinger, A. 2020. "Why Blended Finance Hasn't Taken Off." Devex Blog. February 24. https://www.devex.com/news/why-blended-finance-hasn-t-taken-off-96612.

Sarbib, J.L. 1997. "Privatization in Africa: Present and Future Trends." Paper presented at the African Development Bank Group Annual Meeting Symposium on Private Sector Development in Africa, Abidjan, May 21.

Schloss, M. 1990. "Sub-Saharan Energy Financing: The Need for a New Game Plan." Africa Technical Department, Industry and Energy Division, Division Note 5. Washington, D.C.: World Bank.

Schmitz, J.A. 1996. "The Role Played by Public Enterprises: How Much Does It Differ Across Countries?" *Federal Reserve Bank of Minneapolis Quarterly Review* 20(2): 2–15.

SDIP [Sustainable Development Investment Partnership], United States Trade Development Agency (USTDA), Development Bank of Southern Africa (DBSA). 2018. *Insights on Project Preparation and Development Capital in Africa and the ASEAN Region.* Midrand, South Africa: DBSA. https://www.dbsa.org/sites/default/files/media/documents/2021-03/DBSA%20SDIP%20insights%20into%20Project%20Preparations%20in%20Africa%20and%20ASIAN%20regions.pdf.

Shaoul, J., A. Stafford, P. Stapleton. 2007. "Partnerships and the Role of Financial Advisors: Private Control Over Public Policy?" *The Policy Press*, 35(3): 479–495.

Sherif, Khaled Fouad. 1993. "Public Enterprise Reform and Privatization in Africa." World Bank, Africa Technical Department Working Paper. Washington, D.C.: World Bank.

Shirley, M.M. 1983. "Managing State-Owned Enterprises." World Bank Staff Working Paper No. 577, July. Washington, D.C.: World Bank.

Shirley, M.M. 1995. *Bureaucrats in Business: The Economics and Politics of Government Ownership*. Washington, D.C.: World Bank.

Shirley, M.M., L.C. Xu. 2001. "Empirical Effects of Performance Contracts: Evidence from China." *Journal of Law, Economics and Organization* 17(1): 168–200.

Siemiatycki, M. 2015. "Public-Private Partnership Networks: Exploring Business-Government Relationships in United Kingdom Transportation Projects." *Economic Geography* 87(3): 309–334.

Sirtaine, S., M.E. Pinglo, J.L. Guasch, V. Foster. 2004. *How Profitable Are Infrastructure Concessions in Latin America? Empirical Evidence and Regulatory Implications*. Washington, D.C.: World Bank.

Slobodian, Q. 2018. *Globalists: The End of Empire and the Birth of Neoliberalism.* Cambridge, MA: Harvard University Press.

South Africa Auditor General. 2021. "Consolidated General Report on the Local Government Audit Outcomes, 2019–2020." Pretoria: Auditor General. https://www.agsa.co.za/Reporting/MFMAReports/MFMA2019-2020.aspx.

Spratt, S., L.R. Collins. 2012. "Development Finance Institutions and Infrastructure: A Systematic Review of Evidence for Development Additionality." Report prepared for the Private Infrastructure Development Group, January. https://www.gov.uk/research-for-development-outputs/development-finance-institutions-and-infrastructure-a-systematic-review-of-evidence-for-development-additionality.

Srikumar, S., R. Venkataraman. 2023. "Municipal Bonds: An Analytical Report." In S. Morris (ed.), *India Infrastructure Report 2023: Urban Planning and Development*, 136–150. New Delhi: Bloomsbury Prime.

Stafford, A., P. Stapleton. 2017. "Examining the Use of Corporate Governance Mechanisms in Public-Private Partnerships: Why Do They Not Deliver Public Accountability?" *Australian Journal of Public Administration* 76(3): 378–391.

Thomson Reuters. 2018. "Africa's First Water PPP." *PFI Yearbook 2018*. http://www.pfie.com/africas-first-water-ppp/21320834.fullarticle.

TMP Systems. 2021. "Inga 3, Too High a Cost: A Study of the Socio-Economic Costs of the Inga 3 Dam for South Africa." Johannesburg: International Rivers and WoMin African Alliance.

U.K. Audit Commission. 2003. "PFI in Schools." London: U.K. Audit Commission.

U.K. House of Commons, Committee of Public Accounts. 2003. "Delivering Better Value for Money from the Private Finance Initiative." London: U.K.: House of Commons.

U.K. NAO [National Audit Office]. 2014. "Department for International Development: Oversight of the Private Infrastructure Development Group." Report by the Comptroller and Auditor General. London: National Audit Office.

UN [United Nations]. 2007. *Guidebook on Promoting Good Governance in Public-Private Partnerships*. New York: United Nations.

UN [United Nations]. 2021. *Financing for Sustainable Development Report 2021*. Report of the Inter-agency Task Force on Financing for Development. New York: United Nations.

UNCDF [United Nations Capital Development Fund]. 2018. *Blended Finance in the Least Developed Countries: Case Study 4, Kigali Bulk Water supply PPP*. New York: UNCDF.

UNECE [United Nations Economic Commission for Europe]. 2021. "UNECE PPP Standards." https:// wiki .unece .org/ display/ pppp/ PPP+ Standards+ Development+ Process.

United Nations Millennium Project. 2005. "Investing in Development: A Practical Plan to Achieve the Millennium Development Goals." New York: United Nations Development Programme.

USAID [United States Agency for International Development]. 2018. "Review Study of the Zambia Scaling Solar Program: Final Report." Report prepared for USAID by the USAID Management Support and Technical Analysis Services (MSTAS) Project implemented by the Pragma Corporation and its partners, September. file:///C:/Users/JL/Documents/New%20PPP%20material/USAID%20evaluation%20of%20Scaling%20Solar%20in%20Zambia.%202018.pdf.

Verhoest, K., O.H. Petersen, W. Scherrer, R.M. Soecipto. 2015. "How Do Governments Support the Development of Public Private Partnerships? Measuring and Comparing

PPP Governmental Support in 20 European Countries." *Transport Reviews* 35(2): 118–139.

Washington Post. 2021. "John Kerry is Counting on Private Sector to Solve Climate Change." https://www.washingtonpost.com/politics/2021/12/07/john-kerry-is-counting-private-sector-help-solve-climate-change/.

WBG [World Bank Group]. 2017a. "The G-20 Compact with Africa; a Joint AfDB, IMF and WBG Report." G20 Finance Ministers and Central Bank Governors Meeting, March 17–18, Baden-Baden, Germany.

WGB [World Bank Group]. 2017b. "Maximizing Finance for Development: Leveraging the Private Sector for Growth and Sustainable Development." Washington, D.C.: World Bank.

Williamson, J. 1989. "What Washington Means by Policy Reform." In J. Williamson (ed.), *Latin American Readjustment: How Much has Happened*, Chapter 3. Washington, D.C.: Peterson Institute for International Economics.

Winch, G.M., M. Onishi, S. Schmidt. 2012. *Taking Stock of PPP and PFI around the World*. London, U.K.: The Association of Chartered Certified Accountants.

World Bank. 1981. "Review of Structural Adjustment Lending." Memorandum to the Executive Directors from Robert S. McNamara, President, April 1.

World Bank. 1989. *World Development Report 1989: Financial Systems Development*. New York: Oxford University Press.

World Bank. 1990. "Argentina: Water Supply and Sewerage Sector Project." Staff Appraisal Report 8425-AR, November. Washington, D.C.: World Bank.

World Bank. 1993. "The World Bank's Role in the Electric Power Sector." A World Bank Policy Paper. Washington, D.C.: World Bank.

World Bank. 1994a. *Adjustment in Africa: Reforms, Results, and the Road Ahead*. World Bank Policy Research Report, February. Washington, D.C.: World Bank.

World Bank. 1994b. *World Development Report 1994: Infrastructure for Development*. New York: Oxford University Press.

World Bank. 1995. *Economic Growth in the 1990s*. Washington, D.C.: World Bank.

World Bank. 1999. *World Development Report 1999/2000: Entering the 21st Century: The Changing Development Landscape*. New York: Oxford University Press.

World Bank. 2000. *World Development Report 2000/2001: Attacking Poverty*. New York: Oxford University Press.

World Bank. 2002a. *World Development Report 2002: Building Institutions for Markets*. New York: Oxford University Press.

World Bank. 2002b. "Private Sector Development Strategy: Directions for the World Bank Group." Board Report No. 44933, January. Washington, D.C.: World Bank.

World Bank. 2004. *World Development Report 2004: Making Services Work for Poor People*. New York: Oxford University Press.

World Bank. 2005. *Economic Growth in the 1990s: Learning from a Decade of Reform*. Washington, D.C.: World Bank.

World Bank. 2011a. "Technical Assistance for Delivering Transformational Projects – Draft Concept Note for Discussion," August. SDN Financial Solutions.

World Bank. 2011b. "Transformation Through Infrastructure: World Bank Group Infrastructure Strategy Update FY12–15." Washington, D.C.: World Bank.

World Bank. 2011c. "Project Appraisal Document on a Proposed Credit in the Amount of SDR 73.7 Million to the Federal Republic of Nigeria for the First Phase of the Public/Private Partnership APL Program," February 18. Washington, D.C.: World Bank.

World Bank. 2014. "Project Appraisal Document on a Proposed Grant in the Amount of SDR 47.7 Million (US$ 73.1 Million Equivalent) to the Democratic Republic of Congo for an INGA 3 Basse Chute and Mid-Size Hydropower Development Technical Assistance Project." Report No. 77420-ZR. Washington, D.C.: World Bank.

World Bank. 2015a. "From Billions to Trillions: Transforming Development Finance." Document prepared jointly by the African Development Bank, the Asian Development Bank, the European Bank for Reconstruction and Development, the European Investment Bank, the Inter-American Development Bank, the International Monetary Fund, World Bank Group for the April 18, 2015 Development Committee meeting (April 2). Washington, D.C.: World Bank. https://siteresources.worldbank.org/DEVCOMMINT/Documentation/23659446/DC2015-0002(E)FinancingforDevelopment.pdf.

World Bank. 2015b. "International Development Association Project Appraisal Document on a Proposed Credit in the Amount of SDR 67.70 Million (US$95 Million Equivalent) to the Republic of Rwanda for the Electricity Sector Strengthening Project." Report No: PAD1301. Washington, D.C.: World Bank.

World Bank. 2016. *The World Bank Implementation Status & Results Report: DRC Inga 3 and Mid-Size Hydropower Development TA (P131027)*. Washington, D.C.: World Bank.

World Bank. 2017. *Doing Business 2017*. Washington, D.C.: World Bank.

World Bank. 2019a. *Doing Business 2019*. Washington, D.C.: World Bank.

World Bank. 2019b. "Implementation Completion and Results Report on a Credit in the Amount of SDR 73.7 Million to the Federal Republic of Nigeria for the Nigeria – Public/Private Partnership Program," March 22. Washington, D.C.: World Bank.

World Bank. 2019c. *Who Sponsors Infrastructure Projects? Disentangling Public and Private Contributions 2017*. Washington, D.C.: World Bank and Public-Private Infrastructure Advisory Facility.

World Bank. 2020. *Benchmarking Infrastructure Development 2020*. Washington, D.C.: World Bank.

World Bank. 2022. PPI Project Database. http://ppi.worldbank.org/customquery?mode=1.

World Bank. 2023. "PPP Units Around the World." Public-Private Partnership Legal Resource Center (PPPLRC). https://ppp.worldbank.org/public-private-partnership/overview/international-ppp-units#South%20Africa.

World Bank, Asian Development Bank, Inter-American Development Bank. 2014. *Public-Private Partnerships Reference Guide, Version 2.0*. Washington, D.C.: World Bank.

WSP. 2008. "Desk Review of DFID's Private Sector Infrastructure Investment Facilities." Report prepared for DFID by WSP International Management Consulting Team, March.

Yepes, T. 2007. "New Estimates of Infrastructure Expenditure Requirements." Washington, D.C.: World Bank.

Yusuf, S., A. Deaton, K. Dervis, W. Easterly, T. Ito, J.E. Stiglitz. 2009. *Development Economics through the Decades: A Critical Look at 30 Years of the World Development Report*. Washington, D.C.: World Bank.

Zhang, X., M. Kumaraswamy. 2001. "Procurement Protocols for Public-Private Partnered Projects." *Journal of Construction Engineering and Management* 127(5): 351–358.

Index